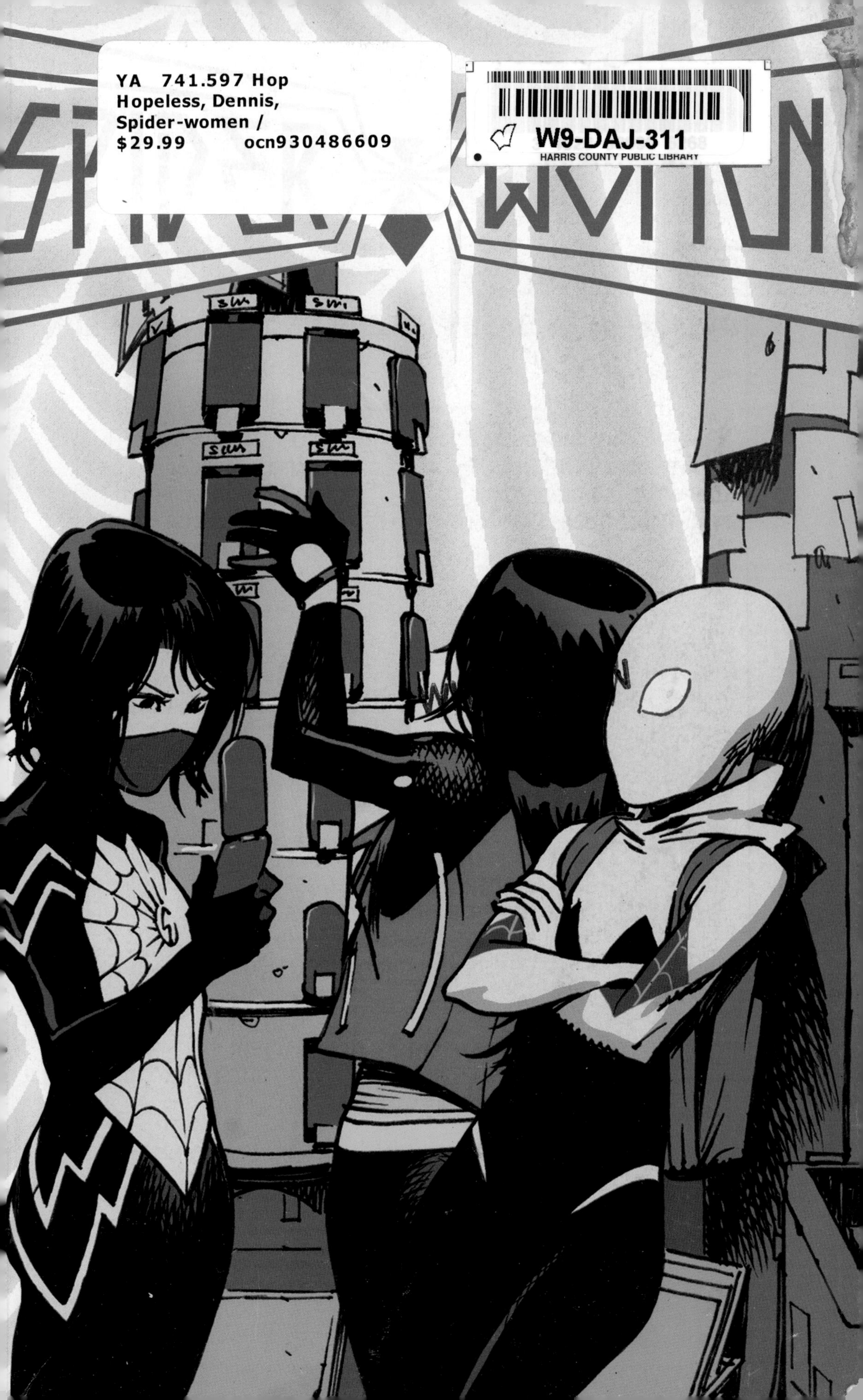

DENNIS HOPELESS, JASON LATOUR & ROBBIE THOMPSON
STORY

SPIDER-WOMEN ALPHA #1
WRITER: ROBBIE THOMPSON
ARTIST: VANESA DEL REY
COLOR ARTIST: JORDIE BELLAIRE
LETTERER: VC'S TRAVIS LANHAM

SPIDER-GWEN #7-8
WRITER: JASON LATOUR
ARTIST: BENGAL
COLOR ARTIST: RICO RENZI
LETTERER: VC'S CLAYTON COWLES
WITH TRAVIS LANHAM [#8]

SILK #7-8
WRITER: ROBBIE THOMPSON
ARTIST: TANA FORD
COLOR ARTIST: IAN HERRING
LETTERER: VC'S TRAVIS LANHAM

SPIDER-WOMAN #6-7
WRITER: DENNIS HOPELESS
PENCILER: JOËLLE JONES
INKERS: JOËLLE JONES [#6]
& LORENZO RUGGIERO [#7]
COLOR ARTIST: RACHELLE ROSENBERG
LETTERER: VC'S TRAVIS LANHAM

SPIDER-WOMEN OMEGA #1
WRITER: DENNIS HOPELESS
ARTIST: NICO LEON
COLOR ARTIST: RACHELLE ROSENBERG
LETTERER: VC'S TRAVIS LANHAM

YASMINE PUTRI
COVER ART

KATHLEEN WISNESKI
ASSISTANT EDITOR

DEVIN LEWIS
ASSOCIATE EDITOR

NICK LOWE
EXECUTIVE EDITOR

COLLECTION EDITOR:
JENNIFER GRÜNWALD

ASSOCIATE EDITOR:
SARAH BRUNSTAD

ASSOCIATE MANAGING EDITOR:
ALEX STARBUCK

EDITOR, SPECIAL PROJECTS:
MARK D. BEAZLEY

VP, PRODUCTION &
SPECIAL PROJECTS:
JEFF YOUNGQUIST

SVP PRINT, SALES &
MARKETING:
DAVID GABRIEL

BOOK DESIGNER:
JAY BOWEN

EDITOR IN CHIEF:
AXEL ALONSO

CHIEF CREATIVE OFFICER:
JOE QUESADA

PUBLISHER:
DAN BUCKLEY

EXECUTIVE PRODUCER:
ALAN FINE

SPIDER-WOMEN. Contains material originally published in magazine form as SPIDER-WOMEN ALPHA #1, SILK #7-8, SPIDER-GWEN #7-8, SPIDER-WOMAN #6-7 and SPIDER-WOMEN OMEGA #1. First printing 2016. ISBN# 978-1-302-90093-9. Published by MARVEL WORLDWIDE, INC., a subsidiary of MARVEL ENTERTAINMENT, LLC. OFFICE OF PUBLICATION: 135 West 50th Street, New York, NY 10020. Copyright © 2016 MARVEL No similarity between any of the names, characters, persons, and/or institutions in this magazine with those of any living or dead person or institution is intended, and any such similarity which may exist is purely coincidental. Printed in the U.S.A. ALAN FINE, President, Marvel Entertainment; DAN BUCKLEY, President, TV, Publishing & Brand Management; JOE QUESADA, Chief Creative Officer; TOM BREVOORT, SVP of Publishing; DAVID BOGART, SVP of Business Affairs & Operations, Publishing & Partnership; C.B. CEBULSKI, VP of Brand Management & Development, Asia; DAVID GABRIEL, SVP of Sales & Marketing, Publishing; JEFF YOUNGQUIST, VP of Production & Special Projects; DAN CARR, Executive Director of Publishing Technology; ALEX MORALES, Director of Publishing Operations; SUSAN CRESPI, Production Manager; STAN LEE, Chairman Emeritus. For information regarding advertising in Marvel Comics or on Marvel.com, please contact Vit DeBellis, Integrated Sales Manager, at vdebellis@marvel.com. For Marvel subscription inquiries, please call 888-511-5480. Manufactured between 5/20/2016 and 6/27/2016 by R.R. DONNELLEY, INC., SALEM, VA, USA.

10 9 8 7 6 5 4 3 2 1

SILK

A RADIOACTIVE SPIDER BITE GAVE TEENAGER CINDY MOON SUPERHUMAN STRENGTH, SPEED, AGILITY, AND THE ABILITY TO SPIN WEBBING FROM HER FINGERTIPS. TO PROTECT HER FROM SPIDER HUNTERS, CINDY WAS LOCKED IN A BUNKER FOR YEARS. NOW FREE, SHE'S TRYING TO FIGURE OUT HOW TO BE AN ADULT AND A HERO.

SPIDER-WOMAN

SPIDER BLOOD CURED JESSICA DREW OF A CHILDHOOD ILLNESS AND GAVE HER ADHESIVE FINGERTIPS AND TOES, ENHANCED AGILITY AND SPEED, AND THE ABILITY TO FIRE BIOKINETIC "VENOM BLASTS" FROM HER FINGERTIPS. SHE'S BEEN A HERO FOR YEARS AND A MOTHER FOR WEEKS.

SPIDER-GWEN

A RADIOACTIVE SPIDER BITE GAVE TEENAGER GWEN STACY A PRECOGNITIVE AWARENESS OF DANGER, ADHESIVE FINGERTIPS AND TOES, AND THE PROPORTIONAL SPEED AND STRENGTH OF A SPIDER. LIFE WAS MESSY BEFORE SHE BECAME HER EARTH'S SPIDER-WOMAN, AND IT HASN'T GOTTEN ANY EASIER.

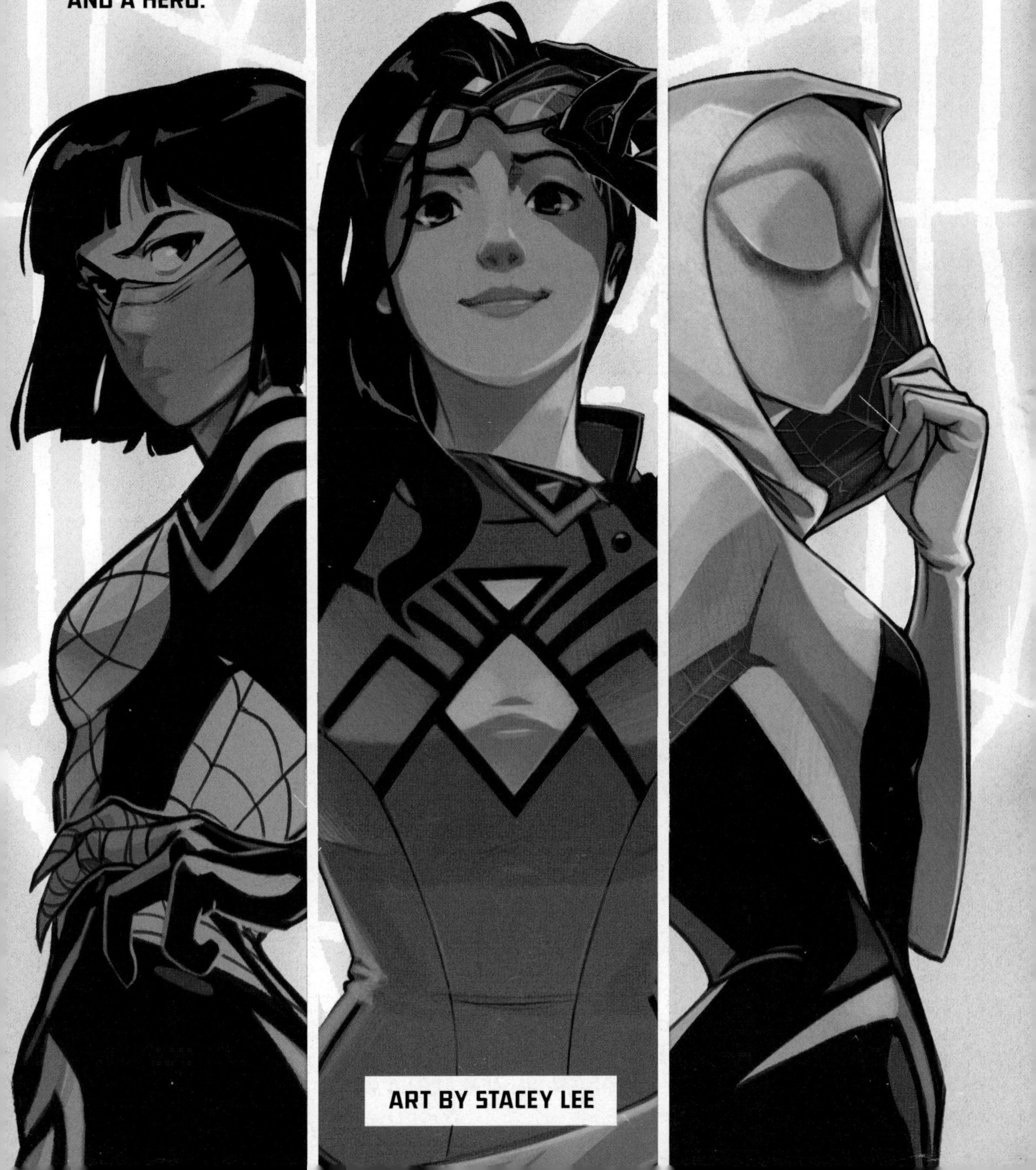

ART BY STACEY LEE

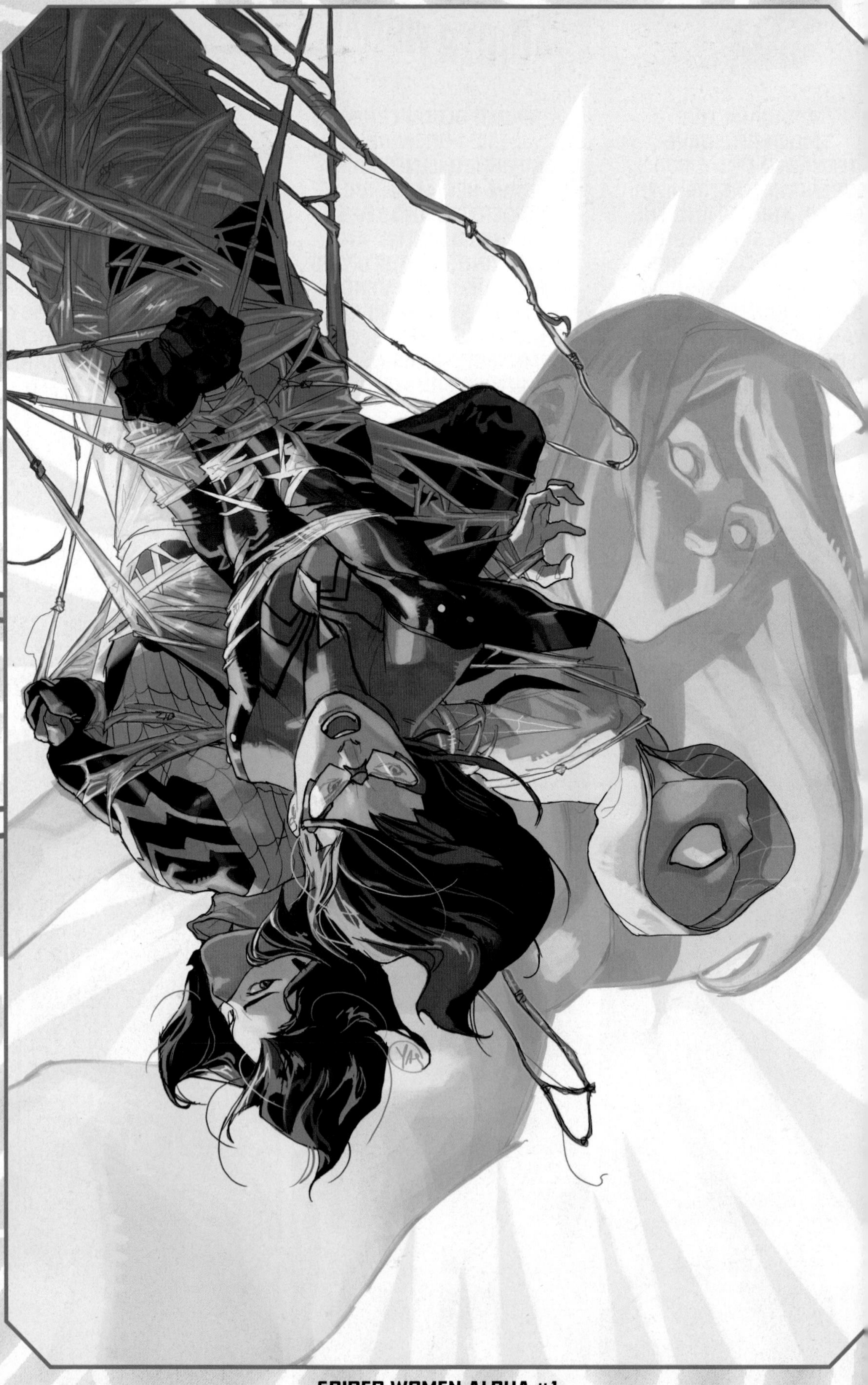

SPIDER-WOMEN ALPHA #1

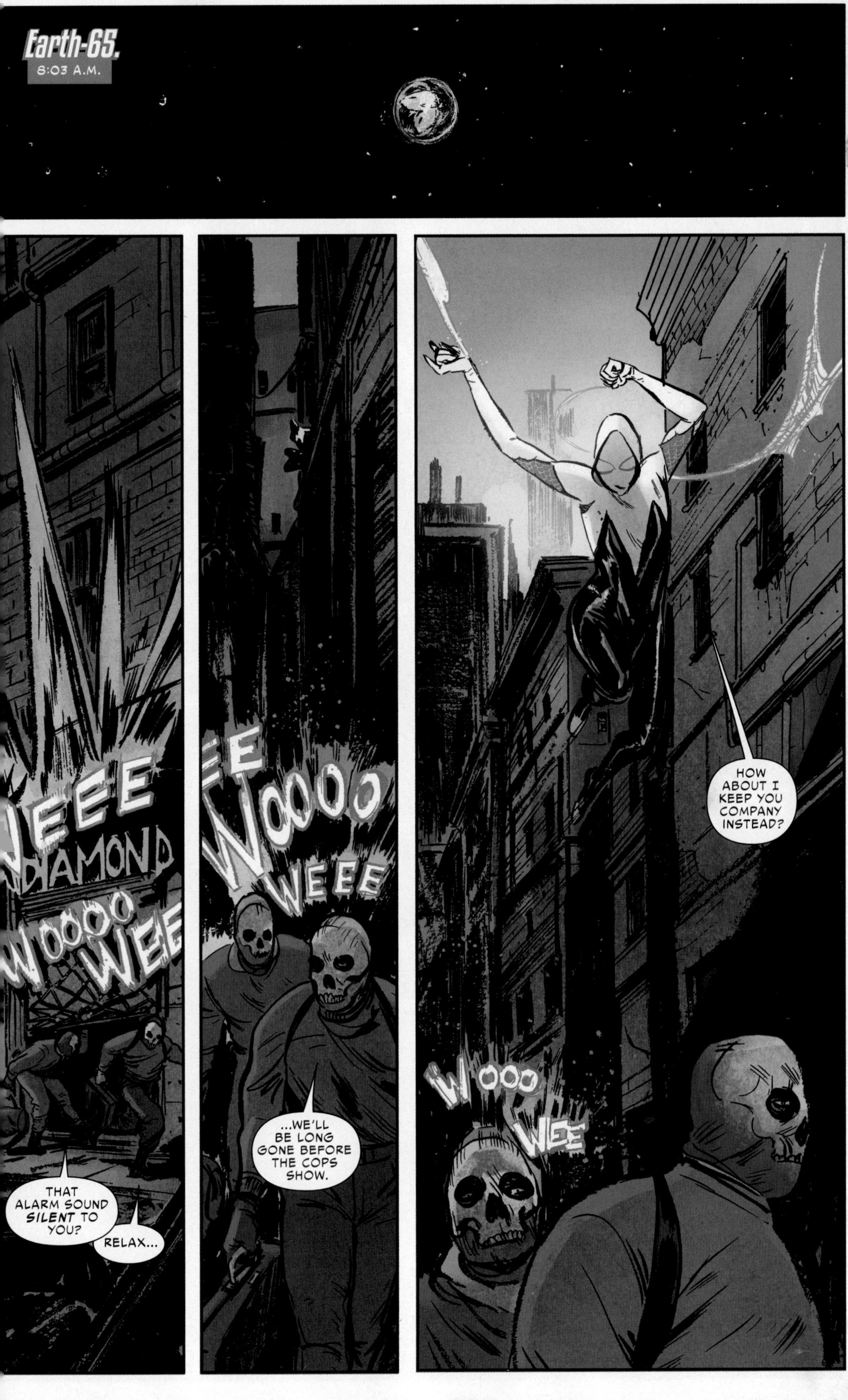
Earth-65.
8:03 A.M.
WEEE
DIAMOND
WOOOO WEE
THAT ALARM SOUND SILENT TO YOU?
RELAX...
EE
WOOOO
WEEE
...WE'LL BE LONG GONE BEFORE THE COPS SHOW.
HOW ABOUT I KEEP YOU COMPANY INSTEAD?
WOOO
WEE

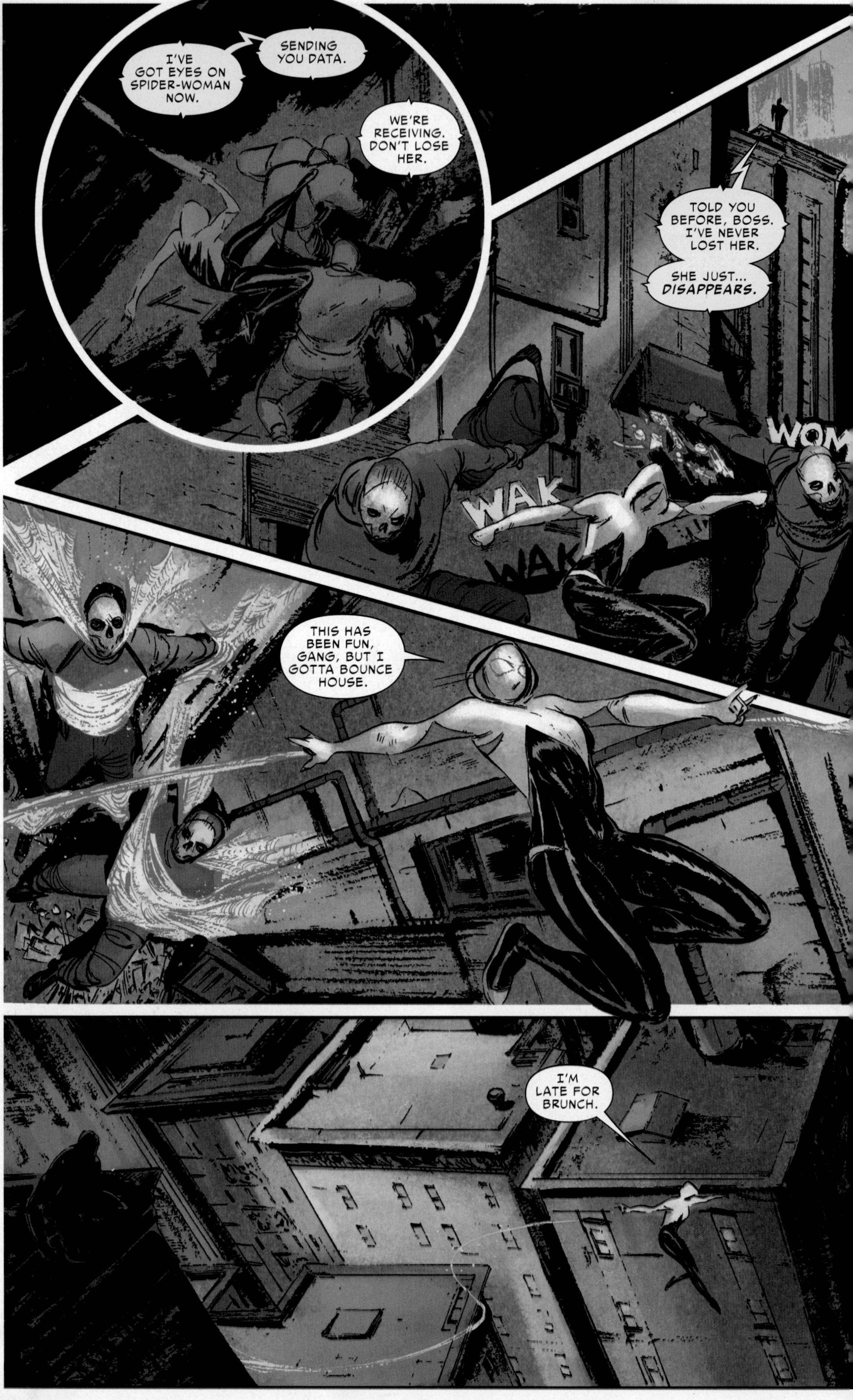
I'VE GOT EYES ON SPIDER-WOMAN NOW.
SENDING YOU DATA.
WE'RE RECEIVING. DON'T LOSE HER.
TOLD YOU BEFORE, BOSS. I'VE NEVER LOST HER.
SHE JUST... DISAPPEARS.
WOM
WAK
WAK
THIS HAS BEEN FUN, GANG, BUT I GOTTA BOUNCE HOUSE.
I'M LATE FOR BRUNCH.

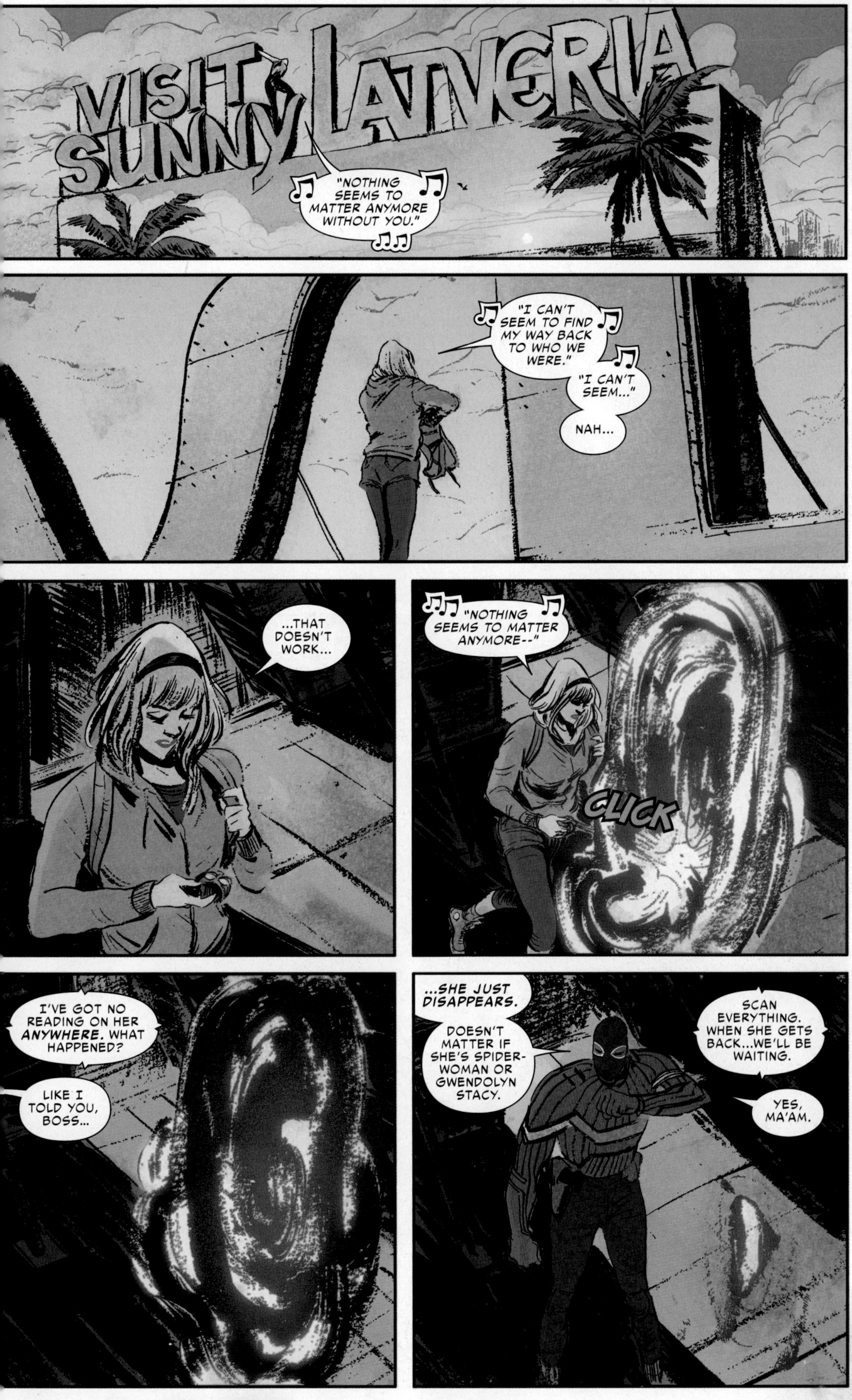
VISIT SUNNY LATVERIA
♫ "NOTHING SEEMS TO MATTER ANYMORE WITHOUT YOU." ♫ ♫♫
♫ "I CAN'T SEEM TO FIND MY WAY BACK TO WHO WE WERE." ♫
♫ "I CAN'T SEEM..."
NAH...
...THAT DOESN'T WORK...
♫♫ "NOTHING SEEMS TO MATTER ANYMORE--" ♫
CLICK
I'VE GOT NO READING ON HER ANYWHERE. WHAT HAPPENED?
LIKE I TOLD YOU, BOSS...
...SHE JUST DISAPPEARS.
DOESN'T MATTER IF SHE'S SPIDER-WOMAN OR GWENDOLYN STACY.
SCAN EVERYTHING. WHEN SHE GETS BACK...WE'LL BE WAITING.
YES, MA'AM.

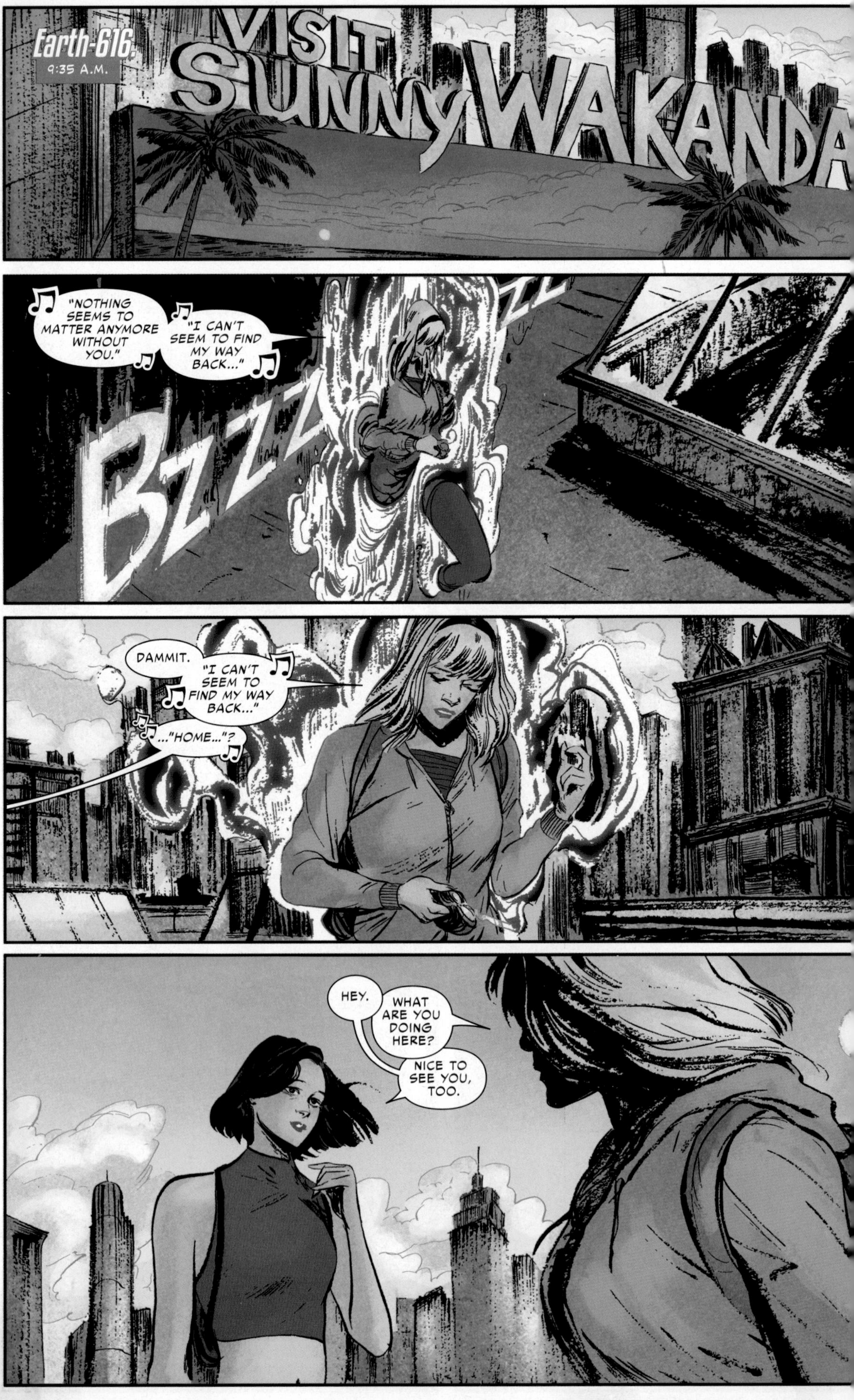
Earth-616.
9:35 A.M.
VISIT SUNNY WAKANDA
"NOTHING SEEMS TO MATTER ANYMORE WITHOUT YOU."
"I CAN'T SEEM TO FIND MY WAY BACK..."
BZZZ
DAMMIT.
"I CAN'T SEEM TO FIND MY WAY BACK..."
..."HOME..."?
HEY.
WHAT ARE YOU DOING HERE?
NICE TO SEE YOU, TOO.

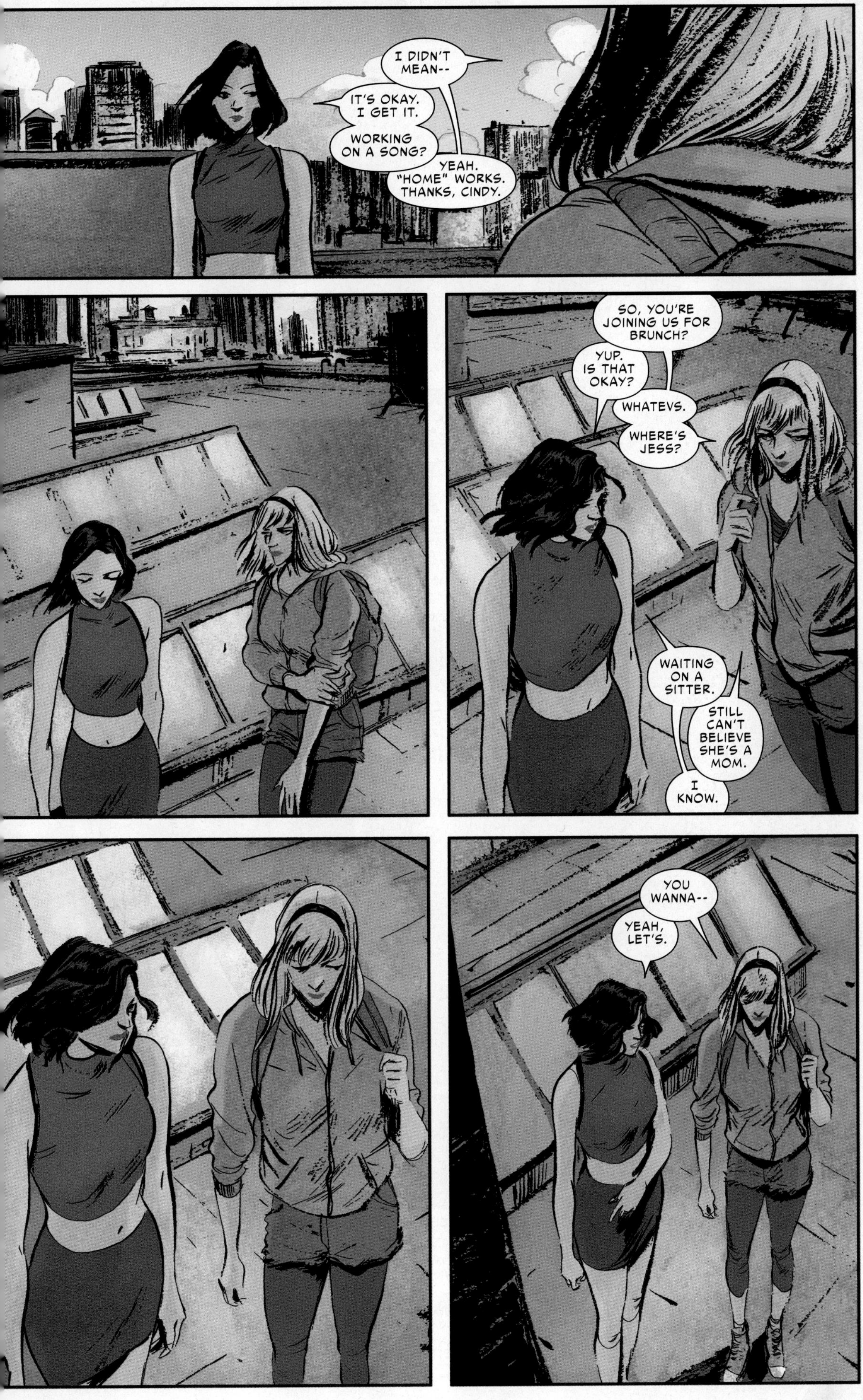
I DIDN'T MEAN--
IT'S OKAY. I GET IT.
WORKING ON A SONG?
YEAH. "HOME" WORKS. THANKS, CINDY.
SO, YOU'RE JOINING US FOR BRUNCH?
YUP. IS THAT OKAY?
WHATEVS.
WHERE'S JESS?
WAITING ON A SITTER.
STILL CAN'T BELIEVE SHE'S A MOM.
I KNOW.
YOU WANNA--
YEAH, LET'S.

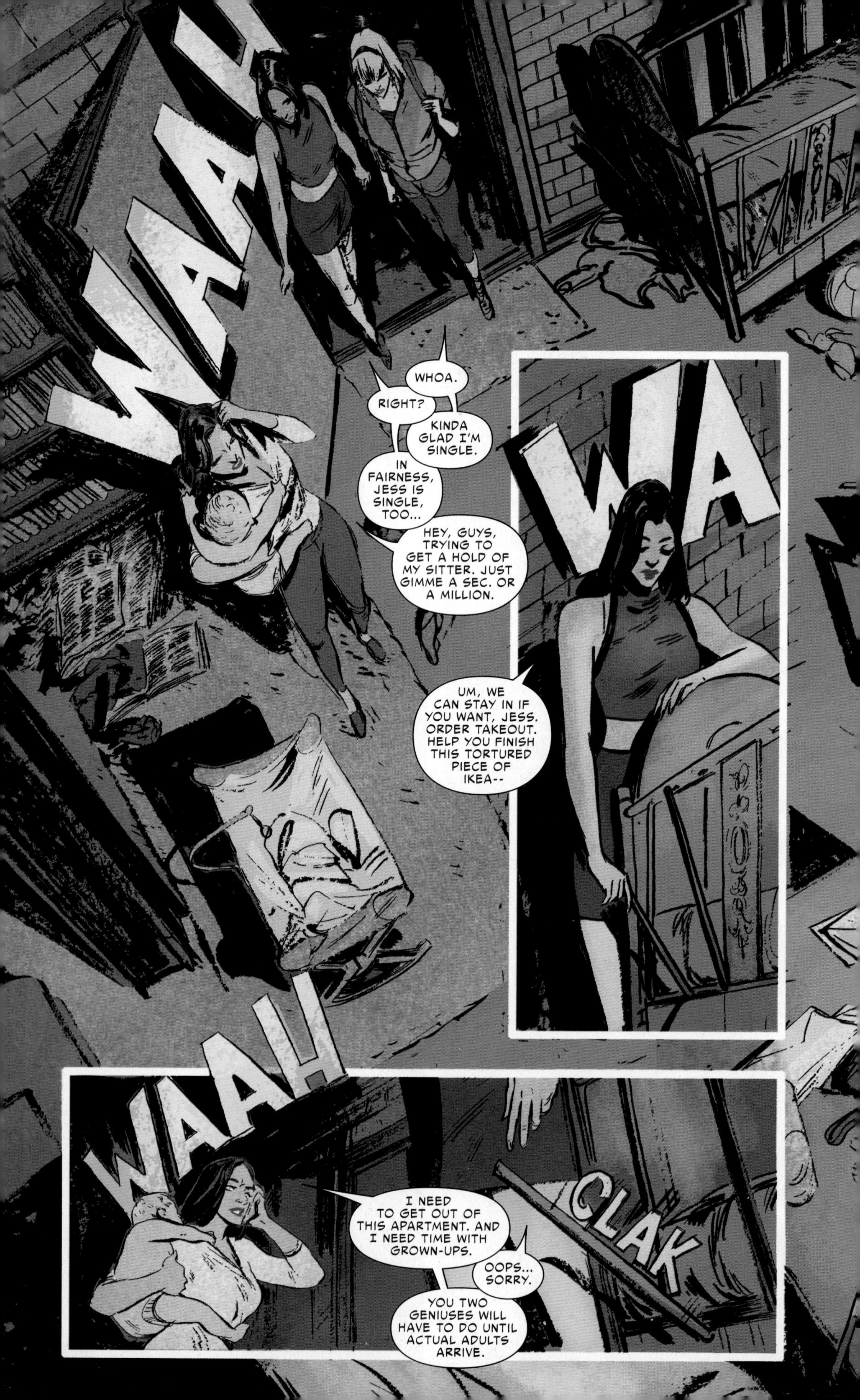
WAAH
WHOA.
RIGHT?
KINDA GLAD I'M SINGLE.
IN FAIRNESS, JESS IS SINGLE, TOO...
HEY, GUYS, TRYING TO GET A HOLD OF MY SITTER. JUST GIMME A SEC. OR A MILLION.
WA
UM, WE CAN STAY IN IF YOU WANT, JESS. ORDER TAKEOUT. HELP YOU FINISH THIS TORTURED PIECE OF IKEA--
WAAH
CLAK
I NEED TO GET OUT OF THIS APARTMENT. AND I NEED TIME WITH GROWN-UPS.
OOPS... SORRY.
YOU TWO GENIUSES WILL HAVE TO DO UNTIL ACTUAL ADULTS ARRIVE.

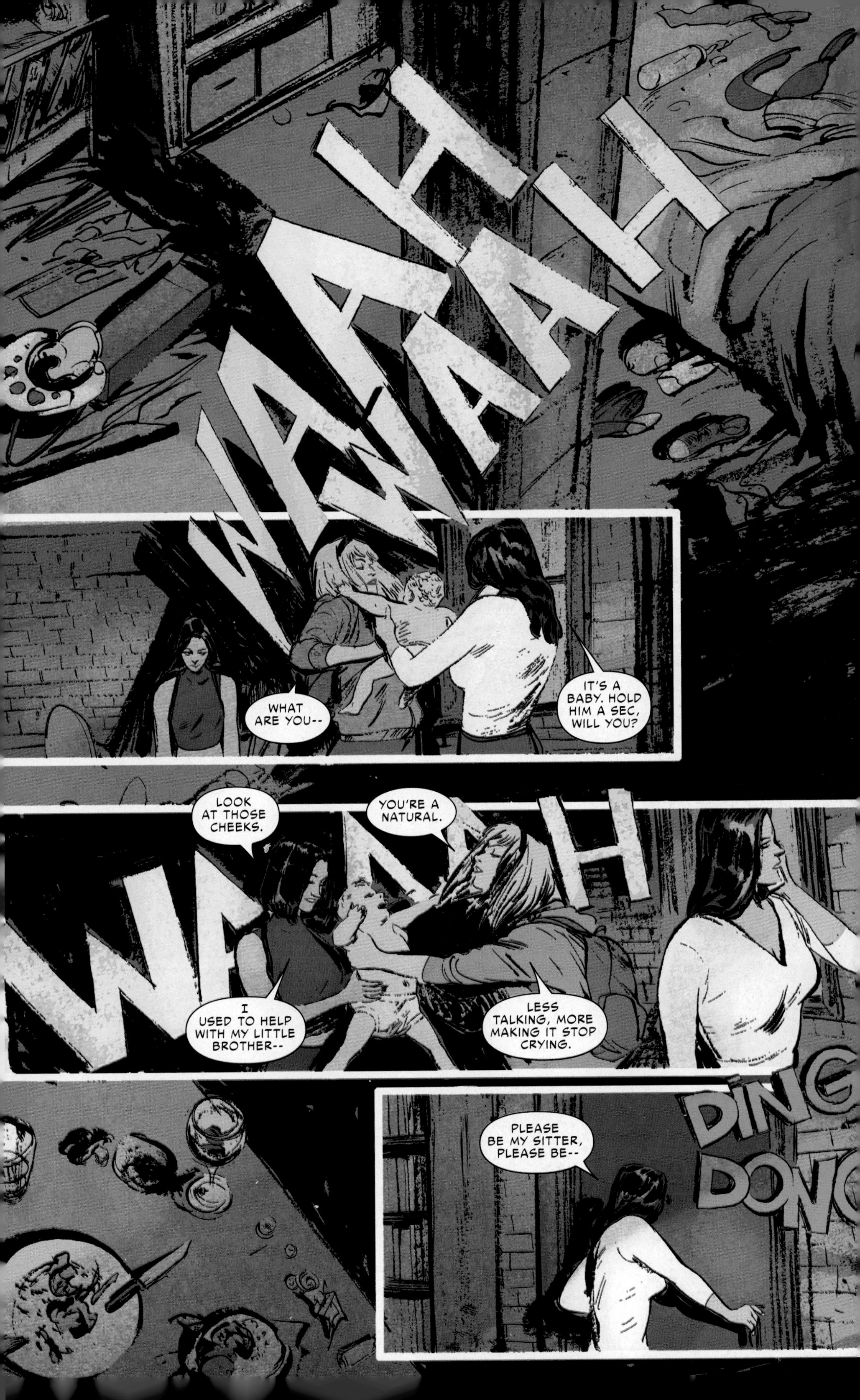
WAAAH
WHAT ARE YOU--
IT'S A BABY. HOLD HIM A SEC, WILL YOU?
WAAAH
LOOK AT THOSE CHEEKS.
YOU'RE A NATURAL.
I USED TO HELP WITH MY LITTLE BROTHER--
LESS TALKING, MORE MAKING IT STOP CRYING.
DING
DONG
PLEASE BE MY SITTER, PLEASE BE--

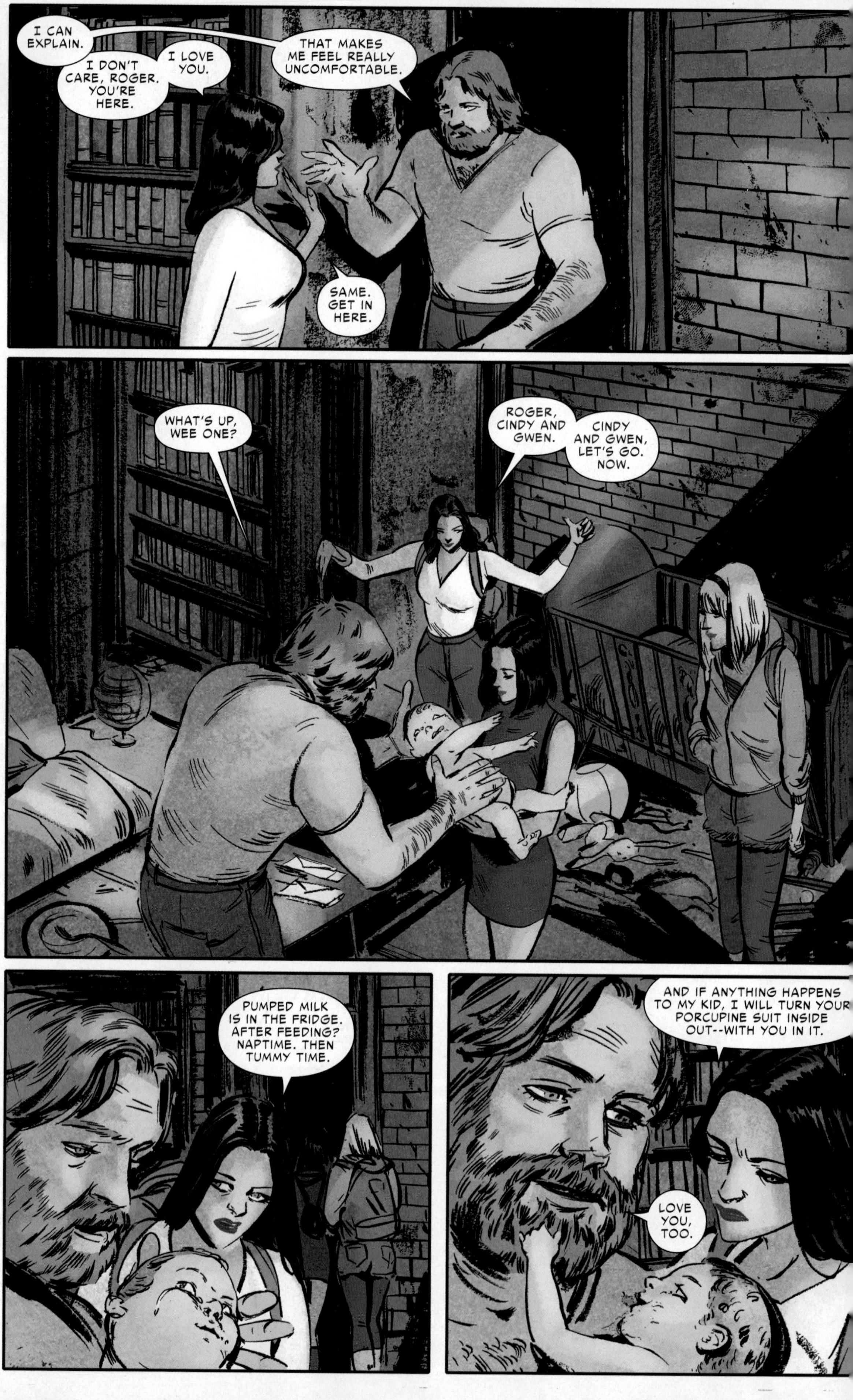
I CAN EXPLAIN.
I DON'T CARE, ROGER. YOU'RE HERE.
I LOVE YOU.
THAT MAKES ME FEEL REALLY UNCOMFORTABLE.
SAME. GET IN HERE.
WHAT'S UP, WEE ONE?
ROGER, CINDY AND GWEN.
CINDY AND GWEN, LET'S GO. NOW.
PUMPED MILK IS IN THE FRIDGE. AFTER FEEDING? NAPTIME. THEN TUMMY TIME.
AND IF ANYTHING HAPPENS TO MY KID, I WILL TURN YOUR PORCUPINE SUIT INSIDE OUT--WITH YOU IN IT.
LOVE YOU, TOO.

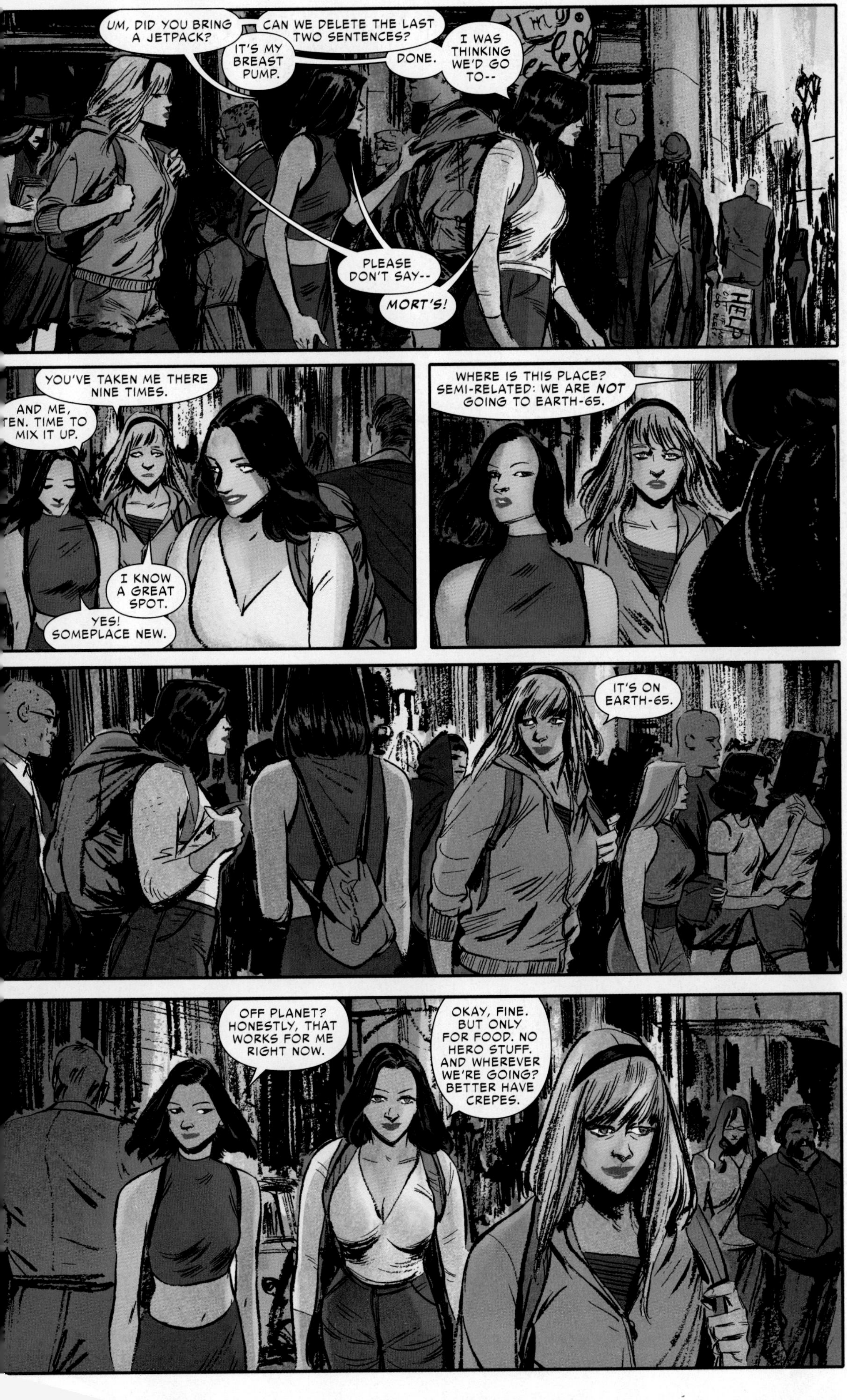
UM, DID YOU BRING A JETPACK?
IT'S MY BREAST PUMP.
CAN WE DELETE THE LAST TWO SENTENCES?
DONE.
I WAS THINKING WE'D GO TO--
PLEASE DON'T SAY--
MORT'S!
YOU'VE TAKEN ME THERE NINE TIMES.
AND ME, TEN. TIME TO MIX IT UP.
I KNOW A GREAT SPOT.
YES! SOMEPLACE NEW.
WHERE IS THIS PLACE? SEMI-RELATED: WE ARE NOT GOING TO EARTH-65.
IT'S ON EARTH-65.
OFF PLANET? HONESTLY, THAT WORKS FOR ME RIGHT NOW.
OKAY, FINE. BUT ONLY FOR FOOD. NO HERO STUFF. AND WHEREVER WE'RE GOING? BETTER HAVE CREPES.

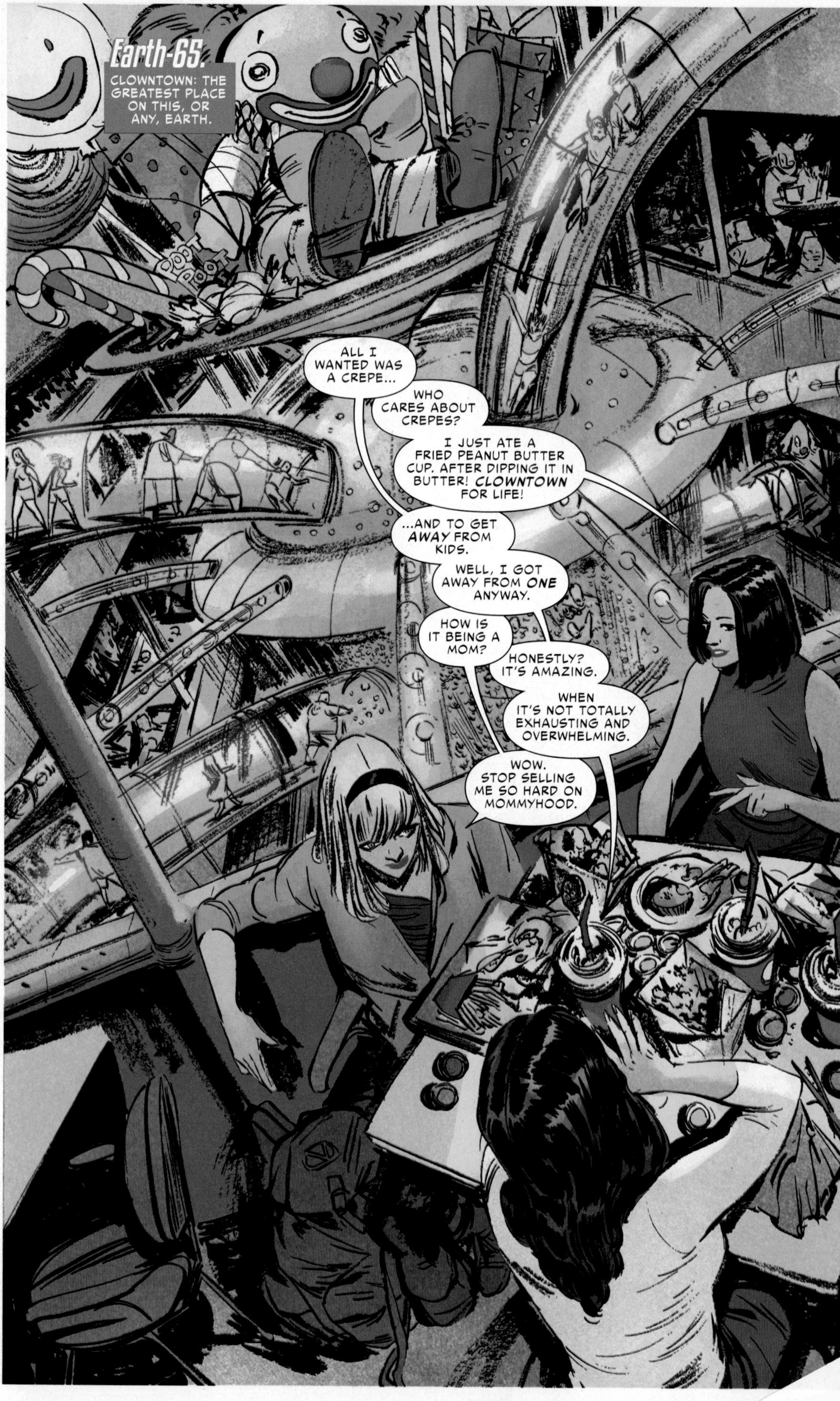
Earth-65.
CLOWNTOWN: THE GREATEST PLACE ON THIS, OR ANY, EARTH.
ALL I WANTED WAS A CREPE...
WHO CARES ABOUT CREPES?
I JUST ATE A FRIED PEANUT BUTTER CUP. AFTER DIPPING IT IN BUTTER! CLOWNTOWN FOR LIFE!
...AND TO GET AWAY FROM KIDS.
WELL, I GOT AWAY FROM ONE ANYWAY.
HOW IS IT BEING A MOM?
HONESTLY? IT'S AMAZING.
WHEN IT'S NOT TOTALLY EXHAUSTING AND OVERWHELMING.
WOW. STOP SELLING ME SO HARD ON MOMMYHOOD.

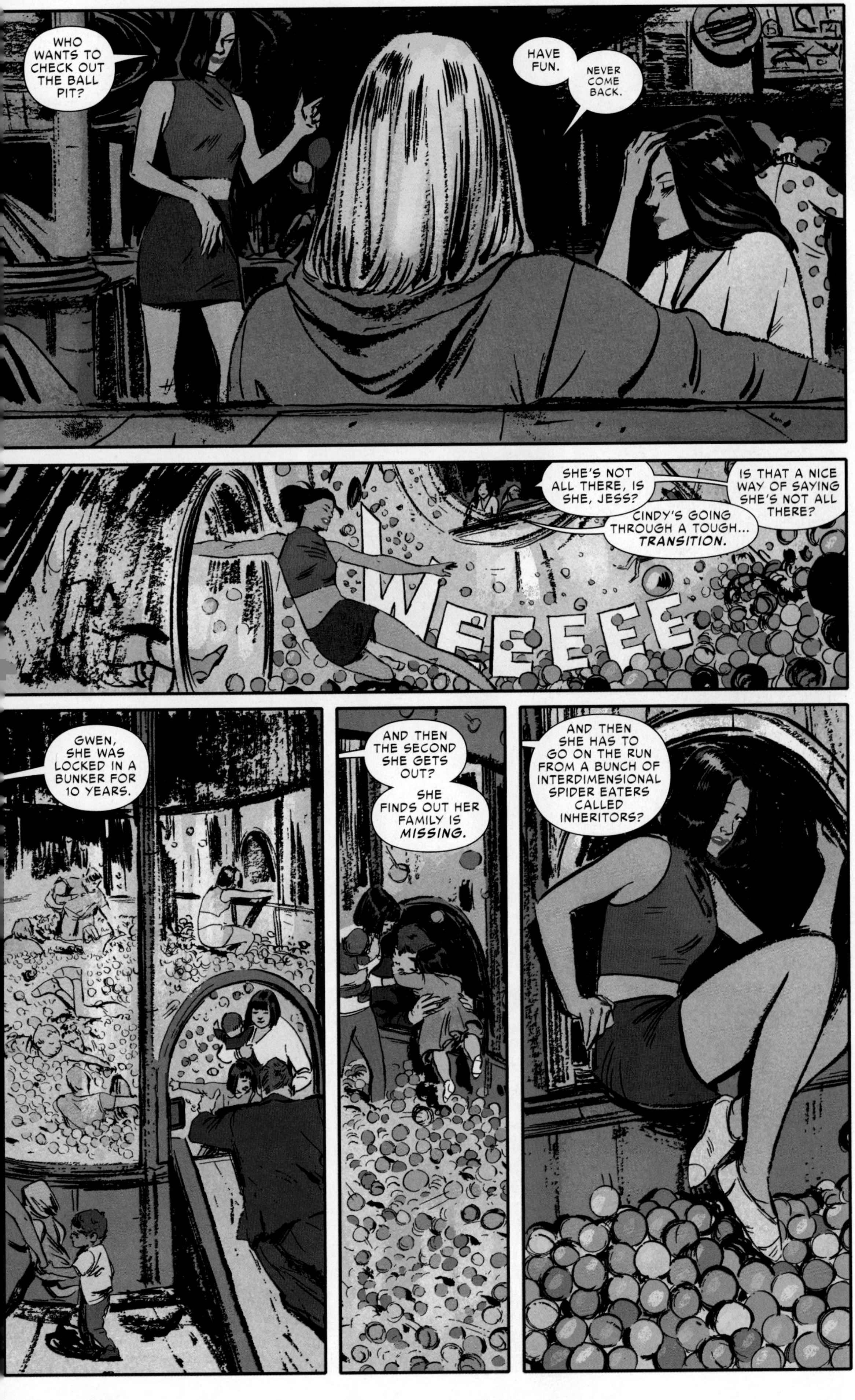
WHO WANTS TO CHECK OUT THE BALL PIT?
HAVE FUN.
NEVER COME BACK.
WEEEEE
SHE'S NOT ALL THERE, IS SHE, JESS?
IS THAT A NICE WAY OF SAYING SHE'S NOT ALL THERE?
CINDY'S GOING THROUGH A TOUGH... *TRANSITION.*
GWEN, SHE WAS LOCKED IN A BUNKER FOR 10 YEARS.
AND THEN THE SECOND SHE GETS OUT?
SHE FINDS OUT HER FAMILY IS *MISSING.*
AND THEN SHE HAS TO GO ON THE RUN FROM A BUNCH OF INTERDIMENSIONAL SPIDER EATERS CALLED INHERITORS?

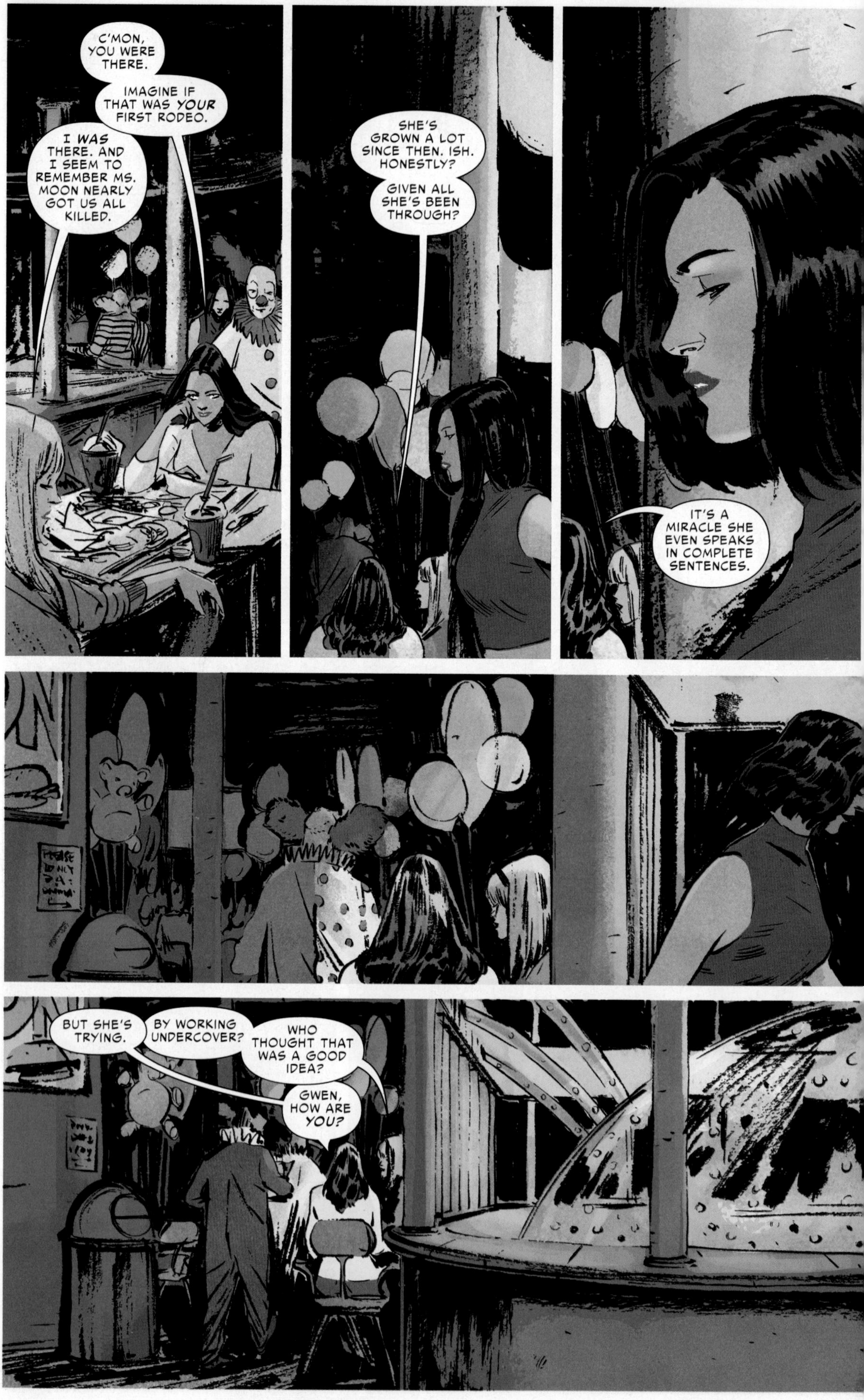
C'MON, YOU WERE THERE.
IMAGINE IF THAT WAS *YOUR* FIRST RODEO.
I *WAS* THERE. AND I SEEM TO REMEMBER MS. MOON NEARLY GOT US ALL KILLED.
SHE'S GROWN A LOT SINCE THEN. ISH. HONESTLY?
GIVEN ALL SHE'S BEEN THROUGH?
IT'S A MIRACLE SHE EVEN SPEAKS IN COMPLETE SENTENCES.
BUT SHE'S TRYING.
BY WORKING UNDERCOVER?
WHO THOUGHT THAT WAS A GOOD IDEA?
GWEN, HOW ARE *YOU*?

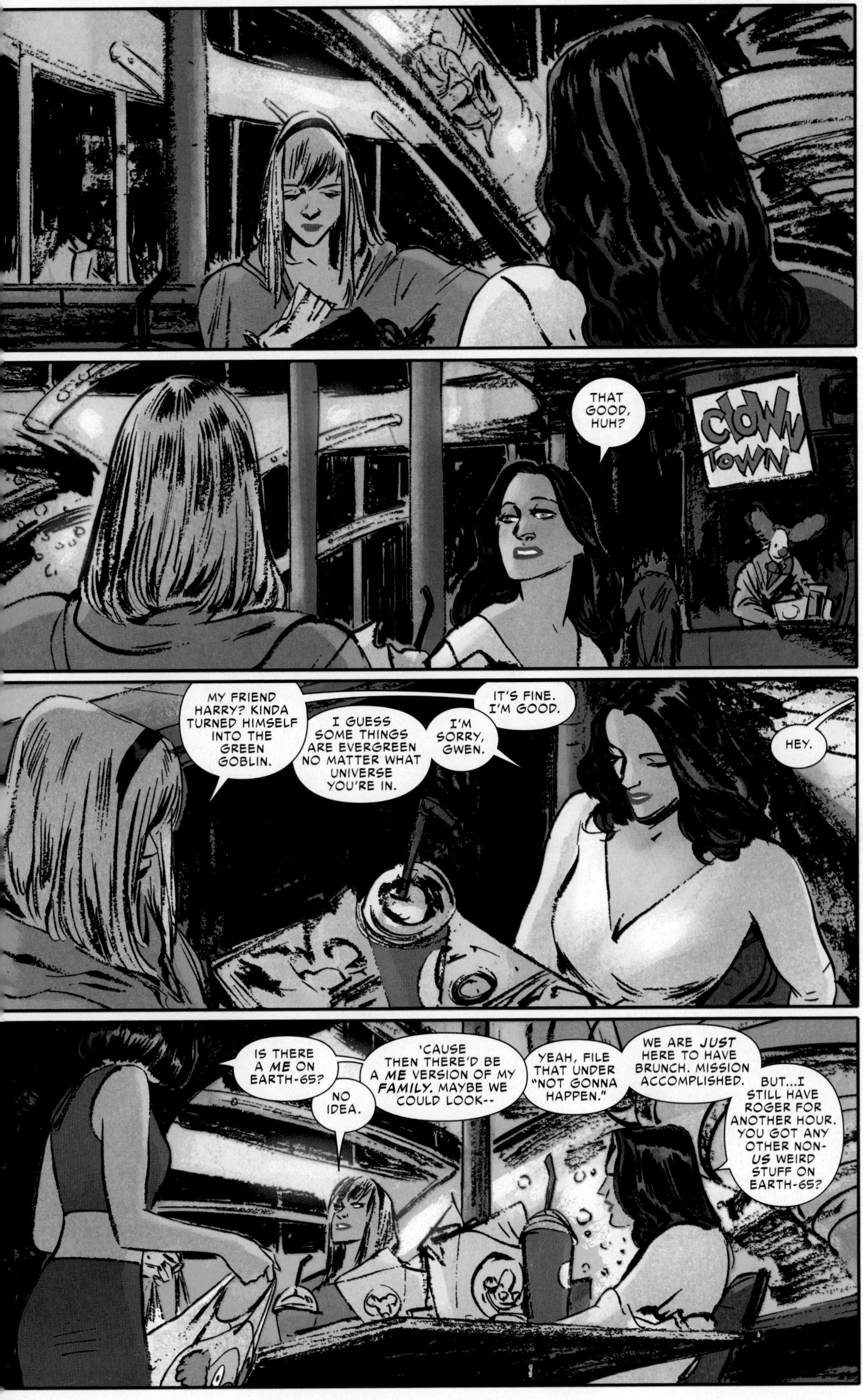
THAT GOOD, HUH?
CLOWN TOWN
MY FRIEND HARRY? KINDA TURNED HIMSELF INTO THE GREEN GOBLIN.
I GUESS SOME THINGS ARE EVERGREEN NO MATTER WHAT UNIVERSE YOU'RE IN.
I'M SORRY, GWEN.
IT'S FINE. I'M GOOD.
HEY.
IS THERE A ME ON EARTH-65?
NO IDEA.
'CAUSE THEN THERE'D BE A ME VERSION OF MY FAMILY. MAYBE WE COULD LOOK--
YEAH, FILE THAT UNDER "NOT GONNA HAPPEN."
WE ARE JUST HERE TO HAVE BRUNCH. MISSION ACCOMPLISHED.
BUT...I STILL HAVE ROGER FOR ANOTHER HOUR. YOU GOT ANY OTHER NON-US WEIRD STUFF ON EARTH-65?

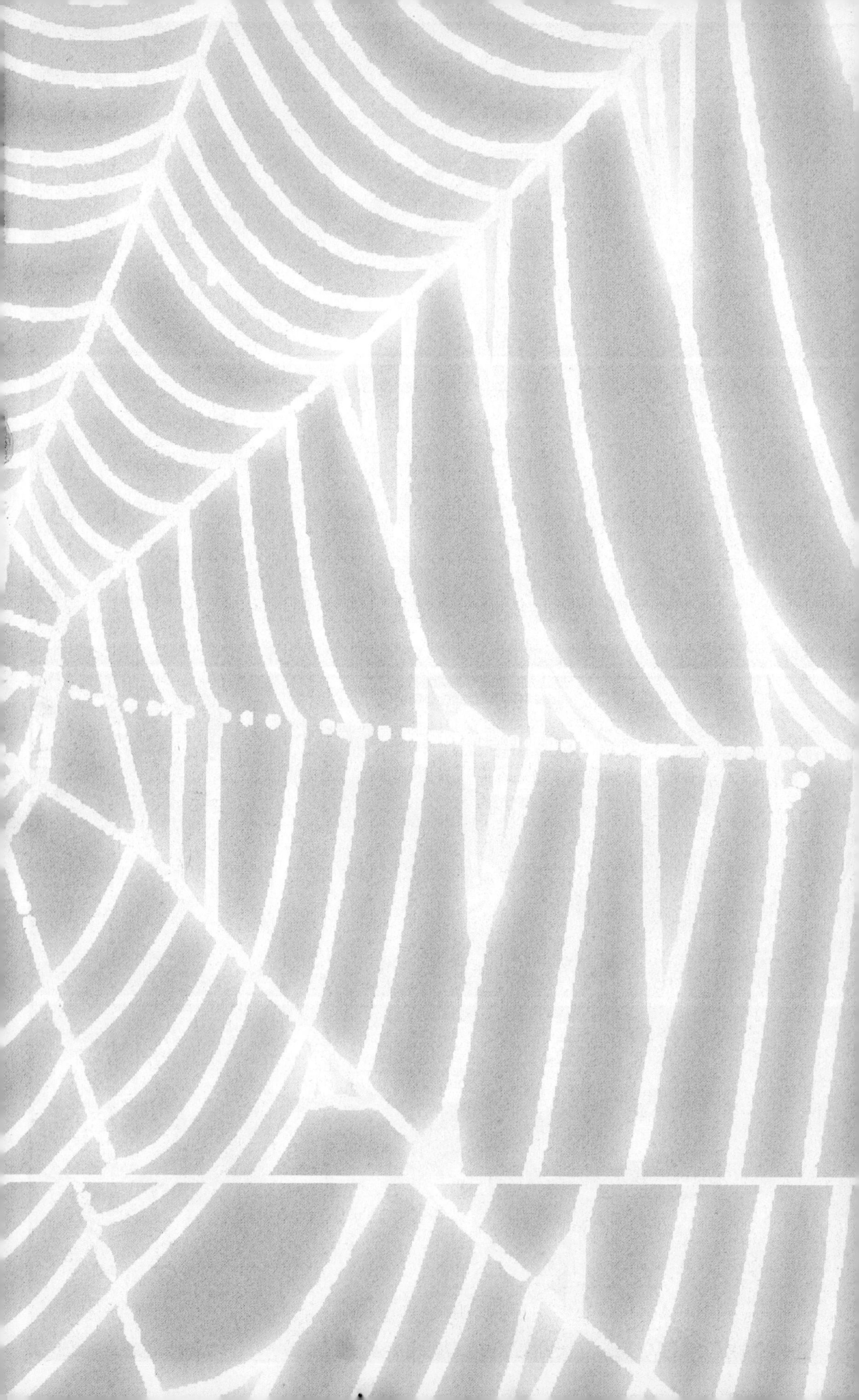

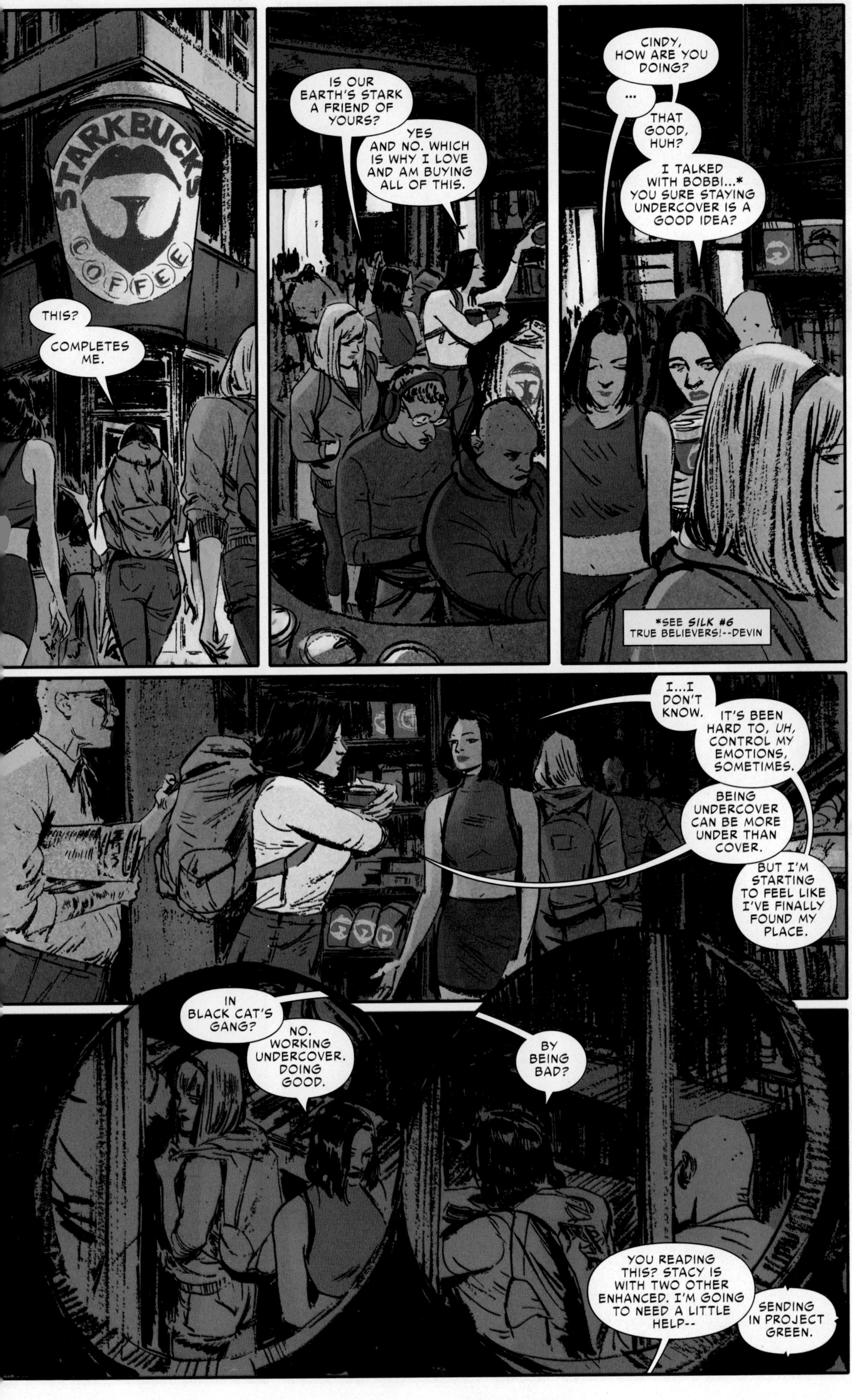

STARKBUCKS COFFEE
THIS?
COMPLETES ME.
IS OUR EARTH'S STARK A FRIEND OF YOURS?
YES AND NO. WHICH IS WHY I LOVE AND AM BUYING ALL OF THIS.
CINDY, HOW ARE YOU DOING?
...
THAT GOOD, HUH?
I TALKED WITH BOBBI...* YOU SURE STAYING UNDERCOVER IS A GOOD IDEA?
*SEE SILK #6 TRUE BELIEVERS!--DEVIN
I...I DON'T KNOW.
IT'S BEEN HARD TO, UH, CONTROL MY EMOTIONS, SOMETIMES.
BEING UNDERCOVER CAN BE MORE UNDER THAN COVER.
BUT I'M STARTING TO FEEL LIKE I'VE FINALLY FOUND MY PLACE.
IN BLACK CAT'S GANG?
NO. WORKING UNDERCOVER. DOING GOOD.
BY BEING BAD?
YOU READING THIS? STACY IS WITH TWO OTHER ENHANCED. I'M GOING TO NEED A LITTLE HELP--
SENDING IN PROJECT GREEN.

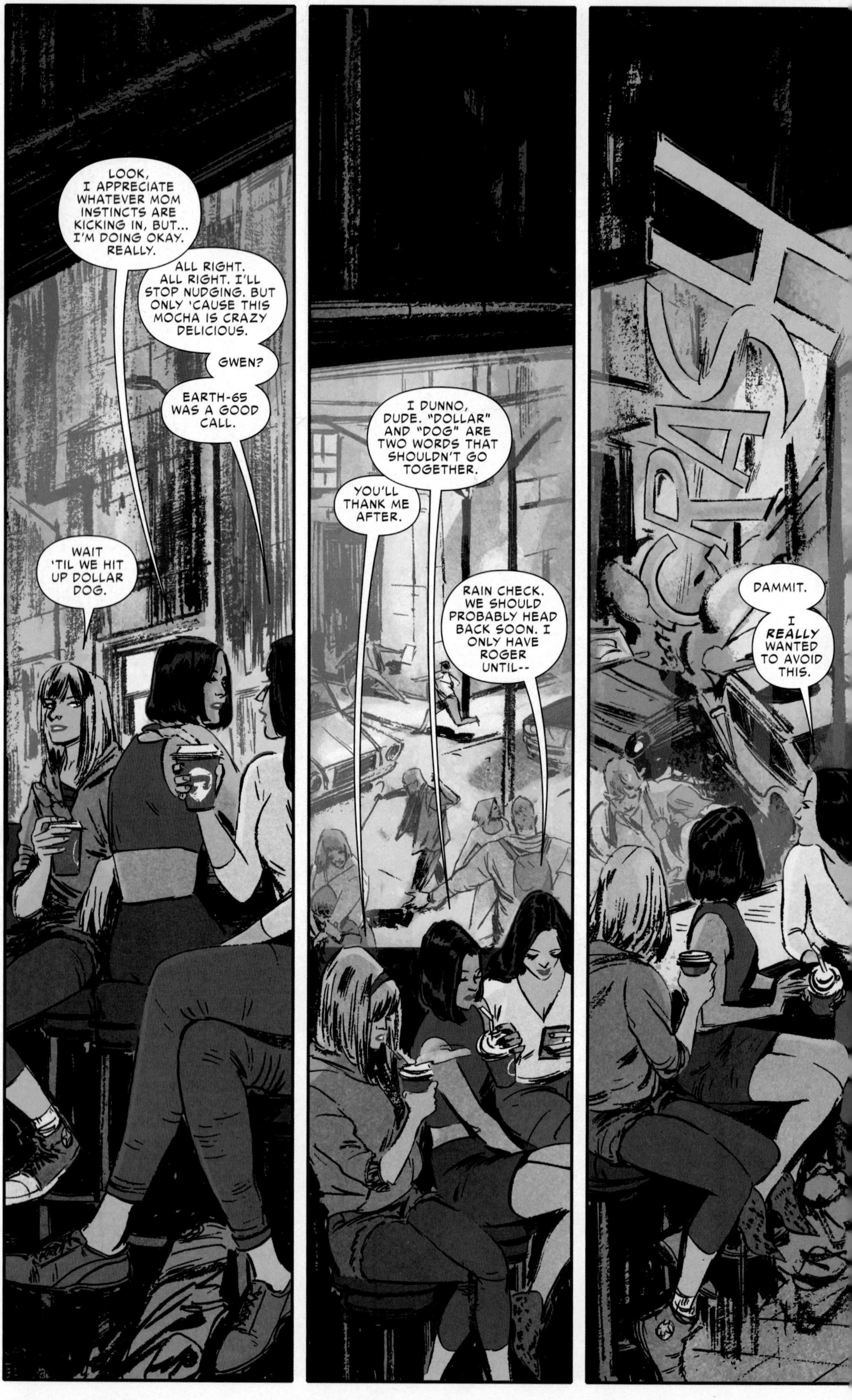
LOOK, I APPRECIATE WHATEVER MOM INSTINCTS ARE KICKING IN, BUT... I'M DOING OKAY. REALLY.
ALL RIGHT. ALL RIGHT. I'LL STOP NUDGING. BUT ONLY 'CAUSE THIS MOCHA IS CRAZY DELICIOUS.
GWEN?
EARTH-65 WAS A GOOD CALL.
WAIT 'TIL WE HIT UP DOLLAR DOG.
I DUNNO, DUDE. "DOLLAR" AND "DOG" ARE TWO WORDS THAT SHOULDN'T GO TOGETHER.
YOU'LL THANK ME AFTER.
RAIN CHECK. WE SHOULD PROBABLY HEAD BACK SOON. I ONLY HAVE ROGER UNTIL--
CRASH
DAMMIT.
I REALLY WANTED TO AVOID THIS.

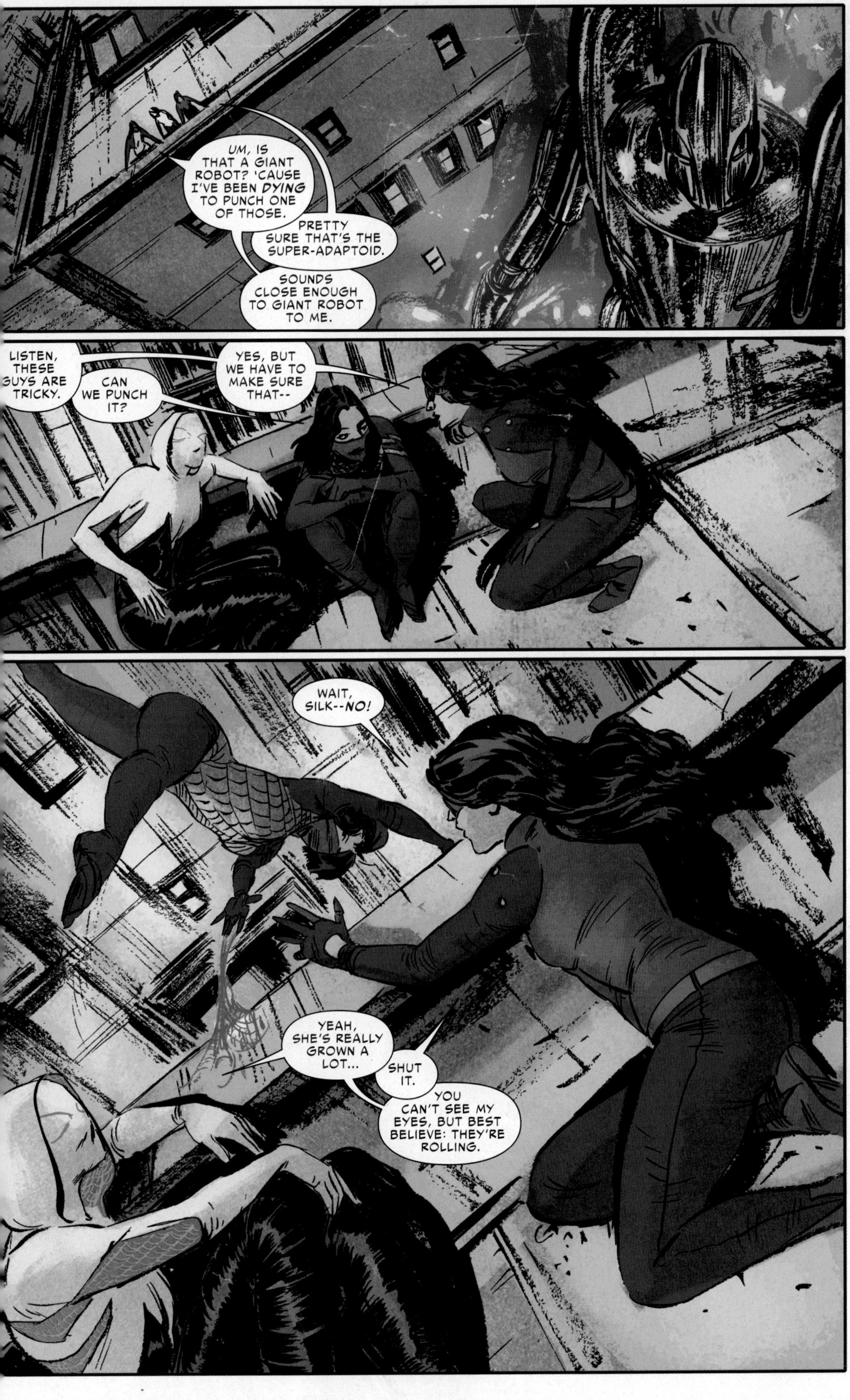
UM, IS THAT A GIANT ROBOT? 'CAUSE I'VE BEEN *DYING* TO PUNCH ONE OF THOSE.
PRETTY SURE THAT'S THE SUPER-ADAPTOID.
SOUNDS CLOSE ENOUGH TO GIANT ROBOT TO ME.
LISTEN, THESE GUYS ARE TRICKY.
CAN WE PUNCH IT?
YES, BUT WE HAVE TO MAKE SURE THAT--
WAIT, SILK--*NO!*
YEAH, SHE'S REALLY GROWN A LOT...
SHUT IT.
YOU CAN'T SEE MY EYES, BUT BEST BELIEVE: THEY'RE ROLLING.

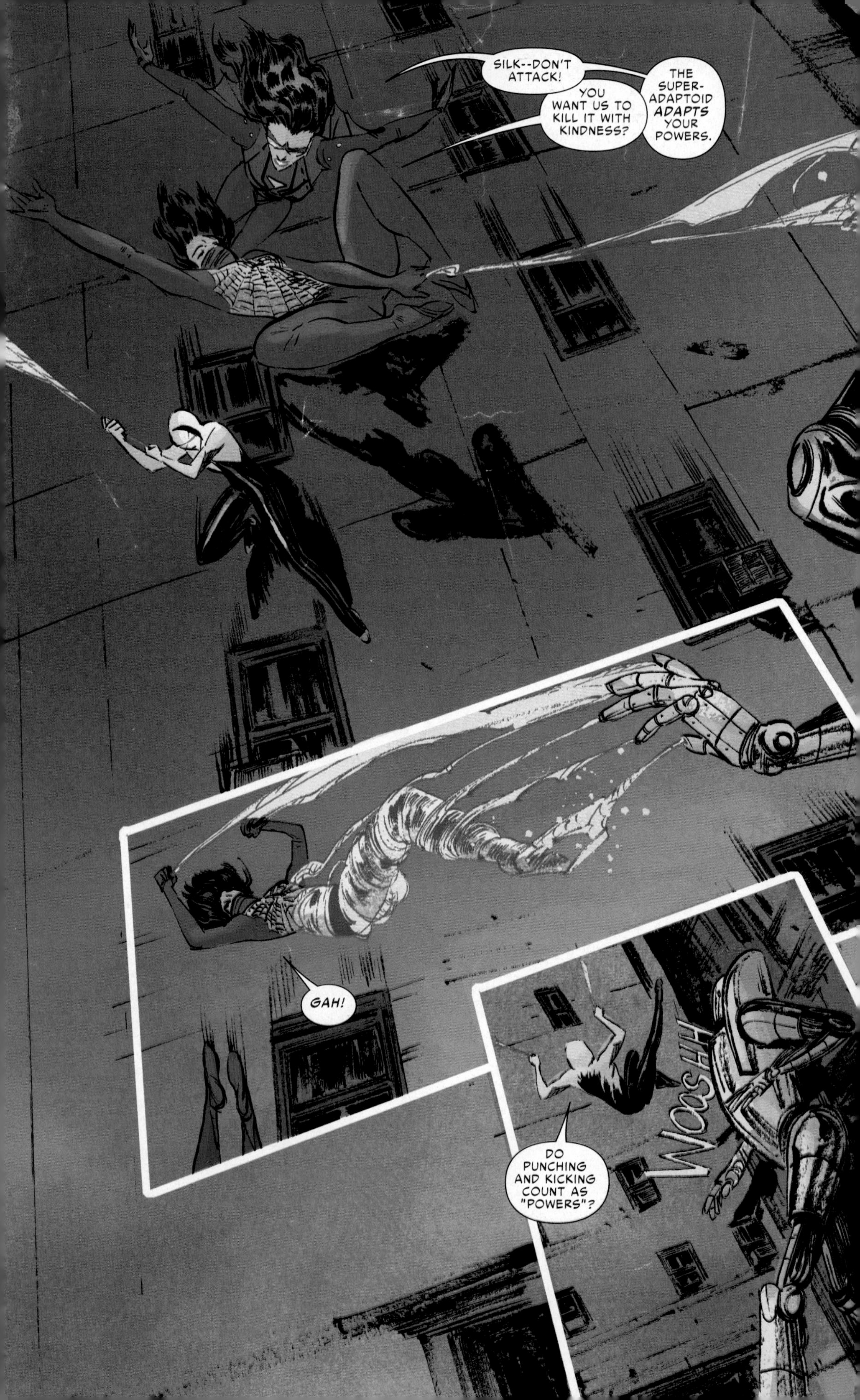
SILK--DON'T ATTACK!
THE SUPER-ADAPTOID ADAPTS YOUR POWERS.
YOU WANT US TO KILL IT WITH KINDNESS?
GAH!
DO PUNCHING AND KICKING COUNT AS "POWERS"?
WOOSHH

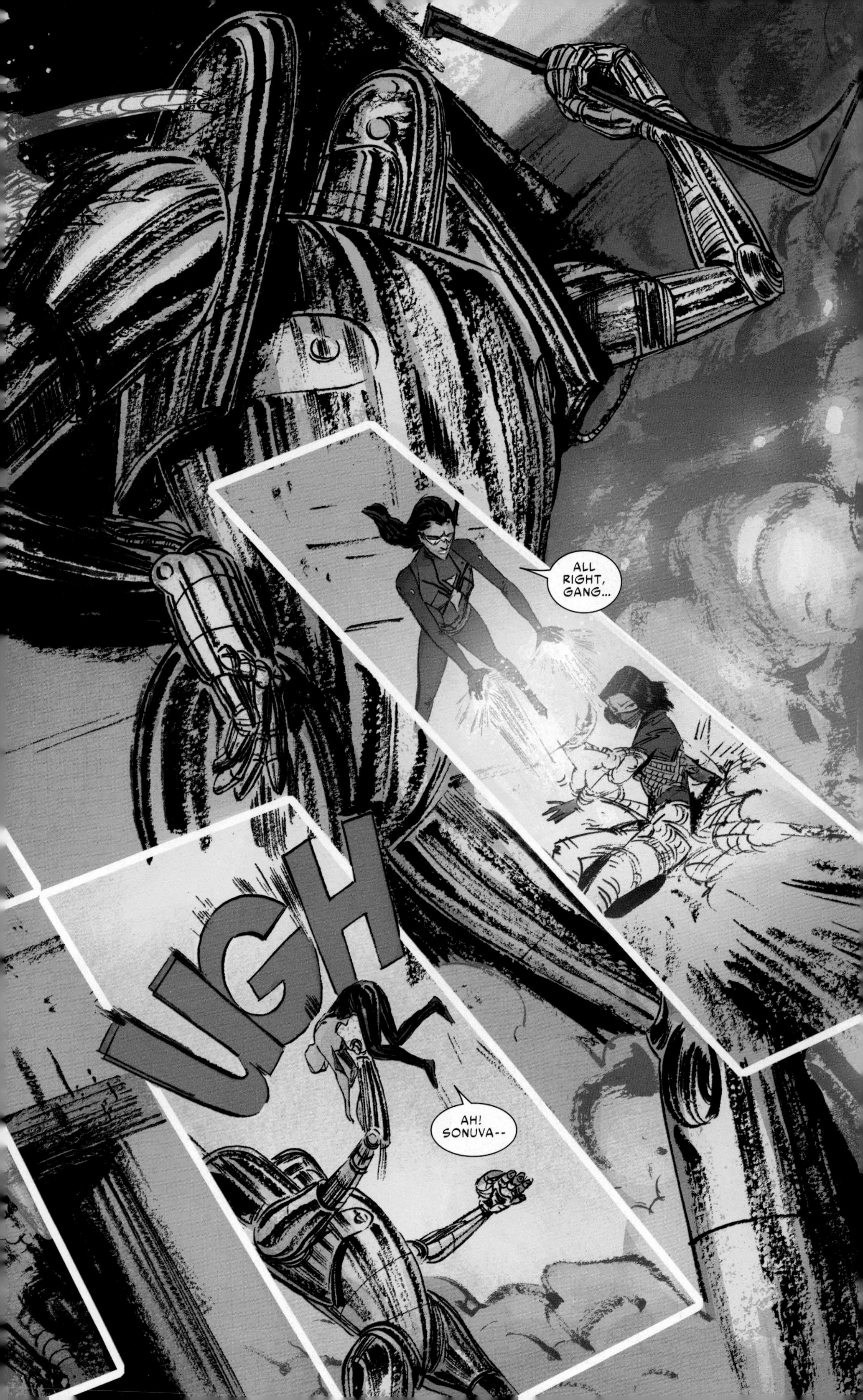
ALL RIGHT, GANG...
UGH
AH! SONUVA--

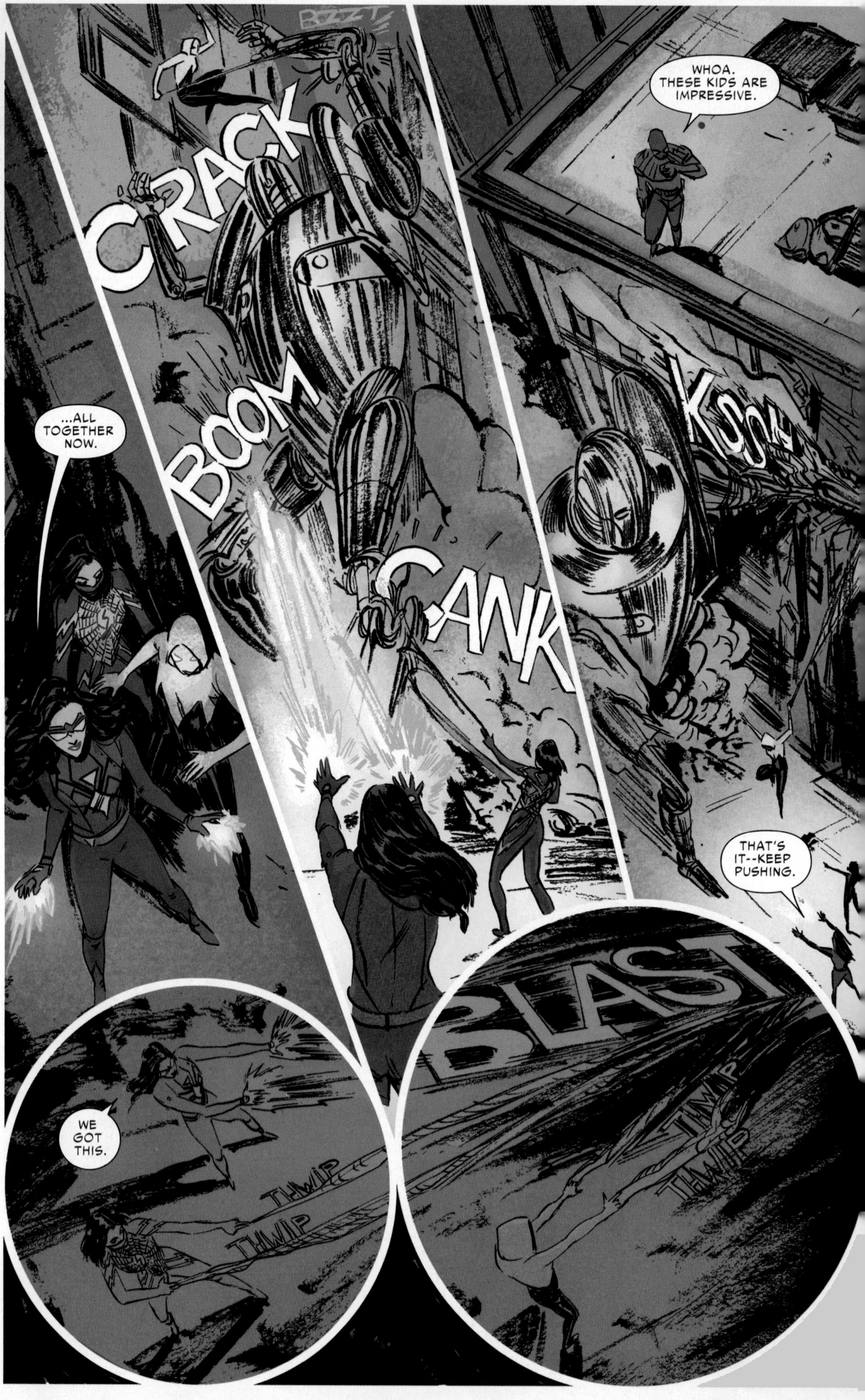
...ALL TOGETHER NOW.
BZZT
CRACK
BOOM
CANK
WHOA. THESE KIDS ARE IMPRESSIVE.
KSSSH
THAT'S IT--KEEP PUSHING.
WE GOT THIS.
THWIP
THWIP
BLAST
THWIP
THWIP

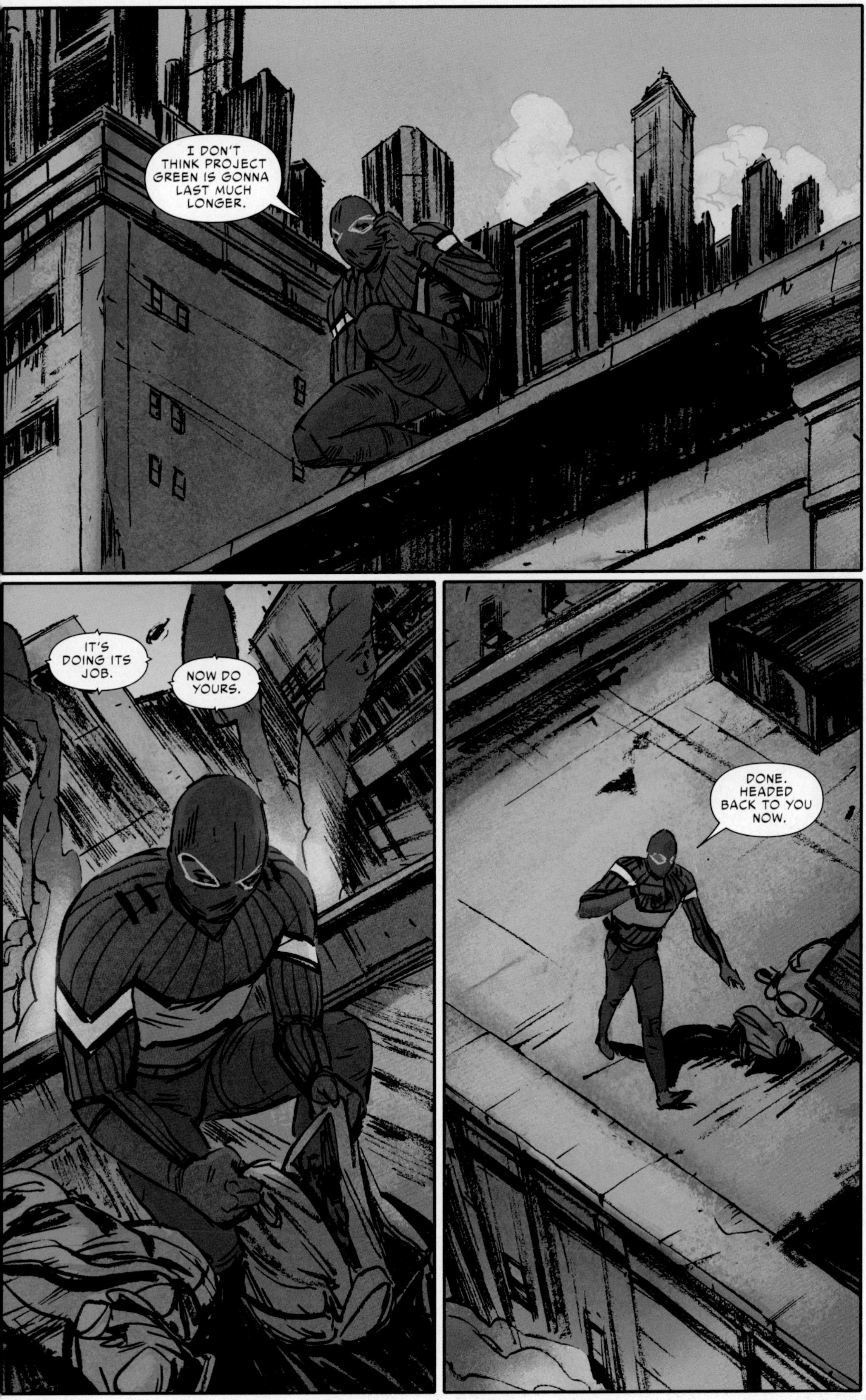
I DON'T THINK PROJECT GREEN IS GONNA LAST MUCH LONGER.
IT'S DOING ITS JOB.
NOW DO YOURS.
DONE. HEADED BACK TO YOU NOW.

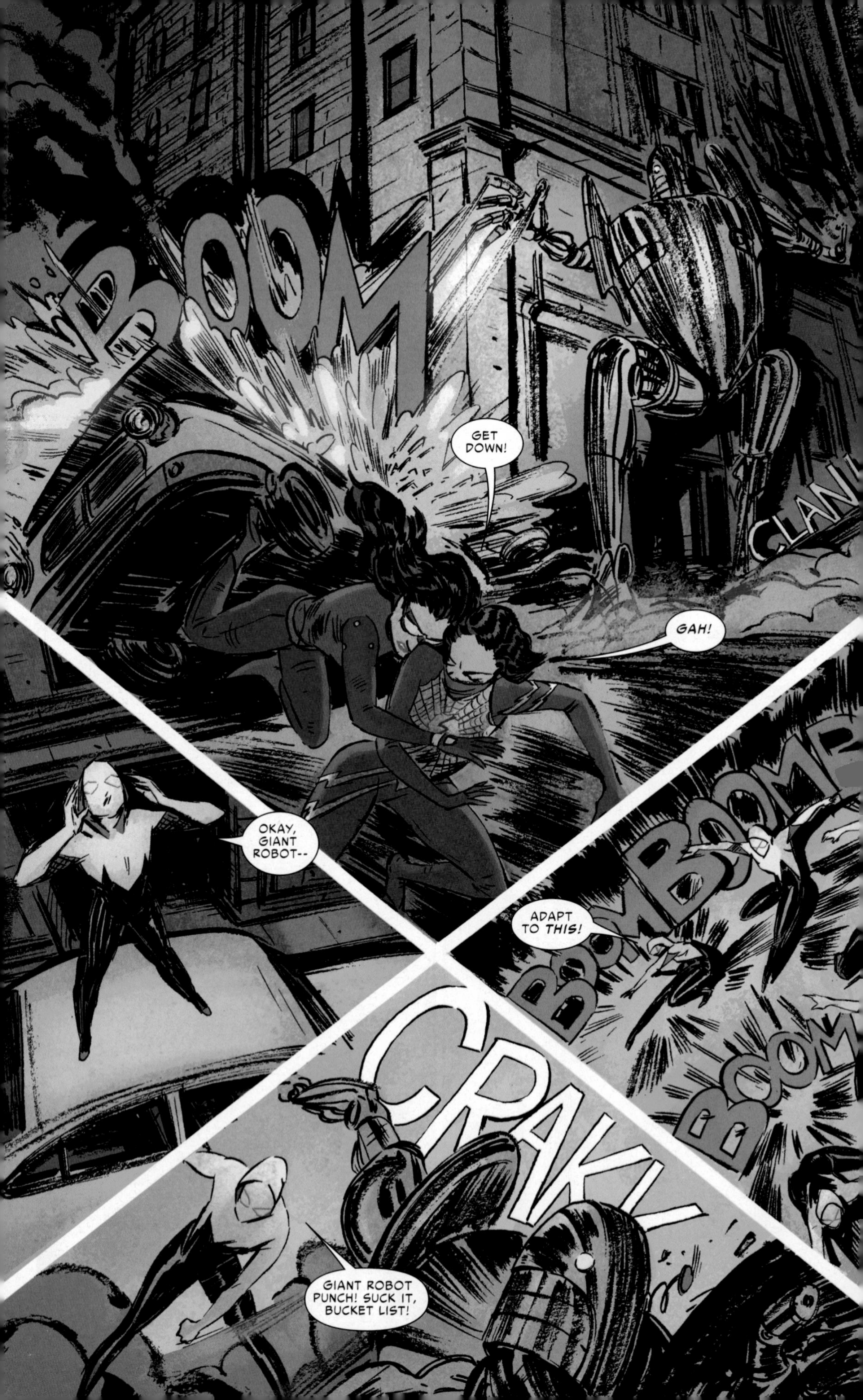
BOOM
GET DOWN!
CLAN
GAH!
OKAY, GIANT ROBOT--
BOOM
ADAPT TO THIS!
BOOM
CRAK!
GIANT ROBOT PUNCH! SUCK IT, BUCKET LIST!

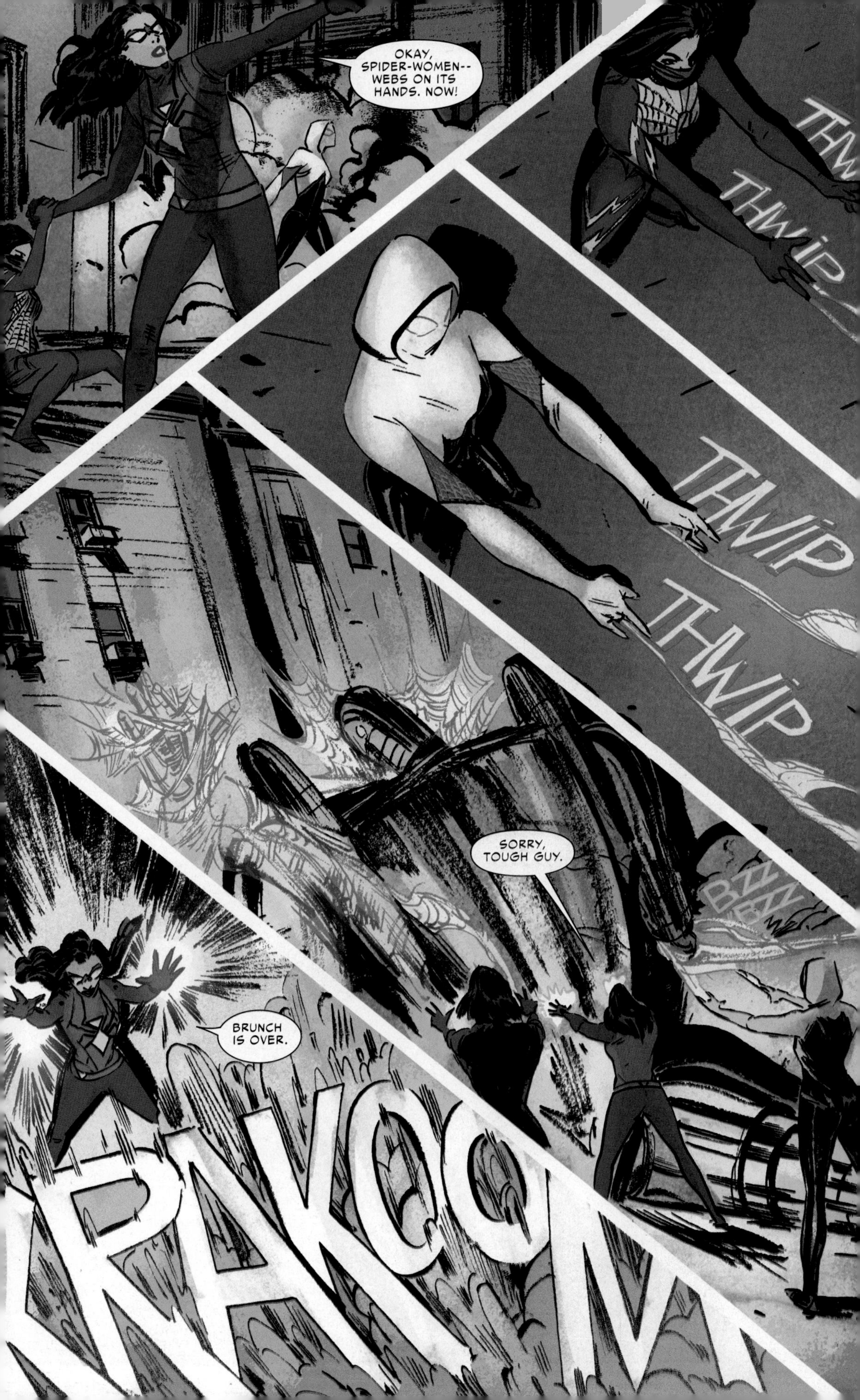
OKAY, SPIDER-WOMEN-- WEBS ON ITS HANDS. NOW!
THWIP
THWIP
THWIP
THWIP
SORRY, TOUGH GUY.
BZZZT
BRUNCH IS OVER.
KRAKOOM

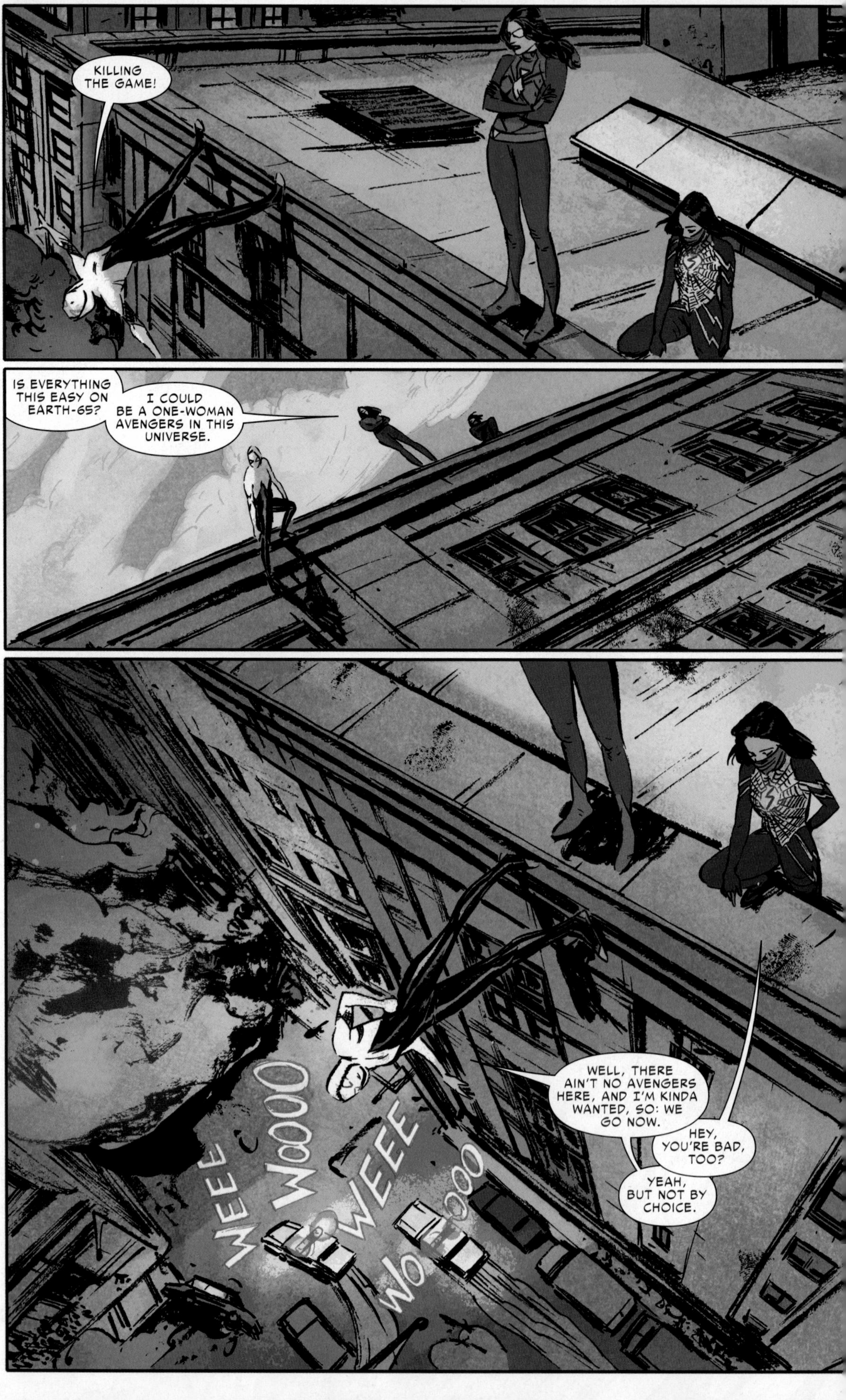

KILLING THE GAME!
IS EVERYTHING THIS EASY ON EARTH-65?
I COULD BE A ONE-WOMAN AVENGERS IN THIS UNIVERSE.
WELL, THERE AIN'T NO AVENGERS HERE, AND I'M KINDA WANTED, SO: WE GO NOW.
HEY, YOU'RE BAD, TOO?
YEAH, BUT NOT BY CHOICE.
WEEE WOOOO WEEE WOOOO

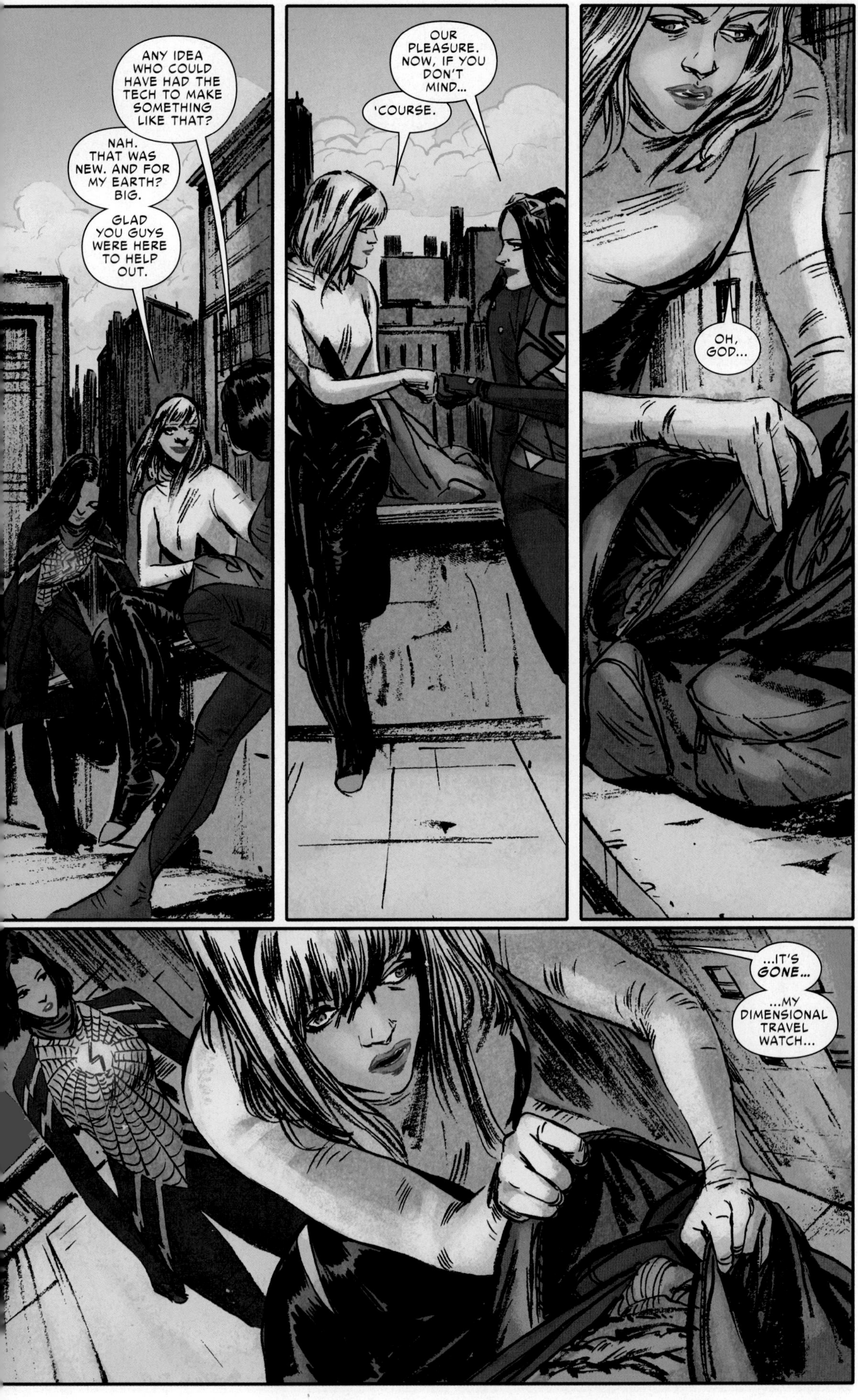
ANY IDEA WHO COULD HAVE HAD THE TECH TO MAKE SOMETHING LIKE THAT?
NAH. THAT WAS NEW. AND FOR MY EARTH? BIG.
GLAD YOU GUYS WERE HERE TO HELP OUT.
OUR PLEASURE. NOW, IF YOU DON'T MIND...
'COURSE.
OH, GOD...
...IT'S GONE...
...MY DIMENSIONAL TRAVEL WATCH...

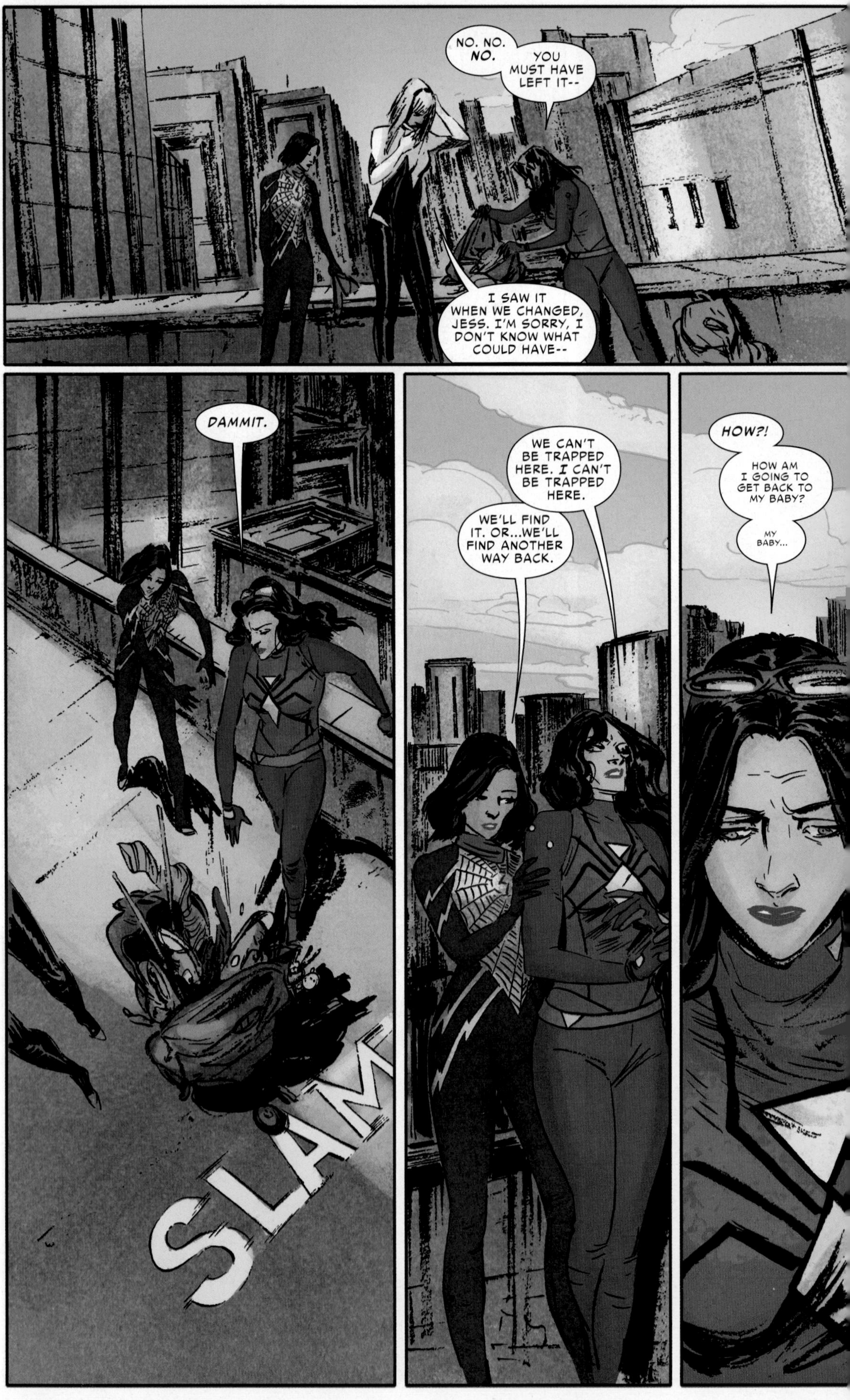

NO. NO. NO.
YOU MUST HAVE LEFT IT--
I SAW IT WHEN WE CHANGED, JESS. I'M SORRY, I DON'T KNOW WHAT COULD HAVE--
DAMMIT.
SLAM
WE CAN'T BE TRAPPED HERE. I CAN'T BE TRAPPED HERE.
WE'LL FIND IT. OR...WE'LL FIND ANOTHER WAY BACK.
HOW?!
HOW AM I GOING TO GET BACK TO MY BABY?
MY BABY...

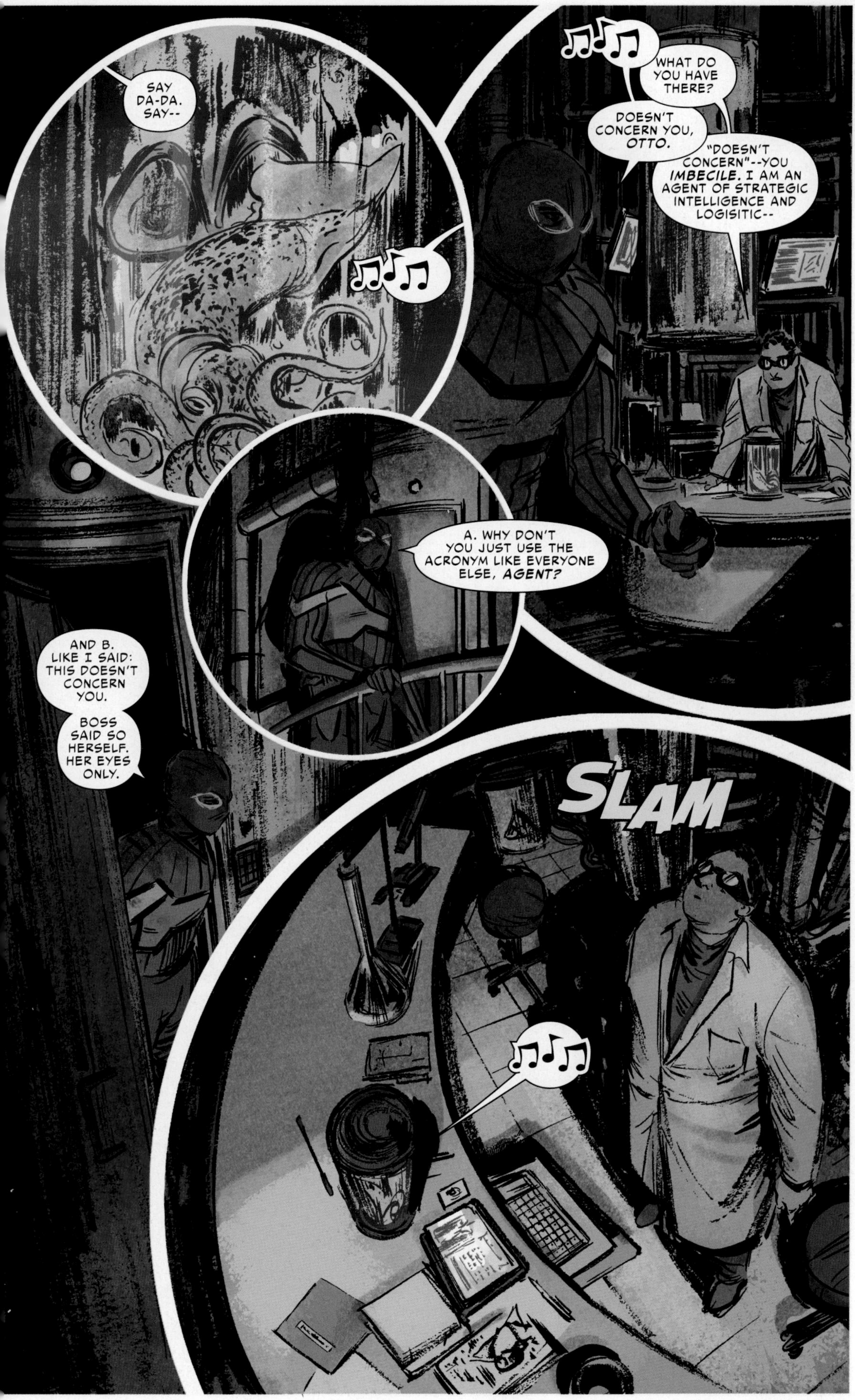
SAY DA-DA. SAY--
♫♩♫
♫♩♫
WHAT DO YOU HAVE THERE?
DOESN'T CONCERN YOU, OTTO.
"DOESN'T CONCERN"--YOU IMBECILE. I AM AN AGENT OF STRATEGIC INTELLIGENCE AND LOGISITIC--
A. WHY DON'T YOU JUST USE THE ACRONYM LIKE EVERYONE ELSE, AGENT?
AND B. LIKE I SAID: THIS DOESN'T CONCERN YOU.
BOSS SAID SO HERSELF. HER EYES ONLY.
SLAM
♫♩♫

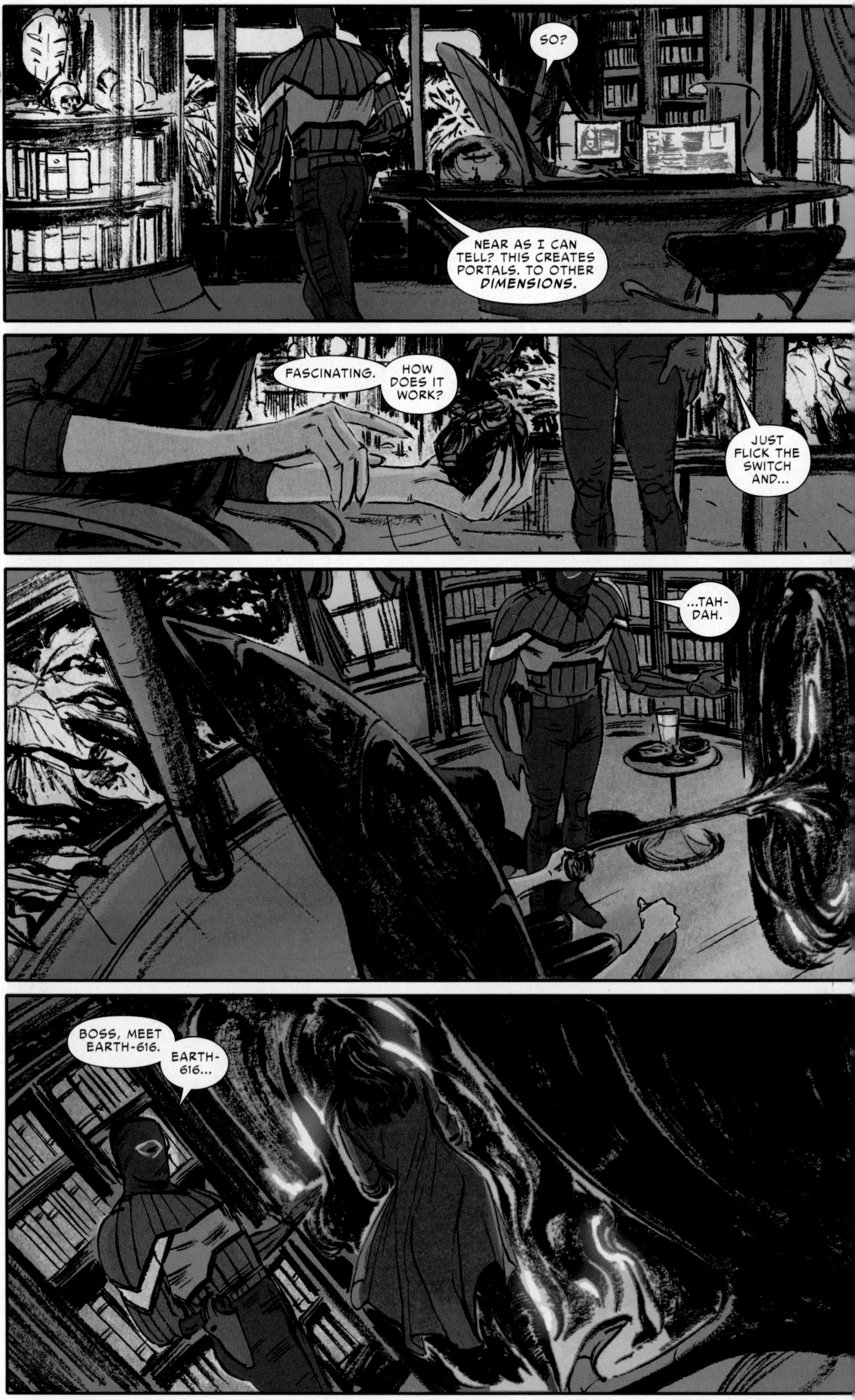
SO?
NEAR AS I CAN TELL? THIS CREATES PORTALS. TO OTHER DIMENSIONS.
FASCINATING.
HOW DOES IT WORK?
JUST FLICK THE SWITCH AND...
...TAH-DAH.
BOSS, MEET EARTH-616.
EARTH-616...

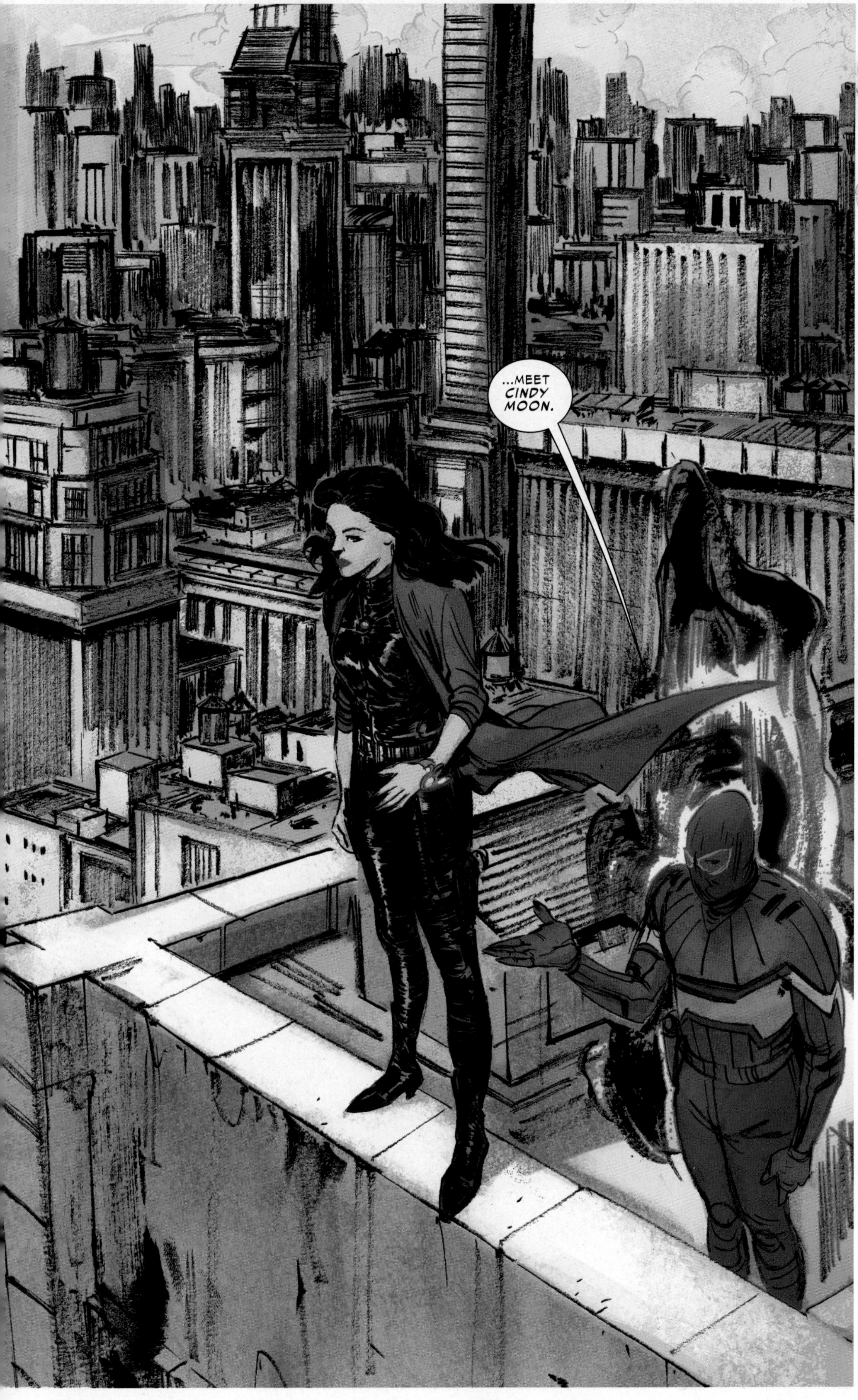
...MEET CINDY MOON.

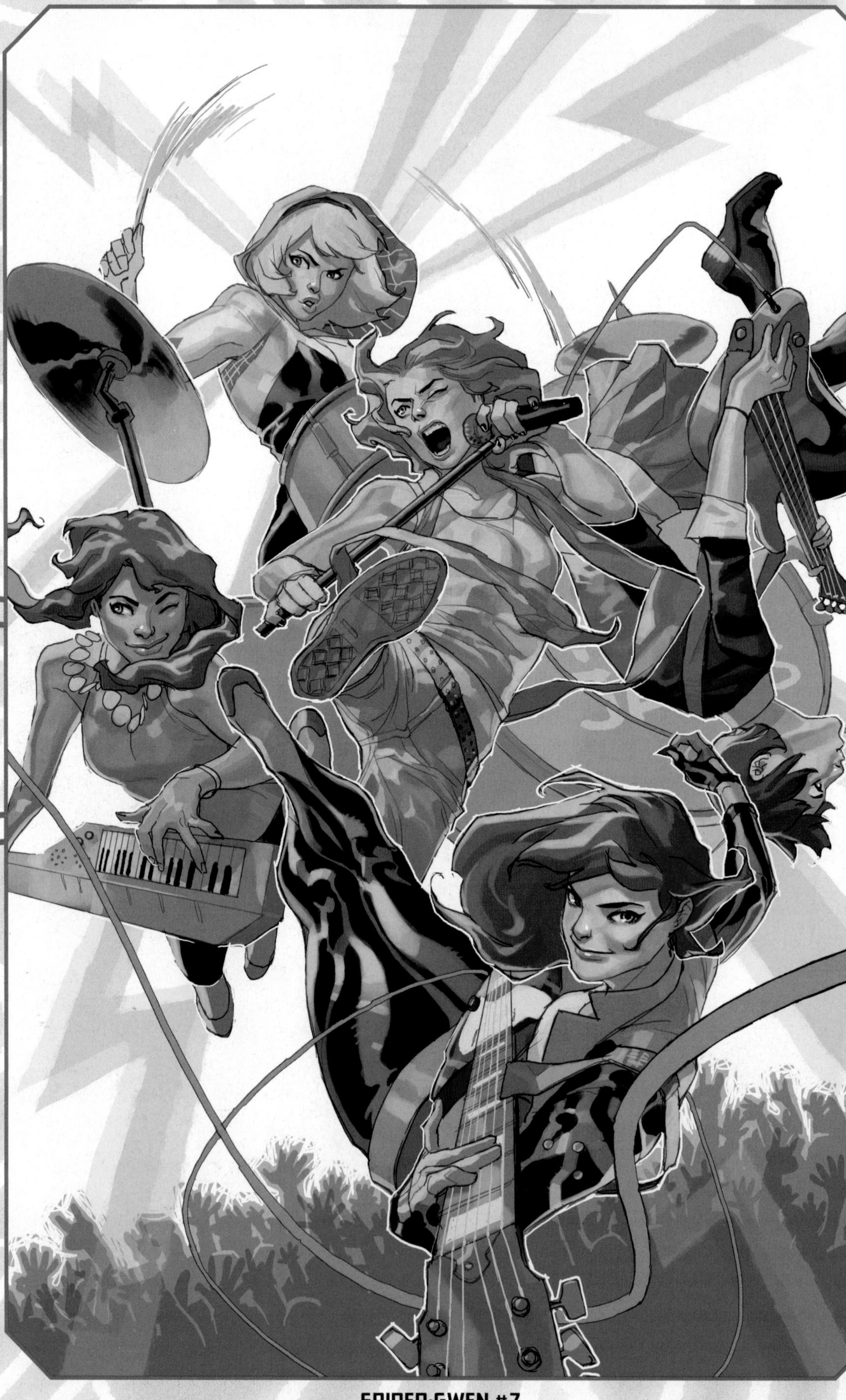

SPIDER-GWEN #7

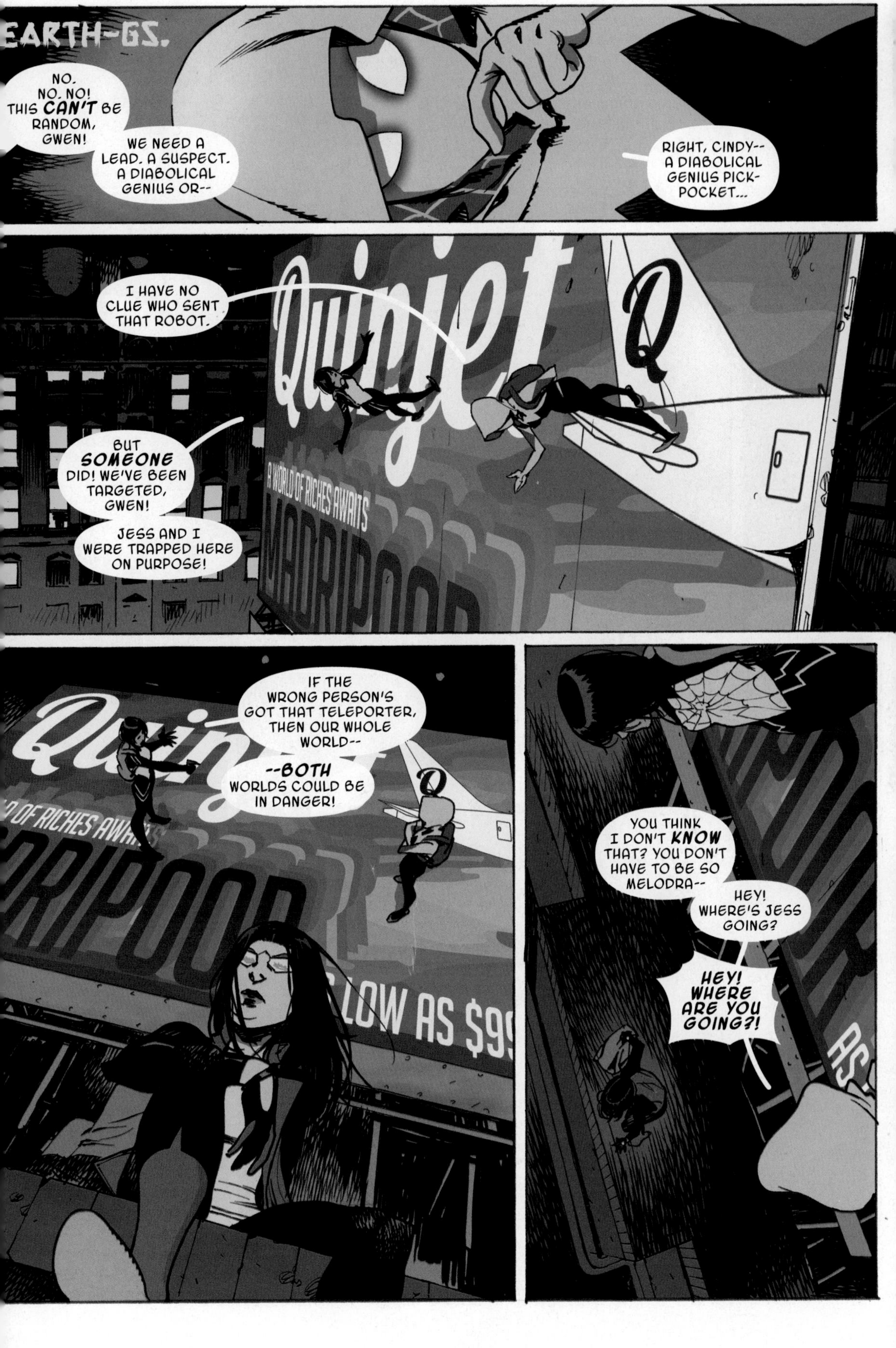
EARTH-GS.
NO. NO. NO! THIS CAN'T BE RANDOM, GWEN!
WE NEED A LEAD. A SUSPECT. A DIABOLICAL GENIUS OR--
RIGHT, CINDY-- A DIABOLICAL GENIUS PICK-POCKET...
I HAVE NO CLUE WHO SENT THAT ROBOT.
Quinjet
Q
A WORLD OF RICHES AWAITS
MADRIPOOR
BUT SOMEONE DID! WE'VE BEEN TARGETED, GWEN!
JESS AND I WERE TRAPPED HERE ON PURPOSE!
IF THE WRONG PERSON'S GOT THAT TELEPORTER, THEN OUR WHOLE WORLD--
--BOTH WORLDS COULD BE IN DANGER!
LOW AS $99
YOU THINK I DON'T KNOW THAT? YOU DON'T HAVE TO BE SO MELODRA--
HEY! WHERE'S JESS GOING?
HEY! WHERE ARE YOU GOING?!

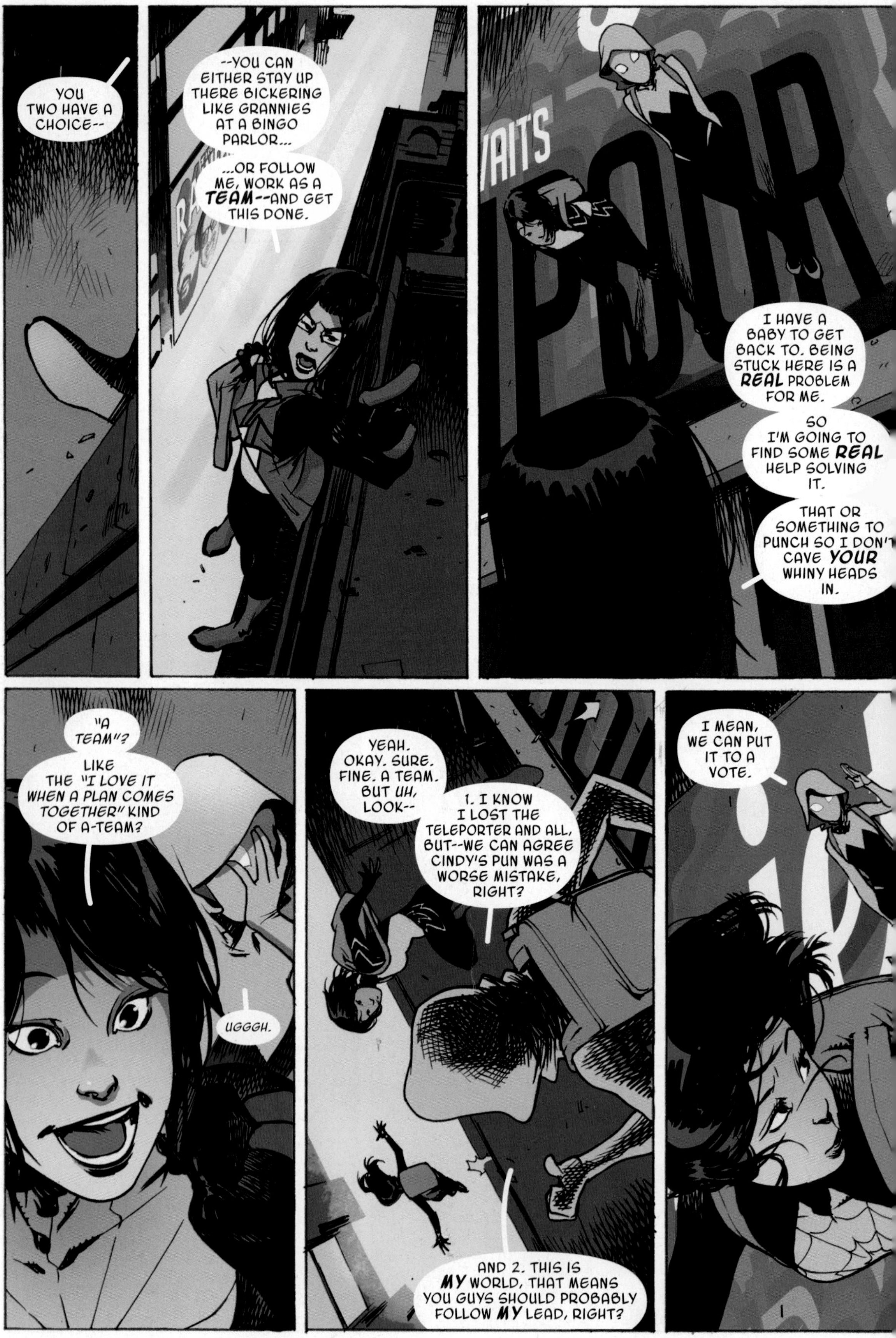
YOU TWO HAVE A CHOICE--
--YOU CAN EITHER STAY UP THERE BICKERING LIKE GRANNIES AT A BINGO PARLOR...
...OR FOLLOW ME, WORK AS A TEAM--AND GET THIS DONE.
VAITS
I HAVE A BABY TO GET BACK TO. BEING STUCK HERE IS A REAL PROBLEM FOR ME.
SO I'M GOING TO FIND SOME REAL HELP SOLVING IT.
THAT OR SOMETHING TO PUNCH SO I DON'T CAVE YOUR WHINY HEADS IN.
"A TEAM"? LIKE THE "I LOVE IT WHEN A PLAN COMES TOGETHER" KIND OF A-TEAM?
UGGGH.
YEAH. OKAY. SURE. FINE. A TEAM. BUT UH, LOOK--
1. I KNOW I LOST THE TELEPORTER AND ALL, BUT--WE CAN AGREE CINDY'S PUN WAS A WORSE MISTAKE, RIGHT?
AND 2. THIS IS MY WORLD, THAT MEANS YOU GUYS SHOULD PROBABLY FOLLOW MY LEAD, RIGHT?
I MEAN, WE CAN PUT IT TO A VOTE.

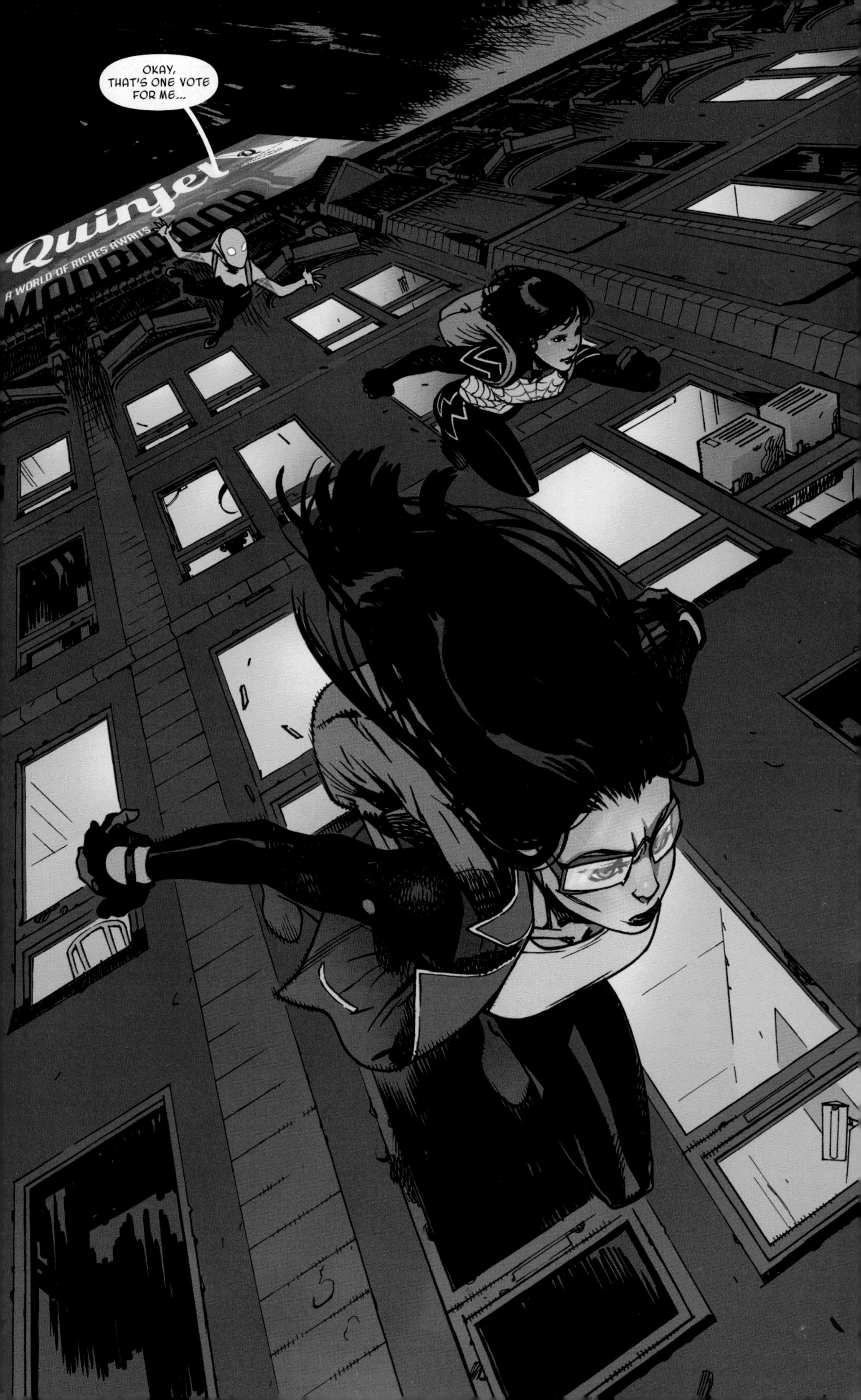

OKAY, THAT'S ONE VOTE FOR ME...
Quinjet
A WORLD OF RICHES AWAITS

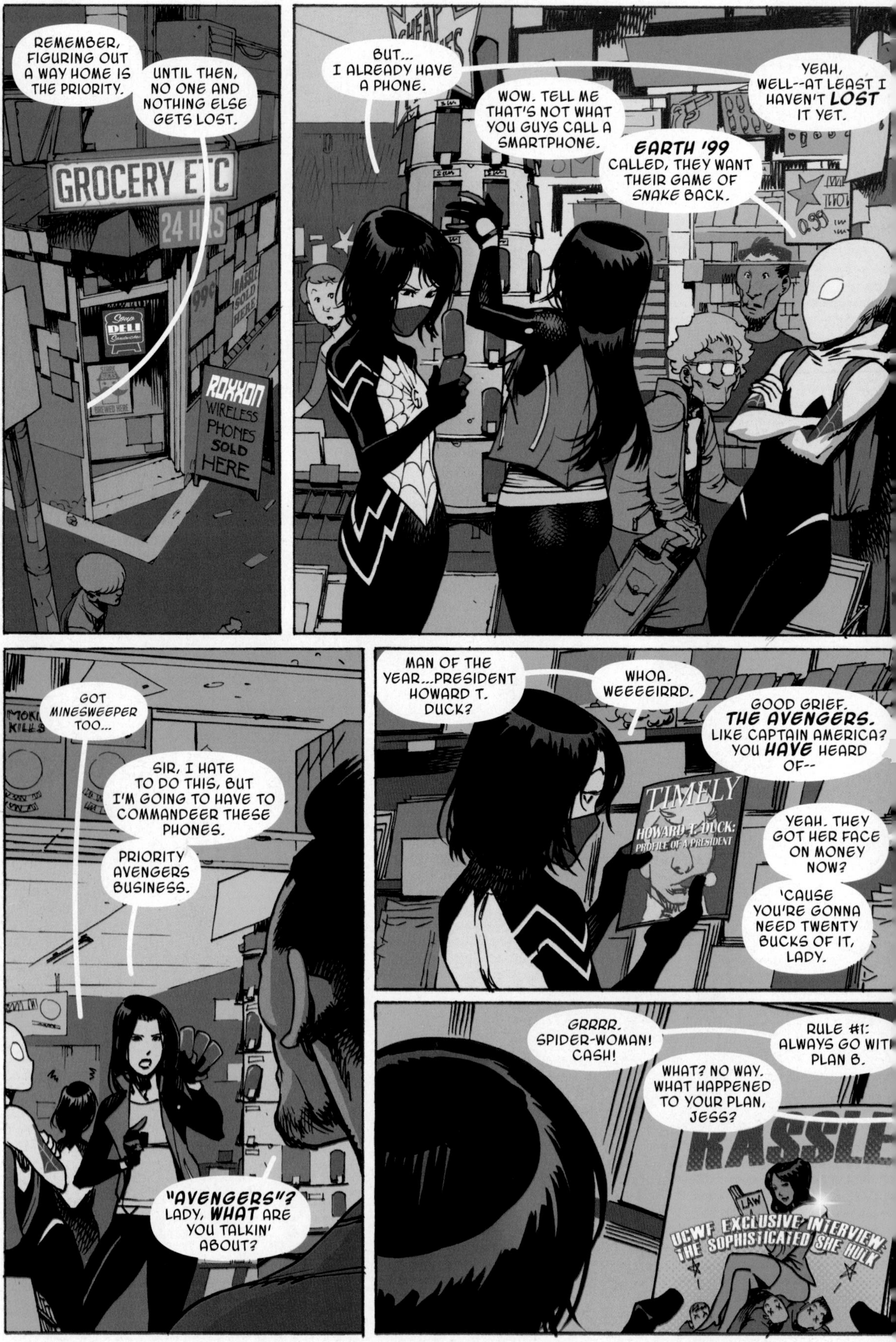
REMEMBER, FIGURING OUT A WAY HOME IS THE PRIORITY.
UNTIL THEN, NO ONE AND NOTHING ELSE GETS LOST.
GROCERY ETC
24 HRS
ROXXON WIRELESS PHONES SOLD HERE
BUT... I ALREADY HAVE A PHONE.
WOW. TELL ME THAT'S NOT WHAT YOU GUYS CALL A SMARTPHONE.
YEAH, WELL--AT LEAST I HAVEN'T LOST IT YET.
EARTH '99 CALLED, THEY WANT THEIR GAME OF SNAKE BACK.
GOT MINESWEEPER TOO...
SIR, I HATE TO DO THIS, BUT I'M GOING TO HAVE TO COMMANDEER THESE PHONES.
PRIORITY AVENGERS BUSINESS.
"AVENGERS"? LADY, WHAT ARE YOU TALKIN' ABOUT?
MAN OF THE YEAR...PRESIDENT HOWARD T. DUCK?
WHOA. WEEEEIRRD.
TIMELY
HOWARD T. DUCK: PROFILE OF A PRESIDENT
GOOD GRIEF. THE AVENGERS. LIKE CAPTAIN AMERICA? YOU HAVE HEARD OF--
YEAH. THEY GOT HER FACE ON MONEY NOW?
'CAUSE YOU'RE GONNA NEED TWENTY BUCKS OF IT, LADY.
GRRRR. SPIDER-WOMAN! CASH!
RULE #1: ALWAYS GO WITH PLAN B.
WHAT? NO WAY. WHAT HAPPENED TO YOUR PLAN, JESS?
RASSLE
UCWF EXCLUSIVE INTERVIEW: THE SOPHISTICATED SHE HULK

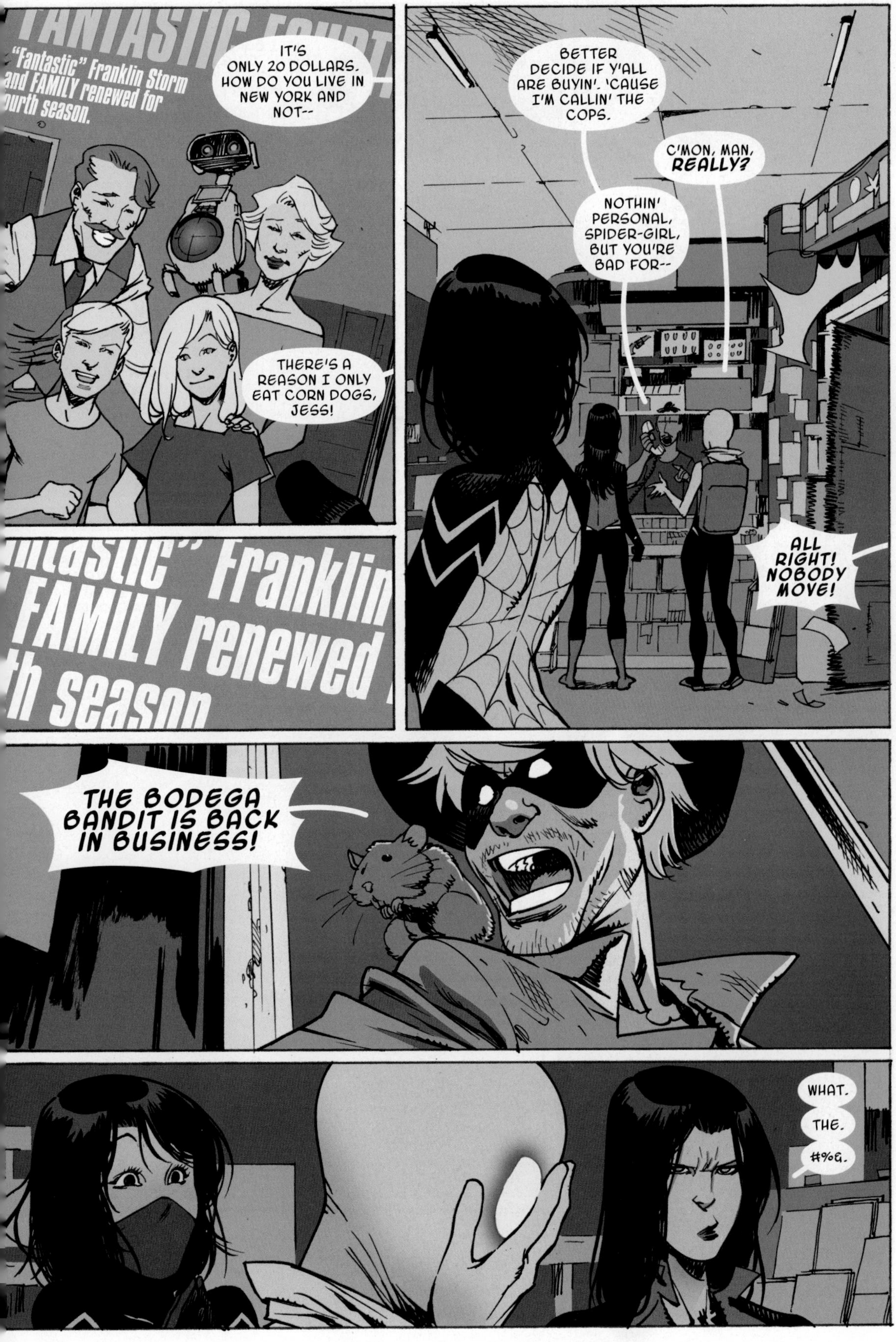
FANTASTIC FOURTH
"Fantastic" Franklin Storm and FAMILY renewed for fourth season.
IT'S ONLY 20 DOLLARS. HOW DO YOU LIVE IN NEW YORK AND NOT--
THERE'S A REASON I ONLY EAT CORN DOGS, JESS!
"Fantastic" Franklin FAMILY renewed th season
BETTER DECIDE IF Y'ALL ARE BUYIN'. 'CAUSE I'M CALLIN' THE COPS.
C'MON, MAN, REALLY?
NOTHIN' PERSONAL, SPIDER-GIRL, BUT YOU'RE BAD FOR--
ALL RIGHT! NOBODY MOVE!
THE BODEGA BANDIT IS BACK IN BUSINESS!
WHAT.
THE.
#%G.

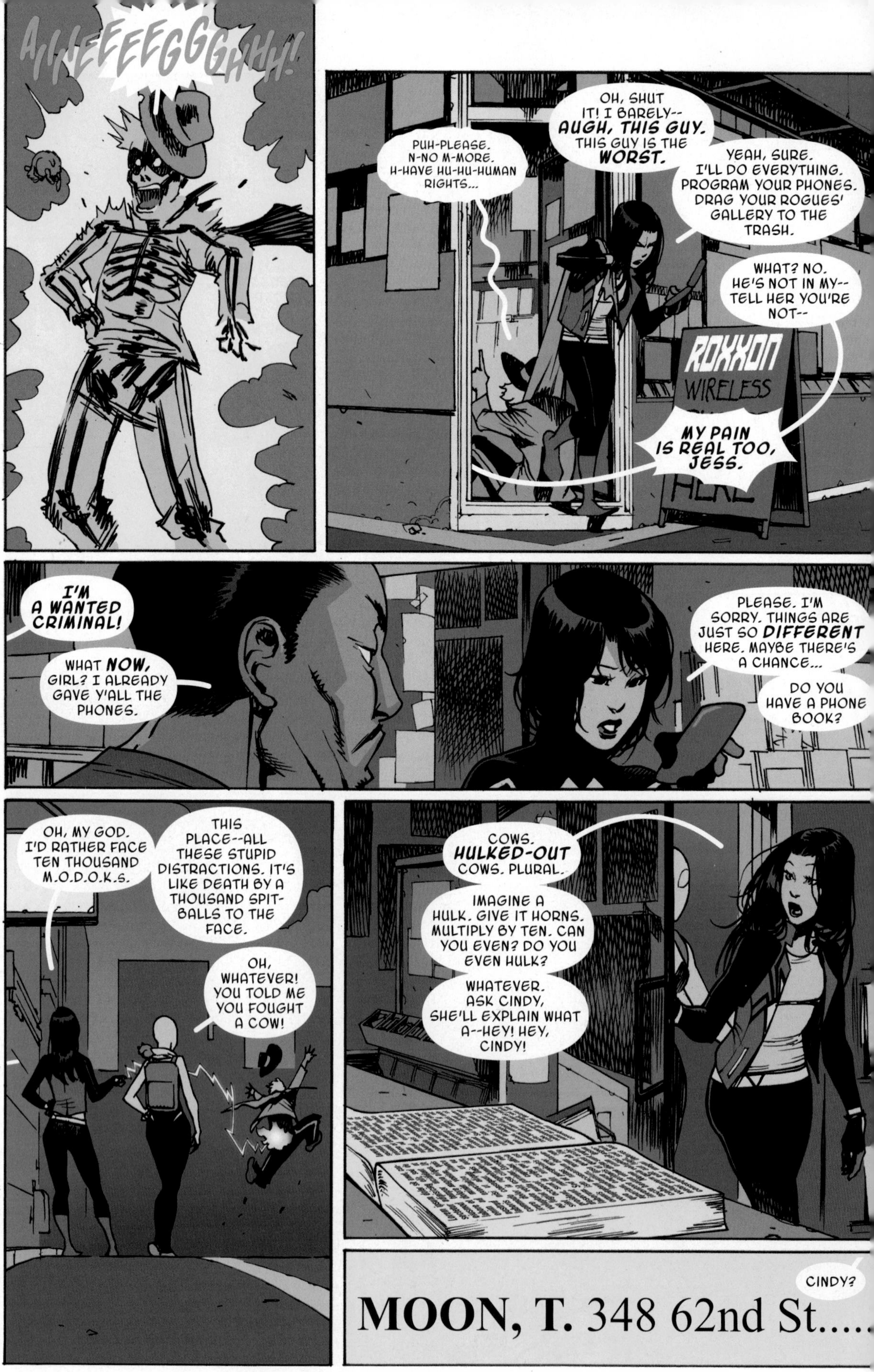
AIIEEEEEGGGHHH!
PUH-PLEASE. N-NO M-MORE. H-HAVE HU-HU-HUMAN RIGHTS...
OH, SHUT IT! I BARELY-- AUGH, THIS GUY. THIS GUY IS THE WORST.
YEAH, SURE. I'LL DO EVERYTHING. PROGRAM YOUR PHONES. DRAG YOUR ROGUES' GALLERY TO THE TRASH.
WHAT? NO. HE'S NOT IN MY-- TELL HER YOU'RE NOT--
ROXXON
WIRELESS
MY PAIN IS REAL TOO, JESS.
I'M A WANTED CRIMINAL!
WHAT NOW, GIRL? I ALREADY GAVE Y'ALL THE PHONES.
PLEASE. I'M SORRY. THINGS ARE JUST SO DIFFERENT HERE. MAYBE THERE'S A CHANCE...
DO YOU HAVE A PHONE BOOK?
OH, MY GOD. I'D RATHER FACE TEN THOUSAND M.O.D.O.K.s.
THIS PLACE--ALL THESE STUPID DISTRACTIONS. IT'S LIKE DEATH BY A THOUSAND SPIT-BALLS TO THE FACE.
OH, WHATEVER! YOU TOLD ME YOU FOUGHT A COW!
COWS. HULKED-OUT COWS. PLURAL.
IMAGINE A HULK. GIVE IT HORNS. MULTIPLY BY TEN. CAN YOU EVEN? DO YOU EVEN HULK?
WHATEVER. ASK CINDY, SHE'LL EXPLAIN WHAT A--HEY! HEY, CINDY!
CINDY?
MOON, T. 348 62nd St.....

RRRGH. I CAN'T BELIEVE CINDY DITCHED US!

AND SHE'S NOT PICKING UP HER PHONE.

SHE'S NOT GOING TO. NOT UNTIL SHE TALKS TO THEM.

TALKS TO WHO?

HEY, WHAT'RE YOU--

GEEZ. PARANOID MUCH? MY SPIDER-SENSE WOULD WARN US OF PEEPING TOMS, JESS.

YEAH. OKAY...

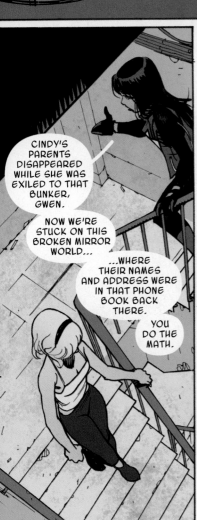

CINDY'S PARENTS DISAPPEARED WHILE SHE WAS EXILED TO THAT BUNKER, GWEN.

NOW WE'RE STUCK ON THIS BROKEN MIRROR WORLD...

...WHERE THEIR NAMES AND ADDRESS WERE IN THAT PHONE BOOK BACK THERE.

YOU DO THE MATH.

BUT, JESS... IF THAT'S WHERE SHE'S GONE--HOW DO WE ASK HER TO--

I MEAN, IF IT WERE ME...I'D GIVE ANYTHING TO REGAIN THE PEOPLE I'VE LOST.

IN ANY UNIVERSE.

YEAH. WELL...ONE EXISTENTIAL CRISIS AT A TIME.

JUST TELL ME YOU HAVE RELIABLE WIFI AND A COUCH FOR ME TO OSTRICH INTO THE CUSHIONS OF AND--

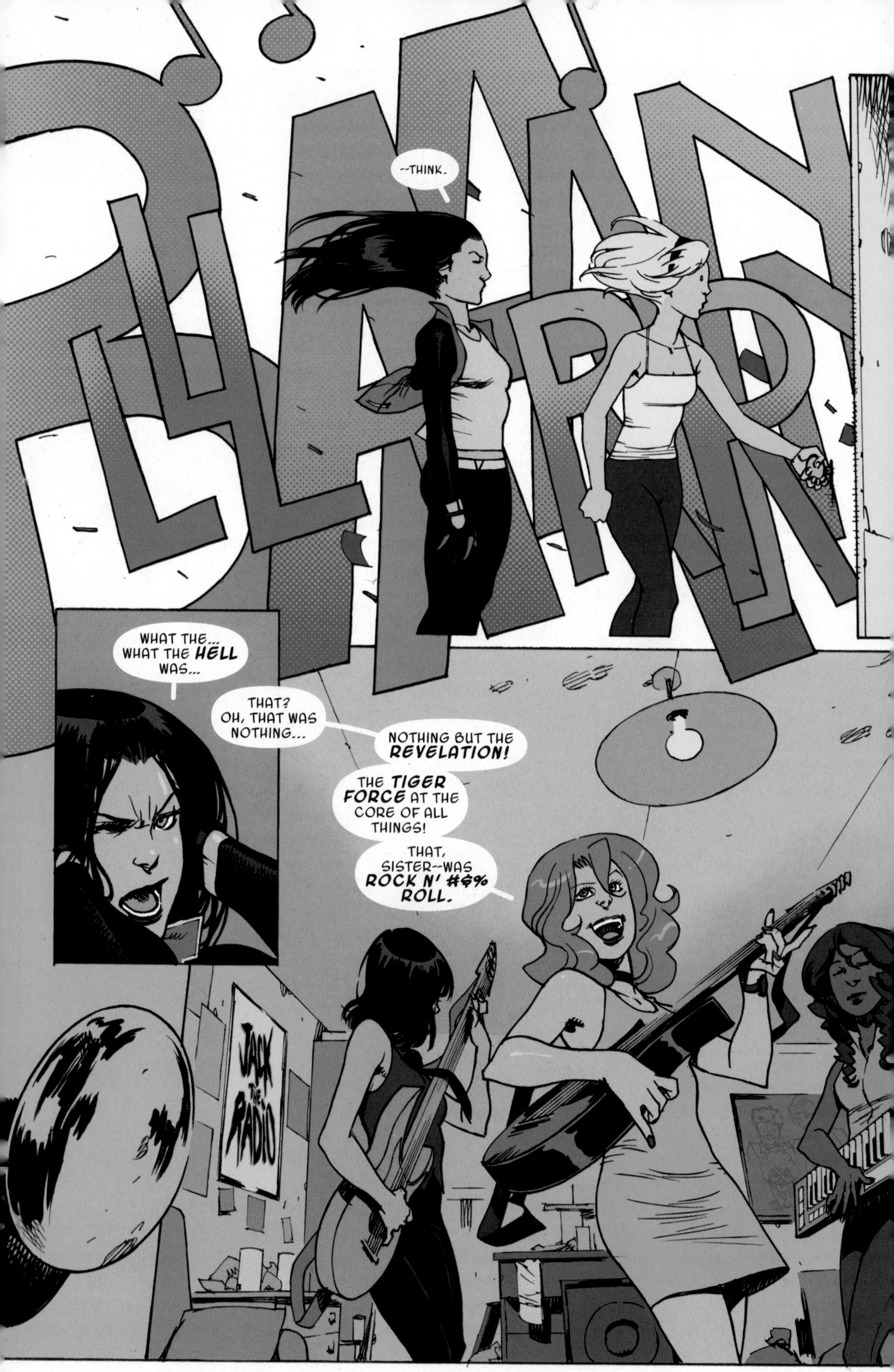
--THINK.
WHAT THE... WHAT THE HELL WAS...
THAT? OH, THAT WAS NOTHING...
NOTHING BUT THE REVELATION!
THE TIGER FORCE AT THE CORE OF ALL THINGS!
THAT, SISTER--WAS ROCK N' #$% ROLL.
JACK THE RADIO

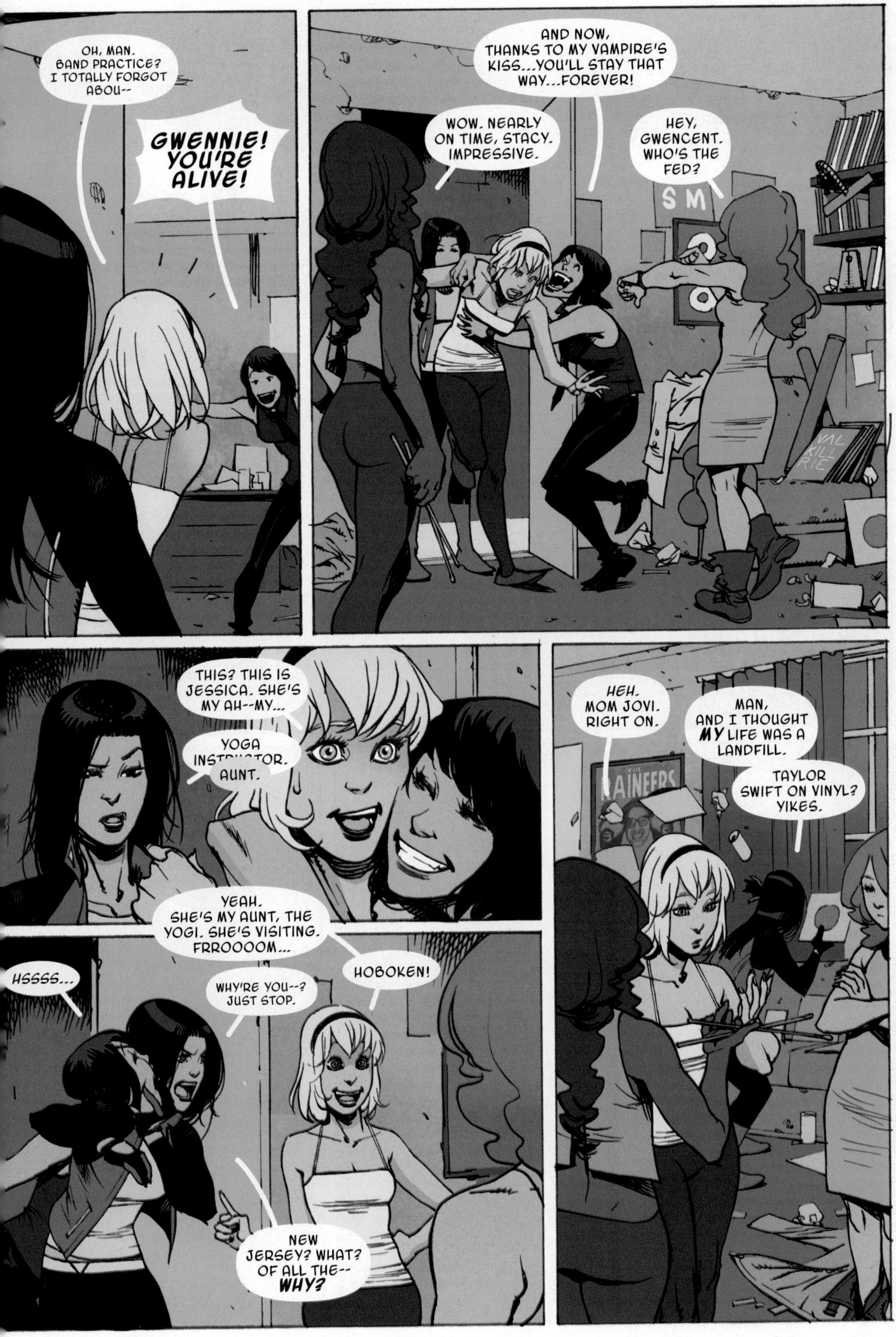
OH, MAN. BAND PRACTICE? I TOTALLY FORGOT ABOU--
GWENNIE! YOU'RE ALIVE!
AND NOW, THANKS TO MY VAMPIRE'S KISS...YOU'LL STAY THAT WAY...FOREVER!
WOW. NEARLY ON TIME, STACY. IMPRESSIVE.
HEY, GWENCENT. WHO'S THE FED?
SM
VAL KILL RIE
THIS? THIS IS JESSICA. SHE'S MY AH--MY...
YOGA INSTRUCTOR.
AUNT.
HEH. MOM JOVI. RIGHT ON.
MAN, AND I THOUGHT MY LIFE WAS A LANDFILL.
TAYLOR SWIFT ON VINYL? YIKES.
YEAH. SHE'S MY AUNT, THE YOGI. SHE'S VISITING. FRROOOOM...
HOBOKEN!
HSSSS...
WHY'RE YOU--? JUST STOP.
NEW JERSEY? WHAT? OF ALL THE-- WHY?

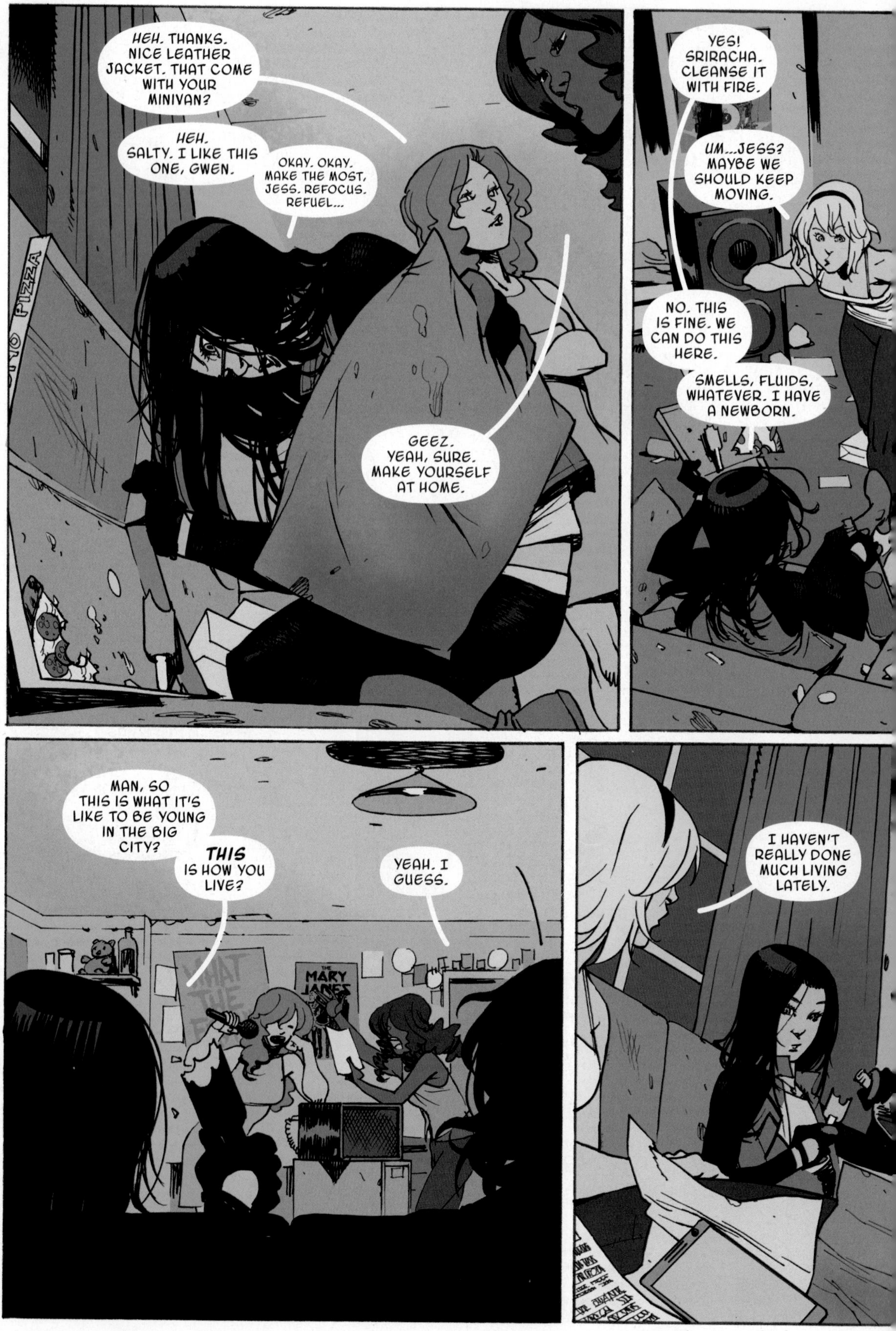
HEH. THANKS. NICE LEATHER JACKET. THAT COME WITH YOUR MINIVAN?
HEH. SALTY. I LIKE THIS ONE, GWEN.
OKAY. OKAY. MAKE THE MOST, JESS. REFOCUS. REFUEL...
PIZZA
GEEZ. YEAH, SURE. MAKE YOURSELF AT HOME.
YES! SRIRACHA. CLEANSE IT WITH FIRE.
UM...JESS? MAYBE WE SHOULD KEEP MOVING.
NO. THIS IS FINE. WE CAN DO THIS HERE.
SMELLS, FLUIDS, WHATEVER. I HAVE A NEWBORN.
MAN, SO THIS IS WHAT IT'S LIKE TO BE YOUNG IN THE BIG CITY?
THIS IS HOW YOU LIVE?
YEAH. I GUESS.
THE MARY JANES
I HAVEN'T REALLY DONE MUCH LIVING LATELY.

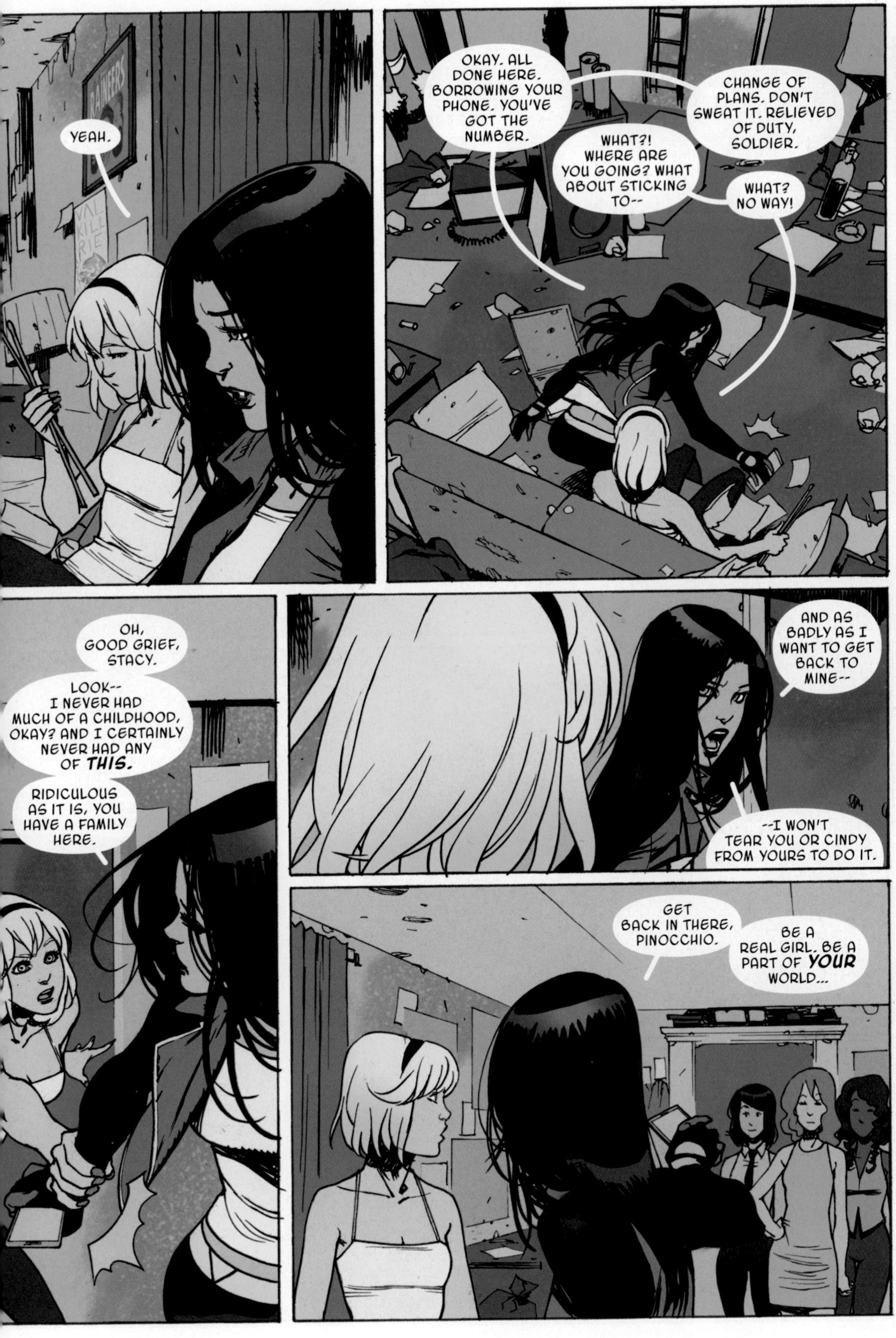
RAINEERS
YEAH.
OKAY. ALL DONE HERE. BORROWING YOUR PHONE. YOU'VE GOT THE NUMBER.
WHAT?! WHERE ARE YOU GOING? WHAT ABOUT STICKING TO--
CHANGE OF PLANS. DON'T SWEAT IT. RELIEVED OF DUTY, SOLDIER.
WHAT? NO WAY!
OH, GOOD GRIEF, STACY.
LOOK-- I NEVER HAD MUCH OF A CHILDHOOD, OKAY? AND I CERTAINLY NEVER HAD ANY OF **THIS.**
RIDICULOUS AS IT IS, YOU HAVE A FAMILY HERE.
AND AS BADLY AS I WANT TO GET BACK TO MINE--
--I WON'T TEAR YOU OR CINDY FROM YOURS TO DO IT.
GET BACK IN THERE, PINOCCHIO.
BE A REAL GIRL. BE A PART OF **YOUR** WORLD...

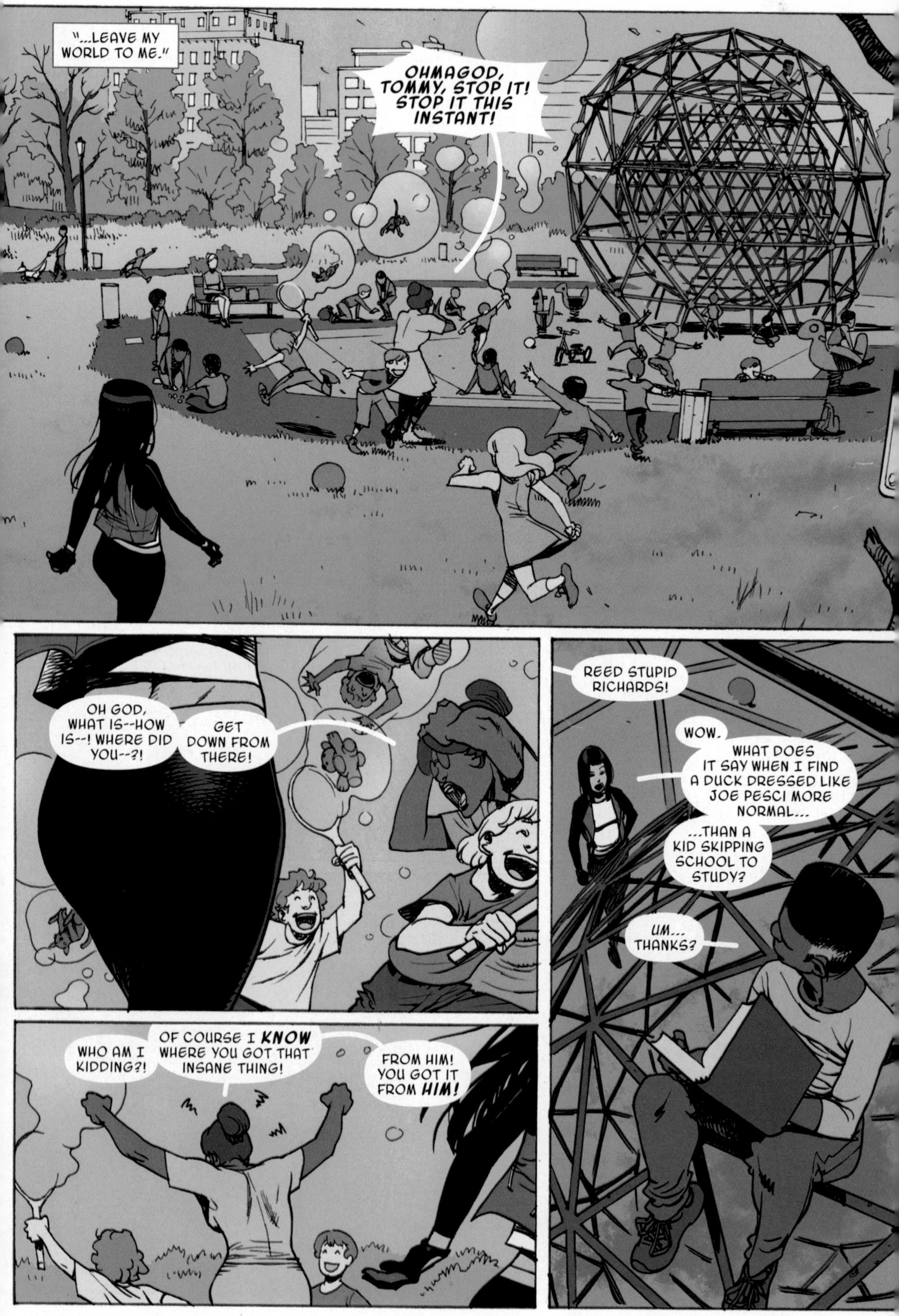

"...LEAVE MY WORLD TO ME."
OHMAGOD, TOMMY, STOP IT! STOP IT THIS INSTANT!
OH GOD, WHAT IS--HOW IS--! WHERE DID YOU--?!
GET DOWN FROM THERE!
REED STUPID RICHARDS!
WOW.
WHAT DOES IT SAY WHEN I FIND A DUCK DRESSED LIKE JOE PESCI MORE NORMAL...
...THAN A KID SKIPPING SCHOOL TO STUDY?
UM... THANKS?
WHO AM I KIDDING?!
OF COURSE I KNOW WHERE YOU GOT THAT INSANE THING!
FROM HIM! YOU GOT IT FROM HIM!

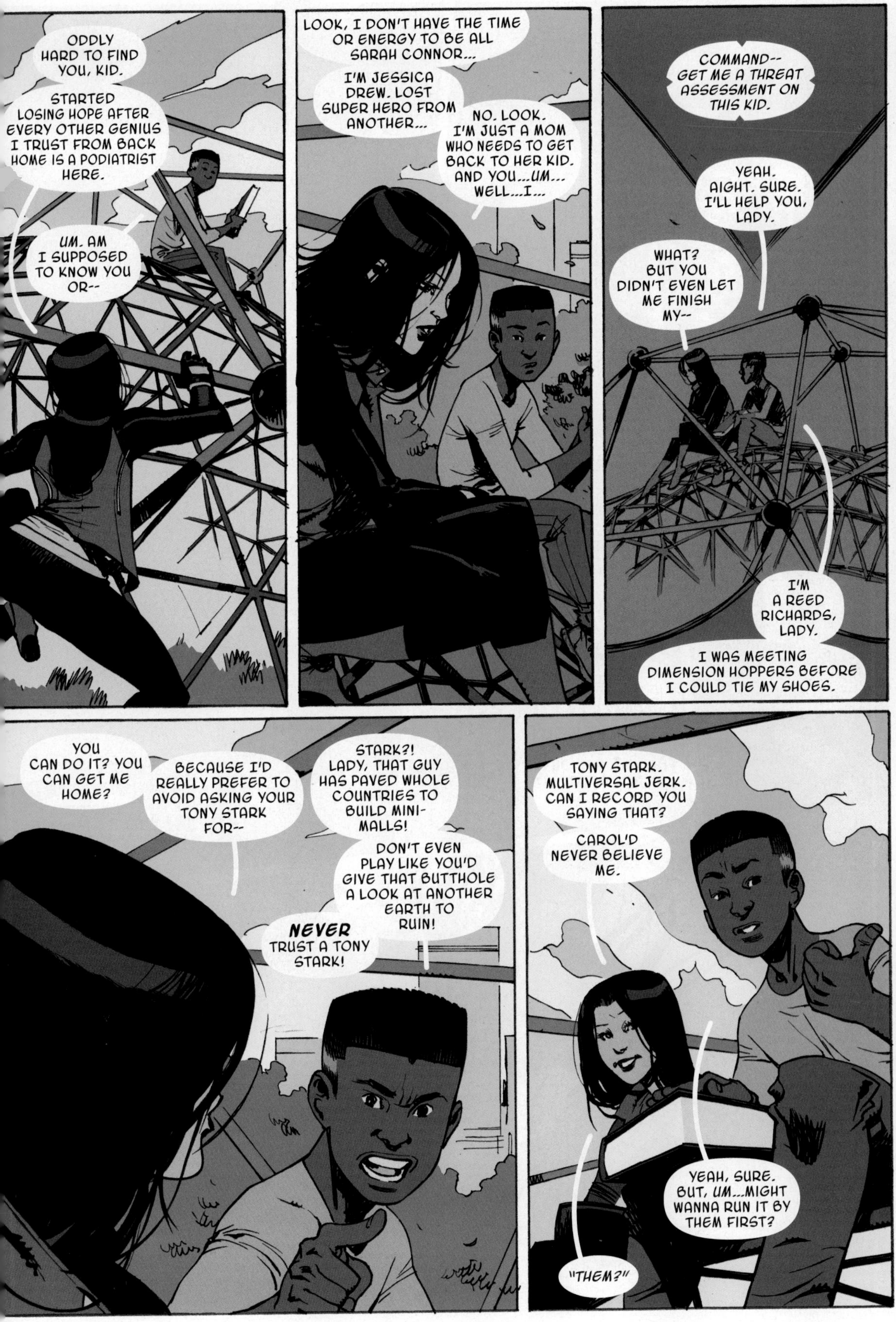
ODDLY HARD TO FIND YOU, KID.
STARTED LOSING HOPE AFTER EVERY OTHER GENIUS I TRUST FROM BACK HOME IS A PODIATRIST HERE.
UM. AM I SUPPOSED TO KNOW YOU OR--
LOOK, I DON'T HAVE THE TIME OR ENERGY TO BE ALL SARAH CONNOR...
I'M JESSICA DREW. LOST SUPER HERO FROM ANOTHER...
NO. LOOK. I'M JUST A MOM WHO NEEDS TO GET BACK TO HER KID. AND YOU...UM... WELL...I...
COMMAND-- GET ME A THREAT ASSESSMENT ON THIS KID.
YEAH. AIGHT. SURE. I'LL HELP YOU, LADY.
WHAT? BUT YOU DIDN'T EVEN LET ME FINISH MY--
I'M A REED RICHARDS, LADY.
I WAS MEETING DIMENSION HOPPERS BEFORE I COULD TIE MY SHOES.
YOU CAN DO IT? YOU CAN GET ME HOME?
BECAUSE I'D REALLY PREFER TO AVOID ASKING YOUR TONY STARK FOR--
STARK?! LADY, THAT GUY HAS PAVED WHOLE COUNTRIES TO BUILD MINI-MALLS!
DON'T EVEN PLAY LIKE YOU'D GIVE THAT BUTTHOLE A LOOK AT ANOTHER EARTH TO RUIN!
NEVER TRUST A TONY STARK!
TONY STARK. MULTIVERSAL JERK. CAN I RECORD YOU SAYING THAT?
CAROL'D NEVER BELIEVE ME.
YEAH, SURE. BUT, UM...MIGHT WANNA RUN IT BY THEM FIRST?
"THEM?"

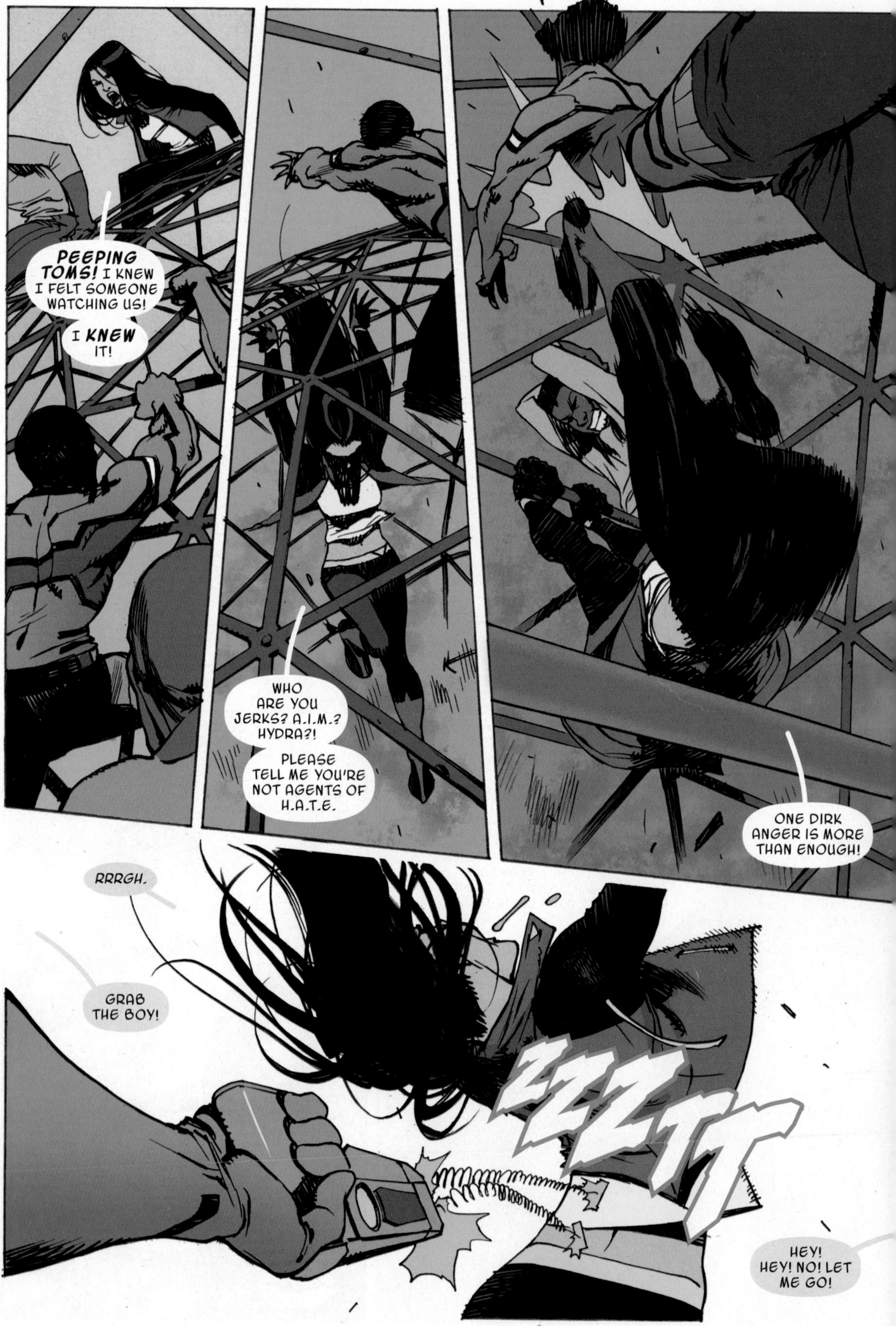
PEEPING TOMS! I KNEW I FELT SOMEONE WATCHING US!
I KNEW IT!
WHO ARE YOU JERKS? A.I.M.? HYDRA?!
PLEASE TELL ME YOU'RE NOT AGENTS OF H.A.T.E.
ONE DIRK ANGER IS MORE THAN ENOUGH!
RRRGH.
GRAB THE BOY!
ZZZTT
HEY! HEY! NO! LET ME GO!

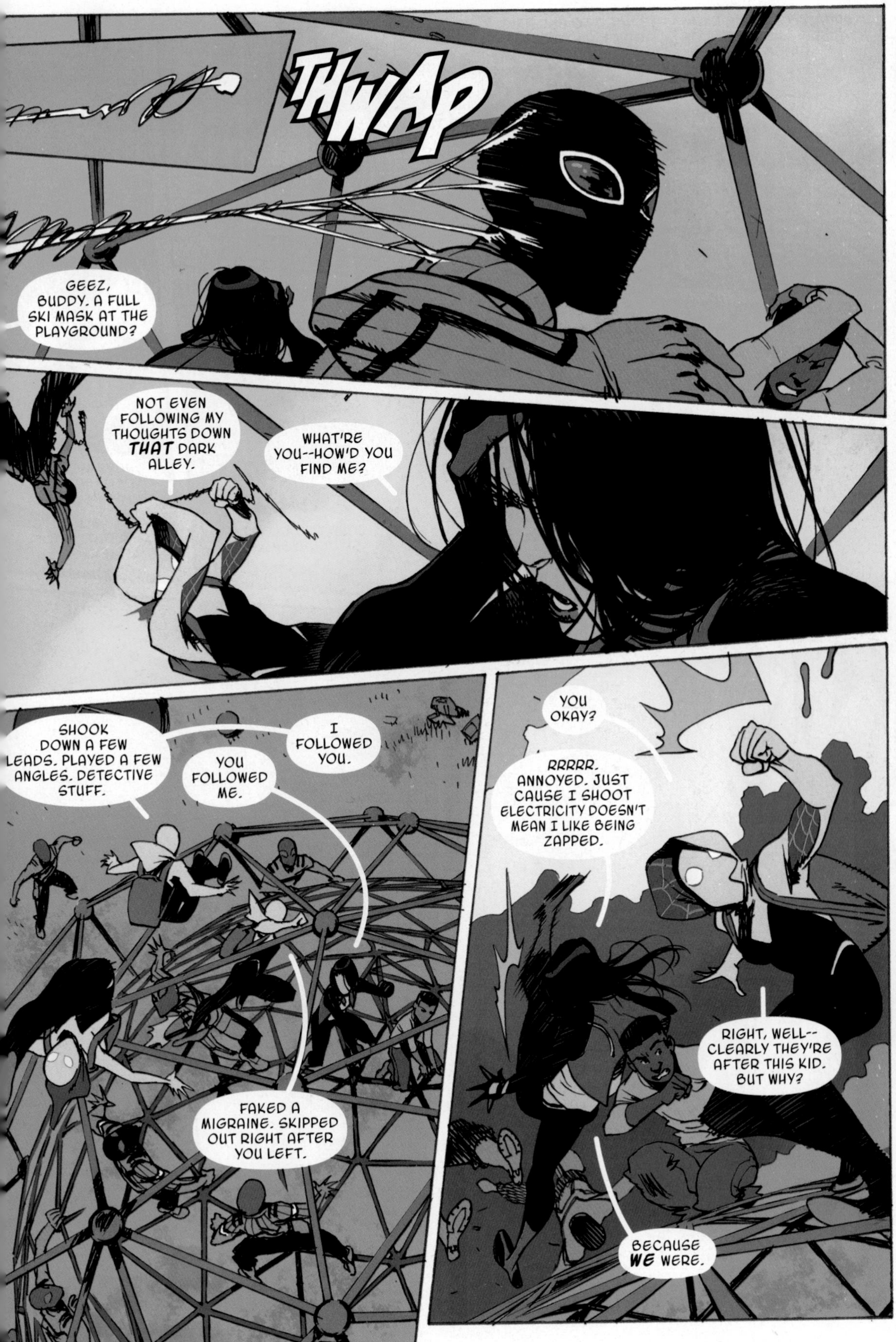
THWAP
GEEZ, BUDDY. A FULL SKI MASK AT THE PLAYGROUND?
NOT EVEN FOLLOWING MY THOUGHTS DOWN THAT DARK ALLEY.
WHAT'RE YOU--HOW'D YOU FIND ME?
SHOOK DOWN A FEW LEADS. PLAYED A FEW ANGLES. DETECTIVE STUFF.
I FOLLOWED YOU.
YOU FOLLOWED ME.
FAKED A MIGRAINE. SKIPPED OUT RIGHT AFTER YOU LEFT.
YOU OKAY?
RRRRR. ANNOYED. JUST CAUSE I SHOOT ELECTRICITY DOESN'T MEAN I LIKE BEING ZAPPED.
RIGHT, WELL-- CLEARLY THEY'RE AFTER THIS KID. BUT WHY?
BECAUSE WE WERE.

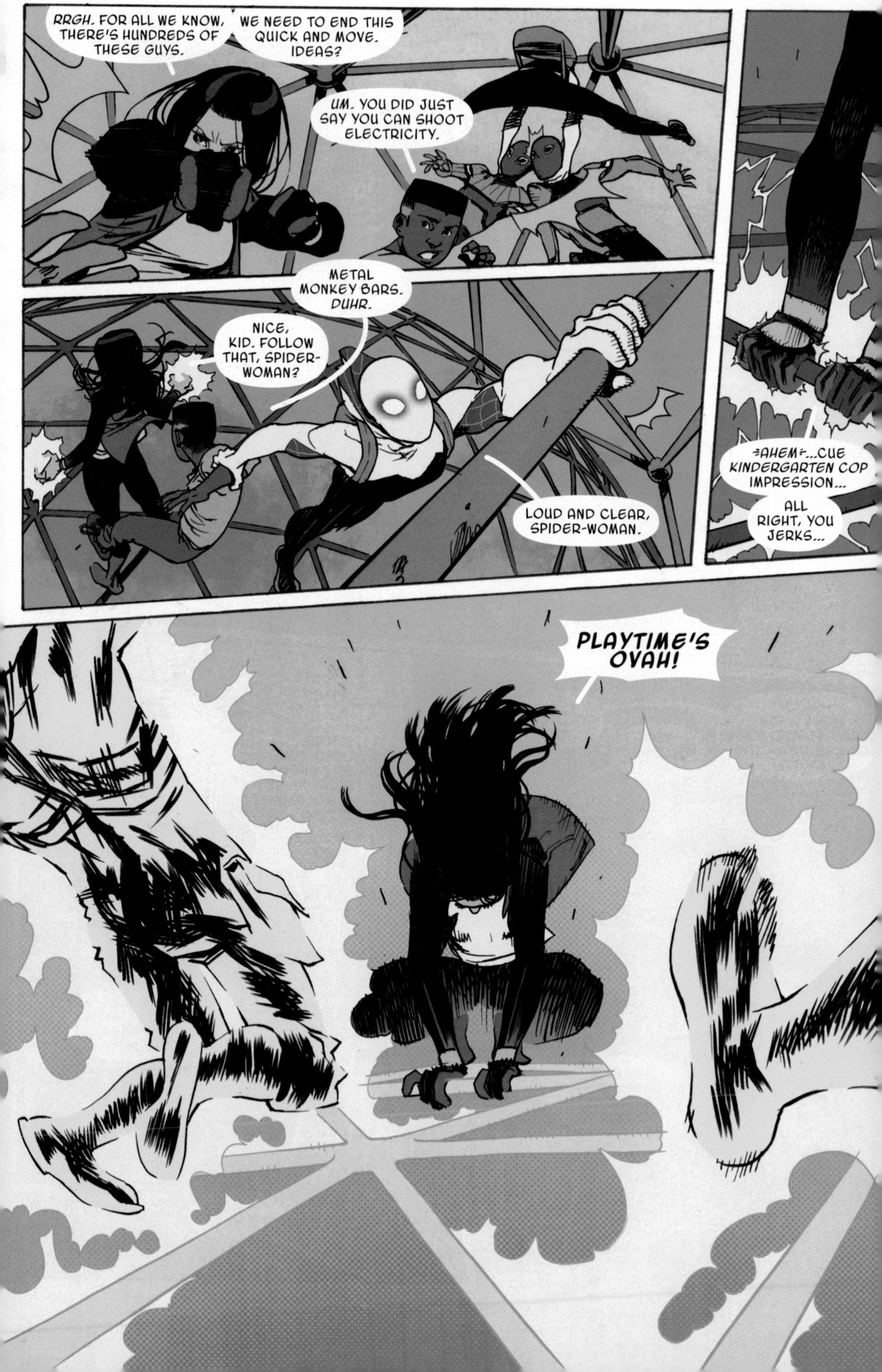
RRGH. FOR ALL WE KNOW, THERE'S HUNDREDS OF THESE GUYS.
WE NEED TO END THIS QUICK AND MOVE. IDEAS?
UM. YOU DID JUST SAY YOU CAN SHOOT ELECTRICITY.
METAL MONKEY BARS. DUHR.
NICE, KID. FOLLOW THAT, SPIDER-WOMAN?
LOUD AND CLEAR, SPIDER-WOMAN.
AHEM...CUE KINDERGARTEN COP IMPRESSION...
ALL RIGHT, YOU JERKS...
PLAYTIME'S OVAH!

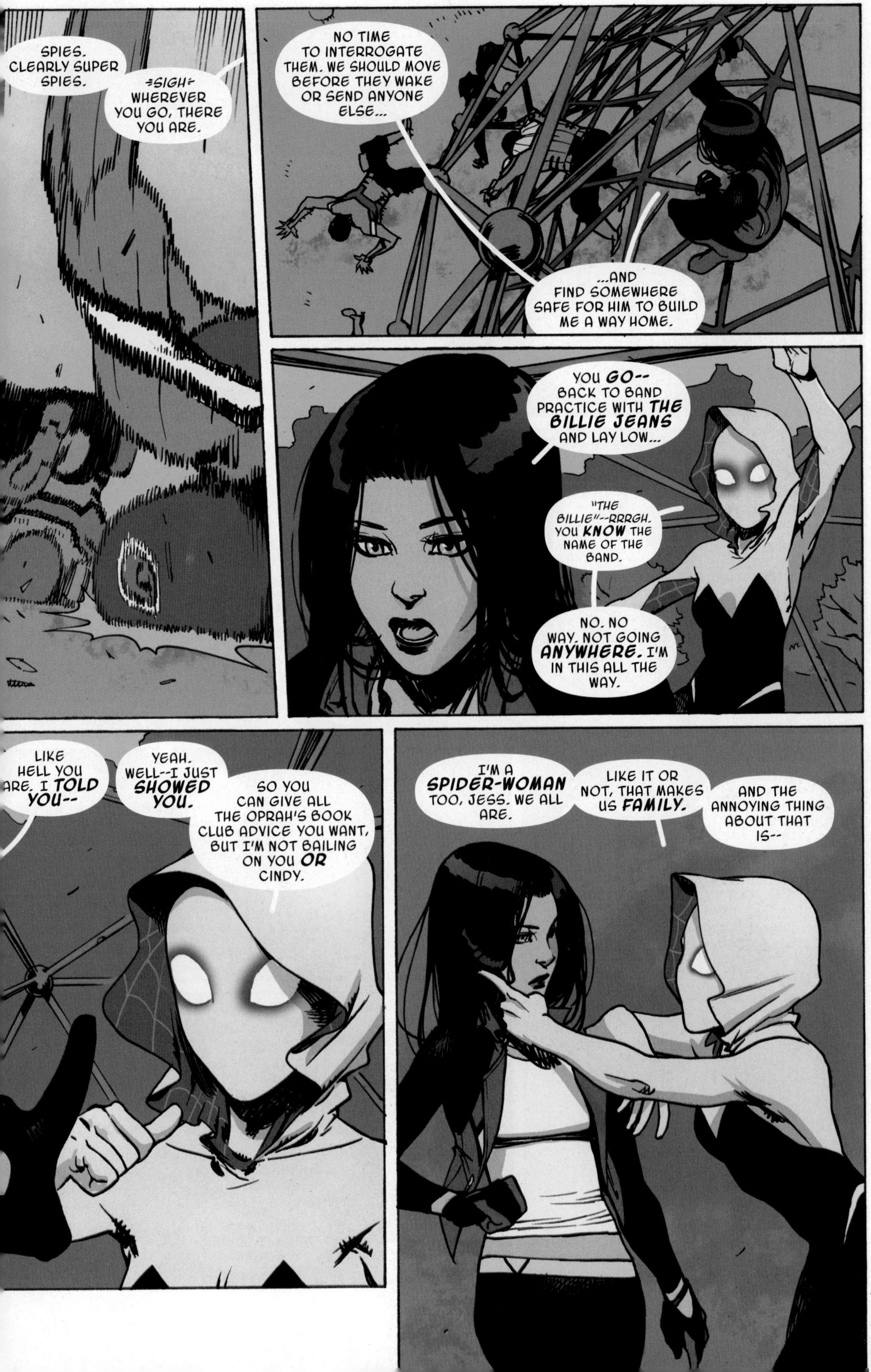
SPIES. CLEARLY SUPER SPIES.
=SIGH= WHEREVER YOU GO, THERE YOU ARE.
NO TIME TO INTERROGATE THEM. WE SHOULD MOVE BEFORE THEY WAKE OR SEND ANYONE ELSE...
...AND FIND SOMEWHERE SAFE FOR HIM TO BUILD ME A WAY HOME.
YOU GO-- BACK TO BAND PRACTICE WITH THE BILLIE JEANS AND LAY LOW...
"THE BILLIE"--RRRGH. YOU KNOW THE NAME OF THE BAND.
NO. NO WAY. NOT GOING ANYWHERE. I'M IN THIS ALL THE WAY.
LIKE HELL YOU ARE. I TOLD YOU--
YEAH. WELL--I JUST SHOWED YOU.
SO YOU CAN GIVE ALL THE OPRAH'S BOOK CLUB ADVICE YOU WANT, BUT I'M NOT BAILING ON YOU OR CINDY.
I'M A SPIDER-WOMAN TOO, JESS. WE ALL ARE.
LIKE IT OR NOT, THAT MAKES US FAMILY.
AND THE ANNOYING THING ABOUT THAT IS--

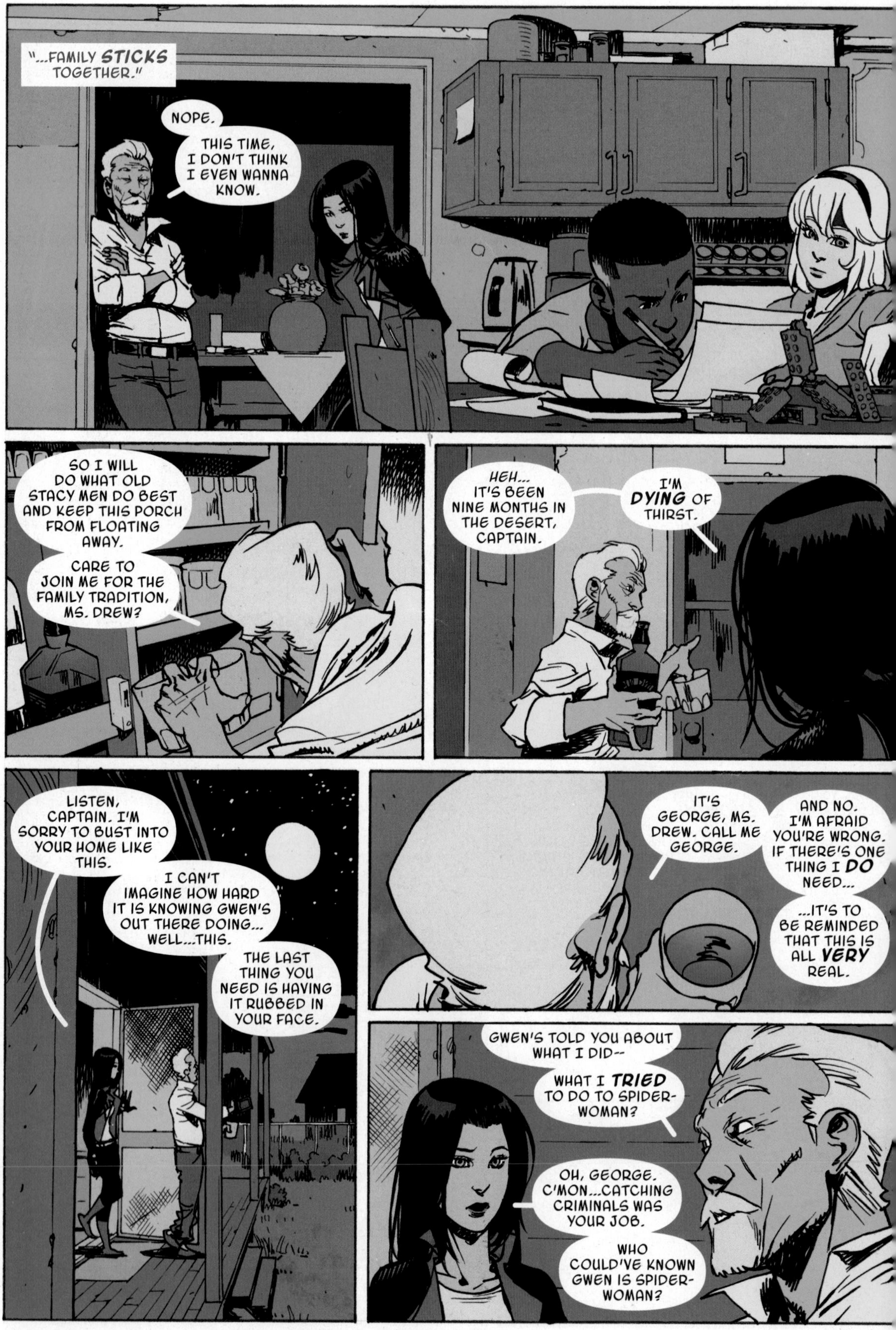
"...FAMILY STICKS TOGETHER."
NOPE.
THIS TIME, I DON'T THINK I EVEN WANNA KNOW.
SO I WILL DO WHAT OLD STACY MEN DO BEST AND KEEP THIS PORCH FROM FLOATING AWAY.
CARE TO JOIN ME FOR THE FAMILY TRADITION, MS. DREW?
HEH... IT'S BEEN NINE MONTHS IN THE DESERT, CAPTAIN.
I'M DYING OF THIRST.
LISTEN, CAPTAIN. I'M SORRY TO BUST INTO YOUR HOME LIKE THIS.
I CAN'T IMAGINE HOW HARD IT IS KNOWING GWEN'S OUT THERE DOING... WELL...THIS.
THE LAST THING YOU NEED IS HAVING IT RUBBED IN YOUR FACE.
IT'S GEORGE, MS. DREW. CALL ME GEORGE.
AND NO. I'M AFRAID YOU'RE WRONG. IF THERE'S ONE THING I DO NEED...
...IT'S TO BE REMINDED THAT THIS IS ALL VERY REAL.
GWEN'S TOLD YOU ABOUT WHAT I DID--
WHAT I TRIED TO DO TO SPIDER-WOMAN?
OH, GEORGE. C'MON...CATCHING CRIMINALS WAS YOUR JOB.
WHO COULD'VE KNOWN GWEN IS SPIDER-WOMAN?

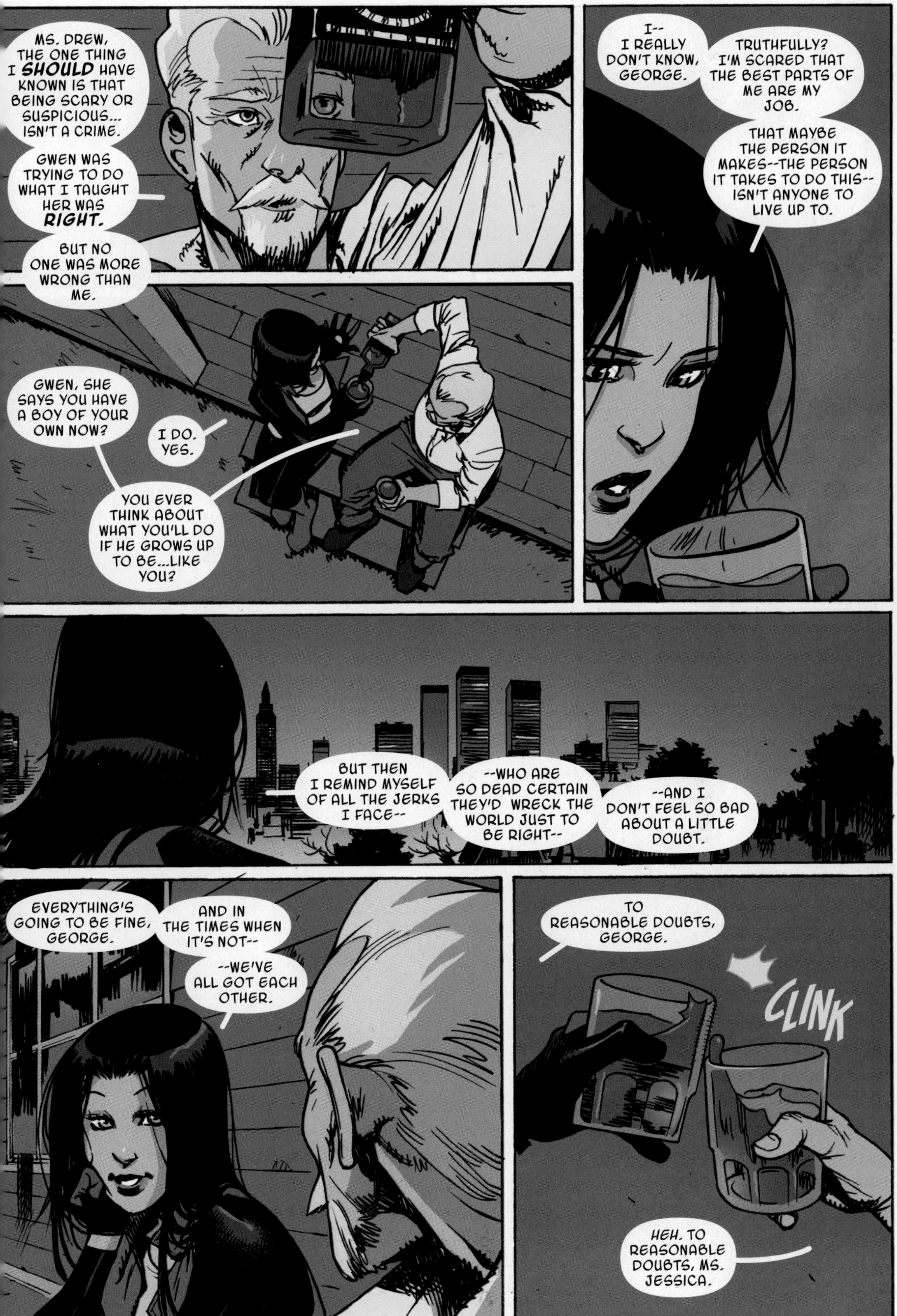
MS. DREW, THE ONE THING I **SHOULD** HAVE KNOWN IS THAT BEING SCARY OR SUSPICIOUS... ISN'T A CRIME.
GWEN WAS TRYING TO DO WHAT I TAUGHT HER WAS **RIGHT.**
BUT NO ONE WAS MORE WRONG THAN ME.
GWEN, SHE SAYS YOU HAVE A BOY OF YOUR OWN NOW?
I DO. YES.
YOU EVER THINK ABOUT WHAT YOU'LL DO IF HE GROWS UP TO BE...LIKE YOU?
I-- I REALLY DON'T KNOW, GEORGE.
TRUTHFULLY? I'M SCARED THAT THE BEST PARTS OF ME ARE MY JOB.
THAT MAYBE THE PERSON IT MAKES--THE PERSON IT TAKES TO DO THIS--ISN'T ANYONE TO LIVE UP TO.
BUT THEN I REMIND MYSELF OF ALL THE JERKS I FACE--
--WHO ARE SO DEAD CERTAIN THEY'D WRECK THE WORLD JUST TO BE RIGHT--
--AND I DON'T FEEL SO BAD ABOUT A LITTLE DOUBT.
EVERYTHING'S GOING TO BE FINE, GEORGE.
AND IN THE TIMES WHEN IT'S NOT--
--WE'VE ALL GOT EACH OTHER.
TO REASONABLE DOUBTS, GEORGE.
CLINK
HEH. TO REASONABLE DOUBTS, MS. JESSICA.

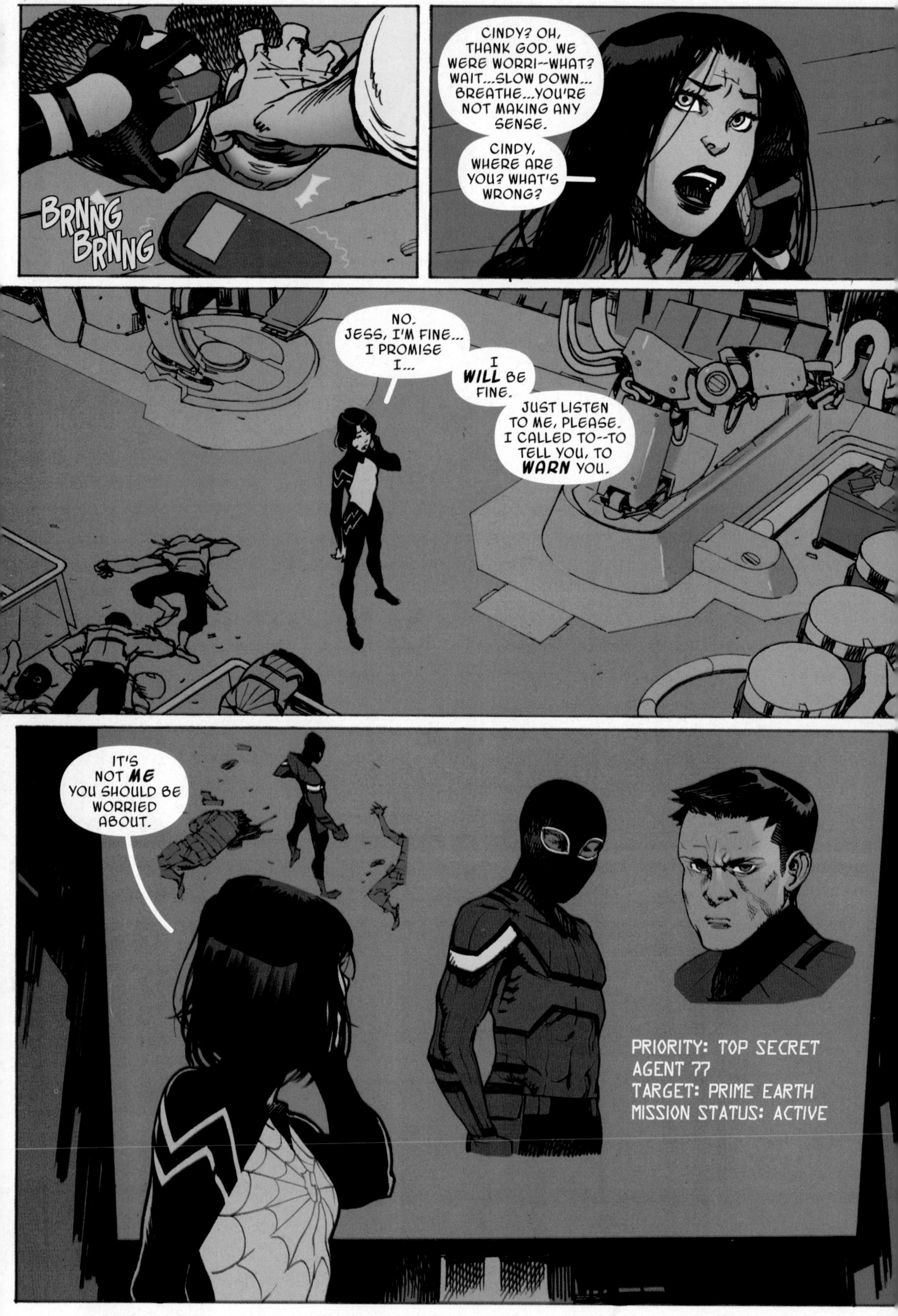
BRNNG BRNNG
CINDY? OH, THANK GOD. WE WERE WORRI--WHAT? WAIT...SLOW DOWN... BREATHE...YOU'RE NOT MAKING ANY SENSE.
CINDY, WHERE ARE YOU? WHAT'S WRONG?
NO. JESS, I'M FINE... I PROMISE I...
I *WILL* BE FINE.
JUST LISTEN TO ME, PLEASE. I CALLED TO--TO TELL YOU, TO *WARN* YOU.
IT'S NOT *ME* YOU SHOULD BE WORRIED ABOUT.
PRIORITY: TOP SECRET
AGENT 77
TARGET: PRIME EARTH
MISSION STATUS: ACTIVE

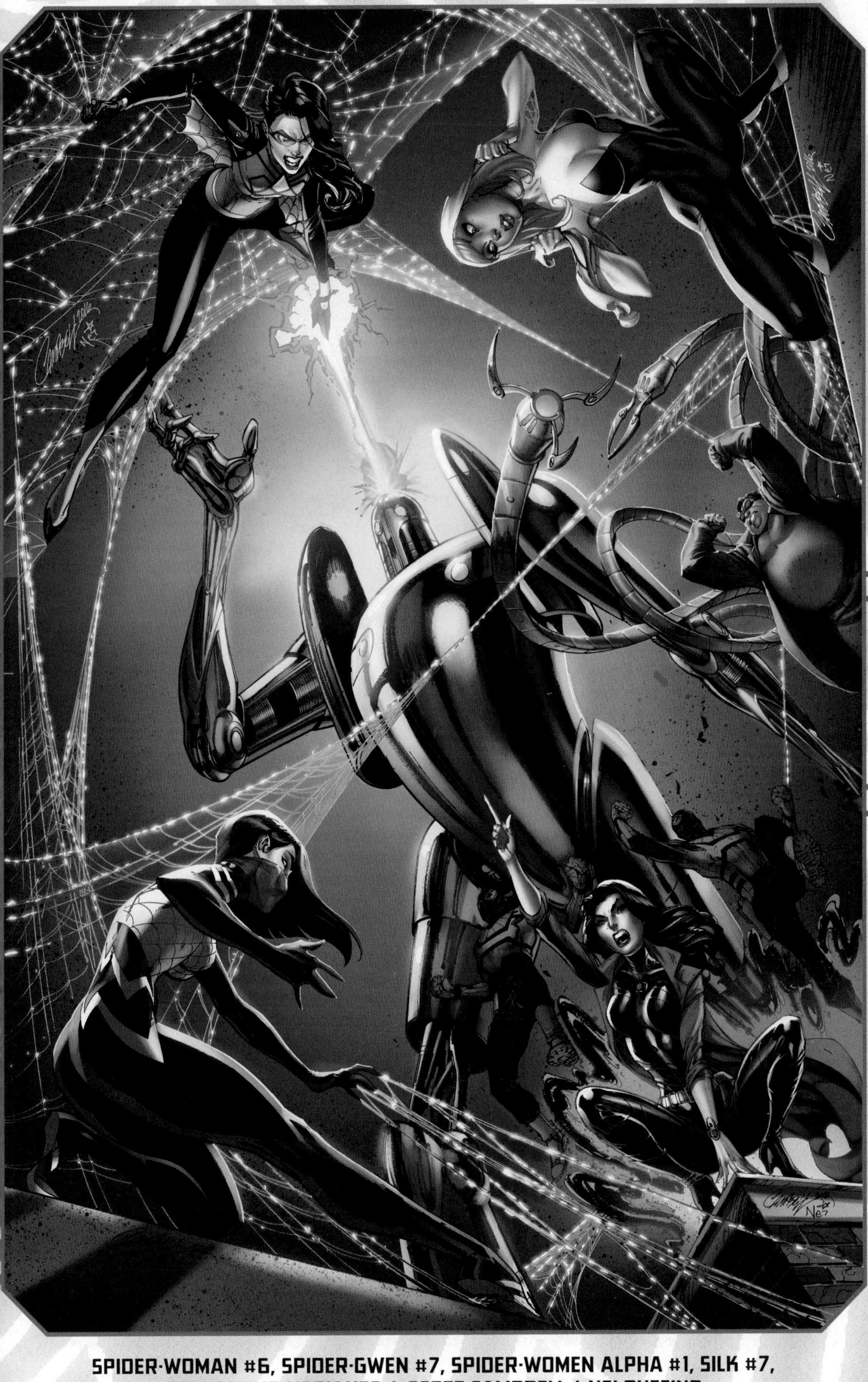

SPIDER-WOMAN #6, SPIDER-GWEN #7, SPIDER-WOMEN ALPHA #1, SILK #7,
CONNECTING VARIANTS J. SCOTT CAMPBELL & NEI RUFFINO

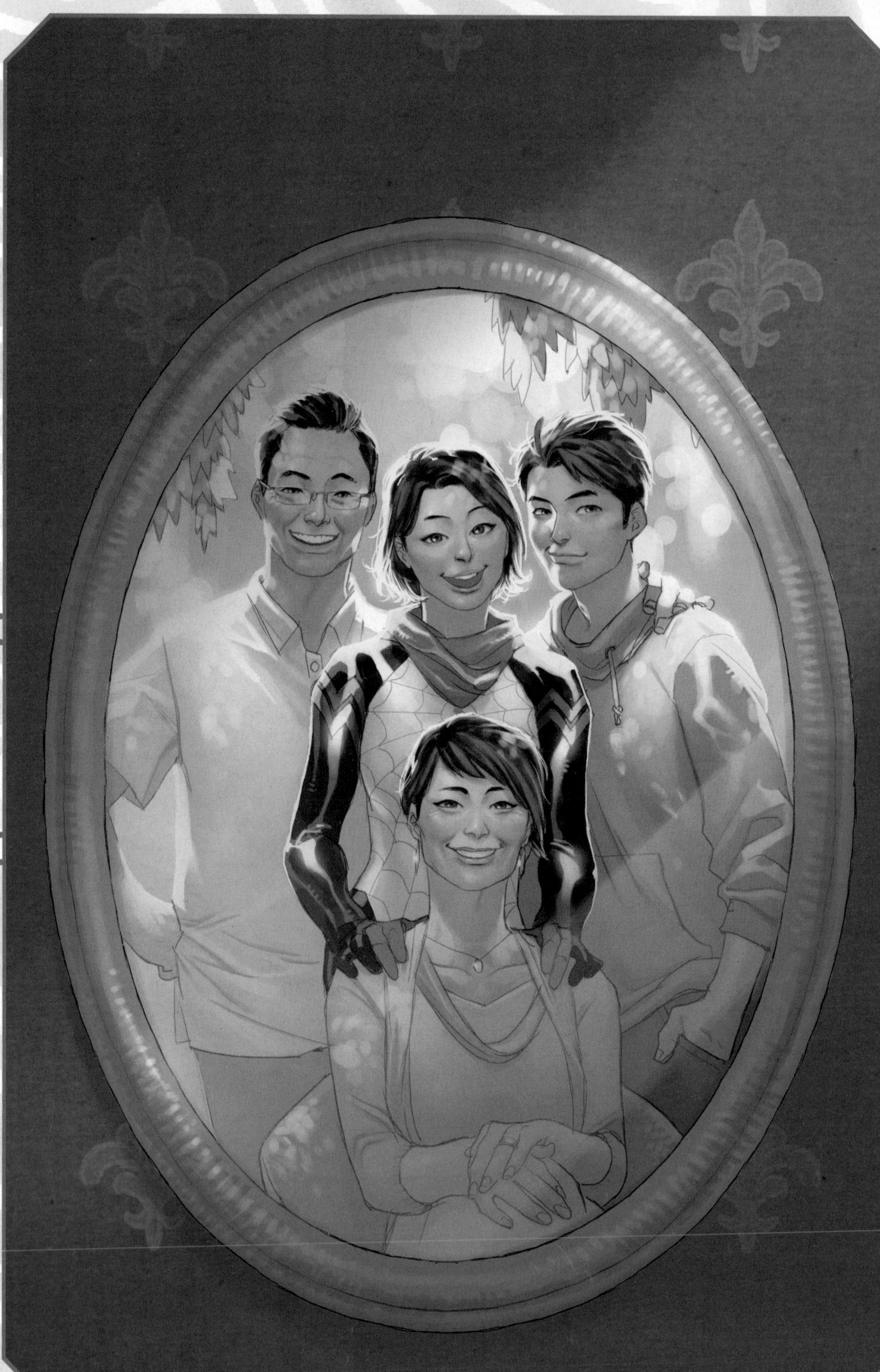

SILK #7

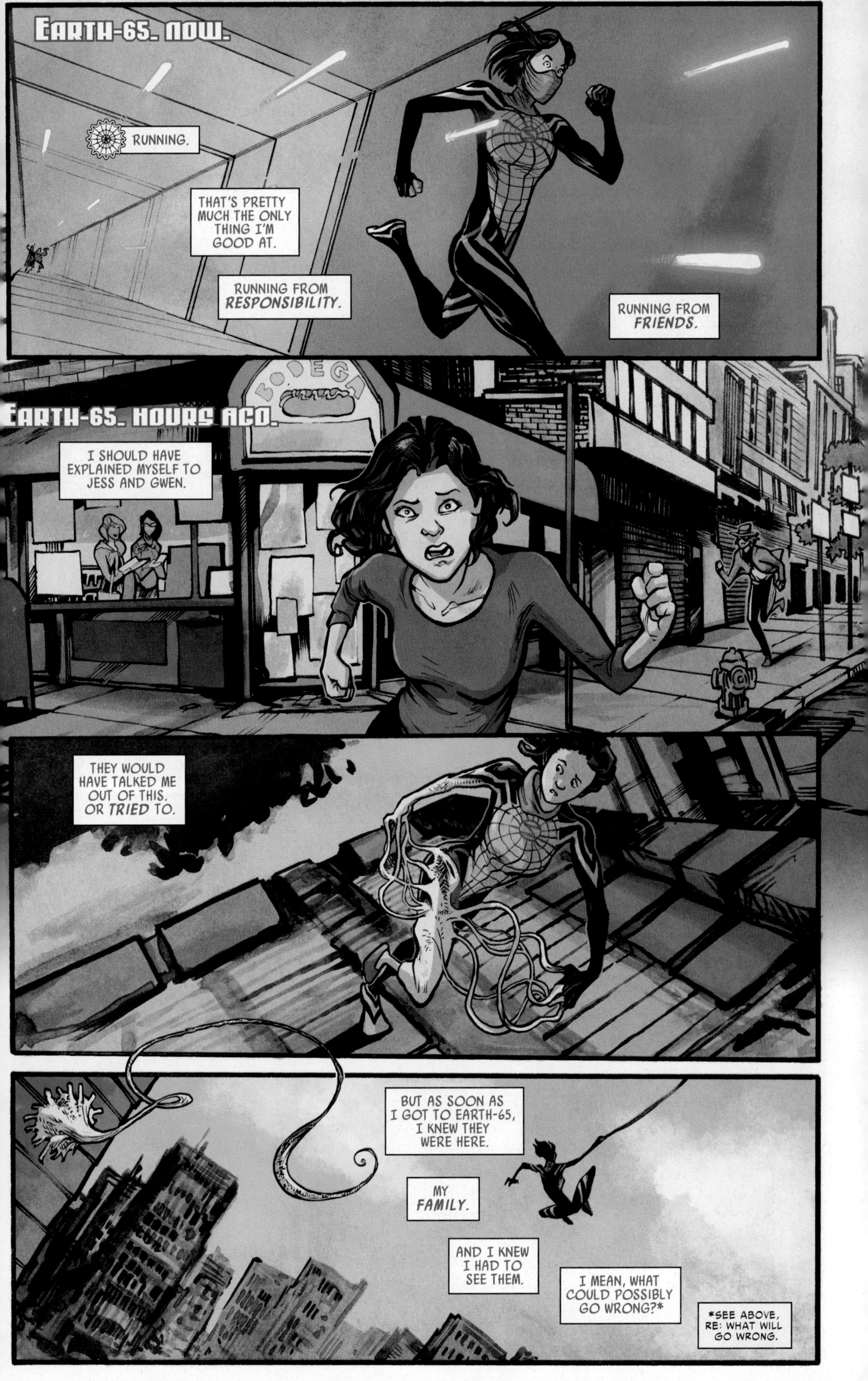
EARTH-65. NOW.
RUNNING.
THAT'S PRETTY MUCH THE ONLY THING I'M GOOD AT.
RUNNING FROM RESPONSIBILITY.
RUNNING FROM FRIENDS.
BODEGA
EARTH-65. HOURS AGO.
I SHOULD HAVE EXPLAINED MYSELF TO JESS AND GWEN.
THEY WOULD HAVE TALKED ME OUT OF THIS. OR TRIED TO.
BUT AS SOON AS I GOT TO EARTH-65, I KNEW THEY WERE HERE.
MY FAMILY.
AND I KNEW I HAD TO SEE THEM.
I MEAN, WHAT COULD POSSIBLY GO WRONG?*
*SEE ABOVE, RE: WHAT WILL GO WRONG.

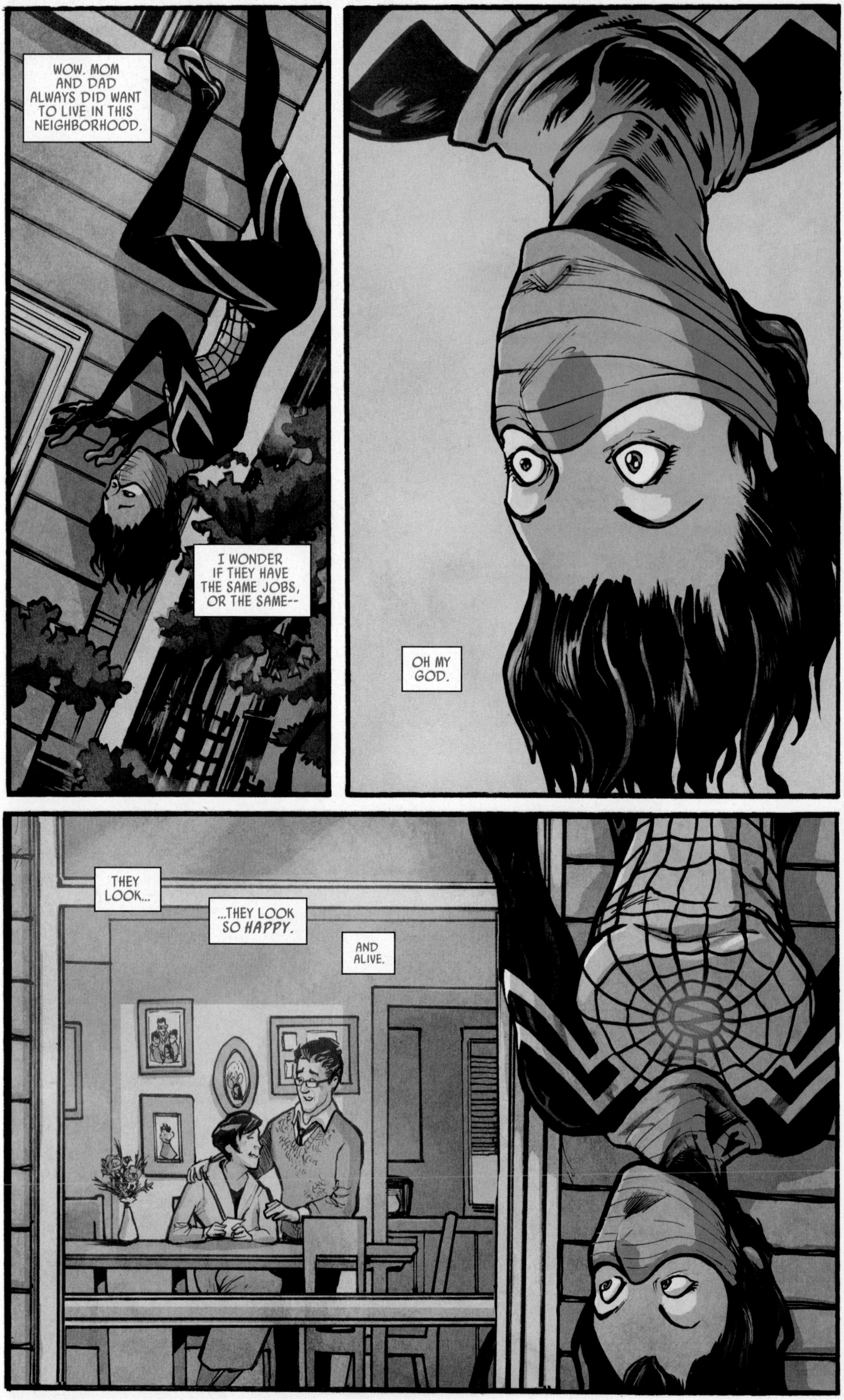
WOW. MOM AND DAD ALWAYS DID WANT TO LIVE IN THIS NEIGHBORHOOD.
I WONDER IF THEY HAVE THE SAME JOBS, OR THE SAME--
OH MY GOD.
THEY LOOK...
...THEY LOOK SO *HAPPY*.
AND ALIVE.

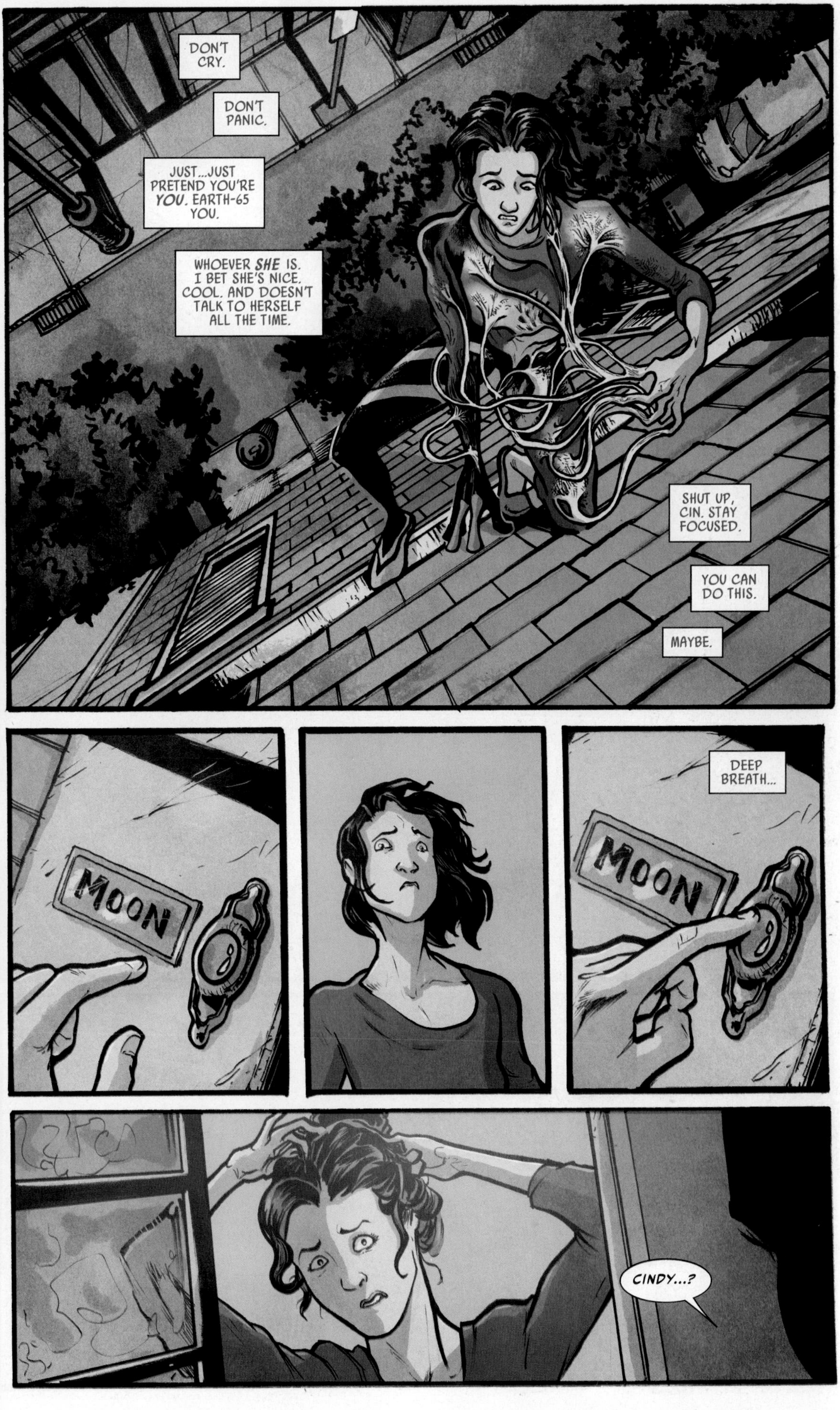
DON'T CRY.
DON'T PANIC.
JUST...JUST PRETEND YOU'RE *YOU*. EARTH-65 YOU.
WHOEVER *SHE* IS. I BET SHE'S NICE. COOL. AND DOESN'T TALK TO HERSELF ALL THE TIME.
SHUT UP, CIN. STAY FOCUSED.
YOU CAN DO THIS.
MAYBE.
MOON
DEEP BREATH...
MOON
CINDY...?

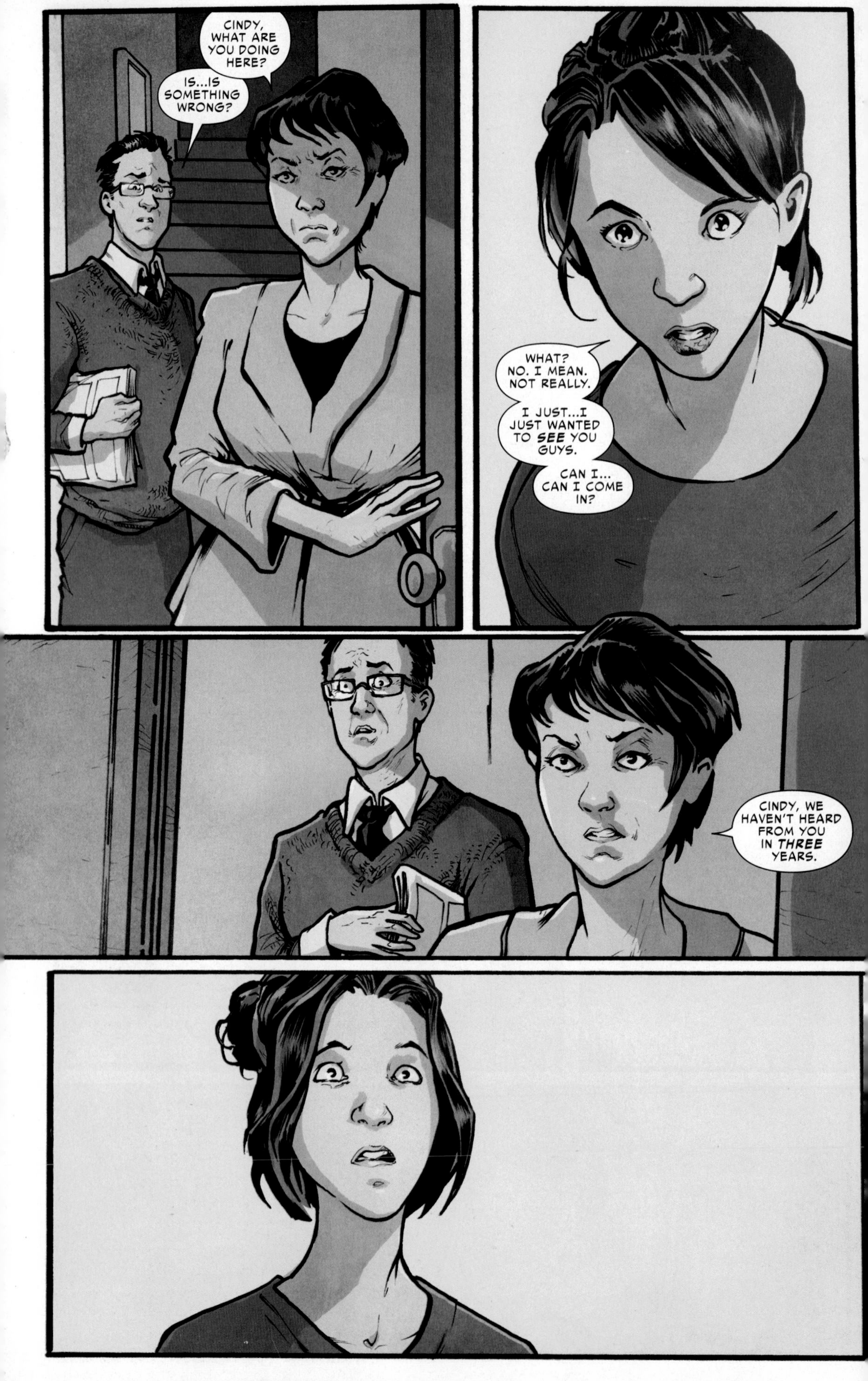
CINDY, WHAT ARE YOU DOING HERE?
IS...IS SOMETHING WRONG?
WHAT? NO. I MEAN. NOT REALLY.
I JUST...I JUST WANTED TO *SEE* YOU GUYS.
CAN I... CAN I COME IN?
CINDY, WE HAVEN'T HEARD FROM YOU IN *THREE* YEARS.

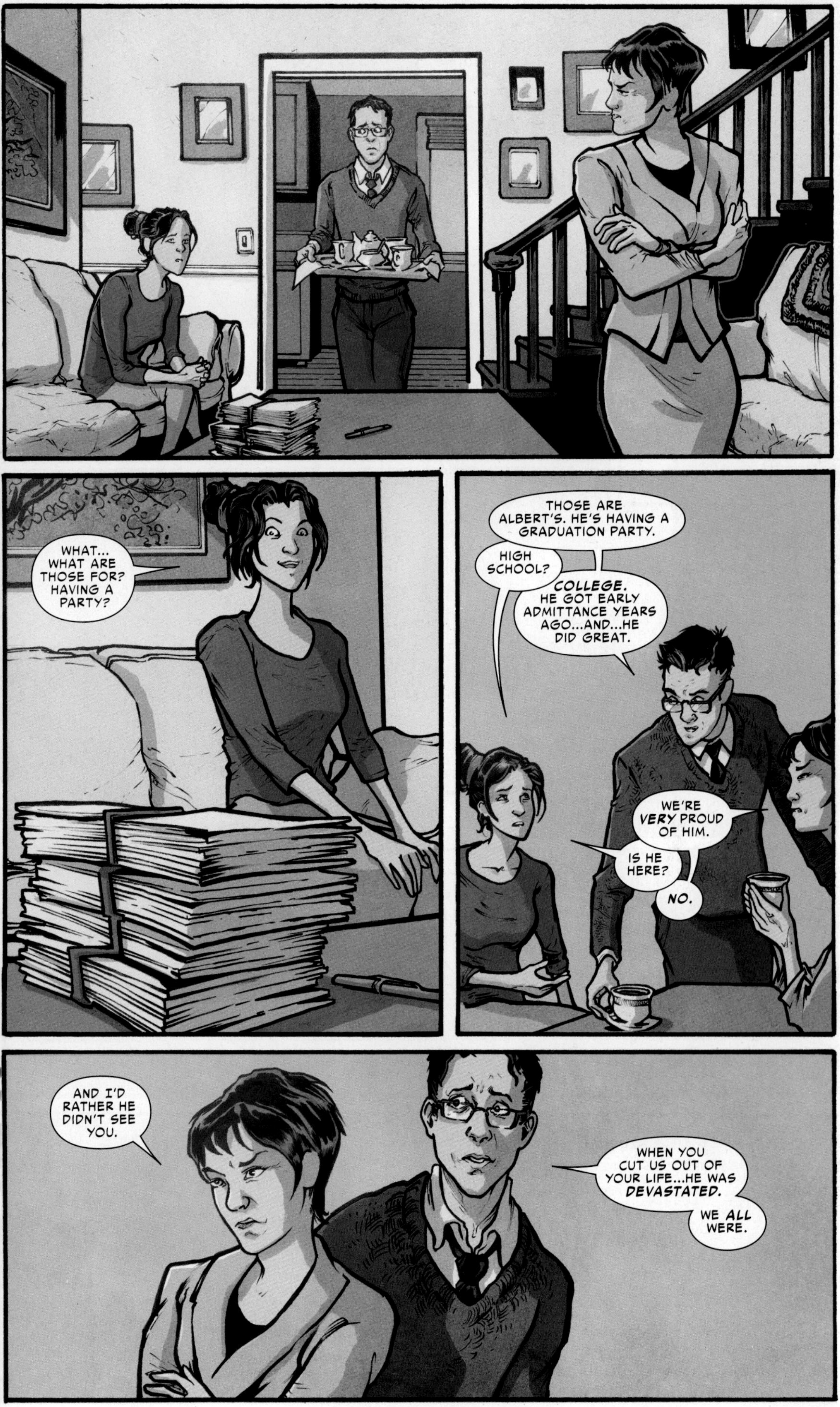
WHAT... WHAT ARE THOSE FOR? HAVING A PARTY?
THOSE ARE ALBERT'S. HE'S HAVING A GRADUATION PARTY.
HIGH SCHOOL?
COLLEGE. HE GOT EARLY ADMITTANCE YEARS AGO...AND...HE DID GREAT.
WE'RE VERY PROUD OF HIM.
IS HE HERE?
NO.
AND I'D RATHER HE DIDN'T SEE YOU.
WHEN YOU CUT US OUT OF YOUR LIFE...HE WAS DEVASTATED.
WE ALL WERE.

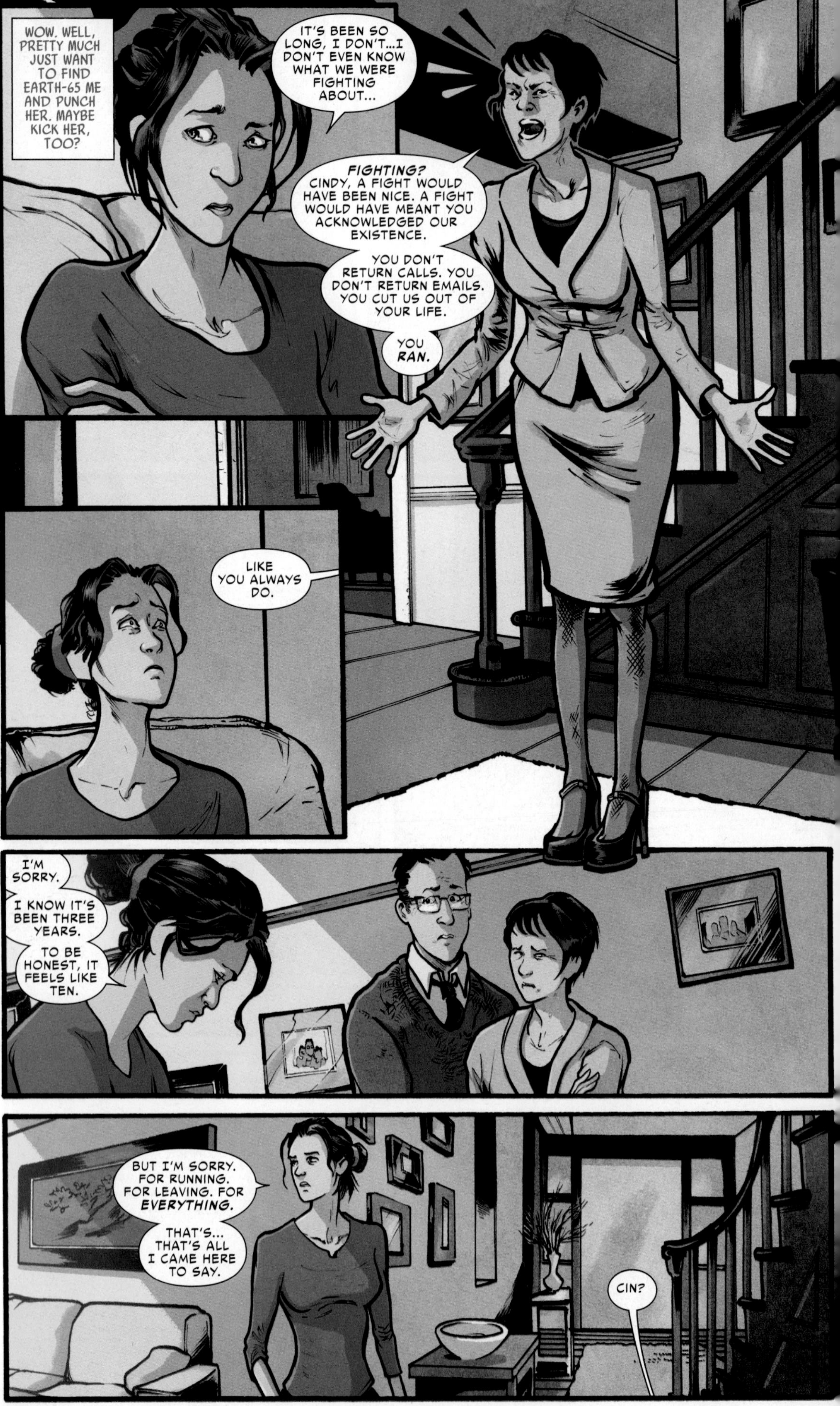

WOW. WELL, PRETTY MUCH JUST WANT TO FIND EARTH-65 ME AND PUNCH HER. MAYBE KICK HER, TOO?
IT'S BEEN SO LONG, I DON'T...I DON'T EVEN KNOW WHAT WE WERE FIGHTING ABOUT...
FIGHTING? CINDY, A FIGHT WOULD HAVE BEEN NICE. A FIGHT WOULD HAVE MEANT YOU ACKNOWLEDGED OUR EXISTENCE.
YOU DON'T RETURN CALLS. YOU DON'T RETURN EMAILS. YOU CUT US OUT OF YOUR LIFE.
YOU RAN.
LIKE YOU ALWAYS DO.
I'M SORRY.
I KNOW IT'S BEEN THREE YEARS.
TO BE HONEST, IT FEELS LIKE TEN.
BUT I'M SORRY. FOR RUNNING. FOR LEAVING. FOR EVERYTHING.
THAT'S... THAT'S ALL I CAME HERE TO SAY.
CIN?

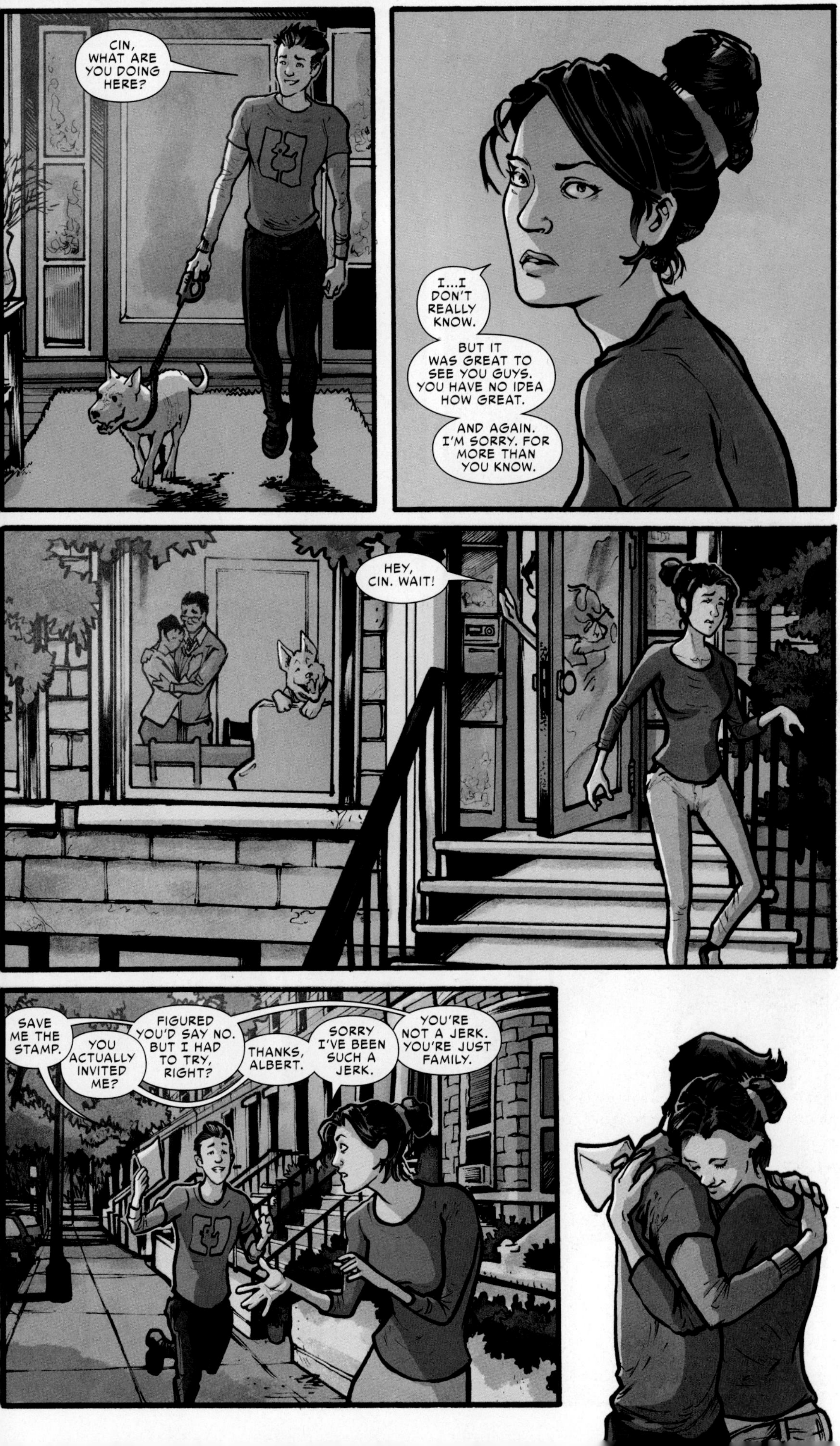
CIN, WHAT ARE YOU DOING HERE?
I...I DON'T REALLY KNOW.
BUT IT WAS GREAT TO SEE YOU GUYS. YOU HAVE NO IDEA HOW GREAT.
AND AGAIN. I'M SORRY. FOR MORE THAN YOU KNOW.
HEY, CIN. WAIT!
SAVE ME THE STAMP.
YOU ACTUALLY INVITED ME?
FIGURED YOU'D SAY NO. BUT I HAD TO TRY, RIGHT?
THANKS, ALBERT.
SORRY I'VE BEEN SUCH A JERK.
YOU'RE NOT A JERK. YOU'RE JUST FAMILY.

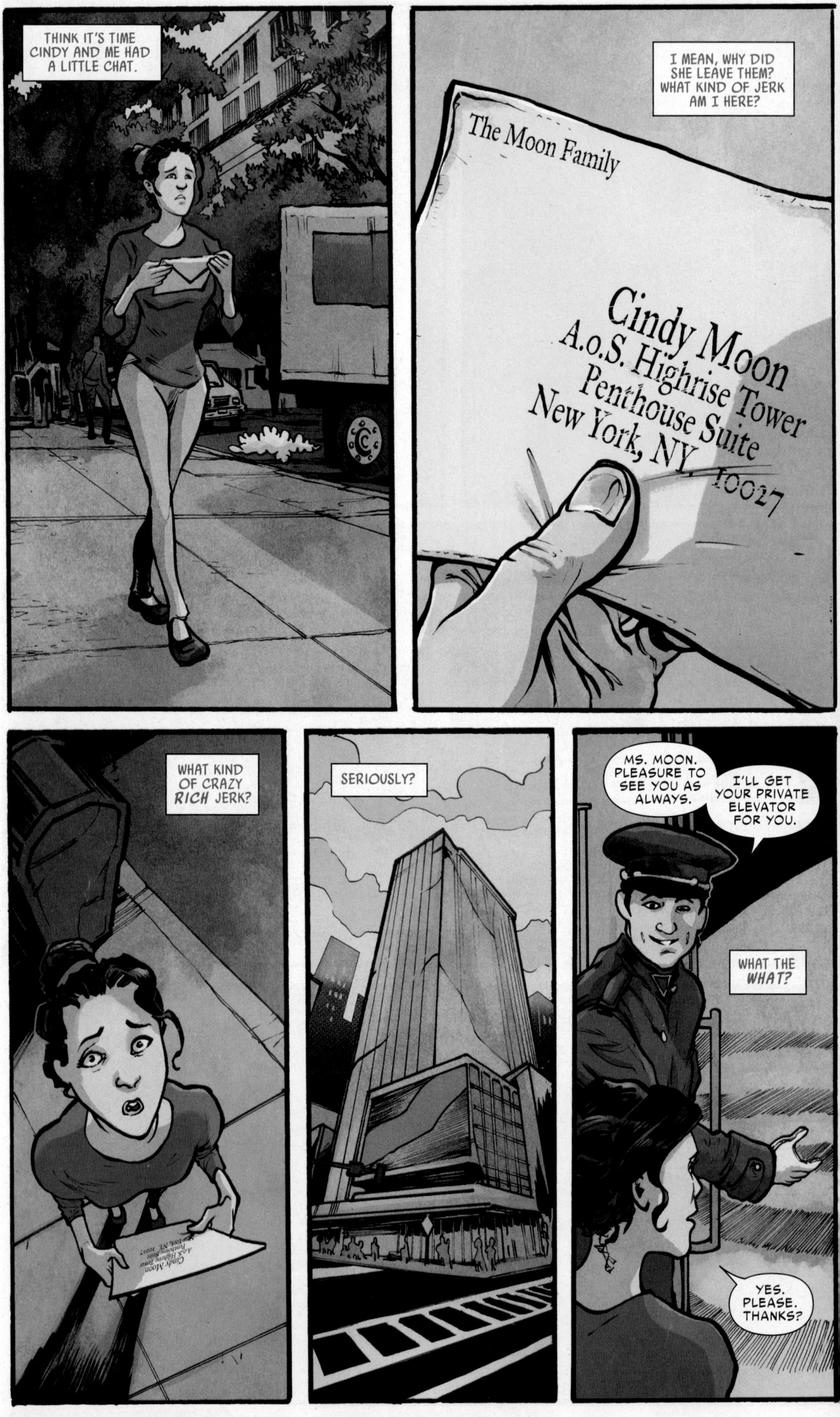
THINK IT'S TIME CINDY AND ME HAD A LITTLE CHAT.
I MEAN, WHY DID SHE LEAVE THEM? WHAT KIND OF JERK AM I HERE?
The Moon Family
Cindy Moon
A.o.S. Highrise Tower
Penthouse Suite
New York, NY 10027
WHAT KIND OF CRAZY RICH JERK?
SERIOUSLY?
MS. MOON. PLEASURE TO SEE YOU AS ALWAYS.
I'LL GET YOUR PRIVATE ELEVATOR FOR YOU.
WHAT THE WHAT?
YES. PLEASE. THANKS?

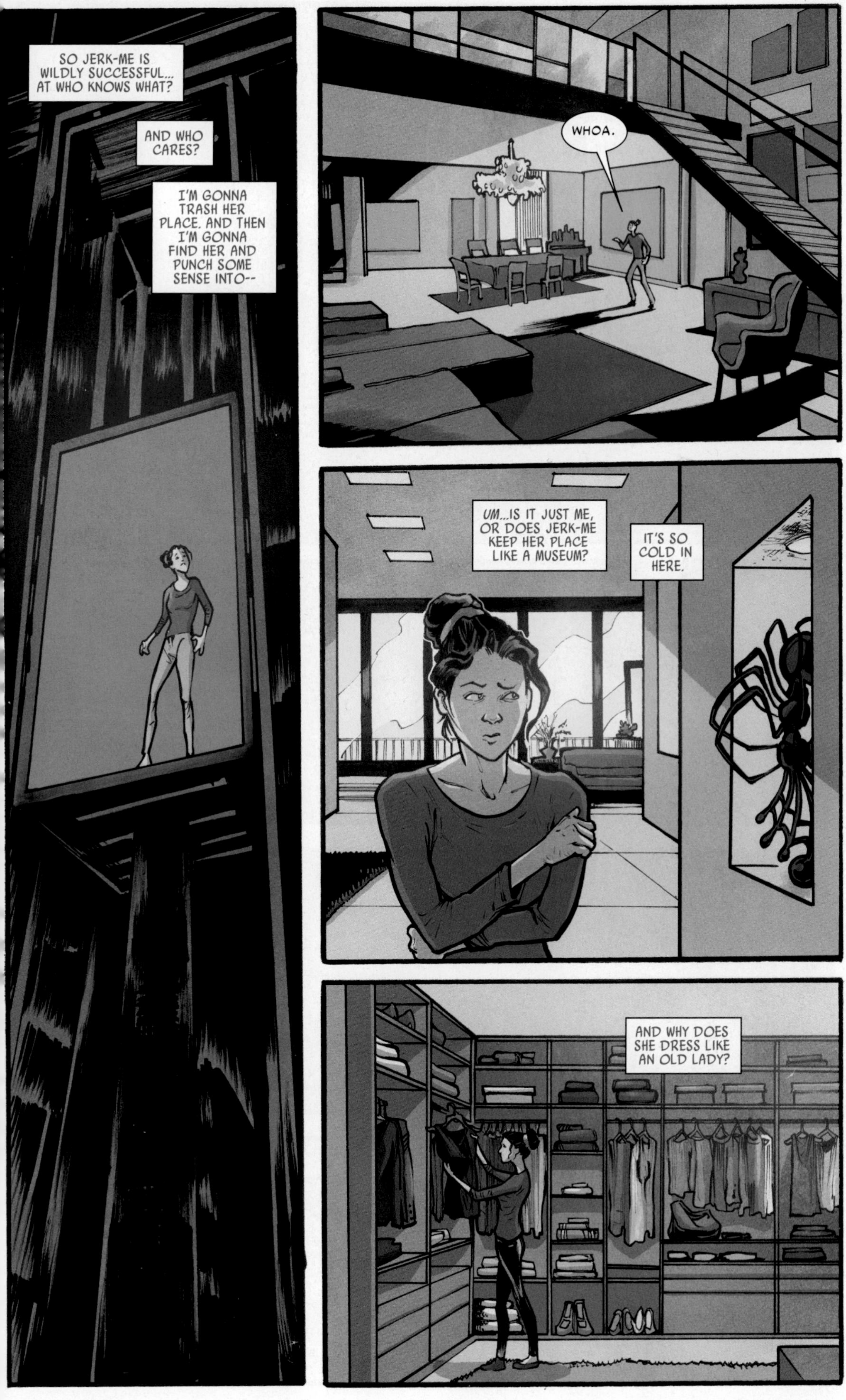
SO JERK-ME IS WILDLY SUCCESSFUL... AT WHO KNOWS WHAT?
AND WHO CARES?
I'M GONNA TRASH HER PLACE. AND THEN I'M GONNA FIND HER AND PUNCH SOME SENSE INTO--
WHOA.
UM...IS IT JUST ME, OR DOES JERK-ME KEEP HER PLACE LIKE A MUSEUM?
IT'S SO COLD IN HERE.
AND WHY DOES SHE DRESS LIKE AN OLD LADY?

AND MOST IMPORTANTLY... WHY DID SHE CUT OFF TIES WITH HER FAMILY?

WHAT COULD POSSIBLY BE MORE IMPORTANT THAN THEM?

WHO AM I TO TALK?

JESS AND GWEN ARE TWO OF MY FEW FRIENDS.

OKAY, GWEN HATES ME, BUT STILL.

I DITCHED THEM.

AM I ANY *BETTER?*

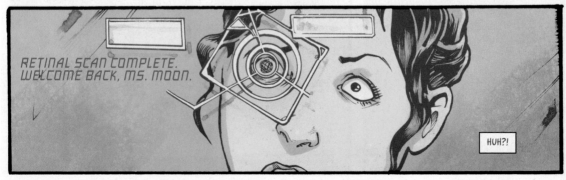

RETINAL SCAN COMPLETE. WELCOME BACK, MS. MOON.

HUH?!

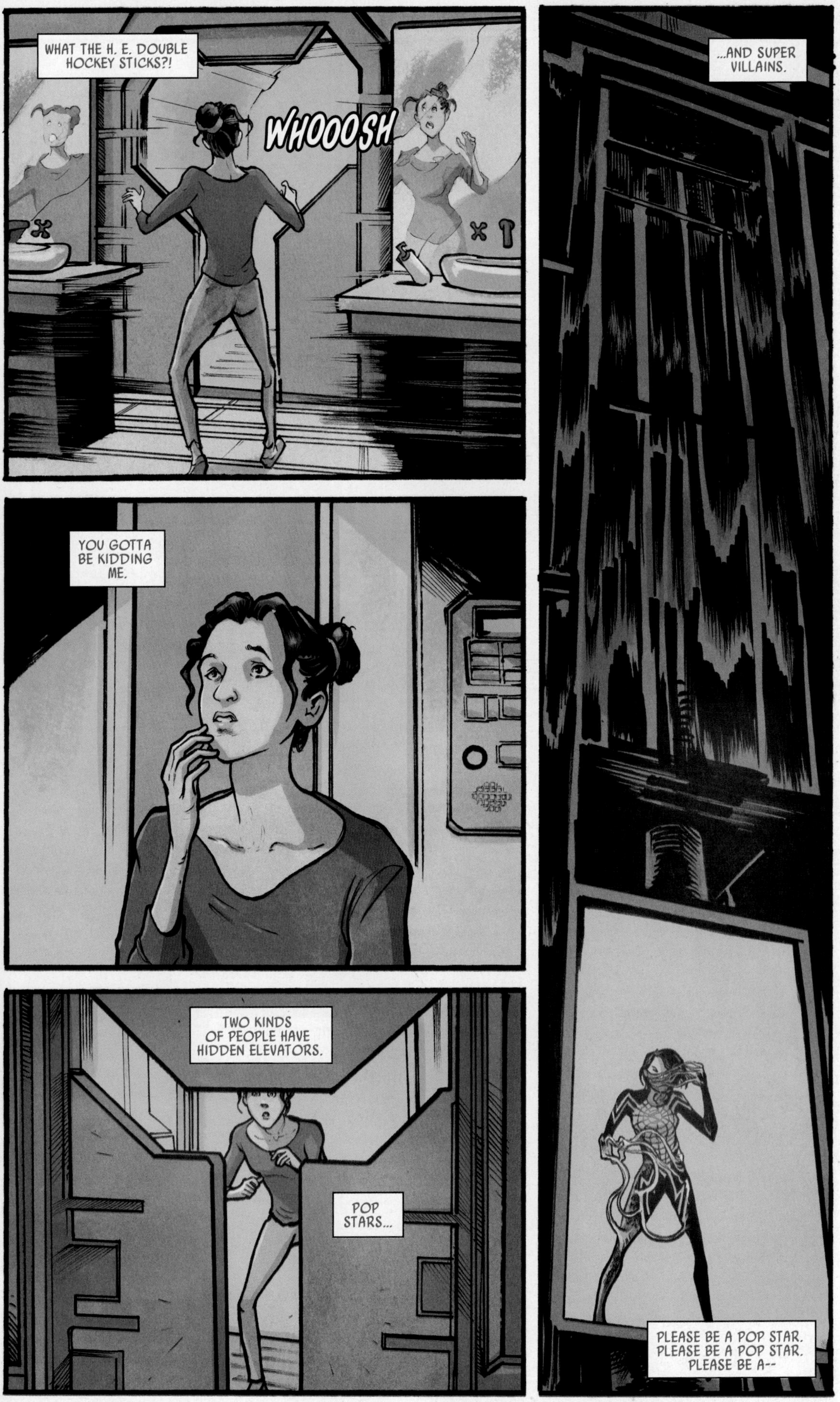

WHAT THE H. E. DOUBLE HOCKEY STICKS?!
WHOOOSH
YOU GOTTA BE KIDDING ME.
TWO KINDS OF PEOPLE HAVE HIDDEN ELEVATORS.
POP STARS...
...AND SUPER VILLAINS.
PLEASE BE A POP STAR. PLEASE BE A POP STAR. PLEASE BE A--

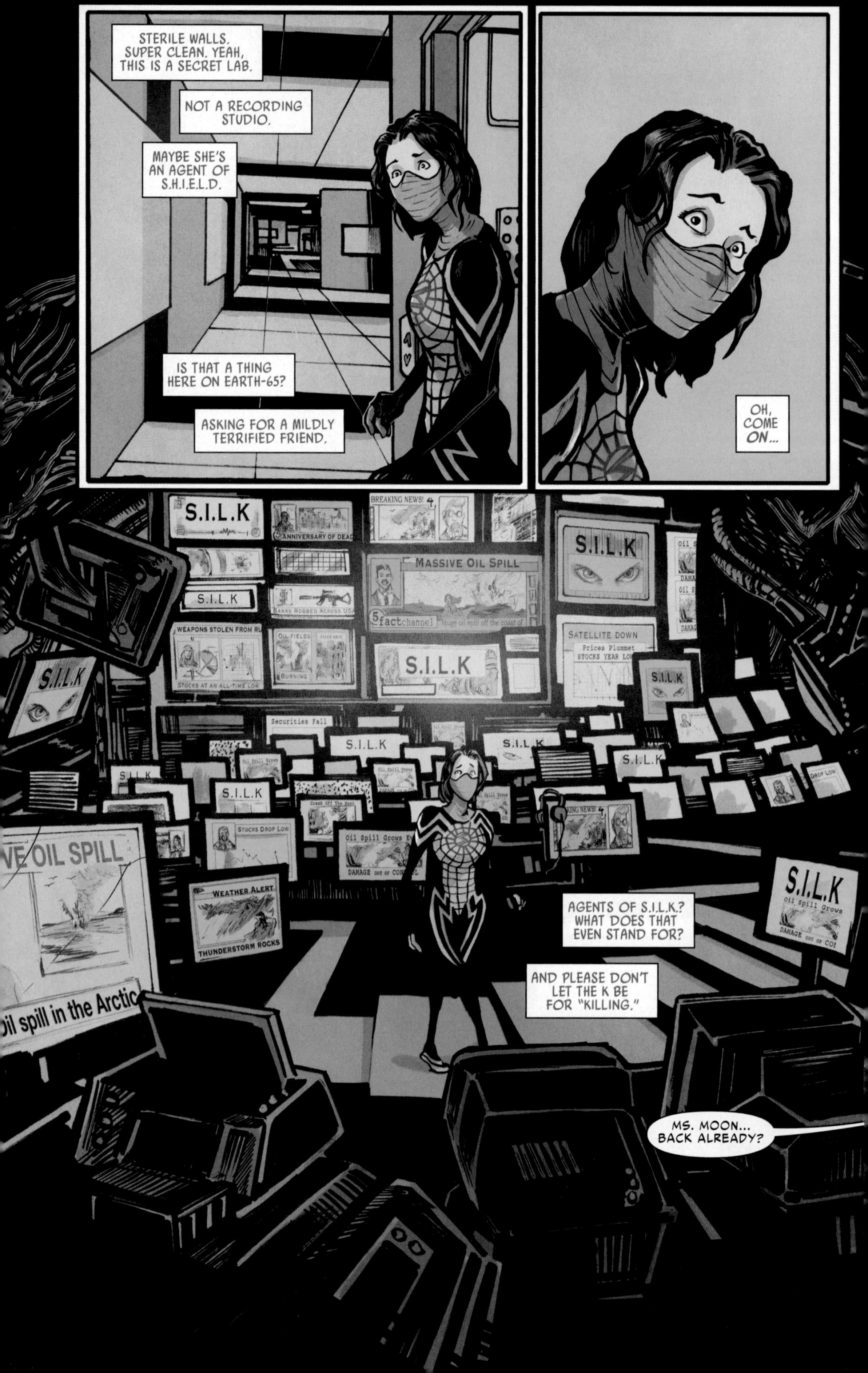
STERILE WALLS. SUPER CLEAN. YEAH, THIS IS A SECRET LAB.
NOT A RECORDING STUDIO.
MAYBE SHE'S AN AGENT OF S.H.I.E.L.D.
IS THAT A THING HERE ON EARTH-65?
ASKING FOR A MILDLY TERRIFIED FRIEND.
OH, COME ON...
S.I.L.K
BREAKING NEWS!
MASSIVE OIL SPILL
factchannel
WEAPONS STOLEN FROM RU
STOCKS AT AN ALL-TIME LOW
SATELLITE DOWN
Prices Plummet
STOCKS YEAR LOW
Securities Fall
STOCKS DROP LOW
WEATHER ALERT
THUNDERSTORM ROCKS
VE OIL SPILL
oil spill in the Arctic
AGENTS OF S.I.L.K.? WHAT DOES THAT EVEN STAND FOR?
AND PLEASE DON'T LET THE K BE FOR "KILLING."
MS. MOON... BACK ALREADY?

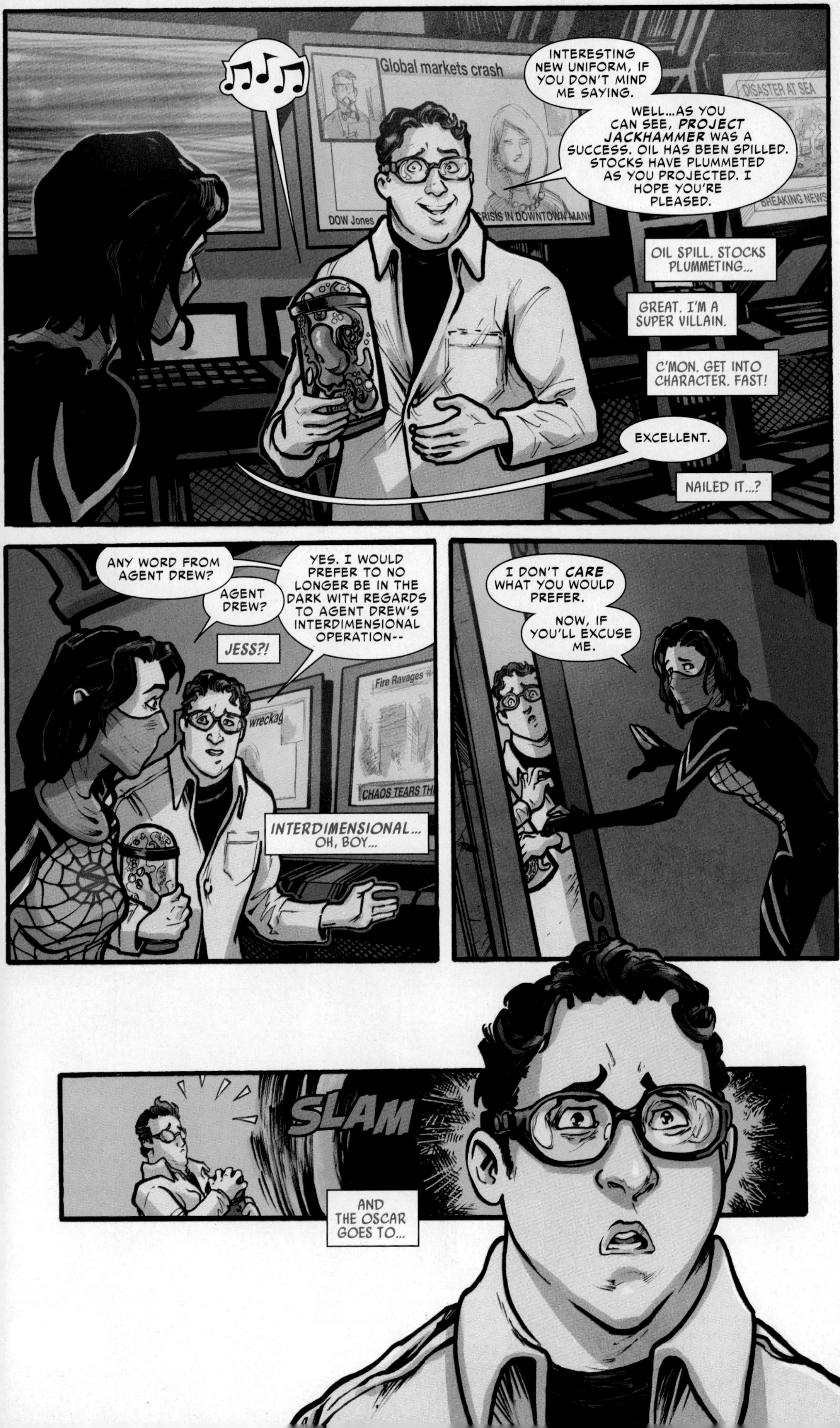
Global markets crash
DISASTER AT SEA
DOW Jones
INTERESTING NEW UNIFORM, IF YOU DON'T MIND ME SAYING.
WELL...AS YOU CAN SEE, *PROJECT JACKHAMMER* WAS A SUCCESS. OIL HAS BEEN SPILLED. STOCKS HAVE PLUMMETED AS YOU PROJECTED. I HOPE YOU'RE PLEASED.
OIL SPILL. STOCKS PLUMMETING...
GREAT. I'M A SUPER VILLAIN.
C'MON. GET INTO CHARACTER. FAST!
EXCELLENT.
NAILED IT...?
ANY WORD FROM AGENT DREW?
AGENT DREW?
JESS?!
YES. I WOULD PREFER TO NO LONGER BE IN THE DARK WITH REGARDS TO AGENT DREW'S INTERDIMENSIONAL OPERATION--
Fire Ravages
INTERDIMENSIONAL... OH, BOY...
I DON'T *CARE* WHAT YOU WOULD PREFER.
NOW, IF YOU'LL EXCUSE ME.
SLAM
AND THE OSCAR GOES TO...

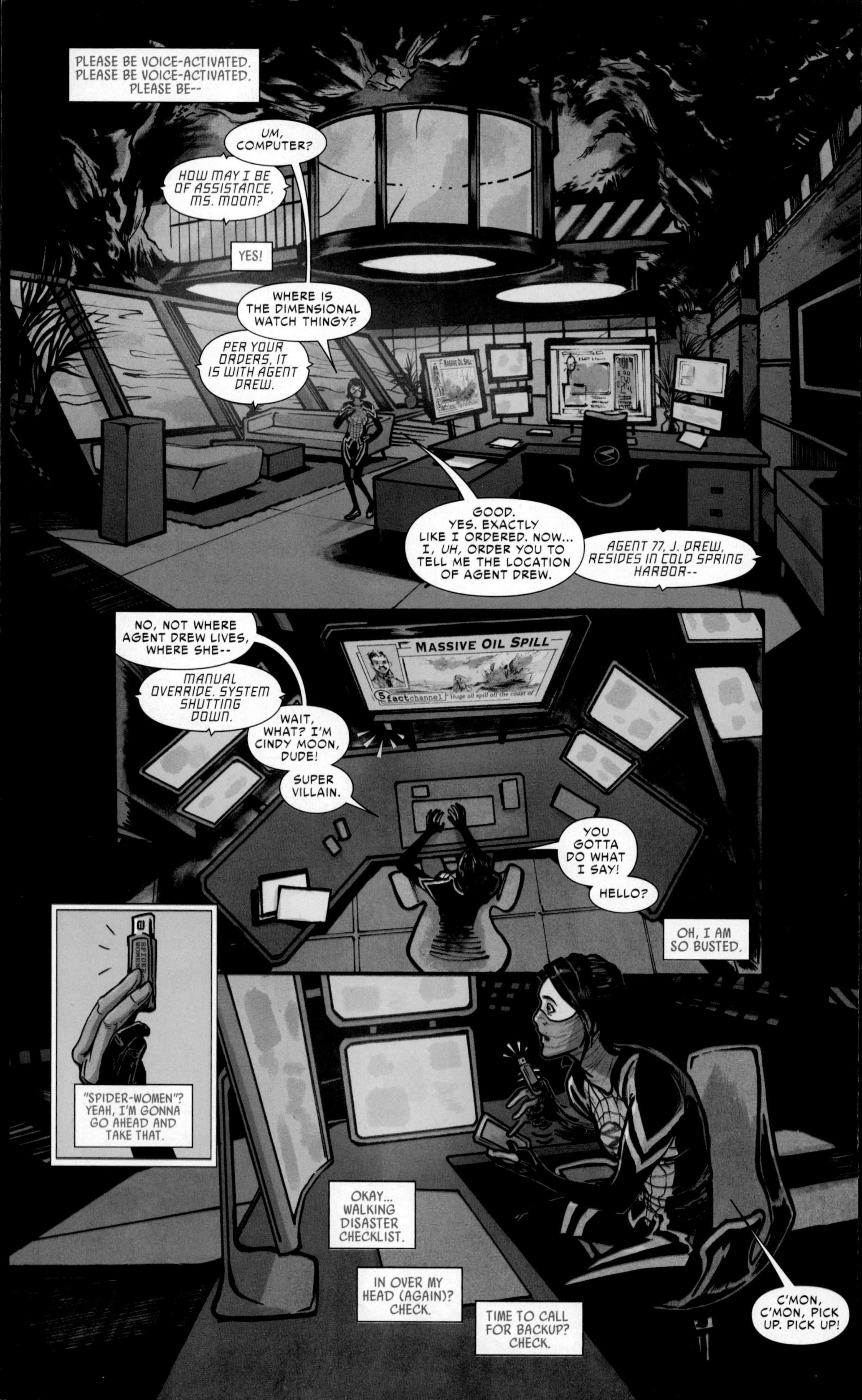
PLEASE BE VOICE-ACTIVATED. PLEASE BE VOICE-ACTIVATED. PLEASE BE--
UM, COMPUTER?
HOW MAY I BE OF ASSISTANCE, MS. MOON?
YES!
WHERE IS THE DIMENSIONAL WATCH THINGY?
PER YOUR ORDERS, IT IS WITH AGENT DREW.
GOOD. YES. EXACTLY LIKE I ORDERED. NOW... I, UH, ORDER YOU TO TELL ME THE LOCATION OF AGENT DREW.
AGENT 77, J. DREW, RESIDES IN COLD SPRING HARBOR--
NO, NOT WHERE AGENT DREW LIVES, WHERE SHE--
MANUAL OVERRIDE. SYSTEM SHUTTING DOWN.
WAIT, WHAT? I'M CINDY MOON, DUDE!
SUPER VILLAIN.
MASSIVE OIL SPILL
5 fact channel Huge oil spill off the coast of
YOU GOTTA DO WHAT I SAY!
HELLO?
OH, I AM SO BUSTED.
SPIDER-WOMEN
"SPIDER-WOMEN"? YEAH, I'M GONNA GO AHEAD AND TAKE THAT.
OKAY... WALKING DISASTER CHECKLIST.
IN OVER MY HEAD (AGAIN)? CHECK.
TIME TO CALL FOR BACKUP? CHECK.
C'MON, C'MON, PICK UP. PICK UP!

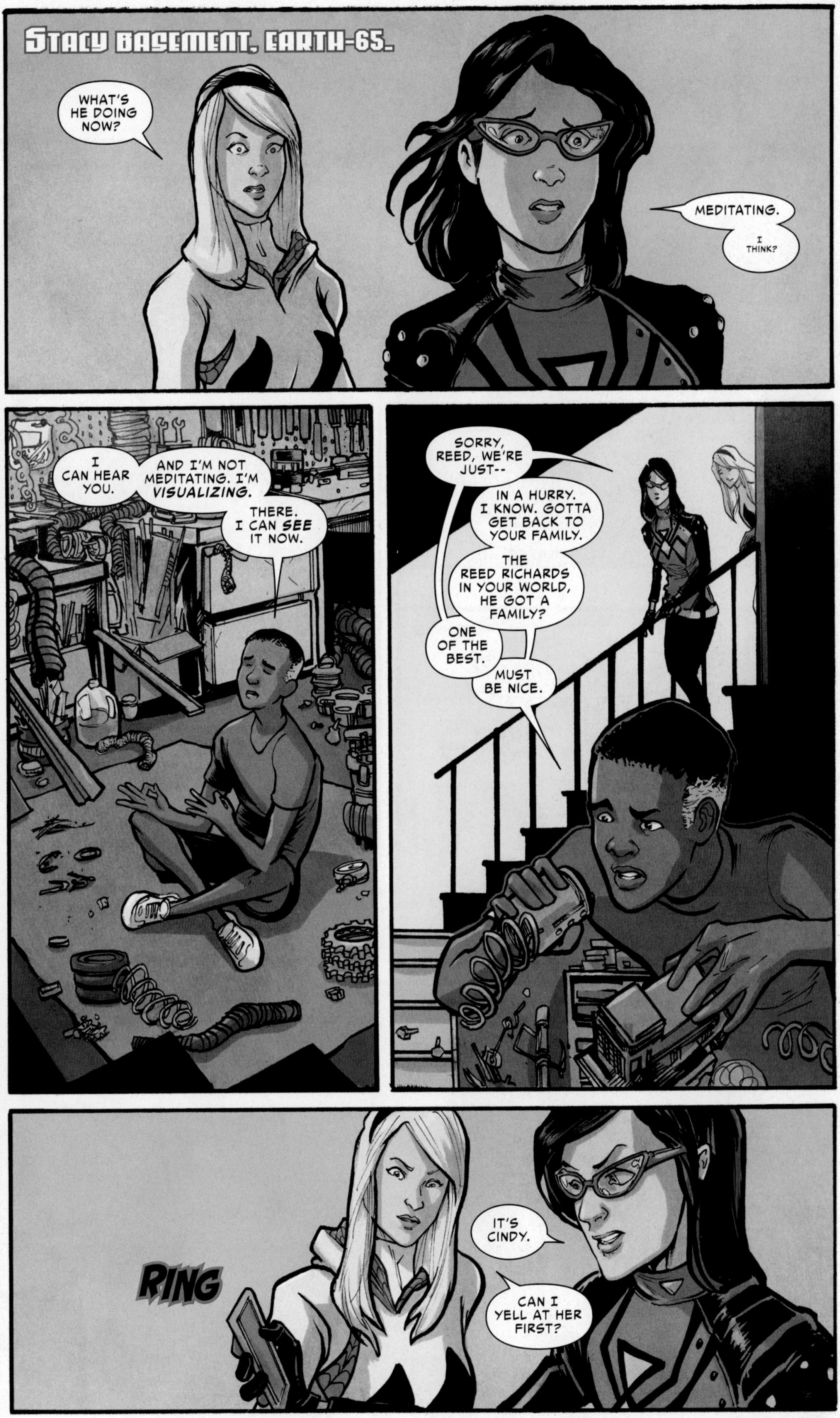
STACY BASEMENT, EARTH-65.
WHAT'S HE DOING NOW?
MEDITATING.
I THINK?
I CAN HEAR YOU.
AND I'M NOT MEDITATING. I'M VISUALIZING.
THERE. I CAN SEE IT NOW.
SORRY, REED, WE'RE JUST--
IN A HURRY. I KNOW. GOTTA GET BACK TO YOUR FAMILY.
THE REED RICHARDS IN YOUR WORLD, HE GOT A FAMILY?
ONE OF THE BEST.
MUST BE NICE.
RING
IT'S CINDY.
CAN I YELL AT HER FIRST?

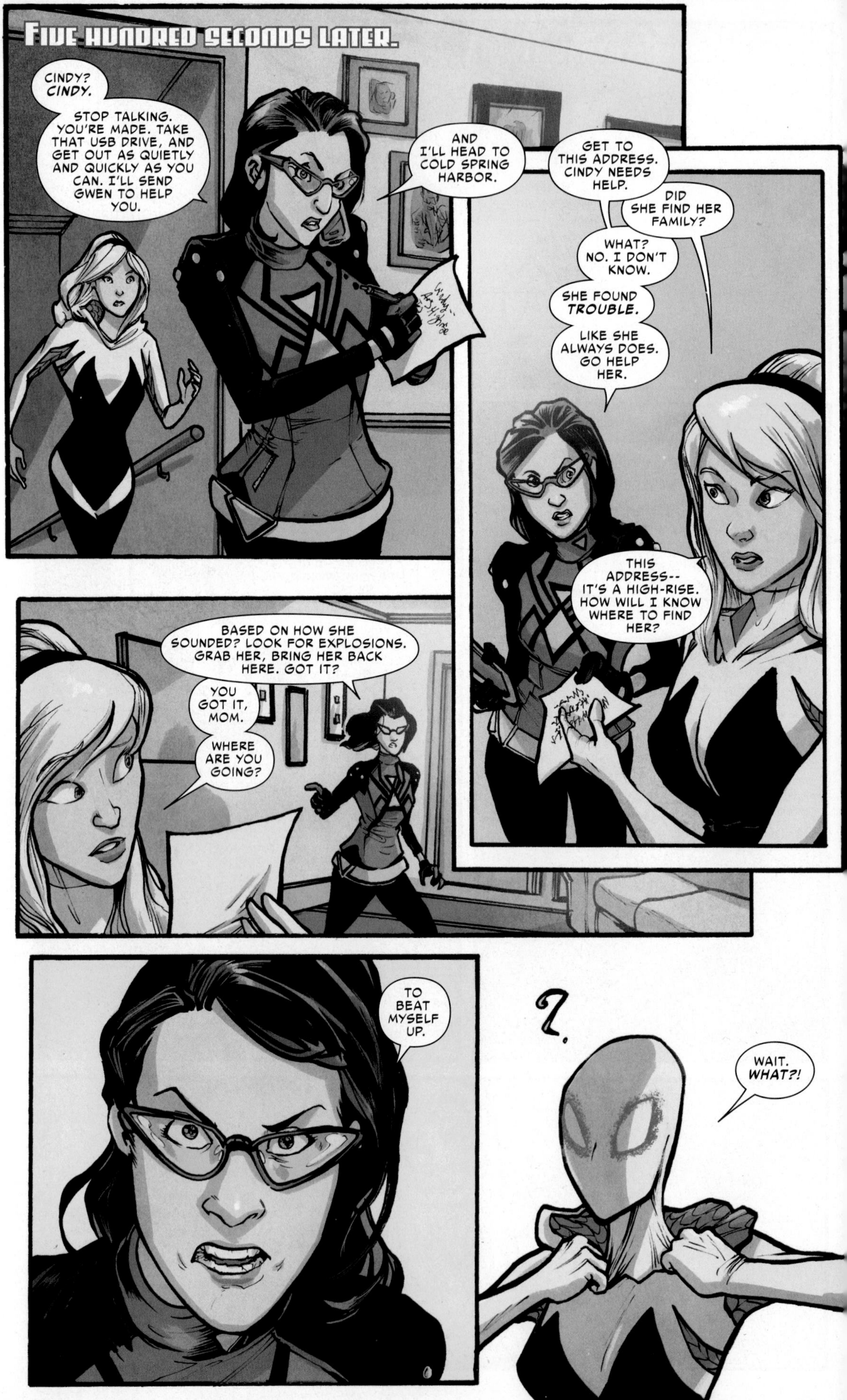
FIVE HUNDRED SECONDS LATER.
CINDY? CINDY.
STOP TALKING. YOU'RE MADE. TAKE THAT USB DRIVE, AND GET OUT AS QUIETLY AND QUICKLY AS YOU CAN. I'LL SEND GWEN TO HELP YOU.
AND I'LL HEAD TO COLD SPRING HARBOR.
GET TO THIS ADDRESS. CINDY NEEDS HELP.
DID SHE FIND HER FAMILY?
WHAT? NO. I DON'T KNOW.
SHE FOUND TROUBLE.
LIKE SHE ALWAYS DOES. GO HELP HER.
THIS ADDRESS-- IT'S A HIGH-RISE. HOW WILL I KNOW WHERE TO FIND HER?
BASED ON HOW SHE SOUNDED? LOOK FOR EXPLOSIONS. GRAB HER, BRING HER BACK HERE. GOT IT?
YOU GOT IT, MOM.
WHERE ARE YOU GOING?
TO BEAT MYSELF UP.
?
WAIT. WHAT?!

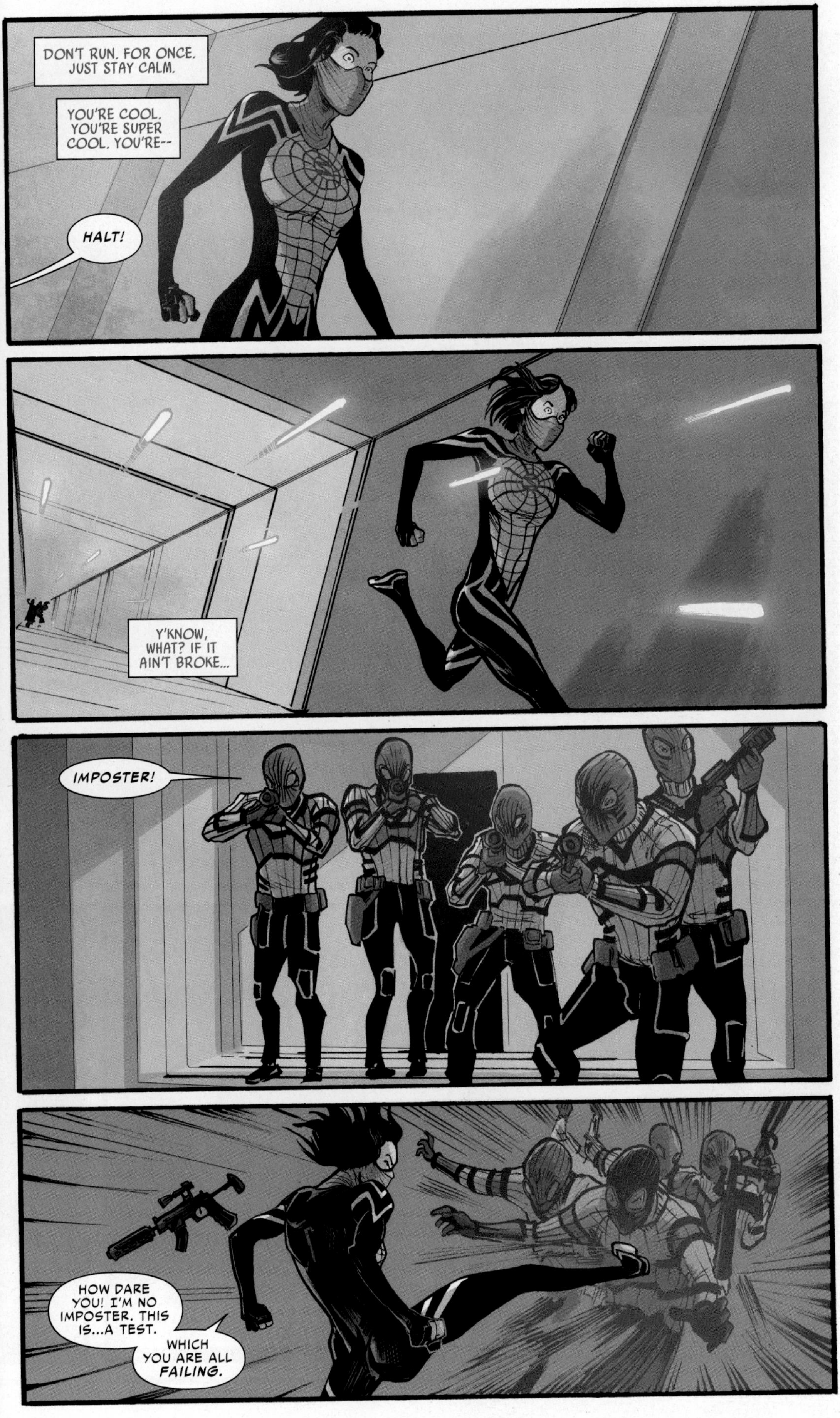
DON'T RUN. FOR ONCE. JUST STAY CALM.
YOU'RE COOL. YOU'RE SUPER COOL. YOU'RE--
HALT!
Y'KNOW, WHAT? IF IT AIN'T BROKE...
IMPOSTER!
HOW DARE YOU! I'M NO IMPOSTER. THIS IS...A TEST.
WHICH YOU ARE ALL FAILING.

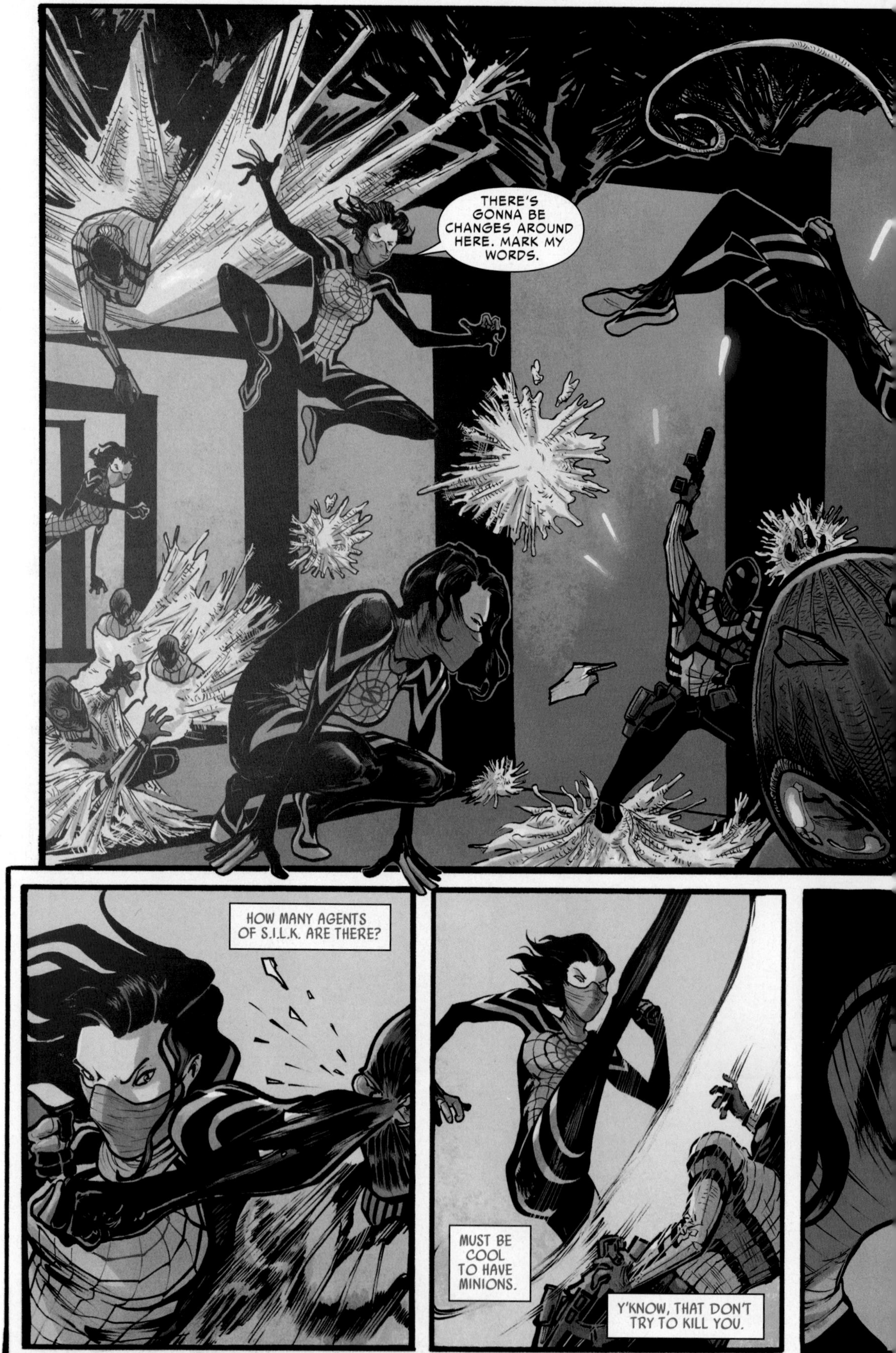
THERE'S GONNA BE CHANGES AROUND HERE. MARK MY WORDS.
HOW MANY AGENTS OF S.I.L.K. ARE THERE?
MUST BE COOL TO HAVE MINIONS.
Y'KNOW, THAT DON'T TRY TO KILL YOU.

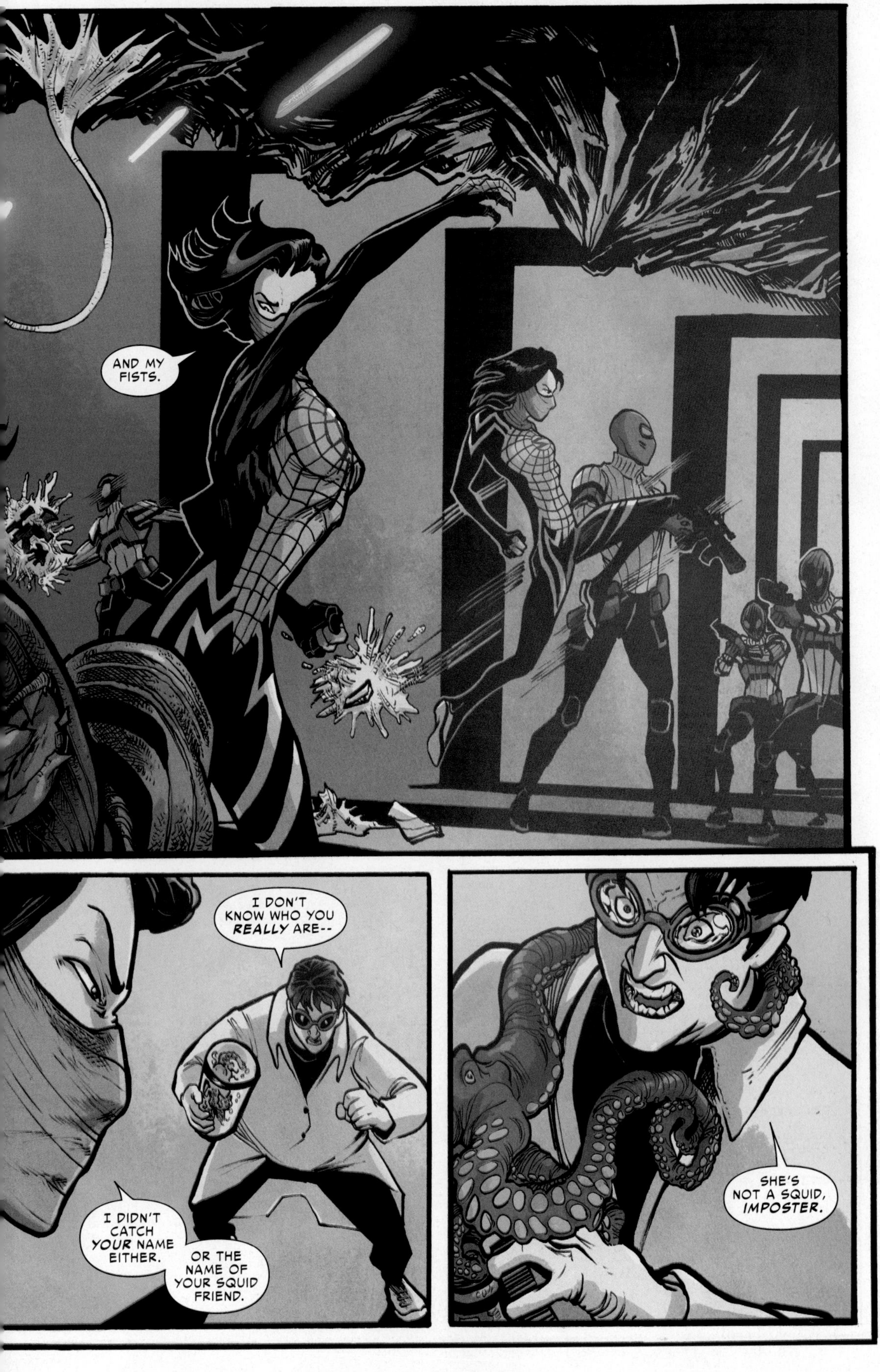
AND MY FISTS.
I DON'T KNOW WHO YOU REALLY ARE--
I DIDN'T CATCH YOUR NAME EITHER.
OR THE NAME OF YOUR SQUID FRIEND.
SHE'S NOT A SQUID, IMPOSTER.

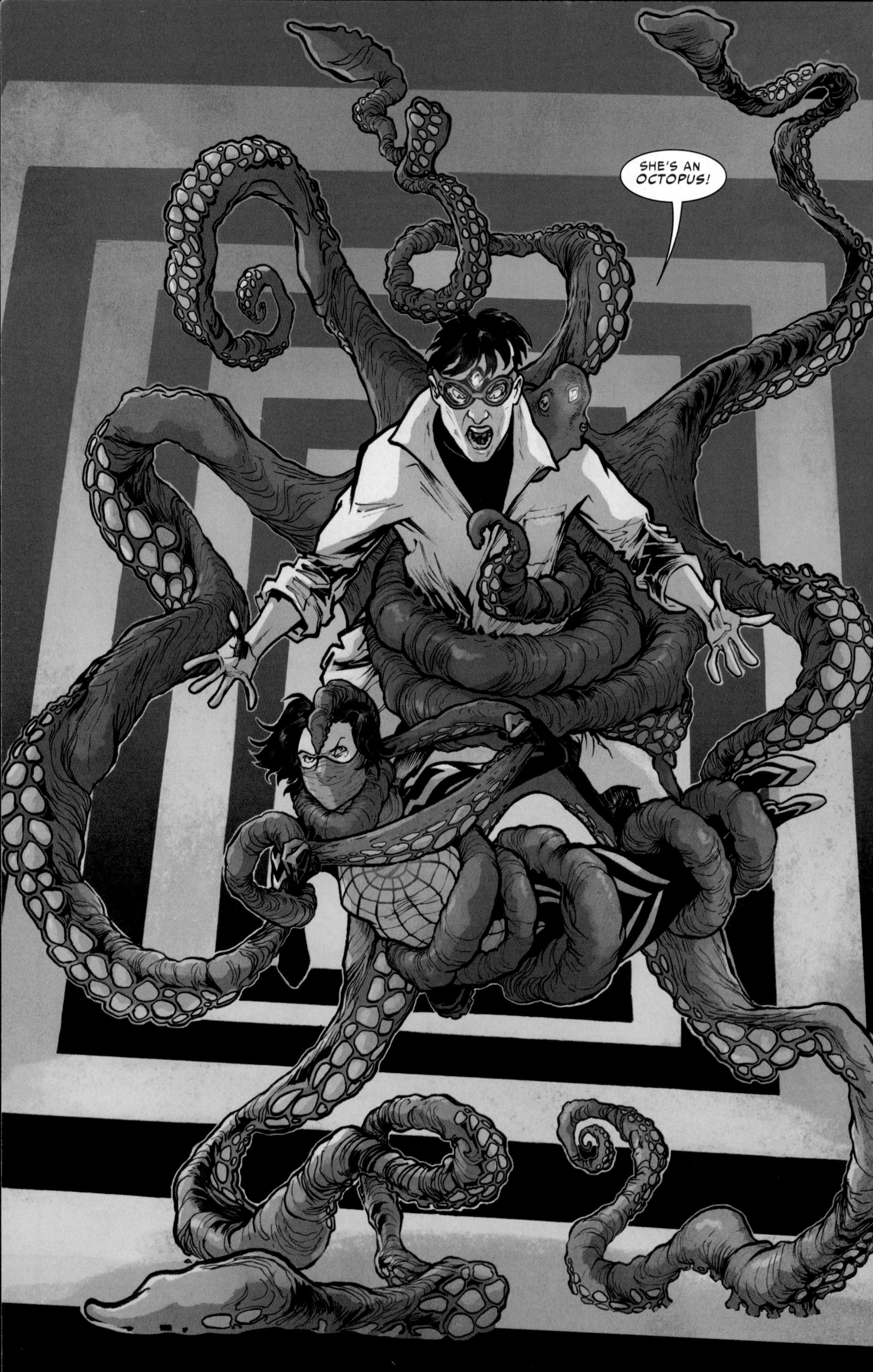
SHE'S AN OCTOPUS!

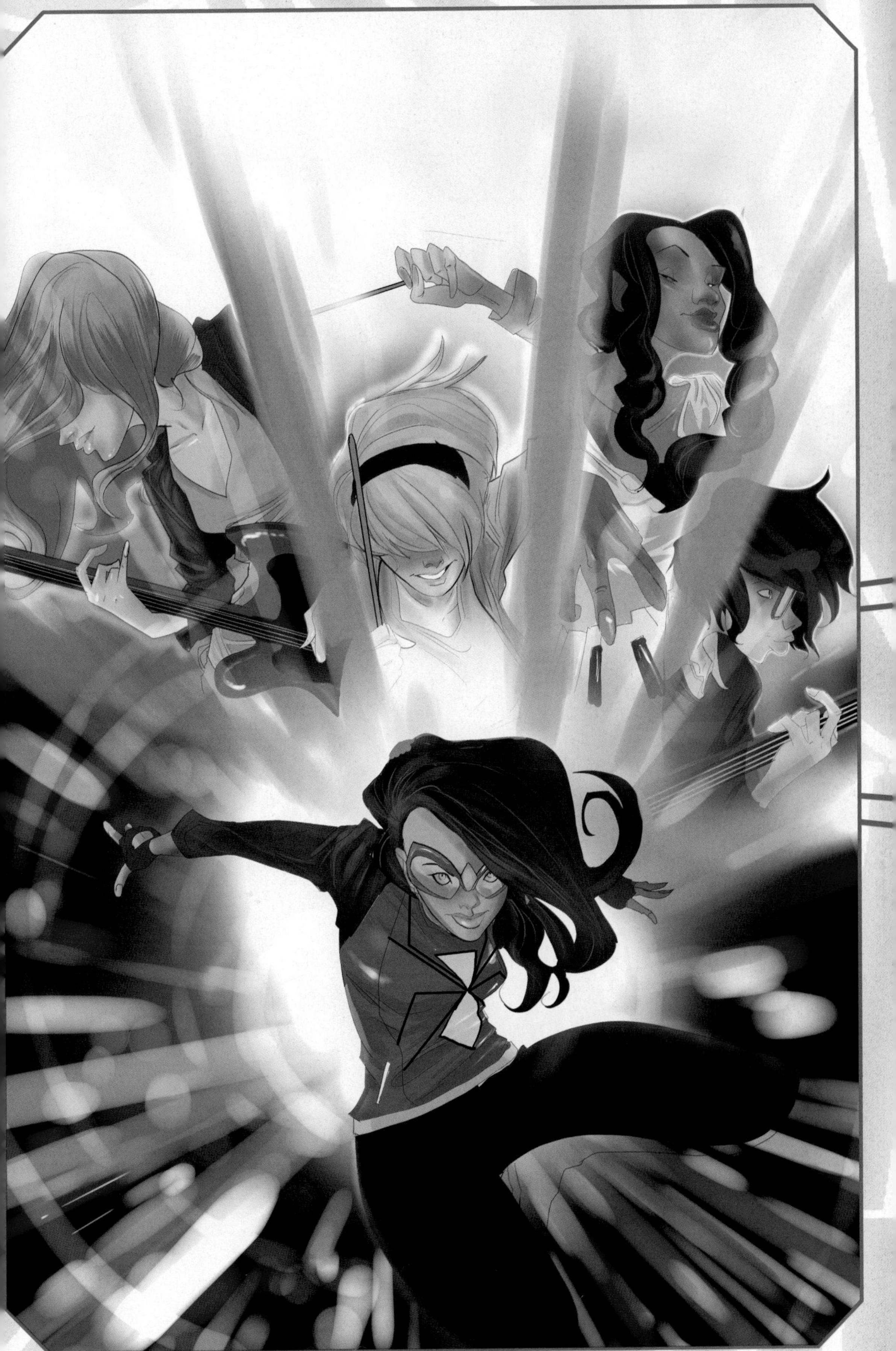

SPIDER-GWEN #7 VARIANT BY ROBBI RODRIGUEZ

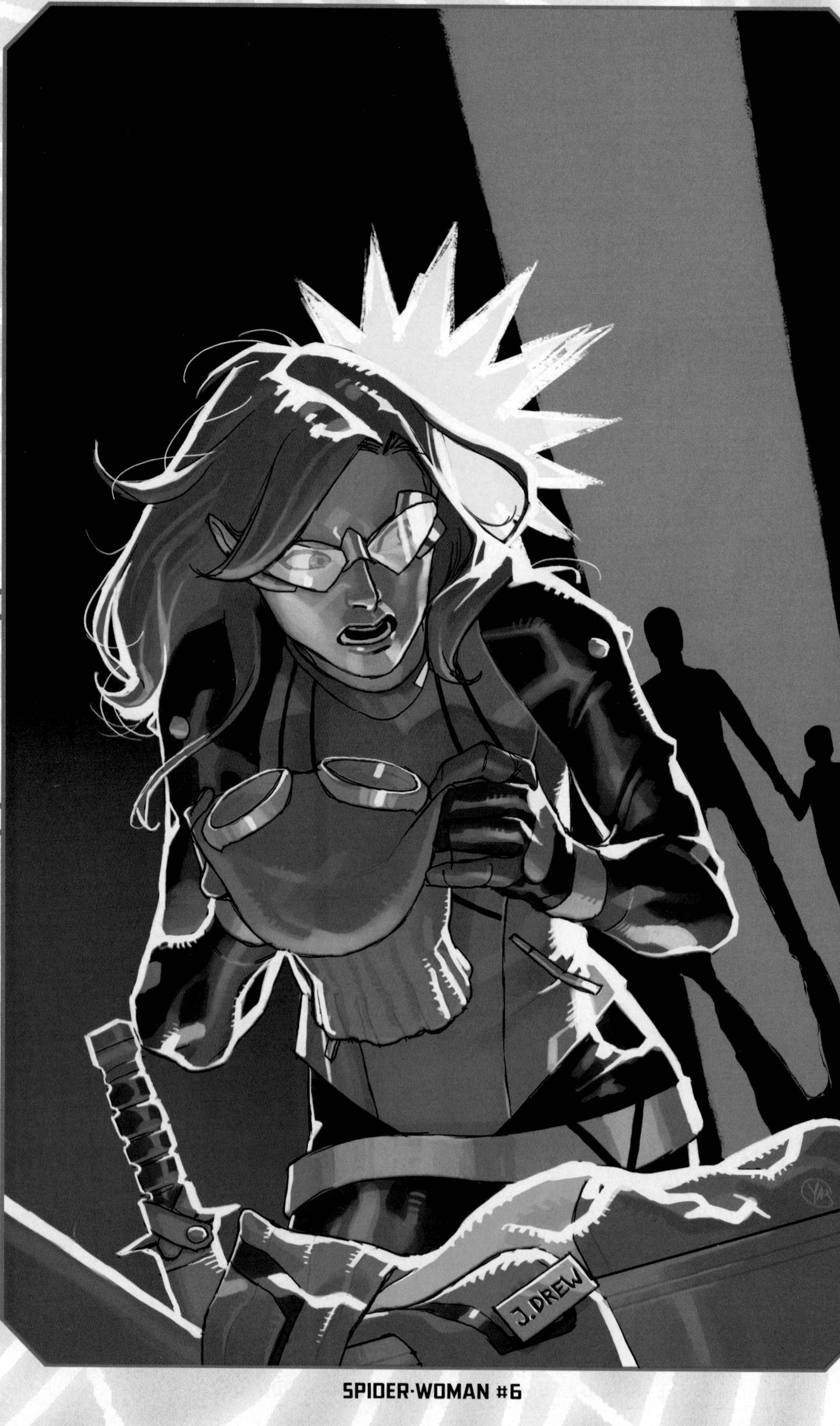
J. DREW

SPIDER-WOMAN #6

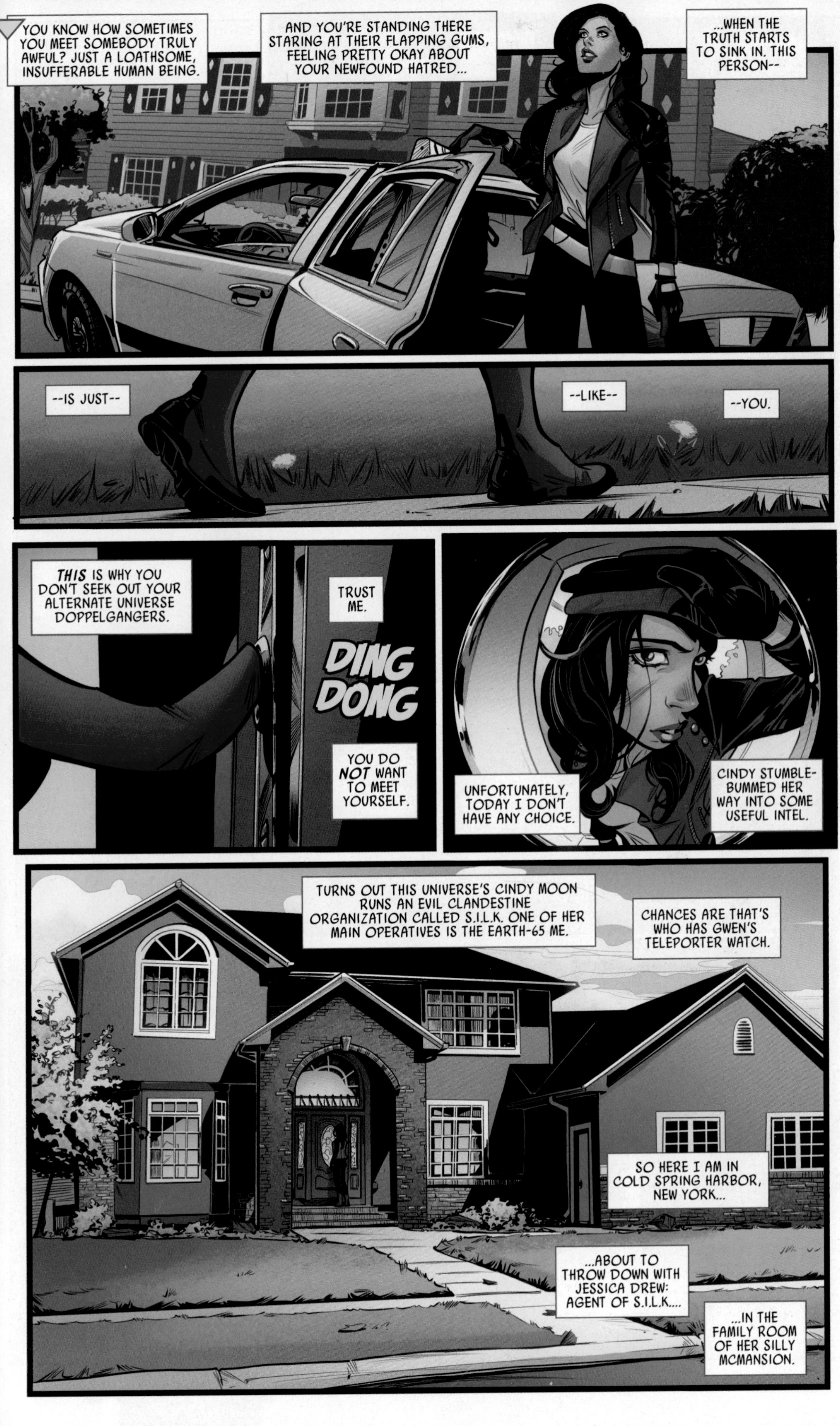
YOU KNOW HOW SOMETIMES YOU MEET SOMEBODY TRULY AWFUL? JUST A LOATHSOME, INSUFFERABLE HUMAN BEING.
AND YOU'RE STANDING THERE STARING AT THEIR FLAPPING GUMS, FEELING PRETTY OKAY ABOUT YOUR NEWFOUND HATRED...
...WHEN THE TRUTH STARTS TO SINK IN. THIS PERSON--
--IS JUST--
--LIKE--
--YOU.
THIS IS WHY YOU DON'T SEEK OUT YOUR ALTERNATE UNIVERSE DOPPELGANGERS.
TRUST ME.
DING DONG
YOU DO NOT WANT TO MEET YOURSELF.
UNFORTUNATELY, TODAY I DON'T HAVE ANY CHOICE.
CINDY STUMBLE-BUMMED HER WAY INTO SOME USEFUL INTEL.
TURNS OUT THIS UNIVERSE'S CINDY MOON RUNS AN EVIL CLANDESTINE ORGANIZATION CALLED S.I.L.K. ONE OF HER MAIN OPERATIVES IS THE EARTH-65 ME.
CHANCES ARE THAT'S WHO HAS GWEN'S TELEPORTER WATCH.
SO HERE I AM IN COLD SPRING HARBOR, NEW YORK...
...ABOUT TO THROW DOWN WITH JESSICA DREW: AGENT OF S.I.L.K....
...IN THE FAMILY ROOM OF HER SILLY MCMANSION.

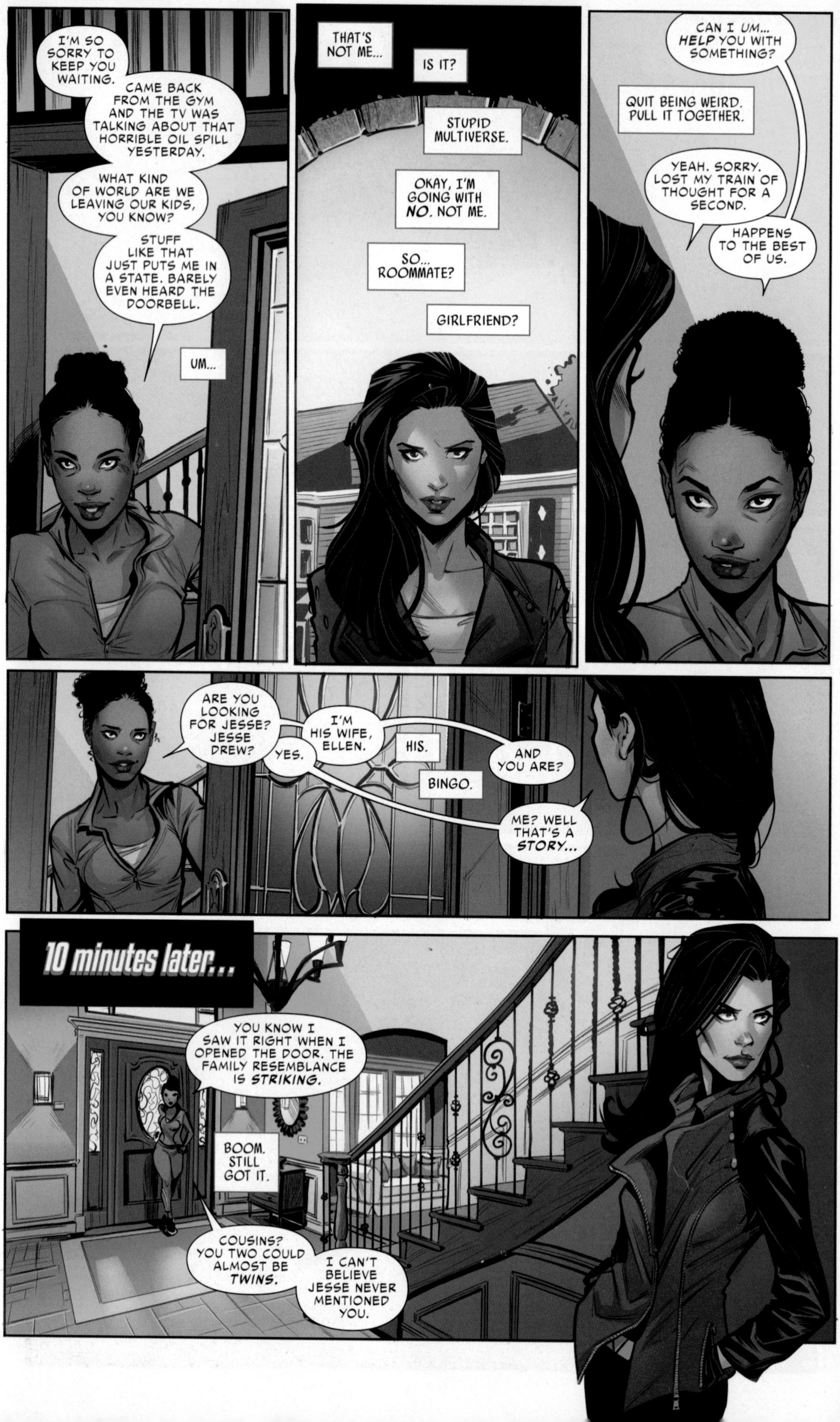
I'M SO SORRY TO KEEP YOU WAITING.
CAME BACK FROM THE GYM AND THE TV WAS TALKING ABOUT THAT HORRIBLE OIL SPILL YESTERDAY.
WHAT KIND OF WORLD ARE WE LEAVING OUR KIDS, YOU KNOW?
STUFF LIKE THAT JUST PUTS ME IN A STATE. BARELY EVEN HEARD THE DOORBELL.
UM...
THAT'S NOT ME...
IS IT?
STUPID MULTIVERSE.
OKAY, I'M GOING WITH NO. NOT ME.
SO... ROOMMATE?
GIRLFRIEND?
CAN I UM... HELP YOU WITH SOMETHING?
QUIT BEING WEIRD. PULL IT TOGETHER.
YEAH. SORRY. LOST MY TRAIN OF THOUGHT FOR A SECOND.
HAPPENS TO THE BEST OF US.
ARE YOU LOOKING FOR JESSE? JESSE DREW?
YES.
I'M HIS WIFE, ELLEN.
HIS.
BINGO.
AND YOU ARE?
ME? WELL THAT'S A STORY...
10 minutes later...
YOU KNOW I SAW IT RIGHT WHEN I OPENED THE DOOR. THE FAMILY RESEMBLANCE IS STRIKING.
BOOM. STILL GOT IT.
COUSINS? YOU TWO COULD ALMOST BE TWINS.
I CAN'T BELIEVE JESSE NEVER MENTIONED YOU.

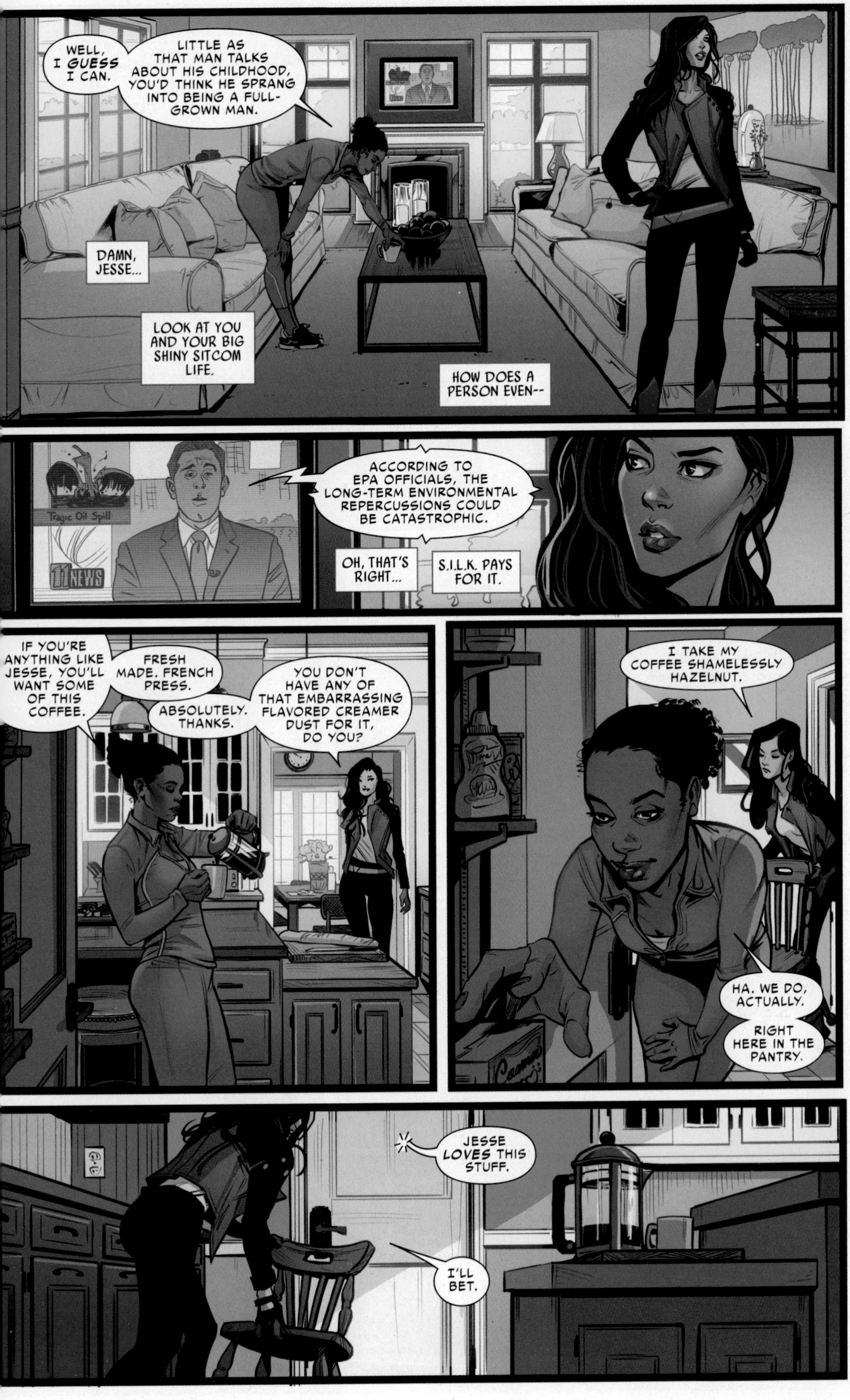

WELL, I *GUESS* I CAN.
LITTLE AS THAT MAN TALKS ABOUT HIS CHILDHOOD, YOU'D THINK HE SPRANG INTO BEING A FULL-GROWN MAN.
DAMN, JESSE...
LOOK AT YOU AND YOUR BIG SHINY SITCOM LIFE.
HOW DOES A PERSON EVEN--
Tragic Oil Spill
11 NEWS
ACCORDING TO EPA OFFICIALS, THE LONG-TERM ENVIRONMENTAL REPERCUSSIONS COULD BE CATASTROPHIC.
OH, THAT'S RIGHT...
S.I.L.K. PAYS FOR IT.
IF YOU'RE ANYTHING LIKE JESSE, YOU'LL WANT SOME OF THIS COFFEE.
FRESH MADE. FRENCH PRESS.
ABSOLUTELY. THANKS.
YOU DON'T HAVE ANY OF THAT EMBARRASSING FLAVORED CREAMER DUST FOR IT, DO YOU?
I TAKE MY COFFEE SHAMELESSLY HAZELNUT.
HA. WE DO, ACTUALLY.
RIGHT HERE IN THE PANTRY.
JESSE *LOVES* THIS STUFF.
I'LL BET.

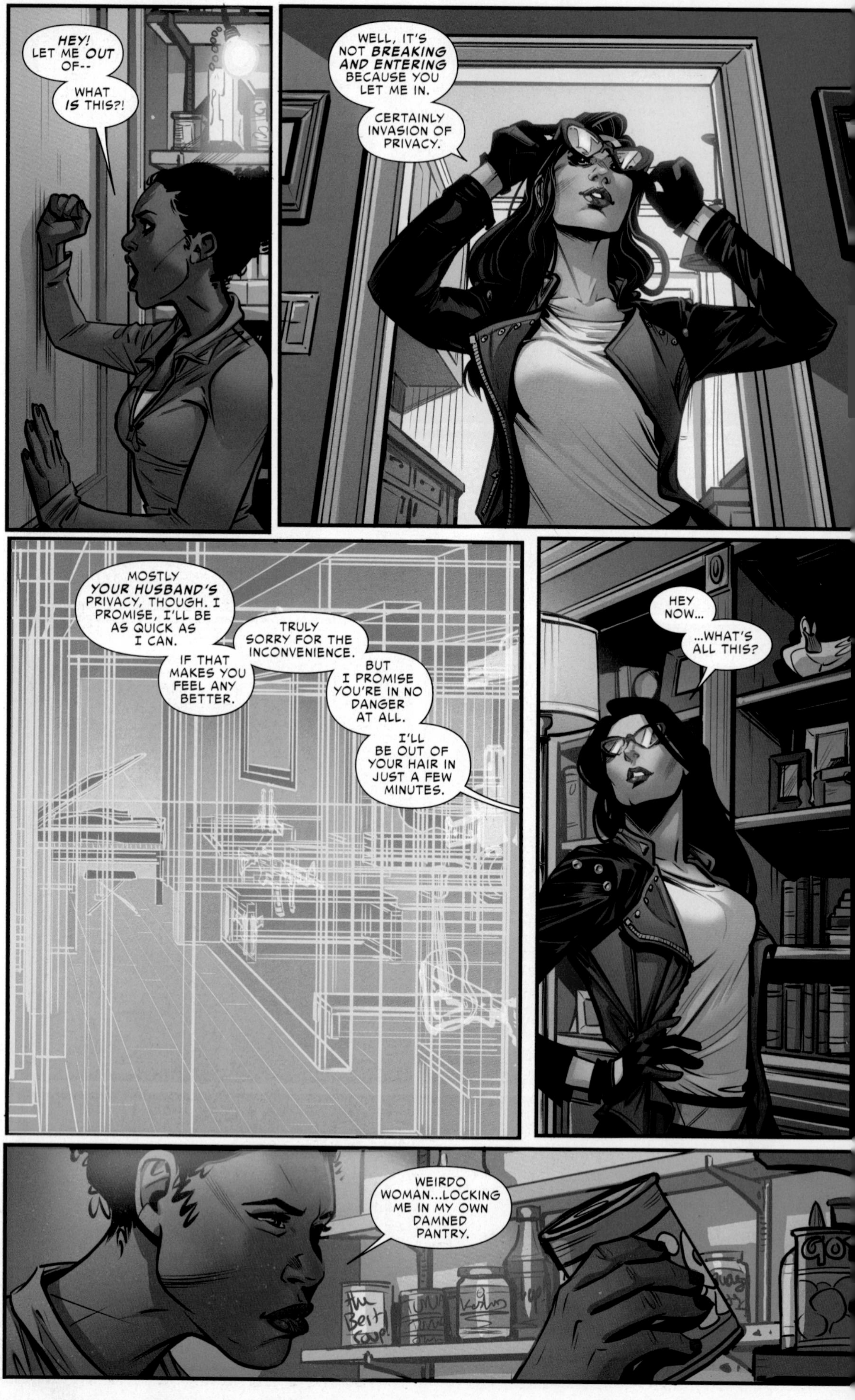
HEY! LET ME OUT OF--
WHAT IS THIS?!
WELL, IT'S NOT BREAKING AND ENTERING BECAUSE YOU LET ME IN.
CERTAINLY INVASION OF PRIVACY.
MOSTLY YOUR HUSBAND'S PRIVACY, THOUGH. I PROMISE, I'LL BE AS QUICK AS I CAN.
IF THAT MAKES YOU FEEL ANY BETTER.
TRULY SORRY FOR THE INCONVENIENCE.
BUT I PROMISE YOU'RE IN NO DANGER AT ALL.
I'LL BE OUT OF YOUR HAIR IN JUST A FEW MINUTES.
HEY NOW...
...WHAT'S ALL THIS?
WEIRDO WOMAN...LOCKING ME IN MY OWN DAMNED PANTRY.
The Best Soup!

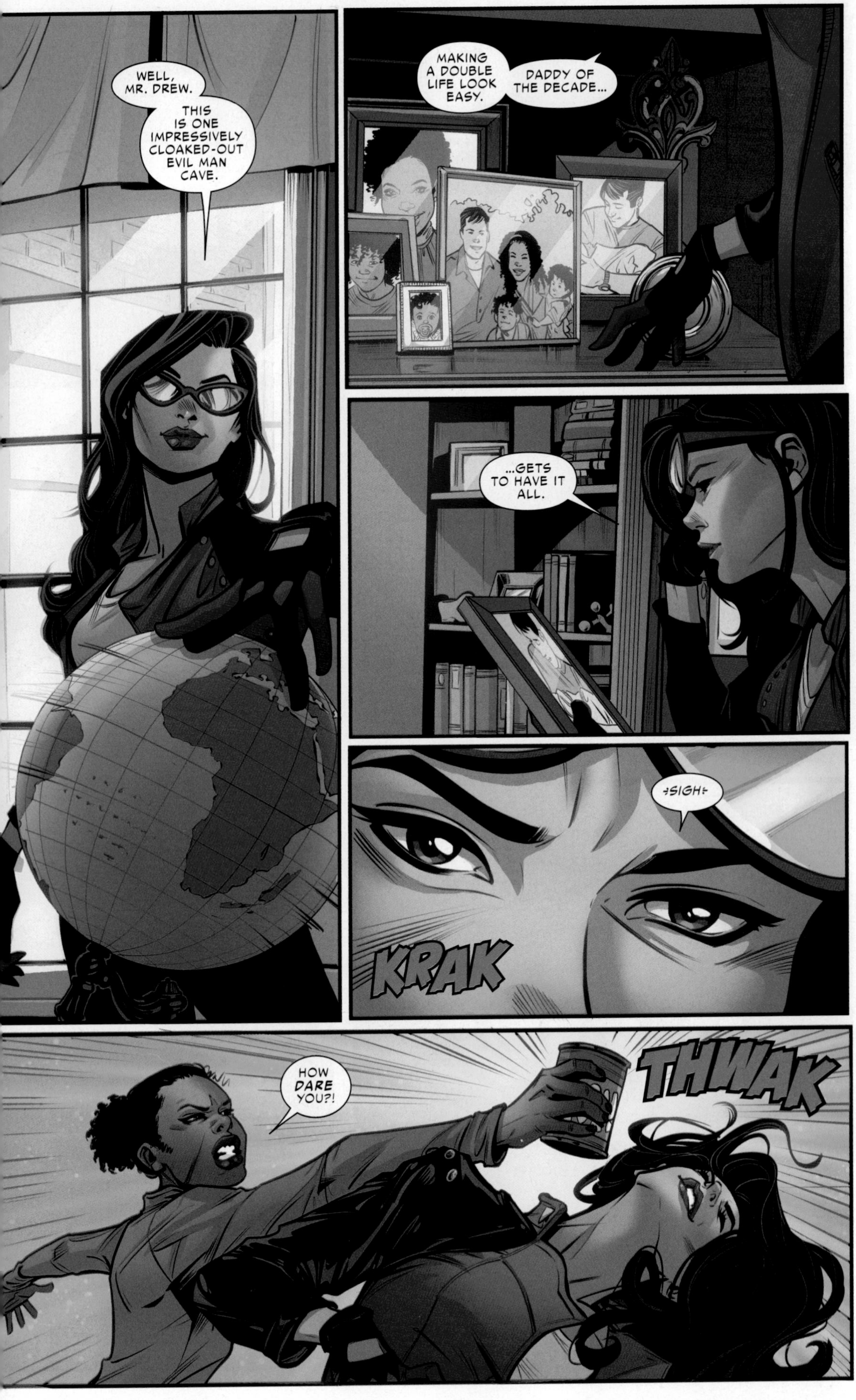
WELL, MR. DREW.
THIS IS ONE IMPRESSIVELY CLOAKED-OUT EVIL MAN CAVE.
MAKING A DOUBLE LIFE LOOK EASY.
DADDY OF THE DECADE...
...GETS TO HAVE IT ALL.
≠SIGH≠
KRAK
HOW DARE YOU?!
THWAK

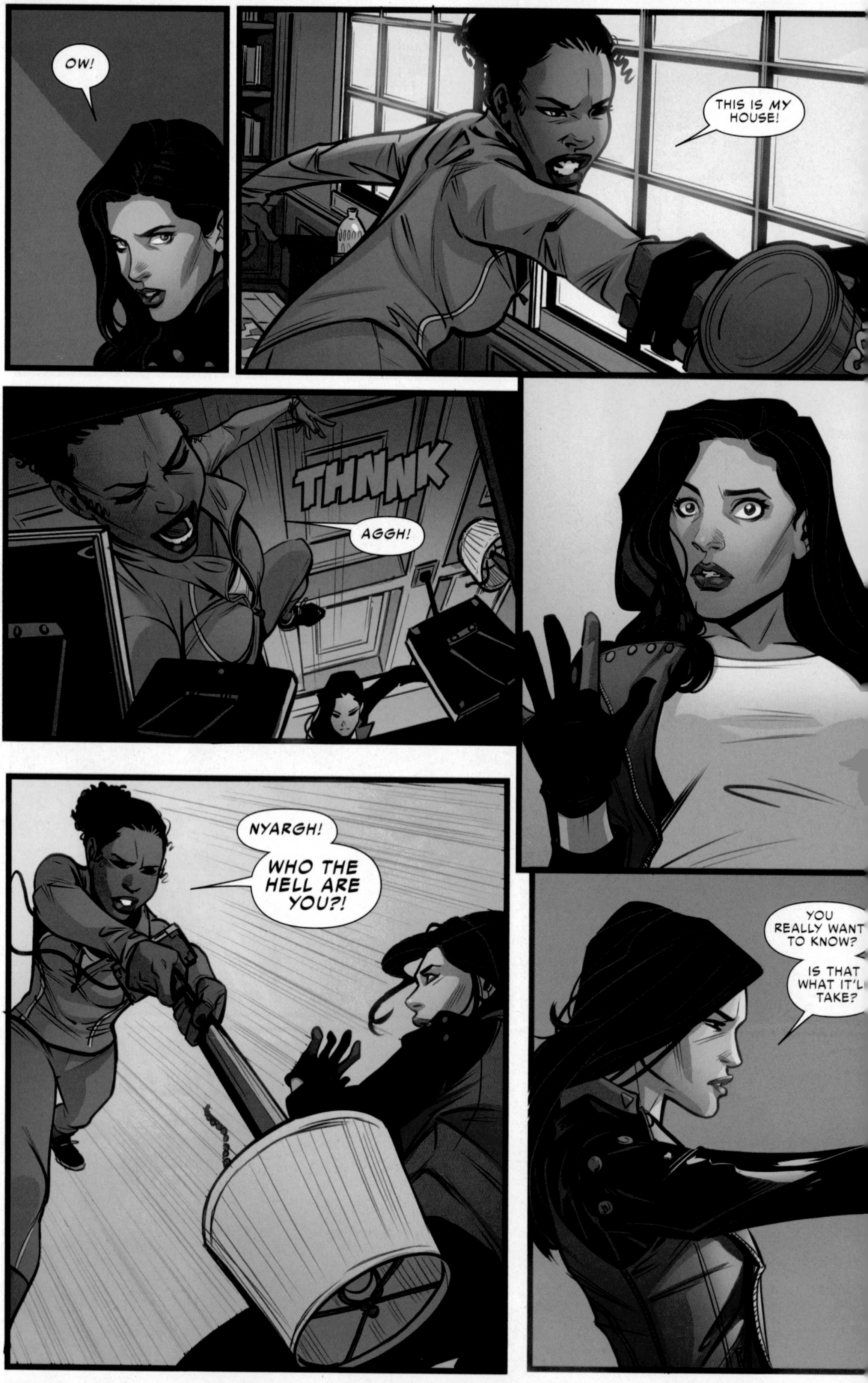
OW!
THIS IS MY HOUSE!
THNNK
AGGH!
NYARGH!
WHO THE HELL ARE YOU?!
YOU REALLY WANT TO KNOW?
IS THAT WHAT IT'LL TAKE?

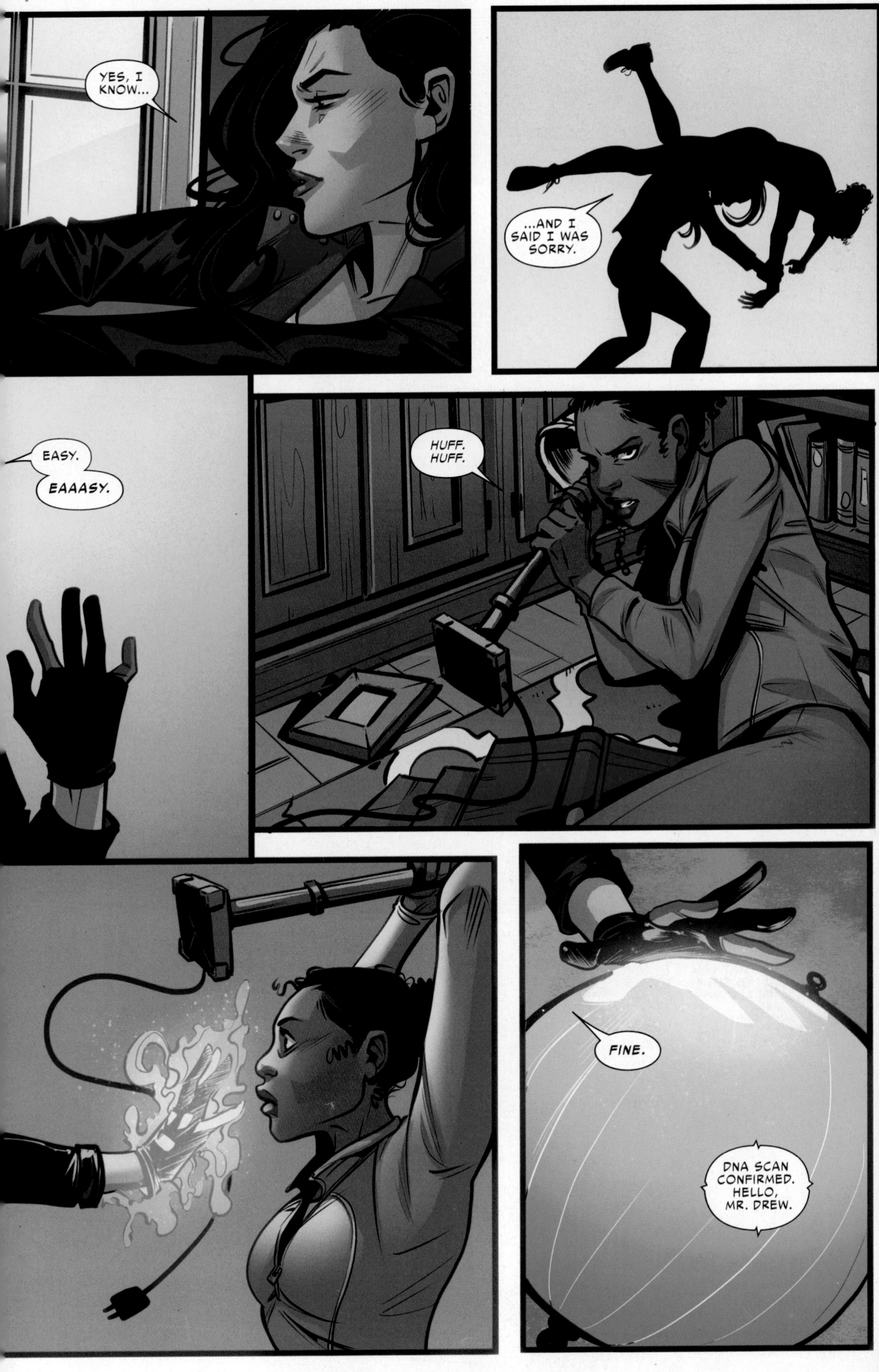
YES, I KNOW...
...AND I SAID I WAS SORRY.
EASY.
EAAASY.
HUFF. HUFF.
FINE.
DNA SCAN CONFIRMED. HELLO, MR. DREW.

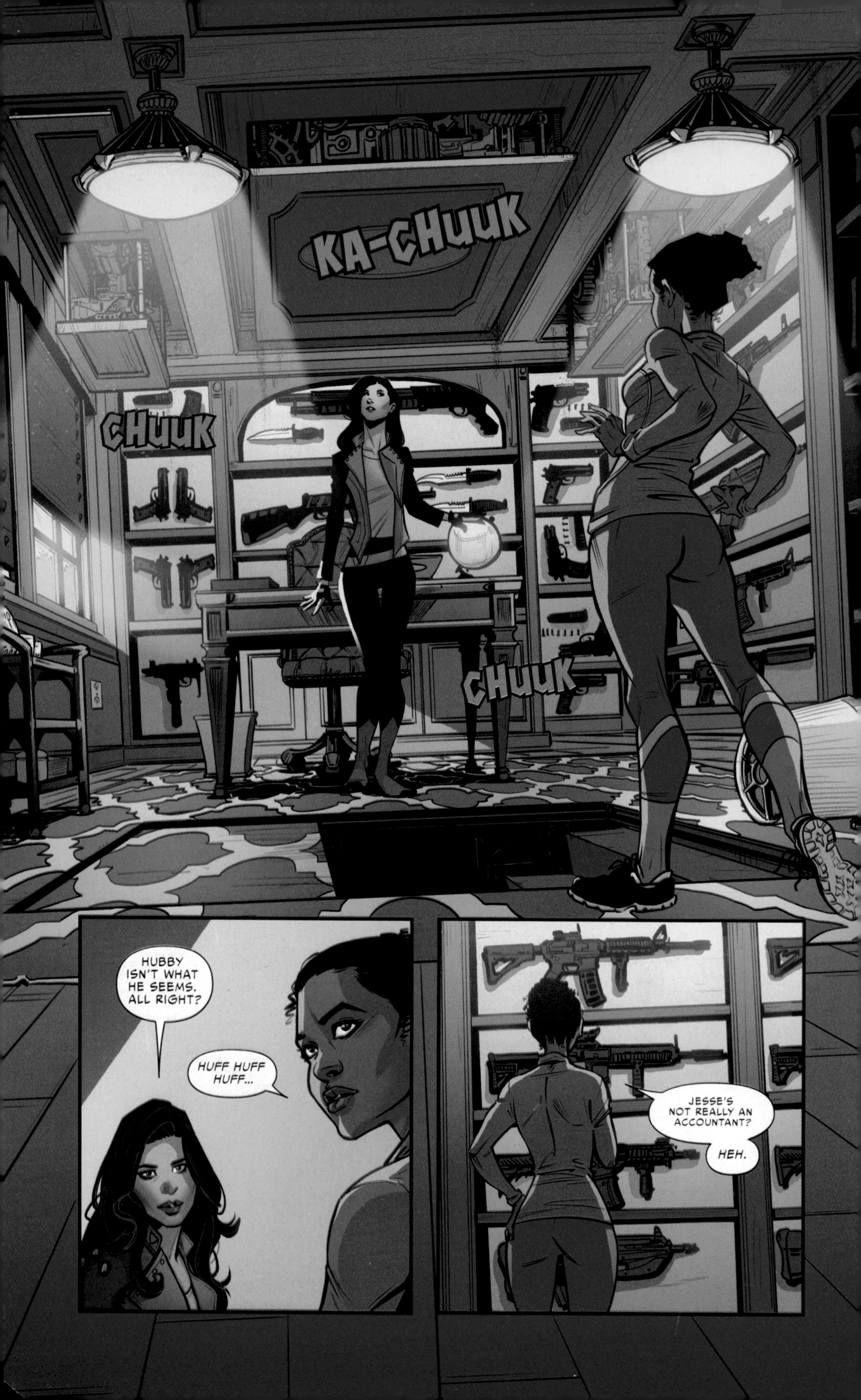
KA-CHUUK
CHUUK
CHUUK
HUBBY ISN'T WHAT HE SEEMS. ALL RIGHT?
HUFF HUFF HUFF...
JESSE'S NOT REALLY AN ACCOUNTANT?
HEH.

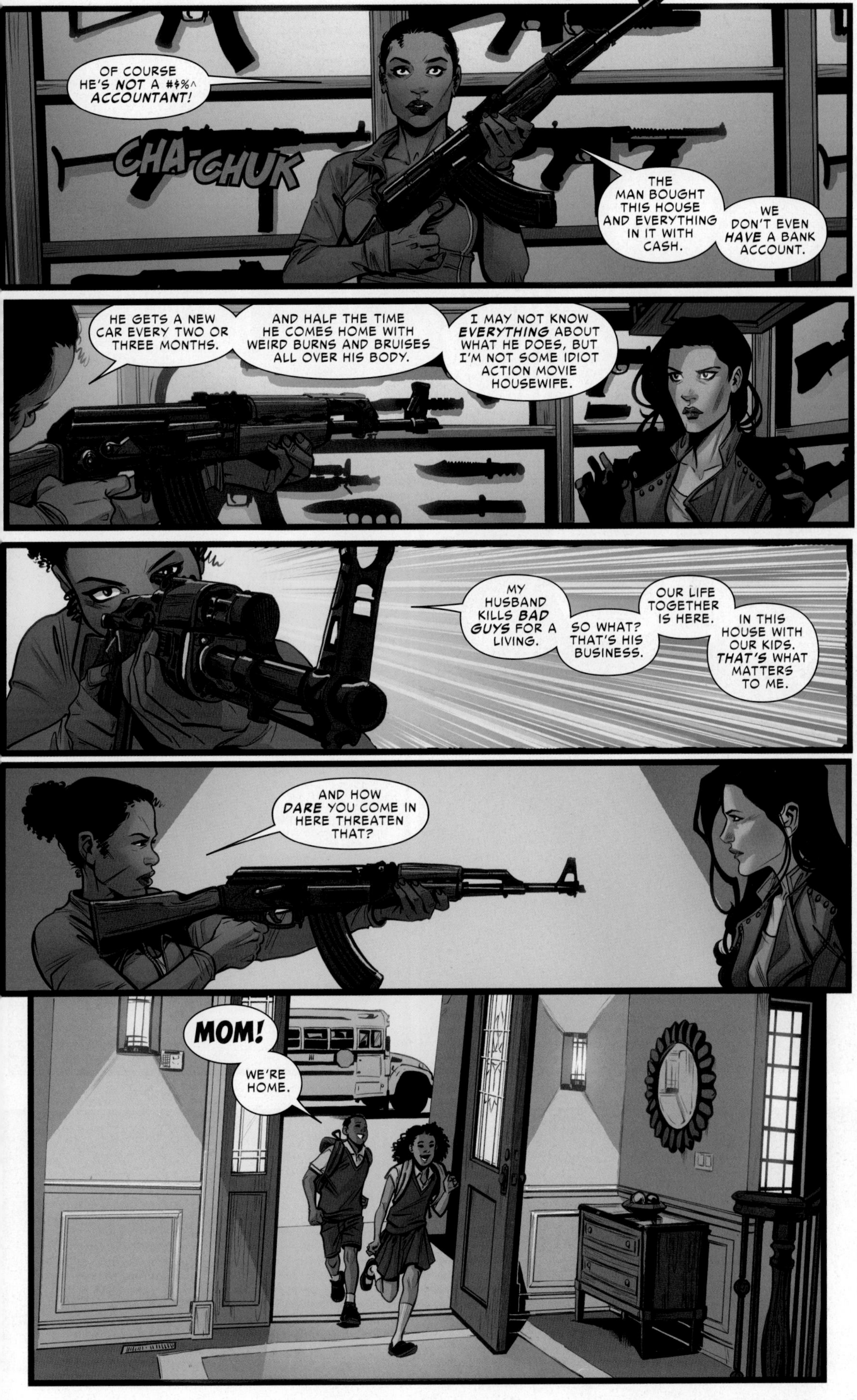
OF COURSE HE'S NOT A #$%^ ACCOUNTANT!
CHA-CHUK
THE MAN BOUGHT THIS HOUSE AND EVERYTHING IN IT WITH CASH.
WE DON'T EVEN HAVE A BANK ACCOUNT.
HE GETS A NEW CAR EVERY TWO OR THREE MONTHS.
AND HALF THE TIME HE COMES HOME WITH WEIRD BURNS AND BRUISES ALL OVER HIS BODY.
I MAY NOT KNOW EVERYTHING ABOUT WHAT HE DOES, BUT I'M NOT SOME IDIOT ACTION MOVIE HOUSEWIFE.
MY HUSBAND KILLS BAD GUYS FOR A LIVING.
SO WHAT? THAT'S HIS BUSINESS.
OUR LIFE TOGETHER IS HERE.
IN THIS HOUSE WITH OUR KIDS. THAT'S WHAT MATTERS TO ME.
AND HOW DARE YOU COME IN HERE THREATEN THAT?
MOM!
WE'RE HOME.

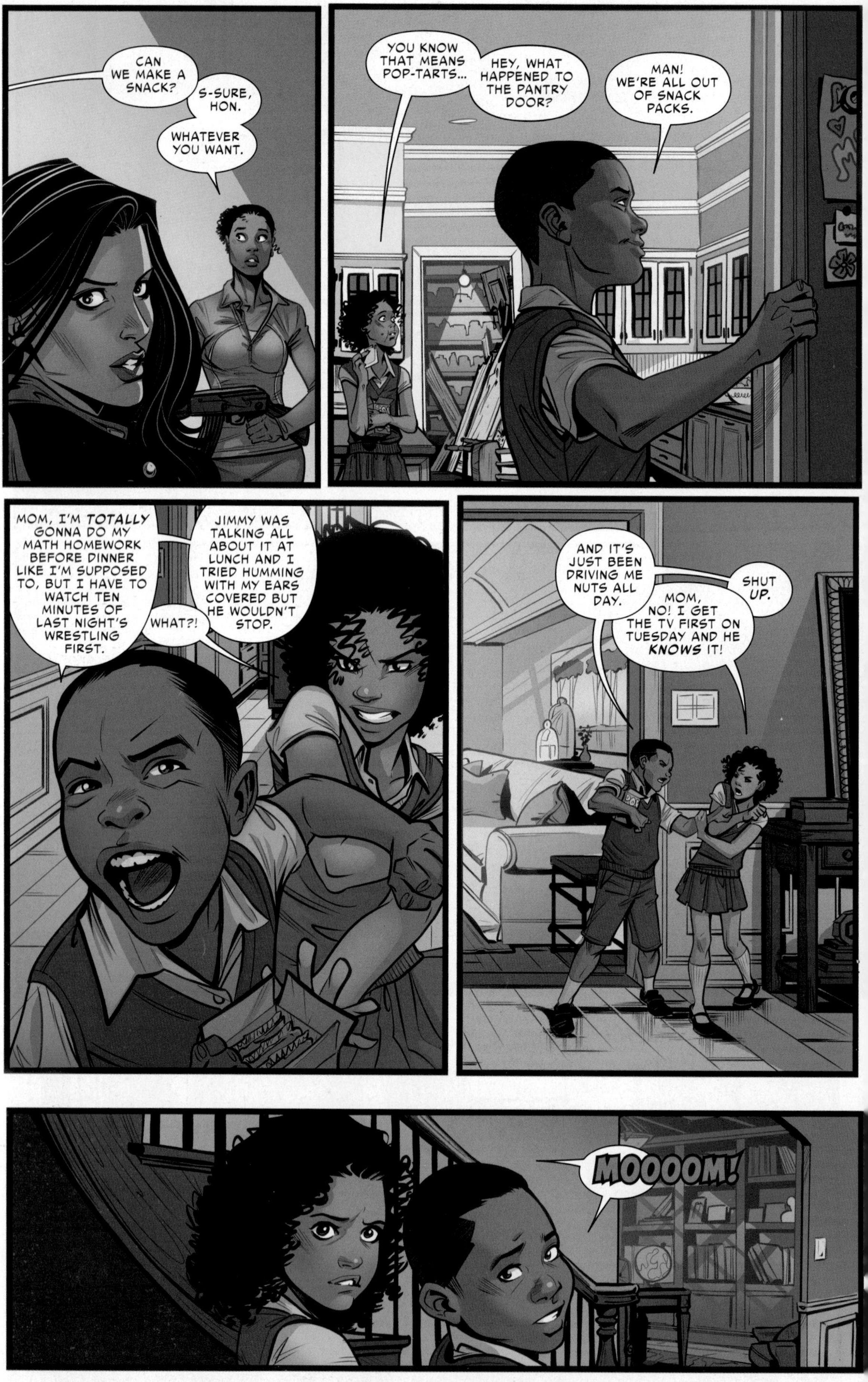
CAN WE MAKE A SNACK?
S-SURE, HON.
WHATEVER YOU WANT.
YOU KNOW THAT MEANS POP-TARTS...
HEY, WHAT HAPPENED TO THE PANTRY DOOR?
MAN! WE'RE ALL OUT OF SNACK PACKS.
MOM, I'M *TOTALLY* GONNA DO MY MATH HOMEWORK BEFORE DINNER LIKE I'M SUPPOSED TO, BUT I HAVE TO WATCH TEN MINUTES OF LAST NIGHT'S WRESTLING FIRST.
WHAT?!
JIMMY WAS TALKING ALL ABOUT IT AT LUNCH AND I TRIED HUMMING WITH MY EARS COVERED BUT HE WOULDN'T STOP.
AND IT'S JUST BEEN DRIVING ME NUTS ALL DAY.
SHUT *UP.*
MOM, NO! I GET THE TV FIRST ON TUESDAY AND HE *KNOWS* IT!
MOOOOM!

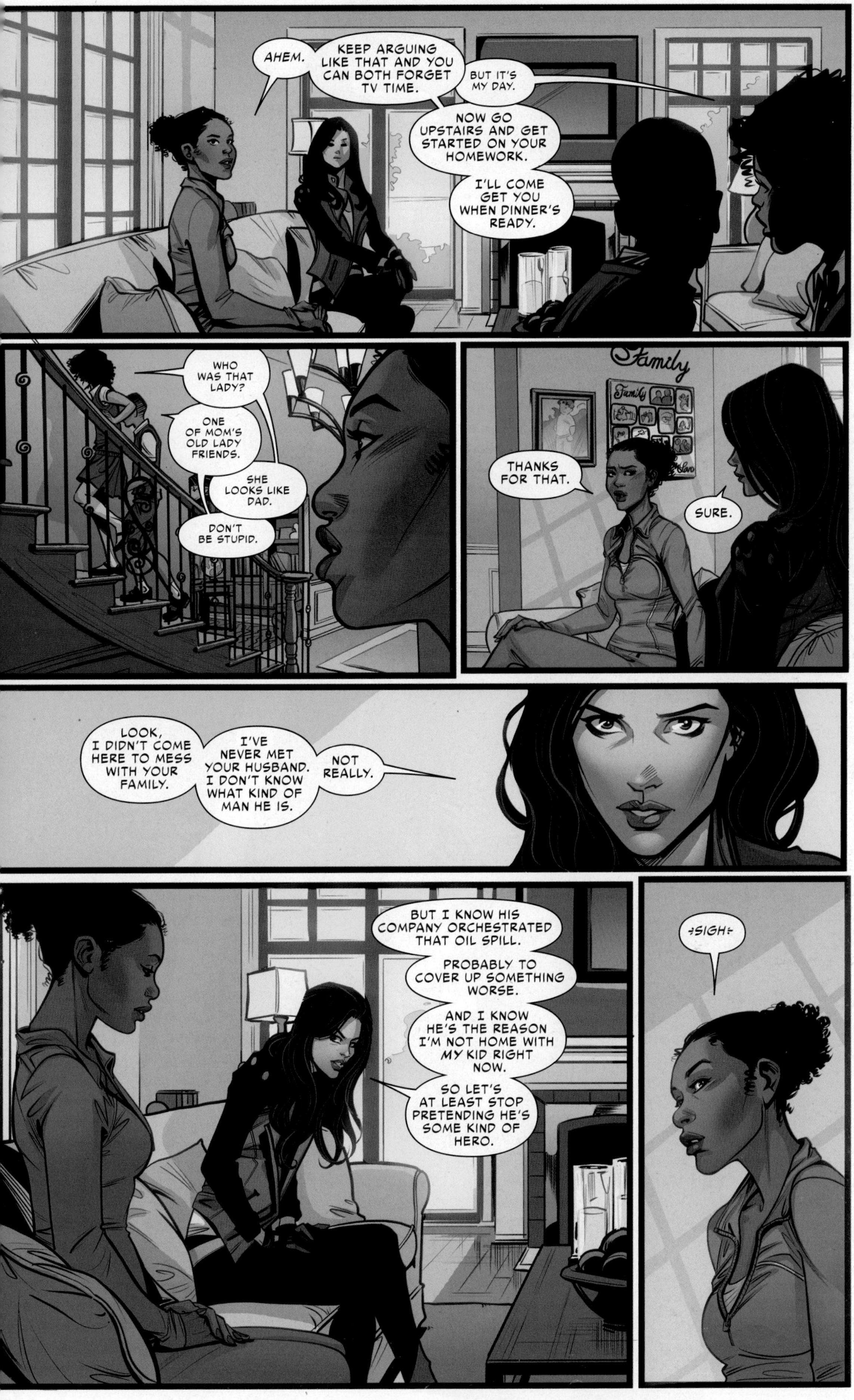
AHEM.
KEEP ARGUING LIKE THAT AND YOU CAN BOTH FORGET TV TIME.
BUT IT'S MY DAY.
NOW GO UPSTAIRS AND GET STARTED ON YOUR HOMEWORK.
I'LL COME GET YOU WHEN DINNER'S READY.
WHO WAS THAT LADY?
ONE OF MOM'S OLD LADY FRIENDS.
SHE LOOKS LIKE DAD.
DON'T BE STUPID.
Family
THANKS FOR THAT.
SURE.
LOOK, I DIDN'T COME HERE TO MESS WITH YOUR FAMILY.
I'VE NEVER MET YOUR HUSBAND. I DON'T KNOW WHAT KIND OF MAN HE IS.
NOT REALLY.
BUT I KNOW HIS COMPANY ORCHESTRATED THAT OIL SPILL.
PROBABLY TO COVER UP SOMETHING WORSE.
AND I KNOW HE'S THE REASON I'M NOT HOME WITH MY KID RIGHT NOW.
SO LET'S AT LEAST STOP PRETENDING HE'S SOME KIND OF HERO.
≠SIGH≠

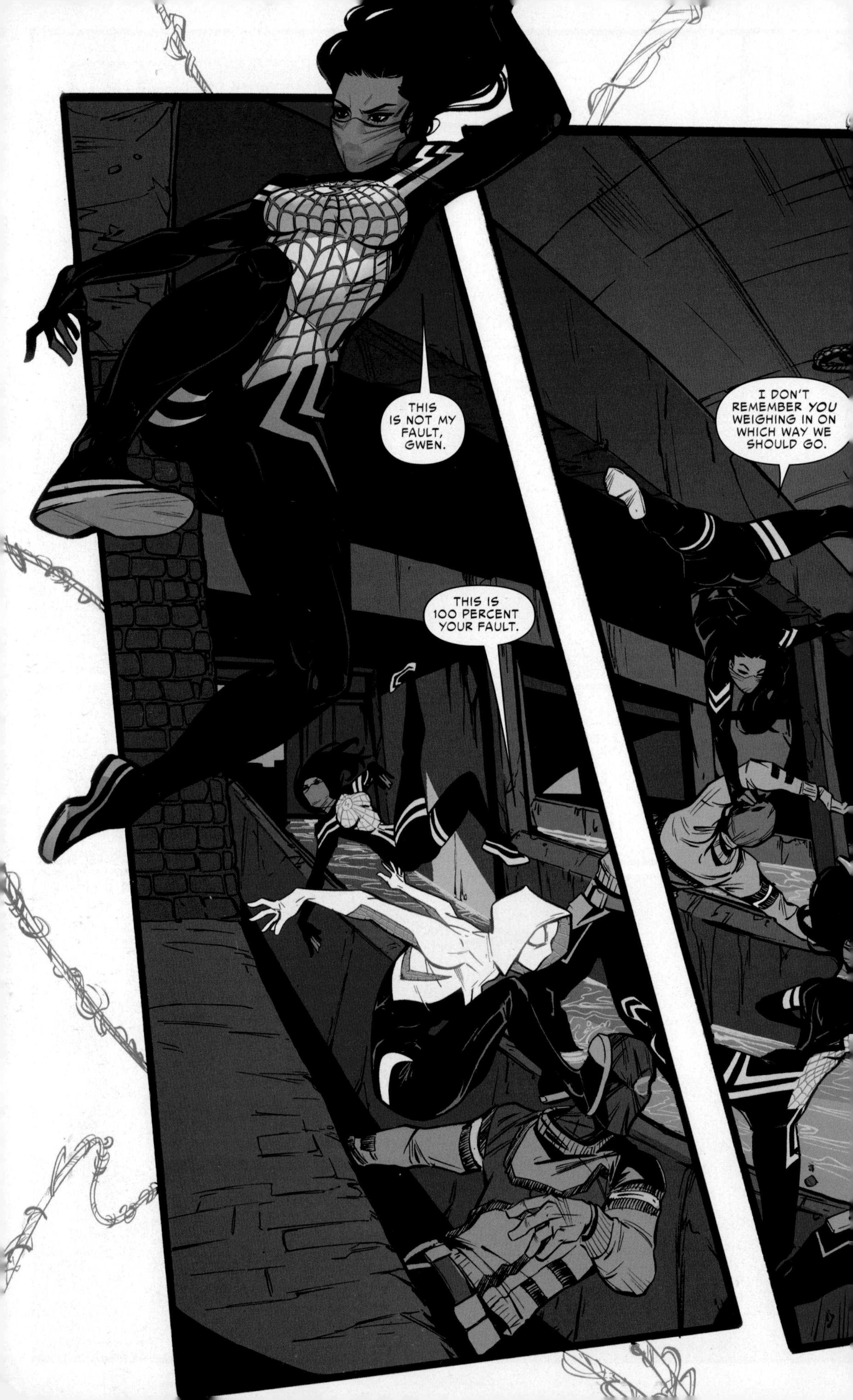
THIS IS NOT MY FAULT, GWEN.
THIS IS 100 PERCENT YOUR FAULT.
I DON'T REMEMBER YOU WEIGHING IN ON WHICH WAY WE SHOULD GO.

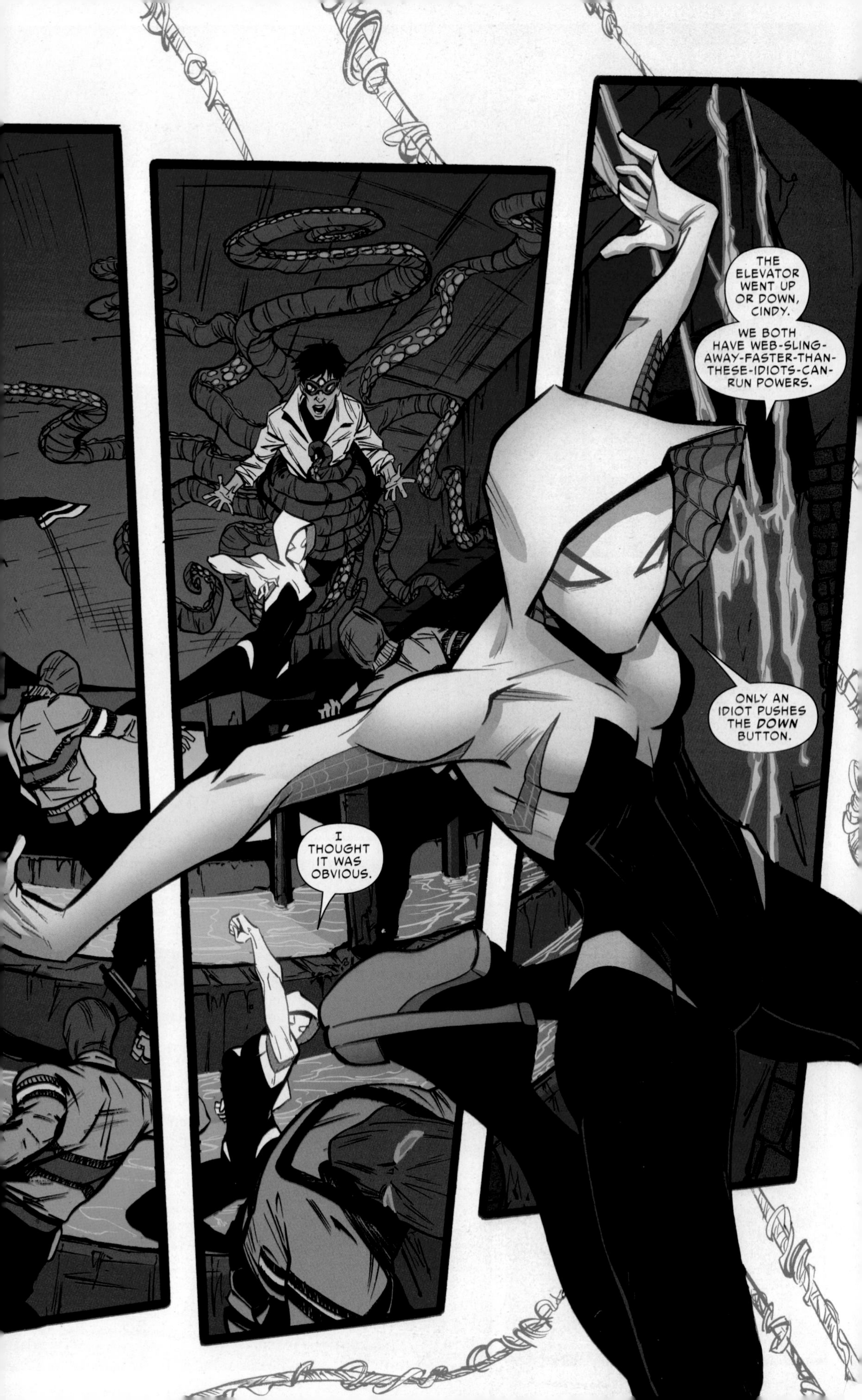

THE ELEVATOR WENT UP OR DOWN, CINDY.
WE BOTH HAVE WEB-SLING-AWAY-FASTER-THAN-THESE-IDIOTS-CAN-RUN POWERS.
ONLY AN IDIOT PUSHES THE *DOWN* BUTTON.
I THOUGHT IT WAS OBVIOUS.

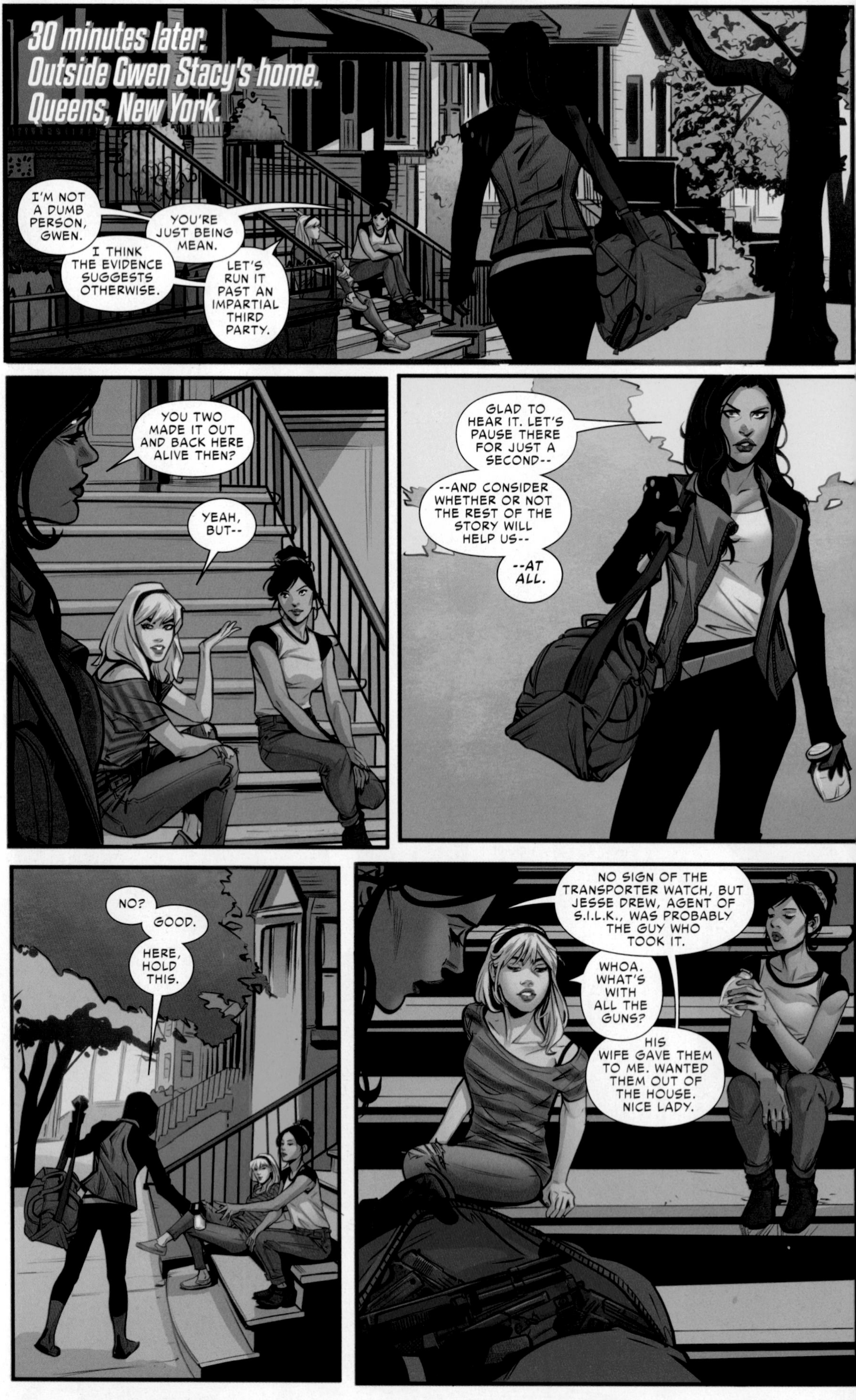
30 minutes later.
Outside Gwen Stacy's home.
Queens, New York.
I'M NOT A DUMB PERSON, GWEN.
YOU'RE JUST BEING MEAN.
I THINK THE EVIDENCE SUGGESTS OTHERWISE.
LET'S RUN IT PAST AN IMPARTIAL THIRD PARTY.
YOU TWO MADE IT OUT AND BACK HERE ALIVE THEN?
YEAH, BUT--
GLAD TO HEAR IT. LET'S PAUSE THERE FOR JUST A SECOND--
--AND CONSIDER WHETHER OR NOT THE REST OF THE STORY WILL HELP US--
--AT ALL.
NO?
GOOD.
HERE, HOLD THIS.
NO SIGN OF THE TRANSPORTER WATCH, BUT JESSE DREW, AGENT OF S.I.L.K., WAS PROBABLY THE GUY WHO TOOK IT.
WHOA. WHAT'S WITH ALL THE GUNS?
HIS WIFE GAVE THEM TO ME. WANTED THEM OUT OF THE HOUSE. NICE LADY.

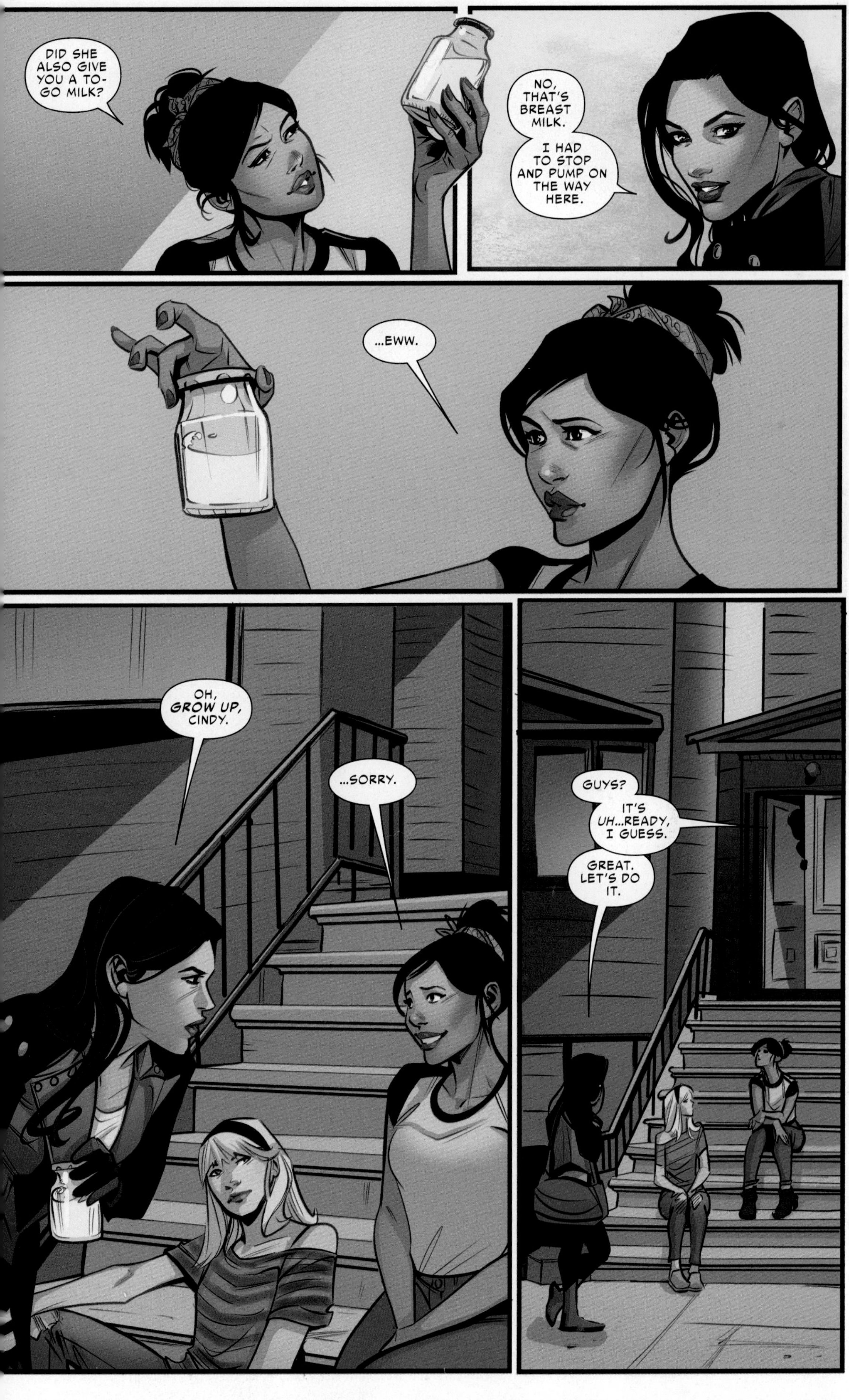
DID SHE ALSO GIVE YOU A TO-GO MILK?
NO, THAT'S BREAST MILK.
I HAD TO STOP AND PUMP ON THE WAY HERE.
...EWW.
OH, GROW UP, CINDY.
...SORRY.
GUYS?
IT'S UH...READY, I GUESS.
GREAT. LET'S DO IT.

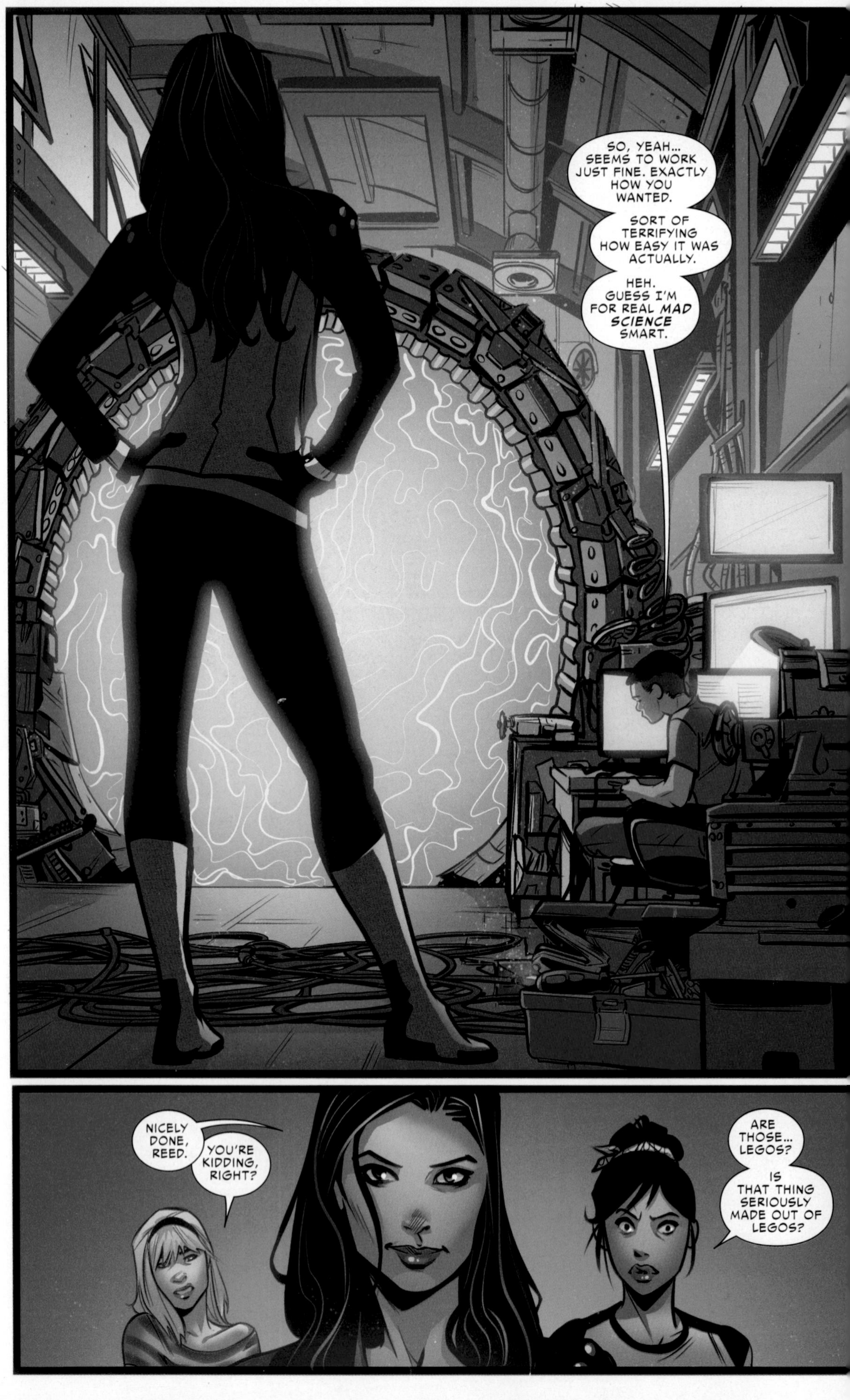
SO, YEAH... SEEMS TO WORK JUST FINE. EXACTLY HOW YOU WANTED.
SORT OF TERRIFYING HOW EASY IT WAS ACTUALLY.
HEH. GUESS I'M FOR REAL MAD SCIENCE SMART.
NICELY DONE, REED.
YOU'RE KIDDING, RIGHT?
ARE THOSE... LEGOS?
IS THAT THING SERIOUSLY MADE OUT OF LEGOS?

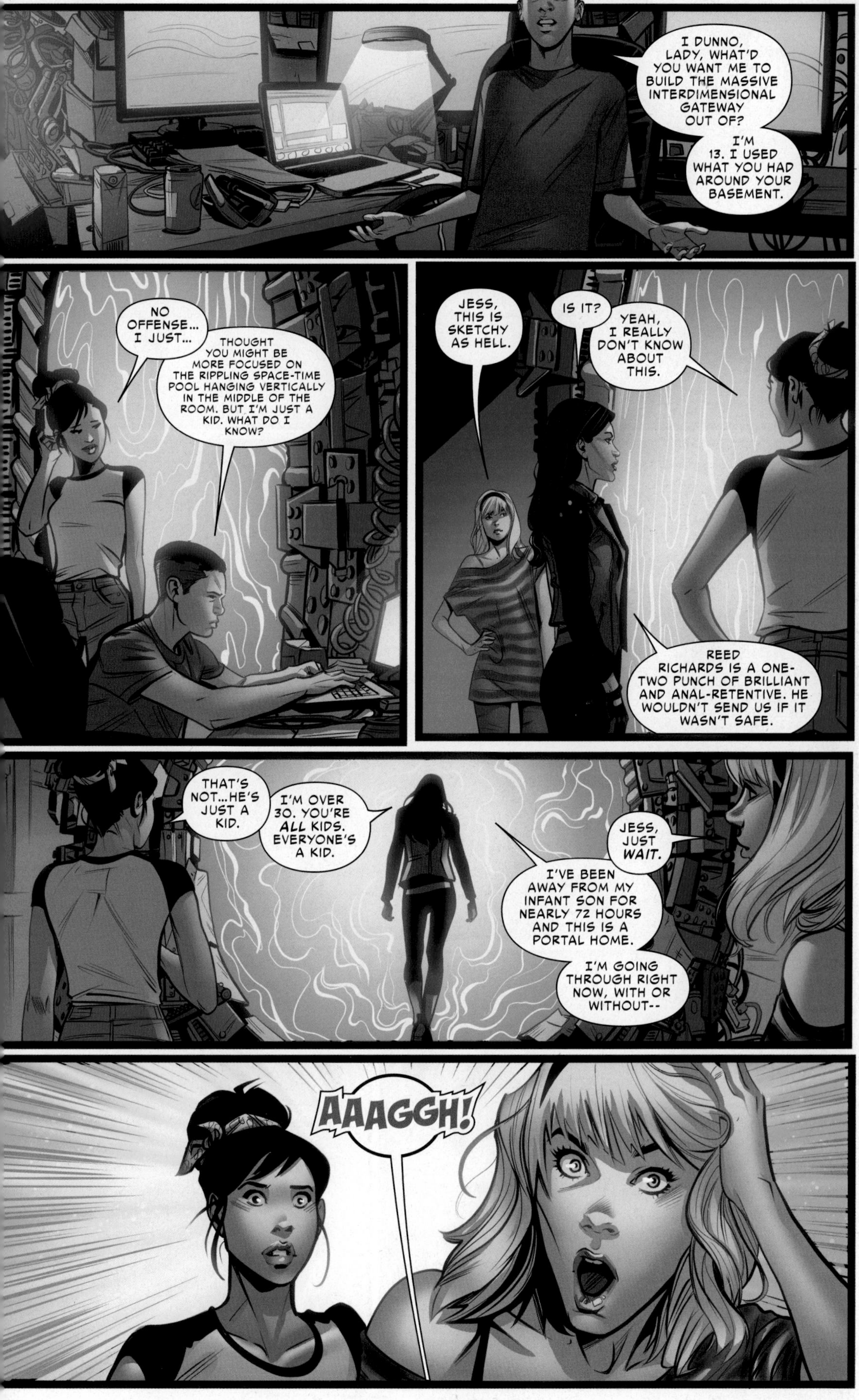
I DUNNO, LADY, WHAT'D YOU WANT ME TO BUILD THE MASSIVE INTERDIMENSIONAL GATEWAY OUT OF?
I'M 13. I USED WHAT YOU HAD AROUND YOUR BASEMENT.
NO OFFENSE... I JUST...
THOUGHT YOU MIGHT BE MORE FOCUSED ON THE RIPPLING SPACE-TIME POOL HANGING VERTICALLY IN THE MIDDLE OF THE ROOM. BUT I'M JUST A KID. WHAT DO I KNOW?
JESS, THIS IS SKETCHY AS HELL.
IS IT?
YEAH, I REALLY DON'T KNOW ABOUT THIS.
REED RICHARDS IS A ONE-TWO PUNCH OF BRILLIANT AND ANAL-RETENTIVE. HE WOULDN'T SEND US IF IT WASN'T SAFE.
THAT'S NOT...HE'S JUST A KID.
I'M OVER 30. YOU'RE ALL KIDS. EVERYONE'S A KID.
JESS, JUST WAIT.
I'VE BEEN AWAY FROM MY INFANT SON FOR NEARLY 72 HOURS AND THIS IS A PORTAL HOME.
I'M GOING THROUGH RIGHT NOW, WITH OR WITHOUT--
AAAGGH!

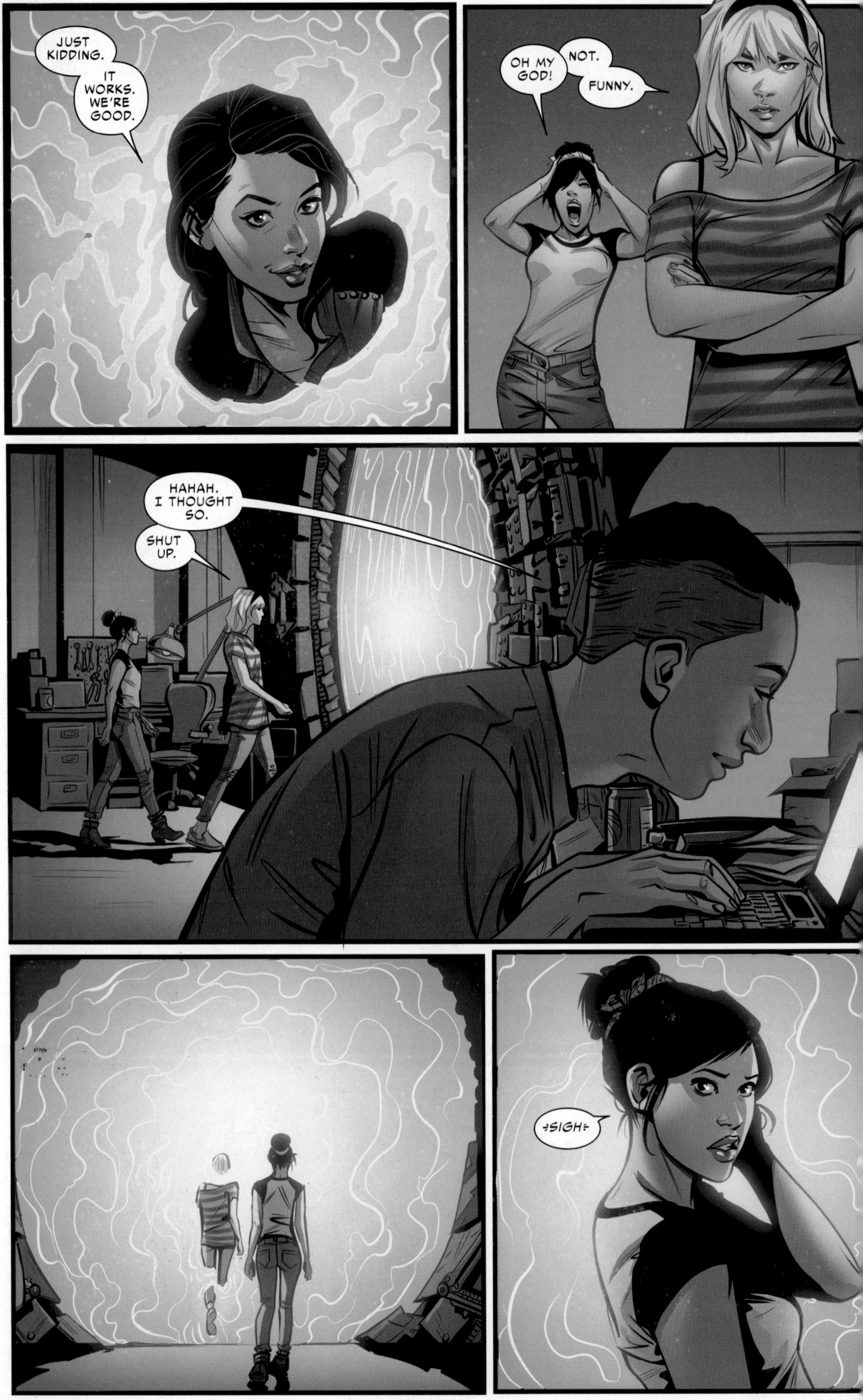
JUST KIDDING.
IT WORKS. WE'RE GOOD.
OH MY GOD!
NOT.
FUNNY.
HAHAH. I THOUGHT SO.
SHUT UP.
=SIGH=

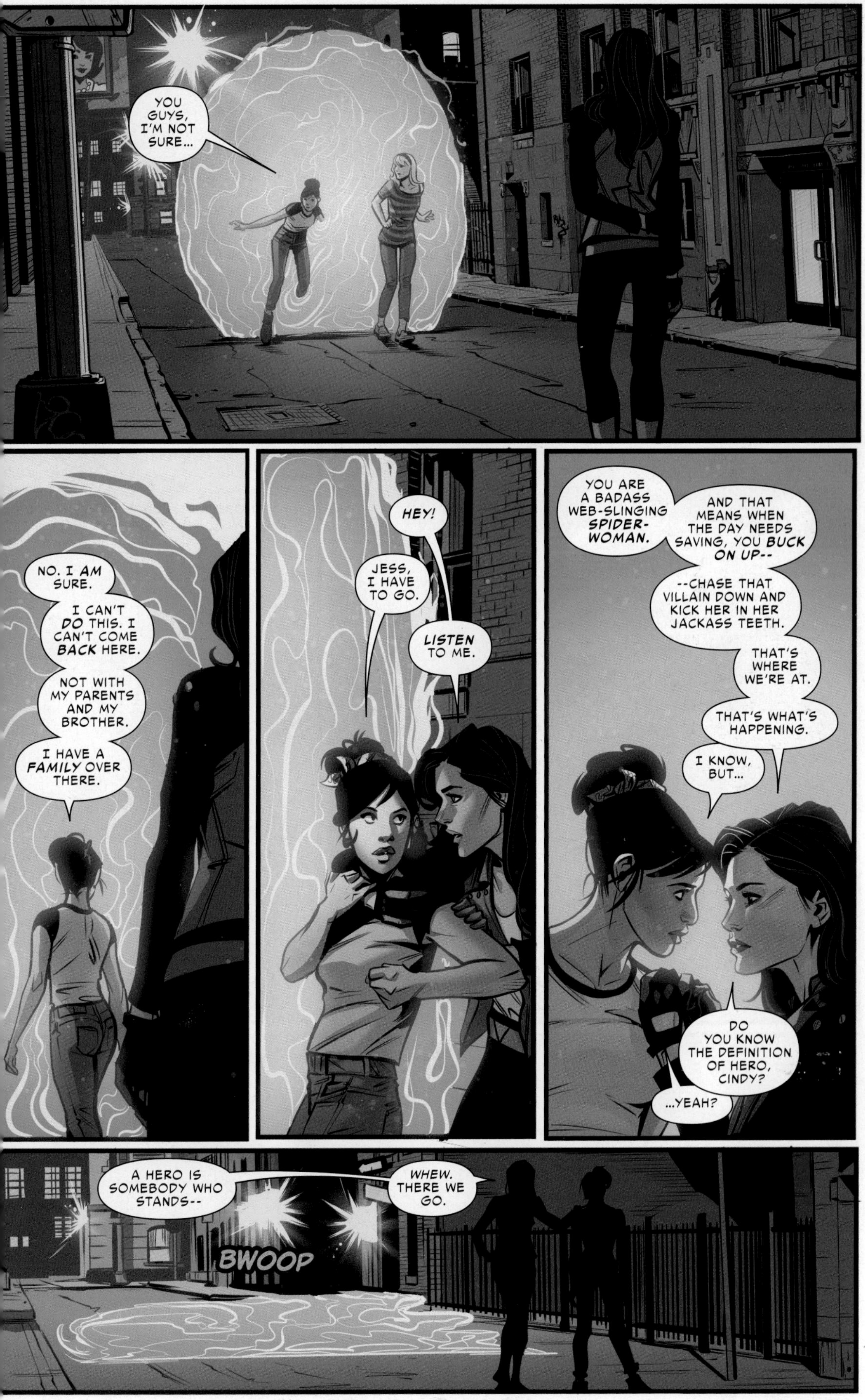
YOU GUYS, I'M NOT SURE...
NO. I AM SURE.
I CAN'T DO THIS. I CAN'T COME BACK HERE.
NOT WITH MY PARENTS AND MY BROTHER.
I HAVE A FAMILY OVER THERE.
HEY!
JESS, I HAVE TO GO.
LISTEN TO ME.
YOU ARE A BADASS WEB-SLINGING SPIDER-WOMAN.
AND THAT MEANS WHEN THE DAY NEEDS SAVING, YOU BUCK ON UP--
--CHASE THAT VILLAIN DOWN AND KICK HER IN HER JACKASS TEETH.
THAT'S WHERE WE'RE AT.
THAT'S WHAT'S HAPPENING.
I KNOW, BUT...
DO YOU KNOW THE DEFINITION OF HERO, CINDY?
...YEAH?
A HERO IS SOMEBODY WHO STANDS--
BWOOP
WHEW. THERE WE GO.

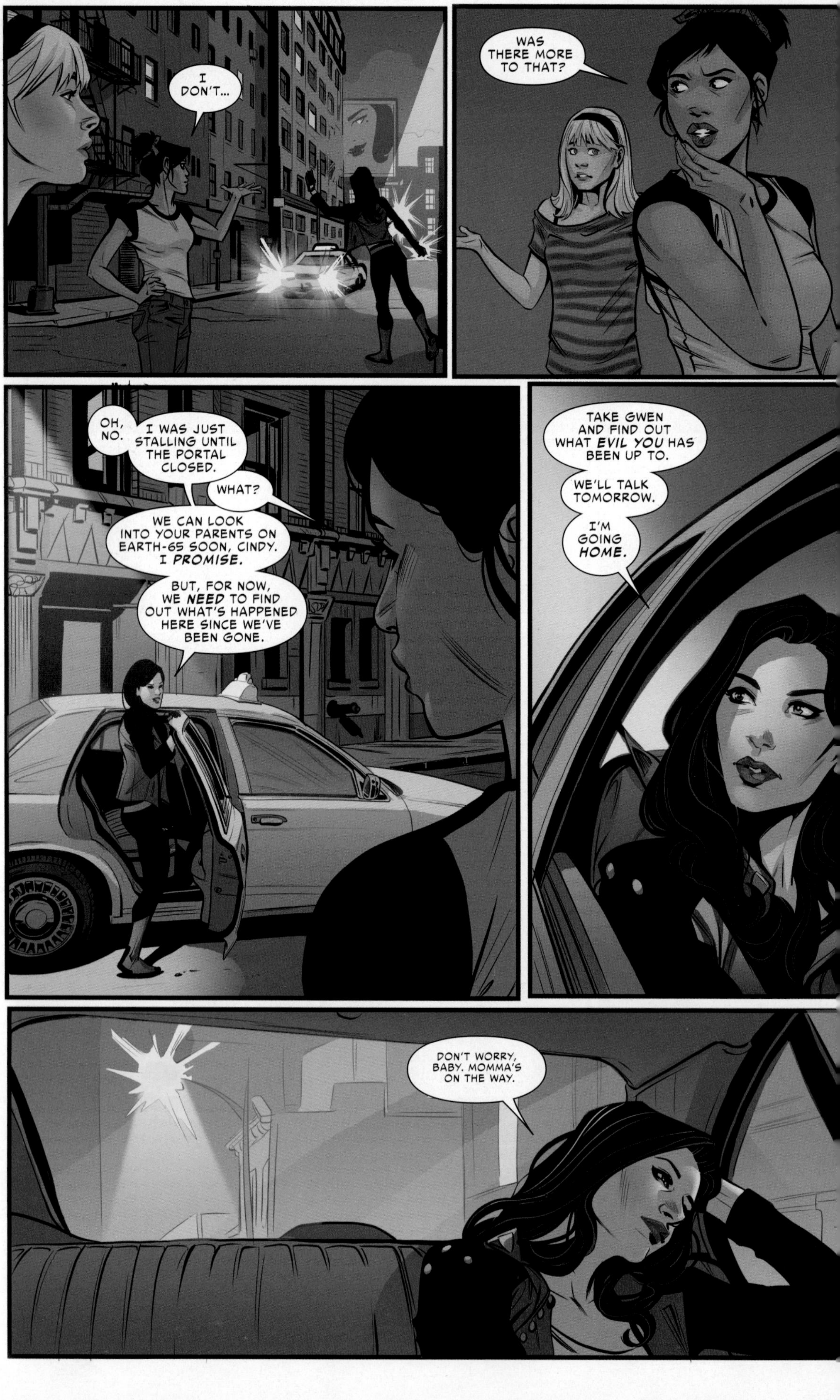
I DON'T...
WAS THERE MORE TO THAT?
OH, NO.
I WAS JUST STALLING UNTIL THE PORTAL CLOSED.
WHAT?
WE CAN LOOK INTO YOUR PARENTS ON EARTH-65 SOON, CINDY. I *PROMISE.*
BUT, FOR NOW, WE *NEED* TO FIND OUT WHAT'S HAPPENED HERE SINCE WE'VE BEEN GONE.
TAKE GWEN AND FIND OUT WHAT *EVIL YOU* HAS BEEN UP TO.
WE'LL TALK TOMORROW.
I'M GOING *HOME.*
DON'T WORRY, BABY. MOMMA'S ON THE WAY.

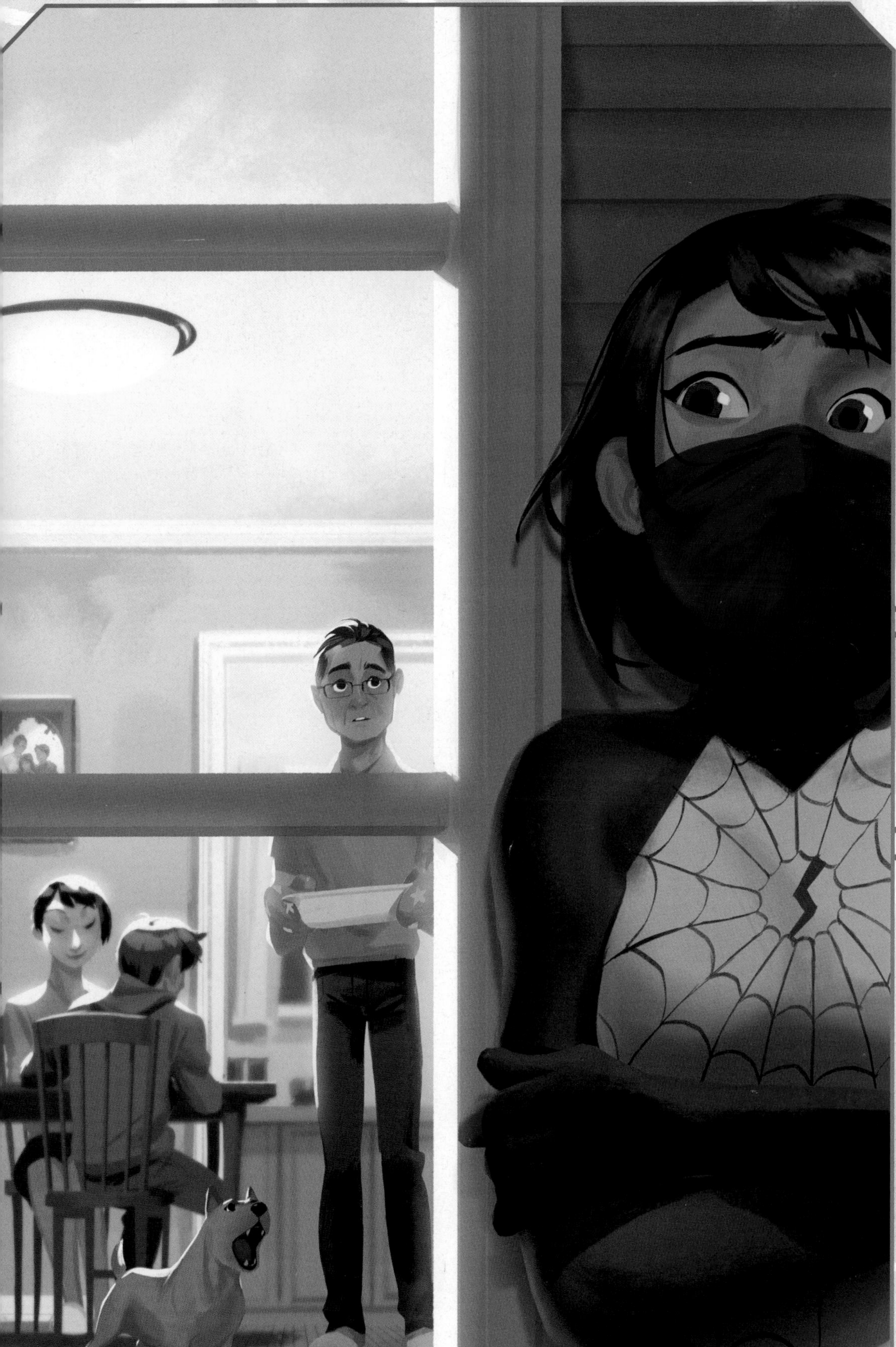

SILK #7 VARIANT BY HELEN CHEN

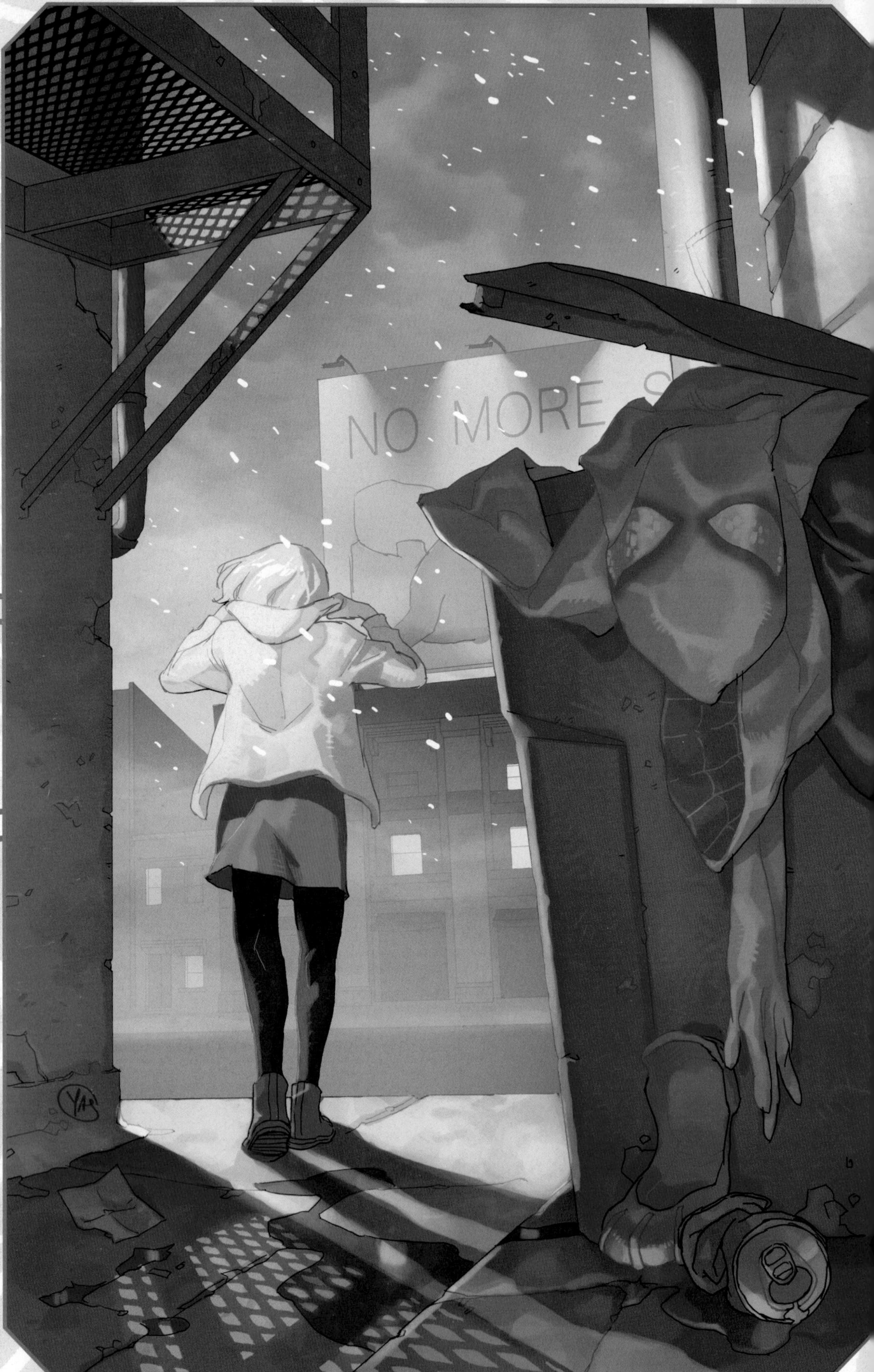
NO MORE

SPIDER-GWEN #8

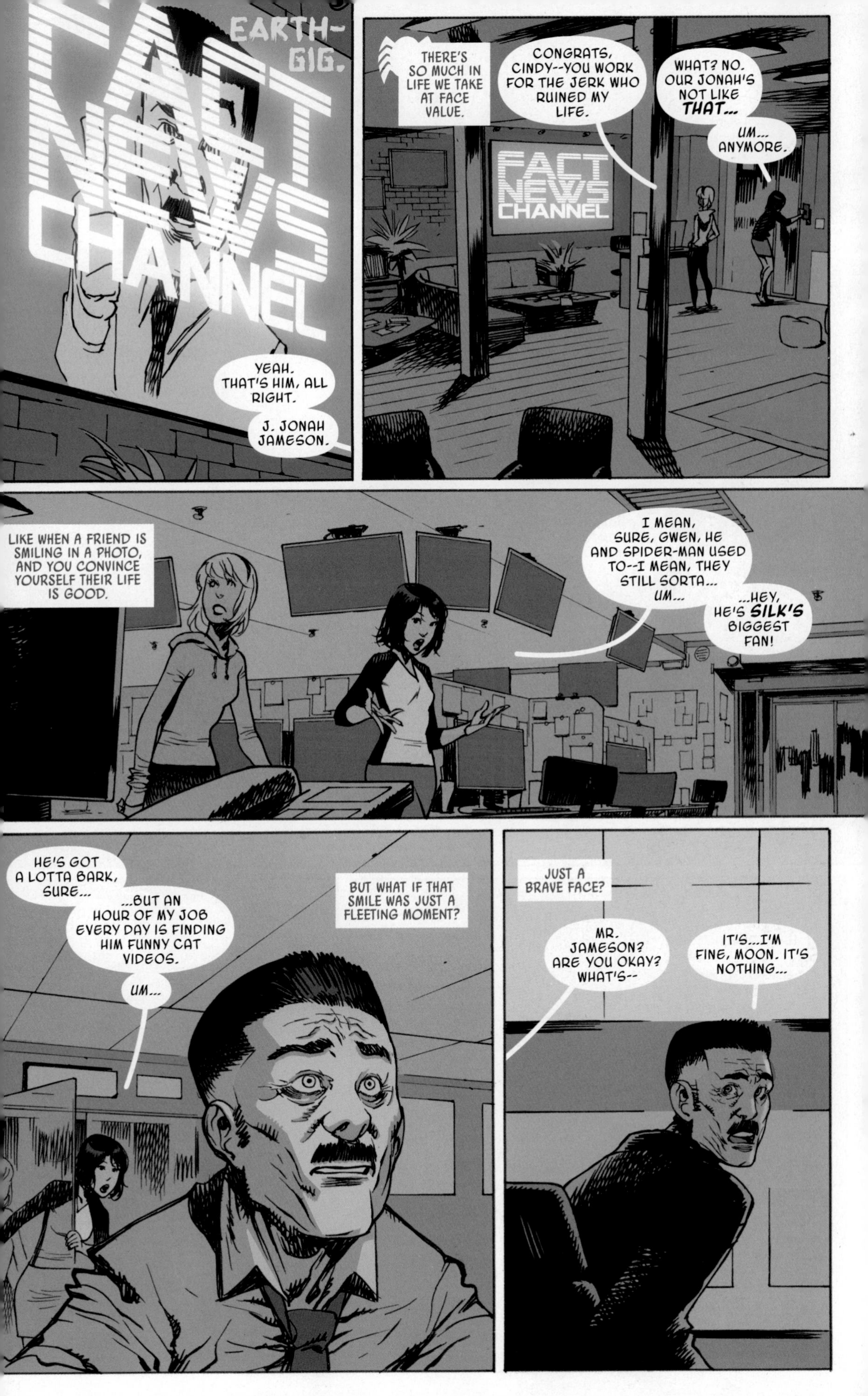
FACT NEWS CHANNEL
EARTH-616.
YEAH. THAT'S HIM, ALL RIGHT.
J. JONAH JAMESON.
THERE'S SO MUCH IN LIFE WE TAKE AT FACE VALUE.
CONGRATS, CINDY--YOU WORK FOR THE JERK WHO RUINED MY LIFE.
FACT NEWS CHANNEL
WHAT? NO. OUR JONAH'S NOT LIKE THAT...
UM... ANYMORE.
LIKE WHEN A FRIEND IS SMILING IN A PHOTO, AND YOU CONVINCE YOURSELF THEIR LIFE IS GOOD.
I MEAN, SURE, GWEN, HE AND SPIDER-MAN USED TO--I MEAN, THEY STILL SORTA... UM...
...HEY, HE'S SILK'S BIGGEST FAN!
HE'S GOT A LOTTA BARK, SURE...
...BUT AN HOUR OF MY JOB EVERY DAY IS FINDING HIM FUNNY CAT VIDEOS.
UM...
BUT WHAT IF THAT SMILE WAS JUST A FLEETING MOMENT?
JUST A BRAVE FACE?
MR. JAMESON? ARE YOU OKAY? WHAT'S--
IT'S...I'M FINE, MOON. IT'S NOTHING...

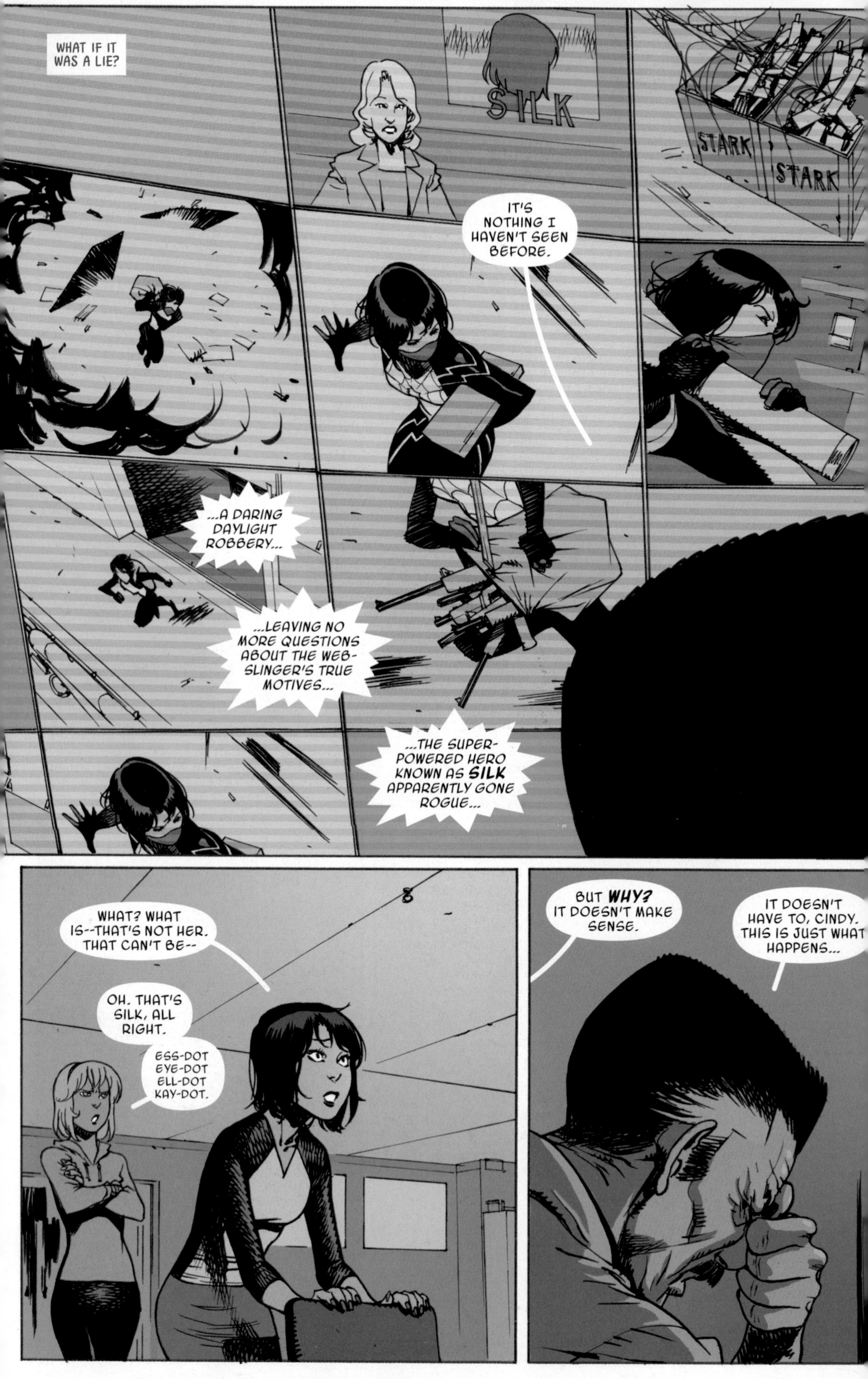
WHAT IF IT WAS A LIE?
SILK
STARK
STARK
IT'S NOTHING I HAVEN'T SEEN BEFORE.
...A DARING DAYLIGHT ROBBERY...
...LEAVING NO MORE QUESTIONS ABOUT THE WEB-SLINGER'S TRUE MOTIVES...
...THE SUPER-POWERED HERO KNOWN AS SILK APPARENTLY GONE ROGUE...
WHAT? WHAT IS--THAT'S NOT HER. THAT CAN'T BE--
OH. THAT'S SILK, ALL RIGHT.
ESS-DOT EYE-DOT ELL-DOT KAY-DOT.
BUT WHY? IT DOESN'T MAKE SENSE.
IT DOESN'T HAVE TO, CINDY. THIS IS JUST WHAT HAPPENS...

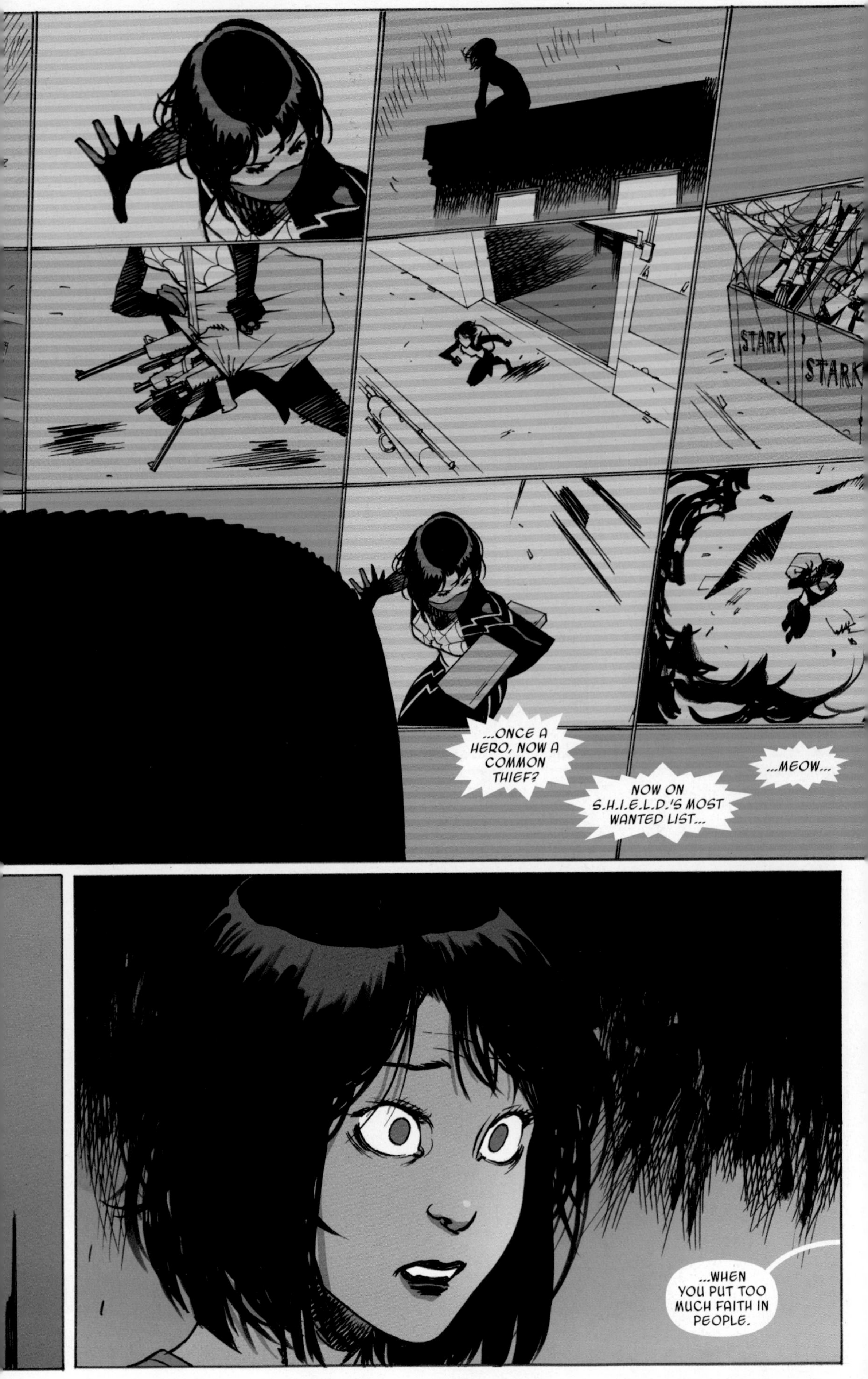
STARK
STARK
...ONCE A HERO, NOW A COMMON THIEF?
NOW ON S.H.I.E.L.D.'S MOST WANTED LIST...
...MEOW...
...WHEN YOU PUT TOO MUCH FAITH IN PEOPLE.

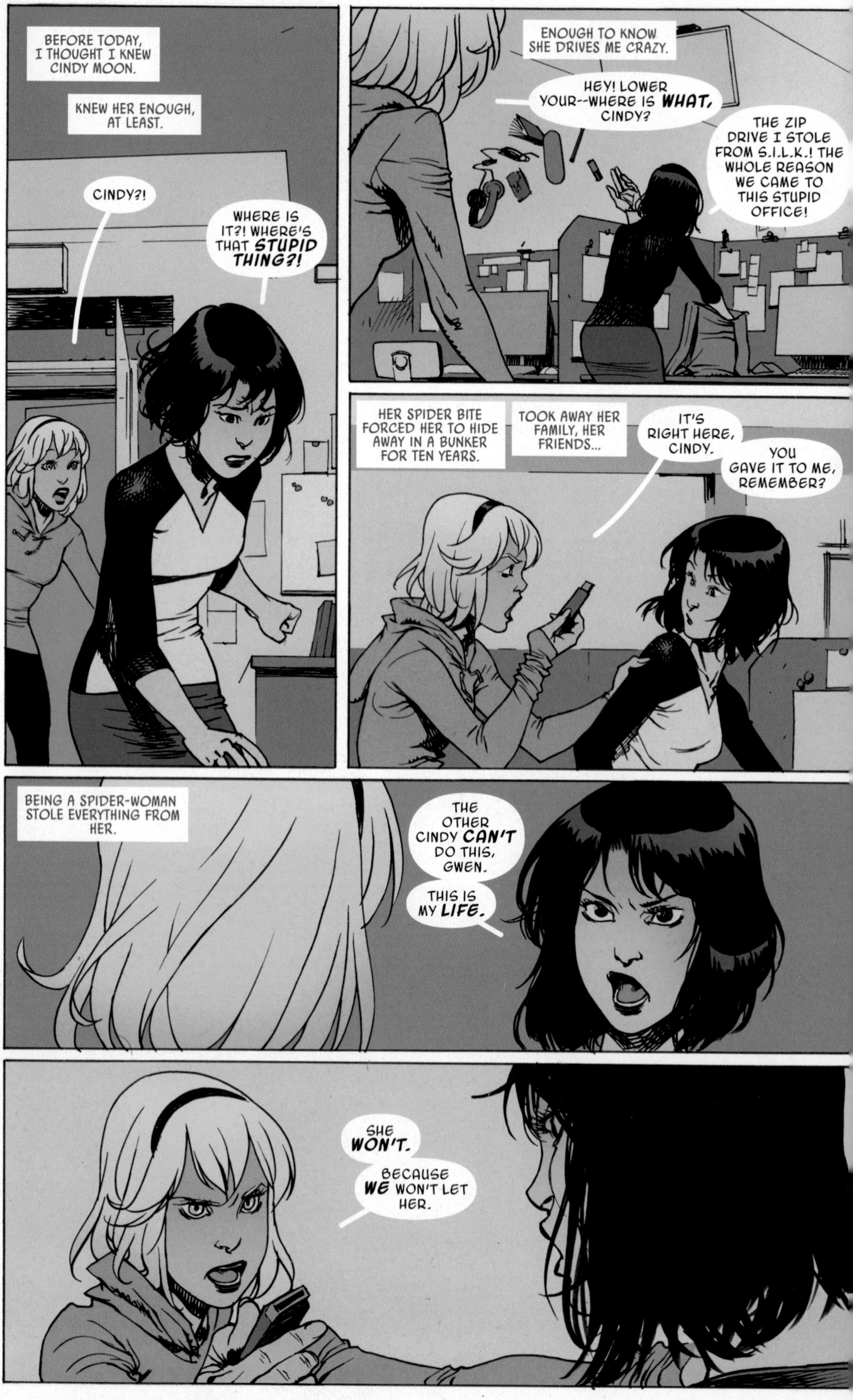

BEFORE TODAY, I THOUGHT I KNEW CINDY MOON.
KNEW HER ENOUGH, AT LEAST.
CINDY?!
WHERE IS IT?! WHERE'S THAT STUPID THING?!
ENOUGH TO KNOW SHE DRIVES ME CRAZY.
HEY! LOWER YOUR--WHERE IS WHAT, CINDY?
THE ZIP DRIVE I STOLE FROM S.I.L.K.! THE WHOLE REASON WE CAME TO THIS STUPID OFFICE!
HER SPIDER BITE FORCED HER TO HIDE AWAY IN A BUNKER FOR TEN YEARS.
TOOK AWAY HER FAMILY, HER FRIENDS...
IT'S RIGHT HERE, CINDY.
YOU GAVE IT TO ME, REMEMBER?
BEING A SPIDER-WOMAN STOLE EVERYTHING FROM HER.
THE OTHER CINDY CAN'T DO THIS, GWEN.
THIS IS MY LIFE.
SHE WON'T.
BECAUSE WE WON'T LET HER.

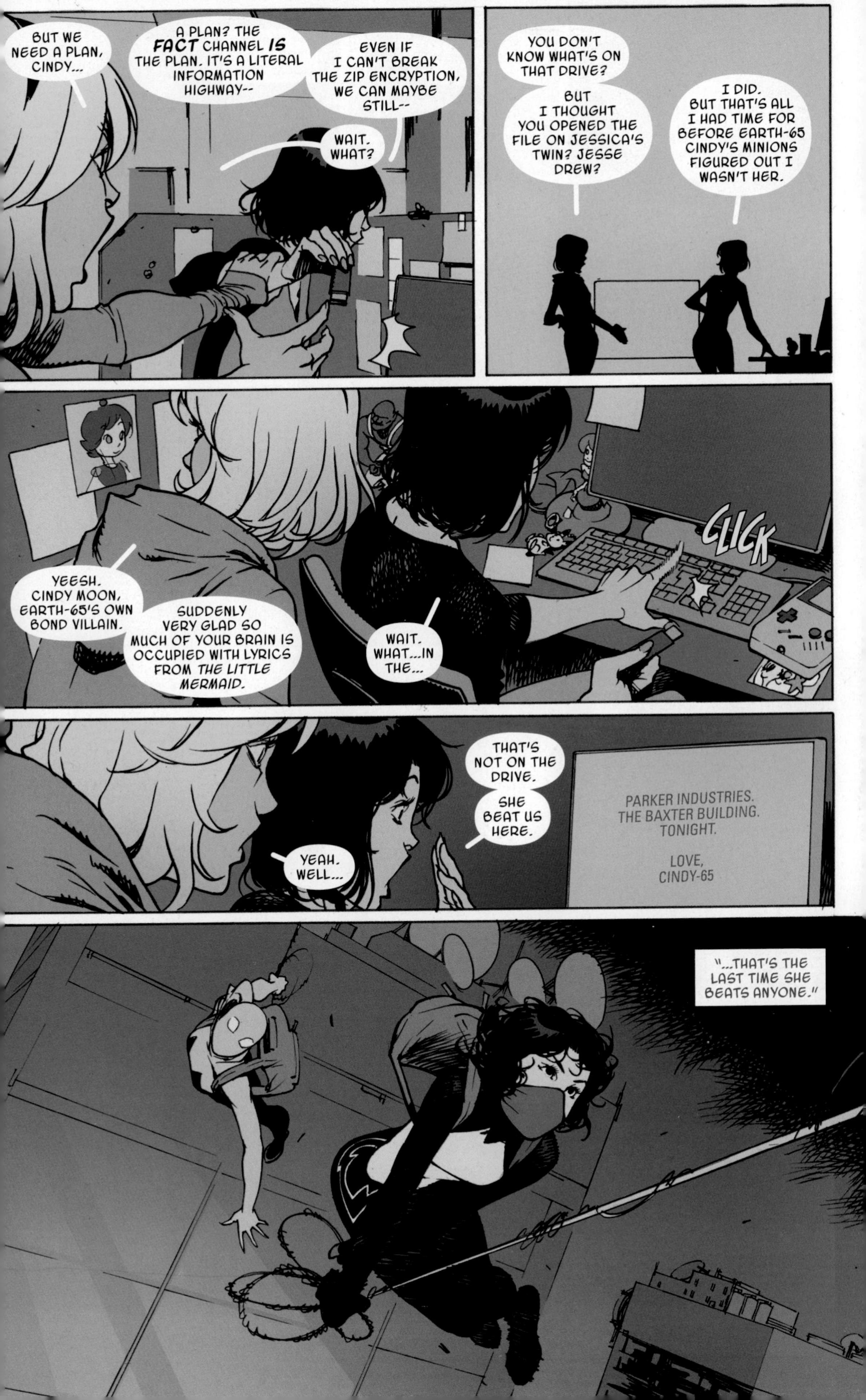
BUT WE NEED A PLAN, CINDY...
A PLAN? THE FACT CHANNEL IS THE PLAN. IT'S A LITERAL INFORMATION HIGHWAY--
EVEN IF I CAN'T BREAK THE ZIP ENCRYPTION, WE CAN MAYBE STILL--
WAIT. WHAT?
YOU DON'T KNOW WHAT'S ON THAT DRIVE?
BUT I THOUGHT YOU OPENED THE FILE ON JESSICA'S TWIN? JESSE DREW?
I DID. BUT THAT'S ALL I HAD TIME FOR BEFORE EARTH-65 CINDY'S MINIONS FIGURED OUT I WASN'T HER.
CLICK
YEESH. CINDY MOON, EARTH-65'S OWN BOND VILLAIN.
SUDDENLY VERY GLAD SO MUCH OF YOUR BRAIN IS OCCUPIED WITH LYRICS FROM THE LITTLE MERMAID.
WAIT. WHAT...IN THE...
THAT'S NOT ON THE DRIVE.
SHE BEAT US HERE.
YEAH. WELL...
PARKER INDUSTRIES.
THE BAXTER BUILDING.
TONIGHT.
LOVE,
CINDY-65
"...THAT'S THE LAST TIME SHE BEATS ANYONE."

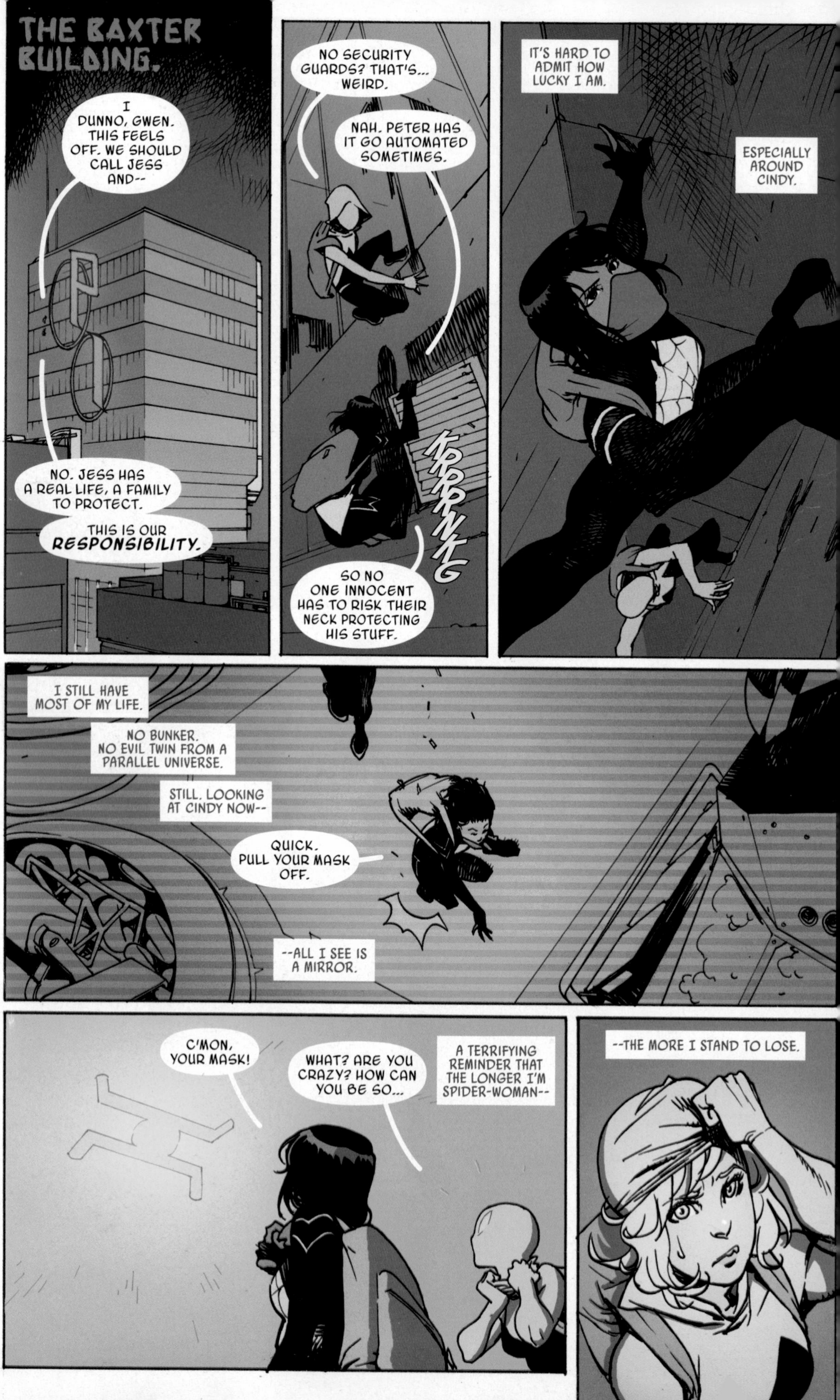
THE BAXTER BUILDING.
I DUNNO, GWEN. THIS FEELS OFF. WE SHOULD CALL JESS AND--
NO. JESS HAS A REAL LIFE, A FAMILY TO PROTECT.
THIS IS OUR RESPONSIBILITY.
NO SECURITY GUARDS? THAT'S... WEIRD.
NAH. PETER HAS IT GO AUTOMATED SOMETIMES.
KRRRNKG
SO NO ONE INNOCENT HAS TO RISK THEIR NECK PROTECTING HIS STUFF.
IT'S HARD TO ADMIT HOW LUCKY I AM.
ESPECIALLY AROUND CINDY.
I STILL HAVE MOST OF MY LIFE.
NO BUNKER. NO EVIL TWIN FROM A PARALLEL UNIVERSE.
STILL. LOOKING AT CINDY NOW--
QUICK. PULL YOUR MASK OFF.
--ALL I SEE IS A MIRROR.
C'MON, YOUR MASK!
WHAT? ARE YOU CRAZY? HOW CAN YOU BE SO...
A TERRIFYING REMINDER THAT THE LONGER I'M SPIDER-WOMAN--
--THE MORE I STAND TO LOSE.

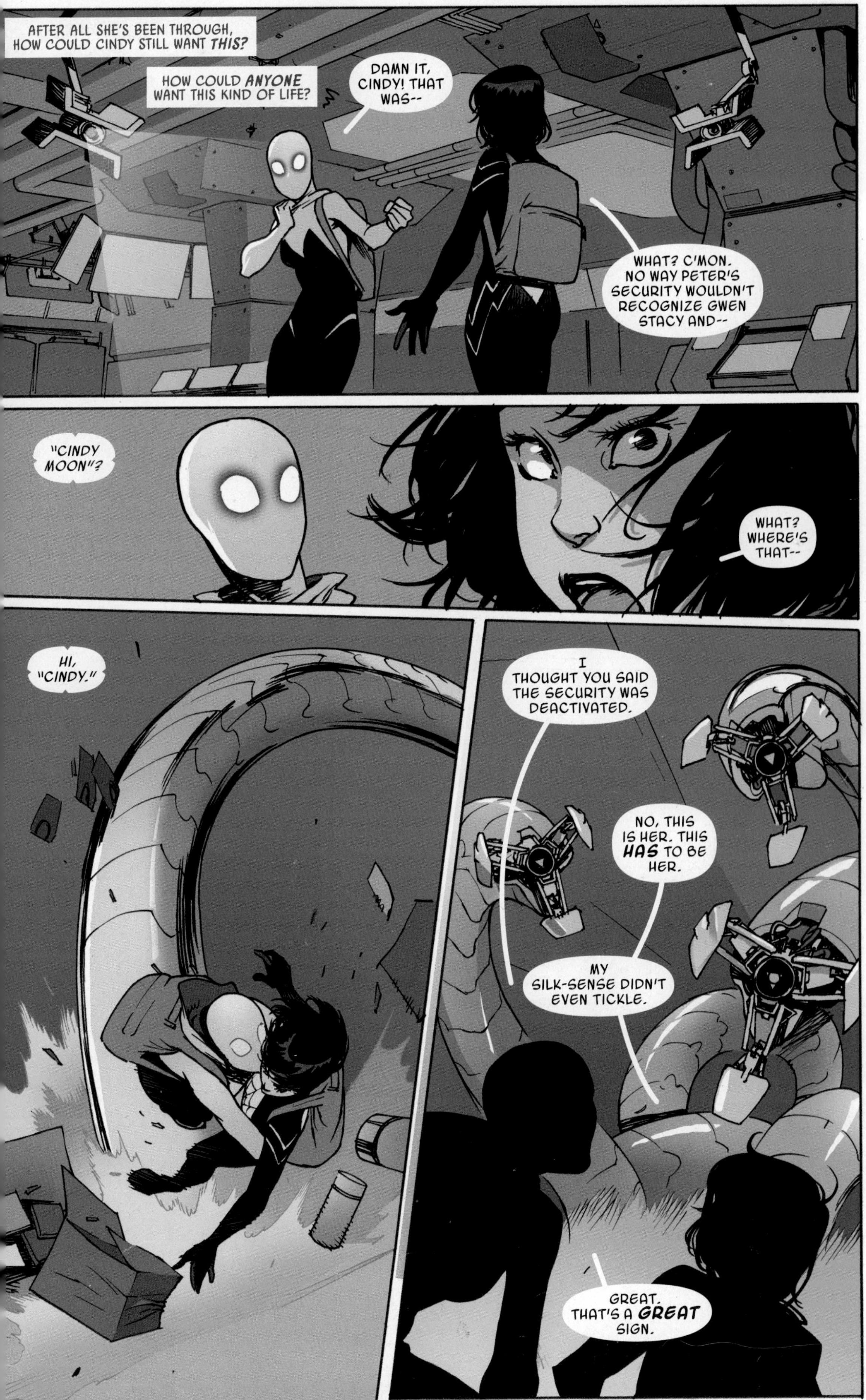
AFTER ALL SHE'S BEEN THROUGH, HOW COULD CINDY STILL WANT *THIS?*
HOW COULD *ANYONE* WANT THIS KIND OF LIFE?
DAMN IT, CINDY! THAT WAS--
WHAT? C'MON. NO WAY PETER'S SECURITY WOULDN'T RECOGNIZE GWEN STACY AND--
"CINDY MOON"?
WHAT? WHERE'S THAT--
HI, "CINDY."
I THOUGHT YOU SAID THE SECURITY WAS DEACTIVATED.
NO, THIS IS HER. THIS **HAS** TO BE HER.
MY SILK-SENSE DIDN'T EVEN TICKLE.
GREAT. THAT'S A **GREAT** SIGN.

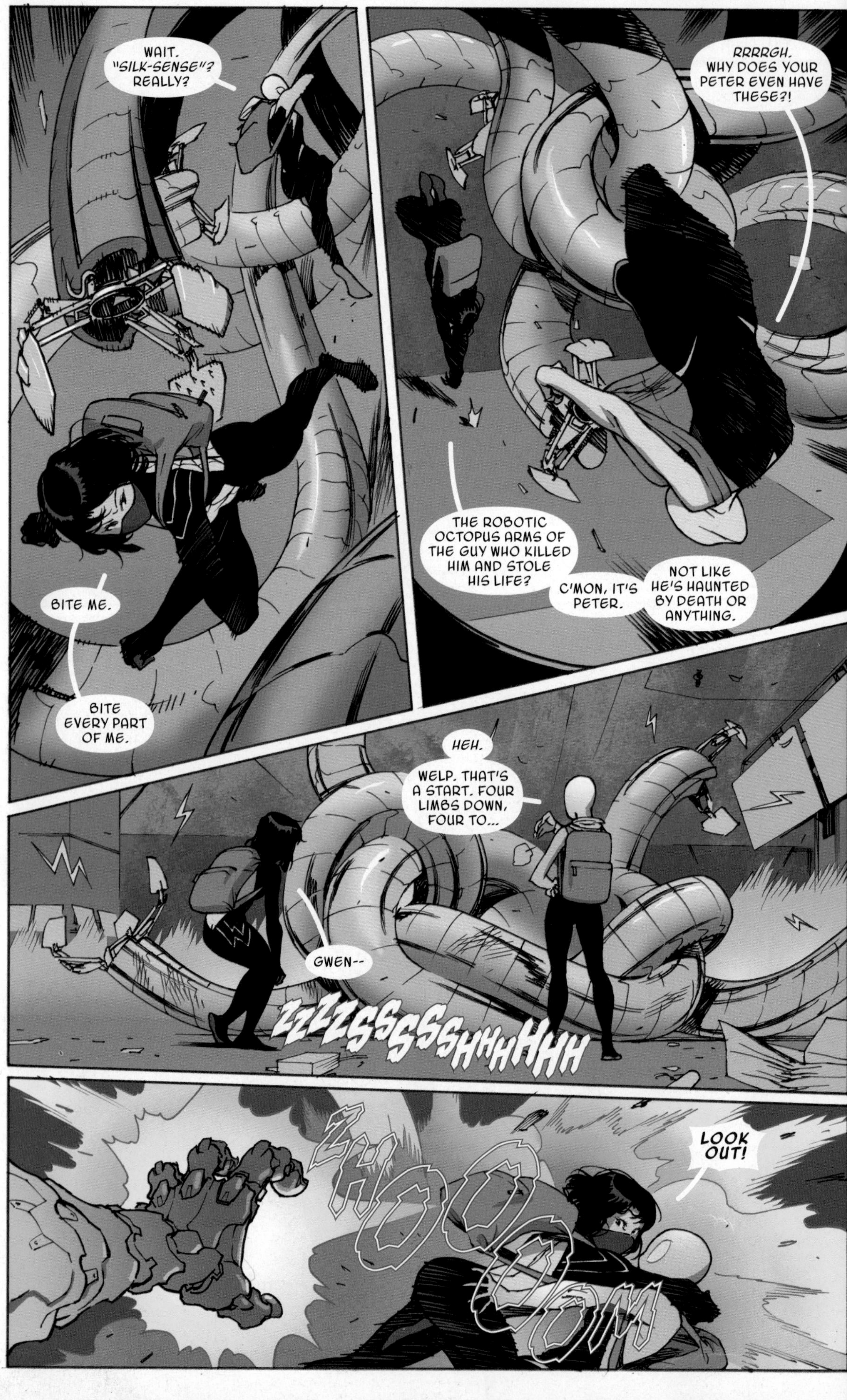
WAIT. "SILK-SENSE"? REALLY?
BITE ME.
BITE EVERY PART OF ME.
RRRRGH. WHY DOES YOUR PETER EVEN HAVE THESE?!
THE ROBOTIC OCTOPUS ARMS OF THE GUY WHO KILLED HIM AND STOLE HIS LIFE?
C'MON, IT'S PETER.
NOT LIKE HE'S HAUNTED BY DEATH OR ANYTHING.
HEH.
WELP. THAT'S A START. FOUR LIMBS DOWN, FOUR TO...
GWEN--
ZZZZSSSSSHHHHHH
LOOK OUT!
THOOOOOM

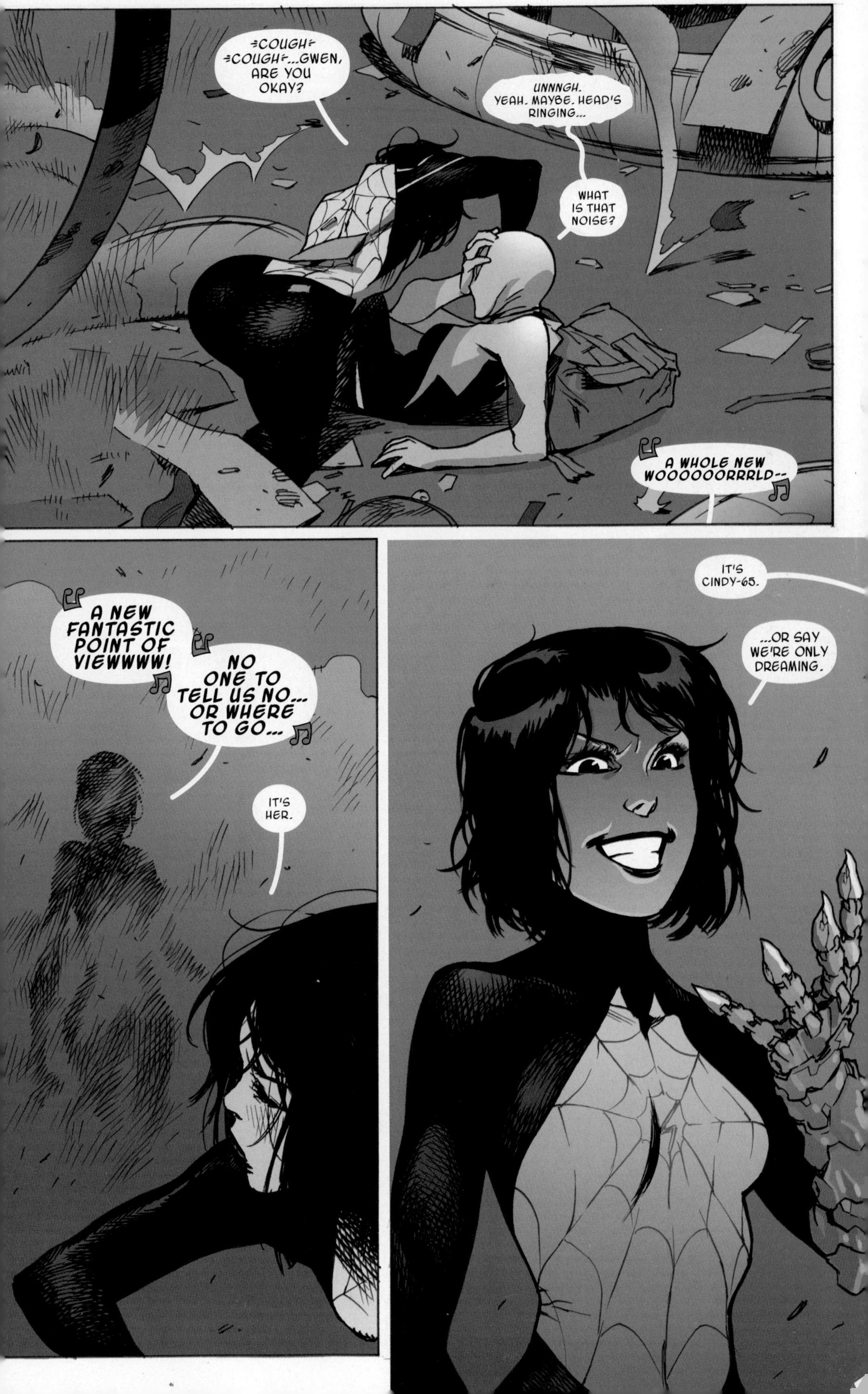

=COUGH= =COUGH=...GWEN, ARE YOU OKAY?
UNNNGH. YEAH. MAYBE. HEAD'S RINGING...
WHAT IS THAT NOISE?
A WHOLE NEW WOOOOOORRRLD--
A NEW FANTASTIC POINT OF VIEWWWW!
NO ONE TO TELL US NO... OR WHERE TO GO...
IT'S HER.
IT'S CINDY-65.
...OR SAY WE'RE ONLY DREAMING.

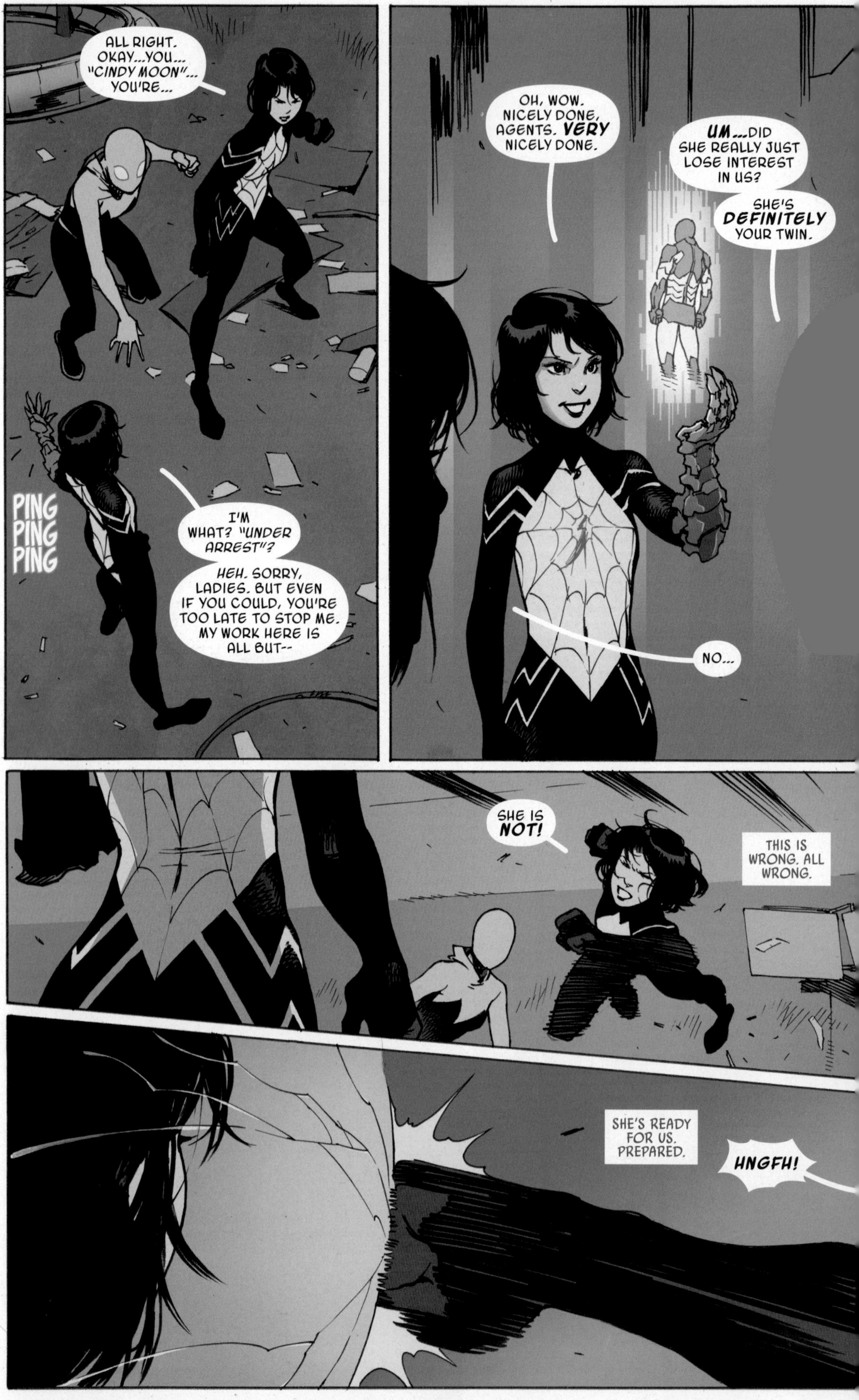
ALL RIGHT. OKAY...YOU... "CINDY MOON"... YOU'RE...
PING PING PING
I'M WHAT? "UNDER ARREST"?
HEH. SORRY, LADIES. BUT EVEN IF YOU COULD, YOU'RE TOO LATE TO STOP ME. MY WORK HERE IS ALL BUT--
OH, WOW. NICELY DONE, AGENTS. VERY NICELY DONE.
UM...DID SHE REALLY JUST LOSE INTEREST IN US?
SHE'S DEFINITELY YOUR TWIN.
NO...
SHE IS NOT!
THIS IS WRONG. ALL WRONG.
SHE'S READY FOR US. PREPARED.
HNGFH!

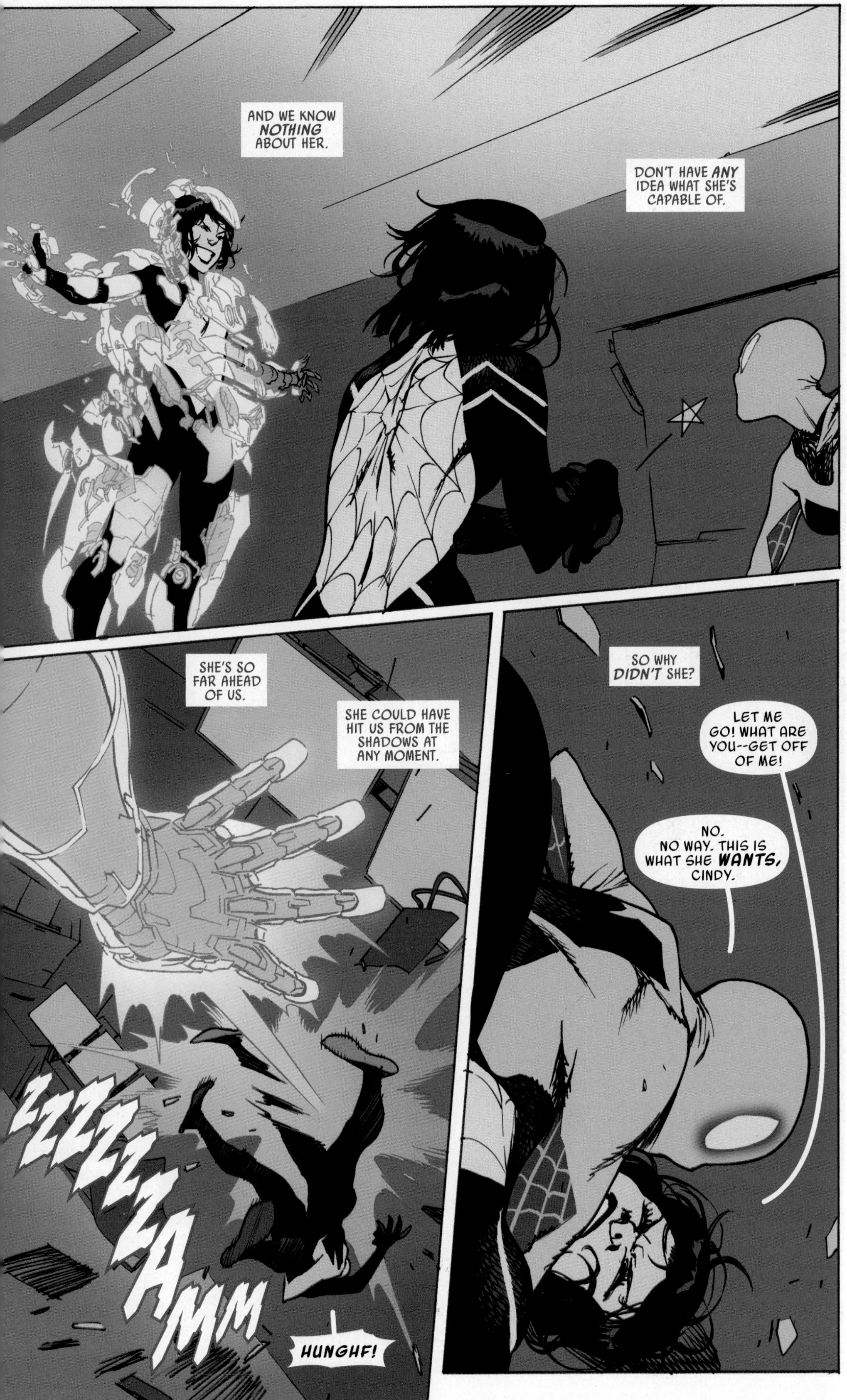
AND WE KNOW NOTHING ABOUT HER.
DON'T HAVE ANY IDEA WHAT SHE'S CAPABLE OF.
SHE'S SO FAR AHEAD OF US.
SHE COULD HAVE HIT US FROM THE SHADOWS AT ANY MOMENT.
ZZZZZZAMM
HUNGHF!
SO WHY DIDN'T SHE?
LET ME GO! WHAT ARE YOU--GET OFF OF ME!
NO. NO WAY. THIS IS WHAT SHE WANTS, CINDY.

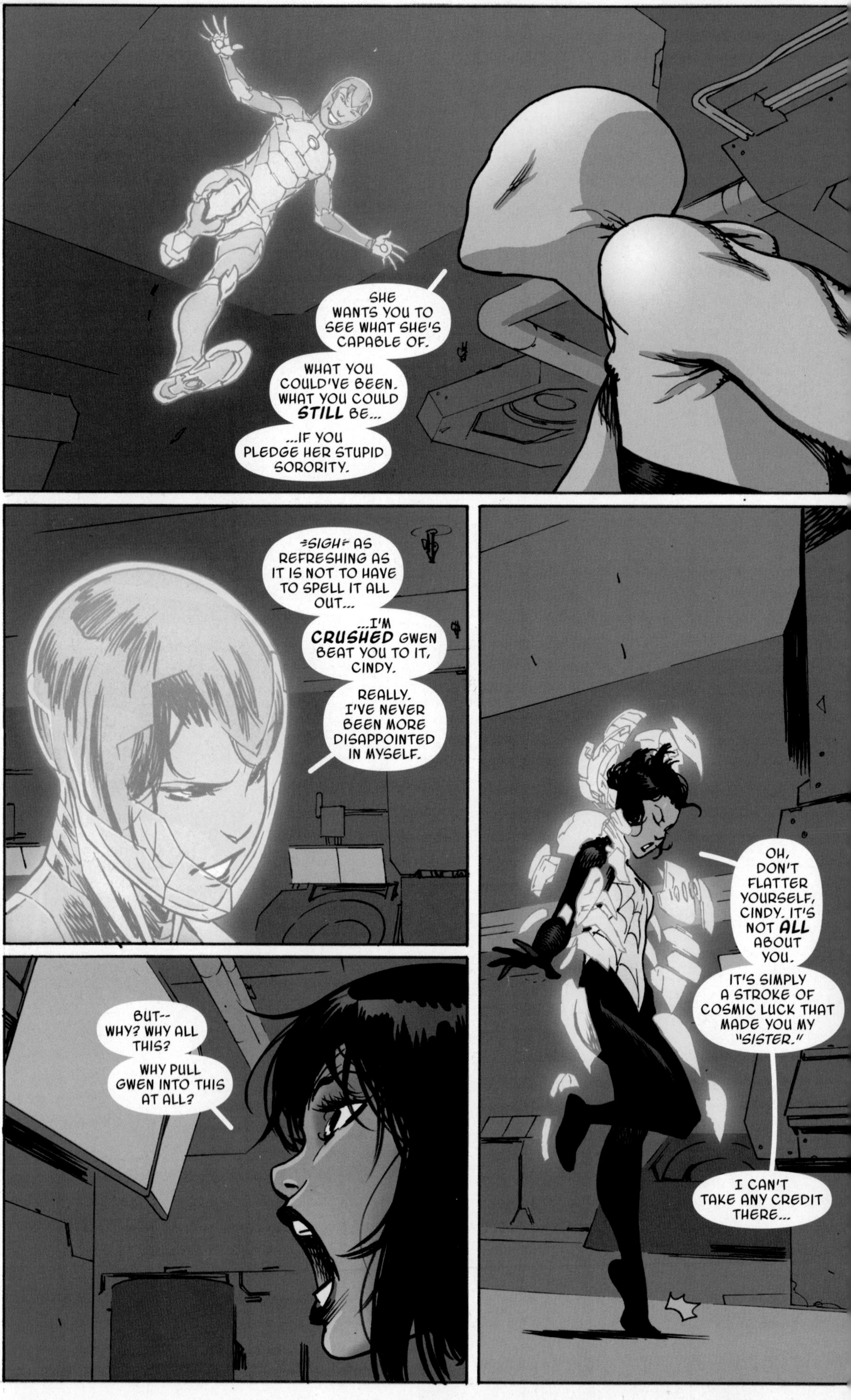
SHE WANTS YOU TO SEE WHAT SHE'S CAPABLE OF.
WHAT YOU COULD'VE BEEN. WHAT YOU COULD **STILL** BE...
...IF YOU PLEDGE HER STUPID SORORITY.
=SIGH= AS REFRESHING AS IT IS NOT TO HAVE TO SPELL IT ALL OUT...
...I'M **CRUSHED** GWEN BEAT YOU TO IT, CINDY.
REALLY. I'VE NEVER BEEN MORE DISAPPOINTED IN MYSELF.
BUT-- WHY? WHY ALL THIS?
WHY PULL GWEN INTO THIS AT ALL?
OH, DON'T FLATTER YOURSELF, CINDY. IT'S NOT **ALL** ABOUT YOU.
IT'S SIMPLY A STROKE OF COSMIC LUCK THAT MADE YOU MY "SISTER."
I CAN'T TAKE ANY CREDIT THERE...

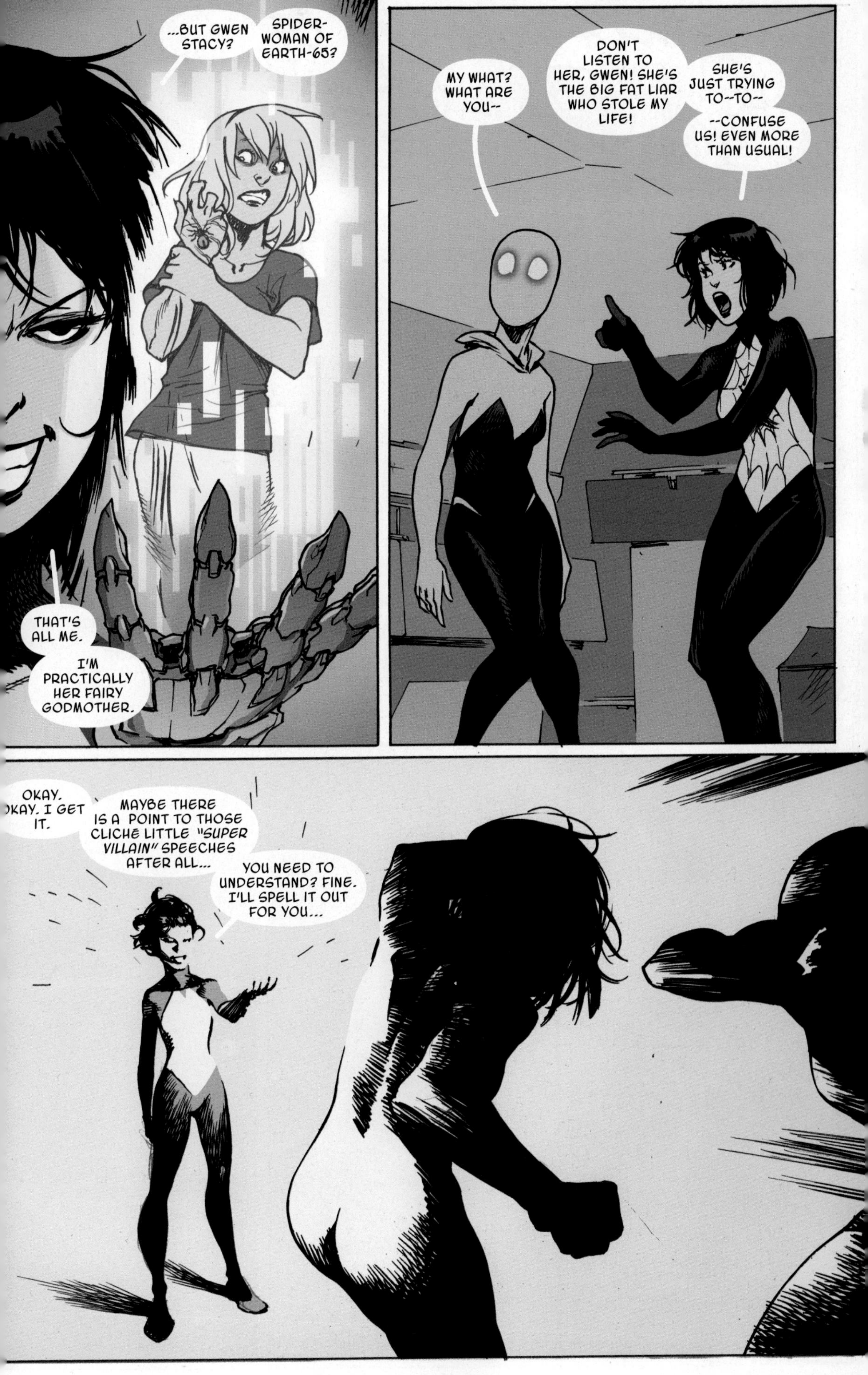

...BUT GWEN STACY?
SPIDER-WOMAN OF EARTH-65?
THAT'S ALL ME.
I'M PRACTICALLY HER FAIRY GODMOTHER.
MY WHAT? WHAT ARE YOU--
DON'T LISTEN TO HER, GWEN! SHE'S THE BIG FAT LIAR WHO STOLE MY LIFE!
SHE'S JUST TRYING TO--TO--
--CONFUSE US! EVEN MORE THAN USUAL!
OKAY. OKAY. I GET IT.
MAYBE THERE IS A POINT TO THOSE CLICHE LITTLE "SUPER VILLAIN" SPEECHES AFTER ALL...
YOU NEED TO UNDERSTAND? FINE. I'LL SPELL IT OUT FOR YOU...

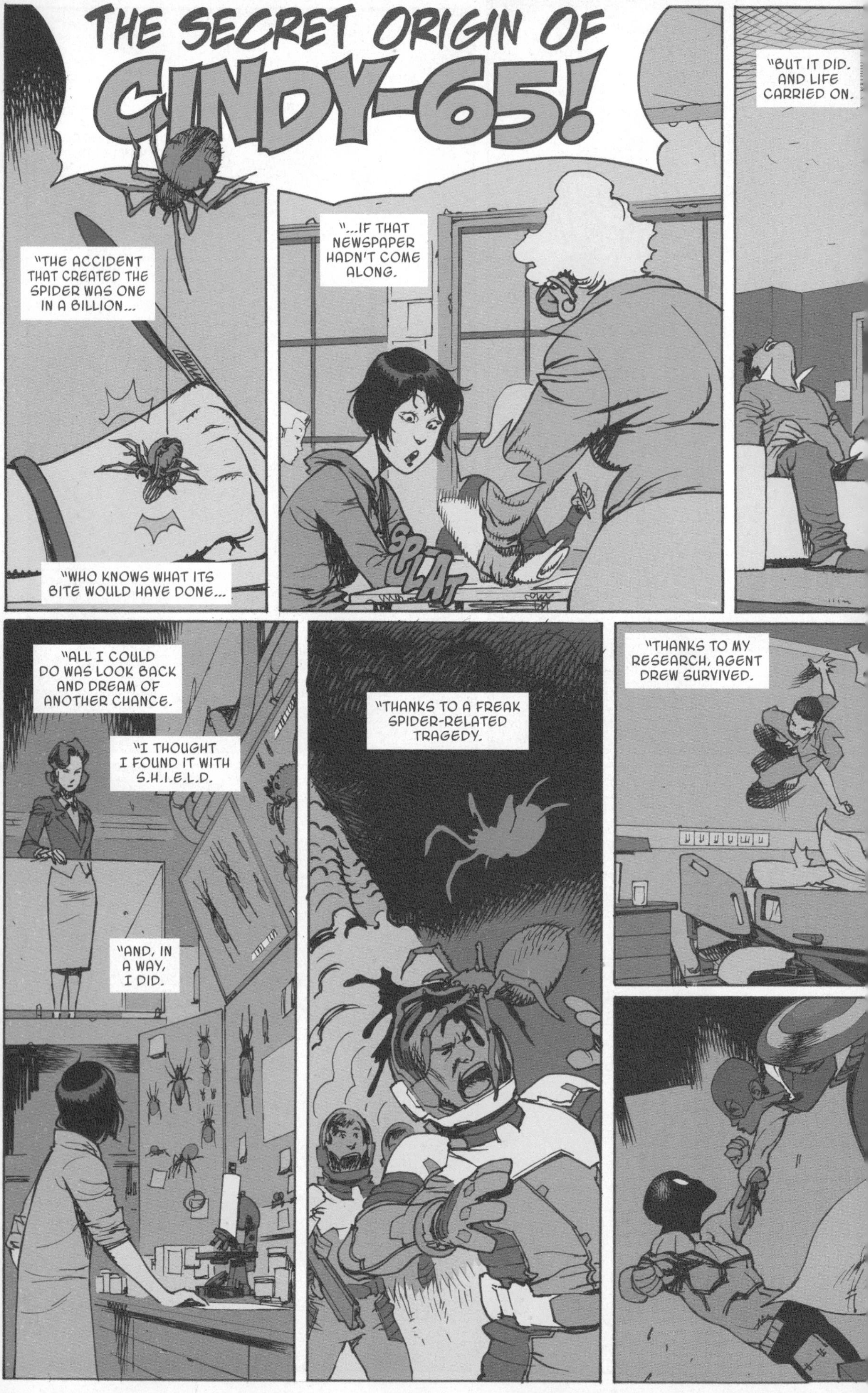
THE SECRET ORIGIN OF CINDY-65!
"THE ACCIDENT THAT CREATED THE SPIDER WAS ONE IN A BILLION...
"WHO KNOWS WHAT ITS BITE WOULD HAVE DONE...
"...IF THAT NEWSPAPER HADN'T COME ALONG.
SPLAT
"BUT IT DID. AND LIFE CARRIED ON.
"ALL I COULD DO WAS LOOK BACK AND DREAM OF ANOTHER CHANCE.
"I THOUGHT I FOUND IT WITH S.H.I.E.L.D.
"AND, IN A WAY, I DID.
"THANKS TO A FREAK SPIDER-RELATED TRAGEDY.
"THANKS TO MY RESEARCH, AGENT DREW SURVIVED.

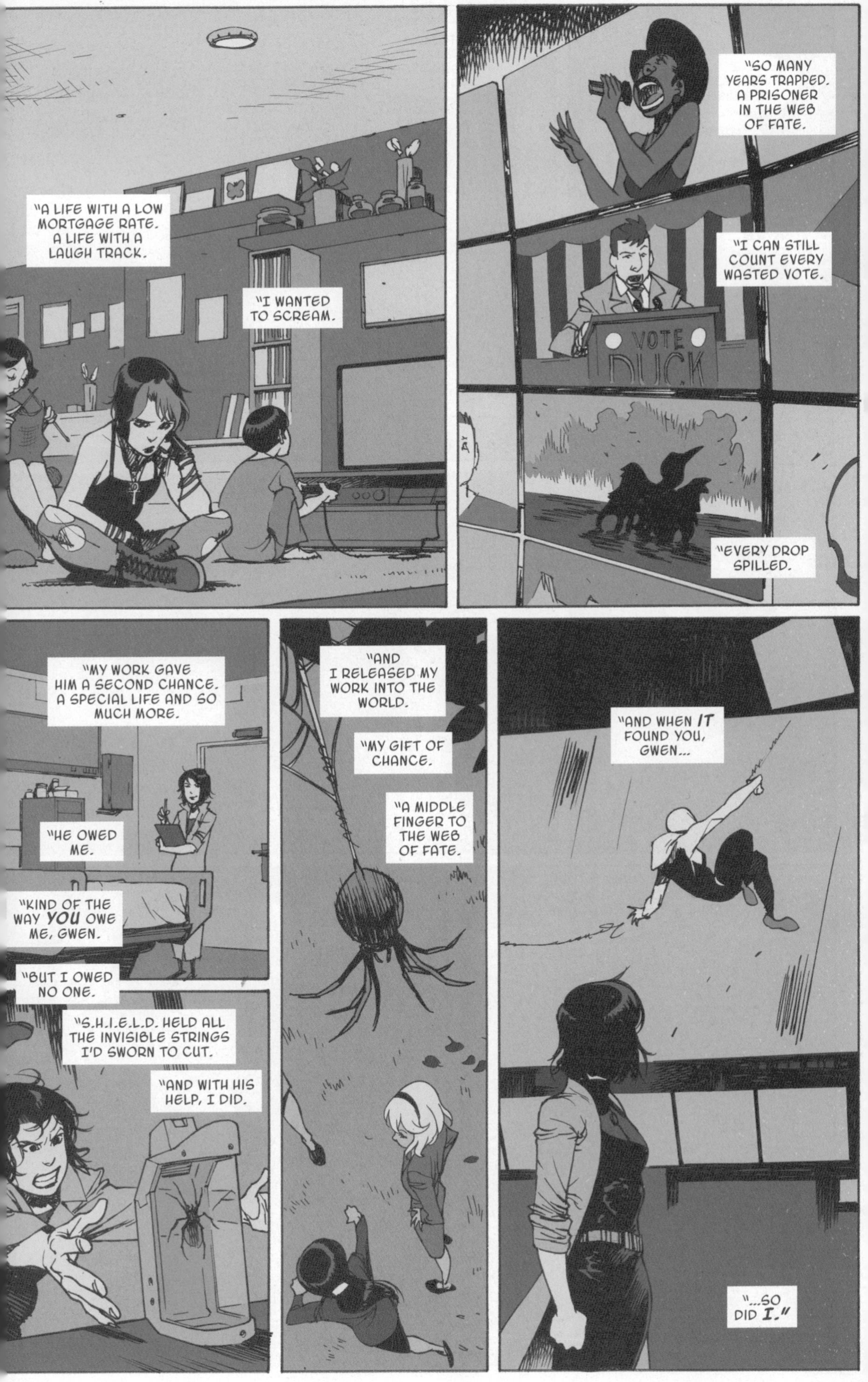
"A LIFE WITH A LOW MORTGAGE RATE. A LIFE WITH A LAUGH TRACK.
"I WANTED TO SCREAM.
"SO MANY YEARS TRAPPED. A PRISONER IN THE WEB OF FATE.
"I CAN STILL COUNT EVERY WASTED VOTE.
VOTE DUCK
"EVERY DROP SPILLED.
"MY WORK GAVE HIM A SECOND CHANCE. A SPECIAL LIFE AND SO MUCH MORE.
"HE OWED ME.
"KIND OF THE WAY YOU OWE ME, GWEN.
"BUT I OWED NO ONE.
"S.H.I.E.L.D. HELD ALL THE INVISIBLE STRINGS I'D SWORN TO CUT.
"AND WITH HIS HELP, I DID.
"AND I RELEASED MY WORK INTO THE WORLD.
"MY GIFT OF CHANCE.
"A MIDDLE FINGER TO THE WEB OF FATE.
"AND WHEN IT FOUND YOU, GWEN...
"...SO DID I."

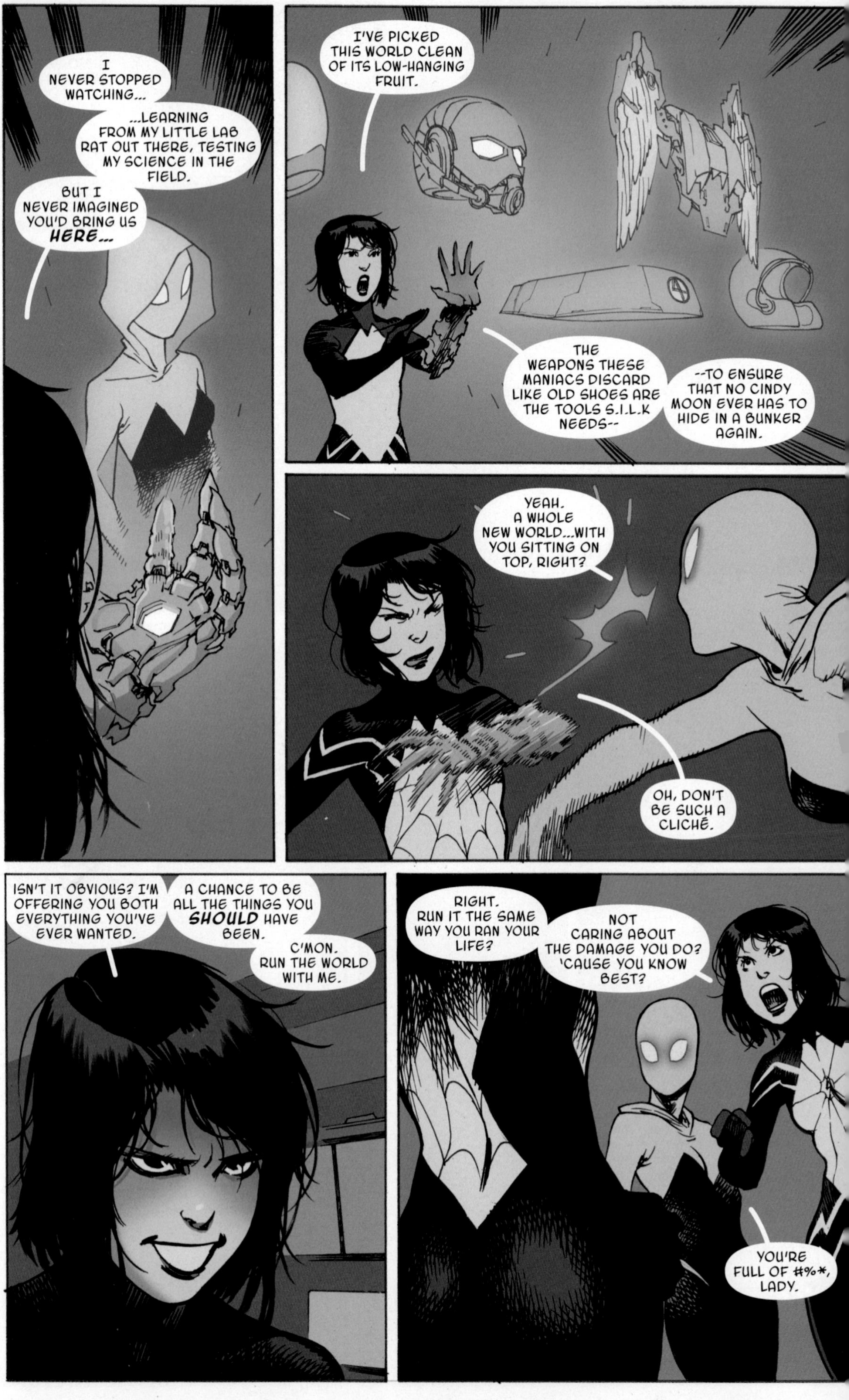
I NEVER STOPPED WATCHING...
...LEARNING FROM MY LITTLE LAB RAT OUT THERE, TESTING MY SCIENCE IN THE FIELD.
BUT I NEVER IMAGINED YOU'D BRING US **HERE...**
I'VE PICKED THIS WORLD CLEAN OF ITS LOW-HANGING FRUIT.
THE WEAPONS THESE MANIACS DISCARD LIKE OLD SHOES ARE THE TOOLS S.I.L.K NEEDS--
--TO ENSURE THAT NO CINDY MOON EVER HAS TO HIDE IN A BUNKER AGAIN.
YEAH. A WHOLE NEW WORLD...WITH YOU SITTING ON TOP, RIGHT?
OH, DON'T BE SUCH A CLICHÉ.
ISN'T IT OBVIOUS? I'M OFFERING YOU BOTH EVERYTHING YOU'VE EVER WANTED.
A CHANCE TO BE ALL THE THINGS YOU **SHOULD** HAVE BEEN.
C'MON. RUN THE WORLD WITH ME.
RIGHT. RUN IT THE SAME WAY YOU RAN YOUR LIFE?
NOT CARING ABOUT THE DAMAGE YOU DO? 'CAUSE YOU KNOW BEST?
YOU'RE FULL OF #%*, LADY.

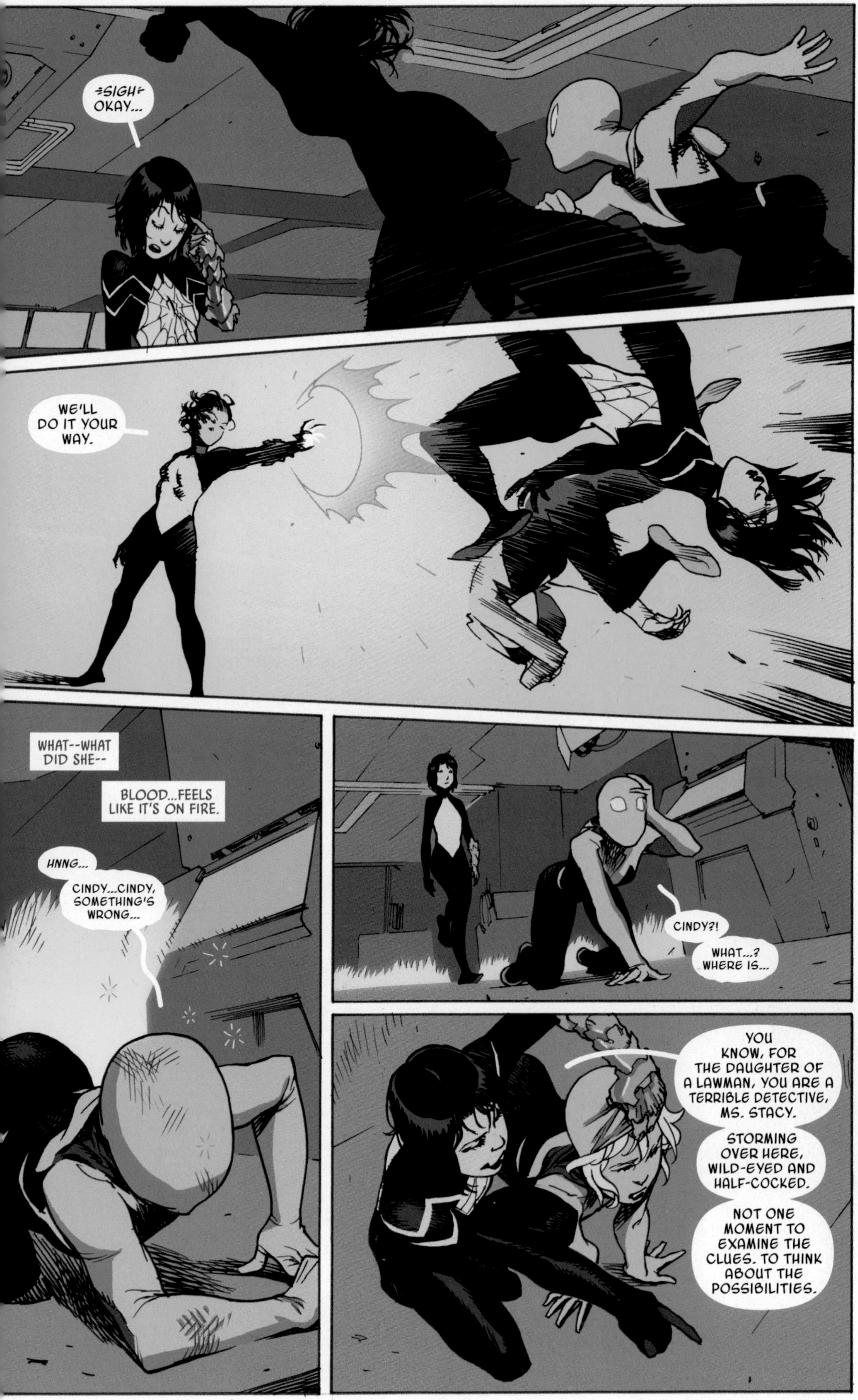

=SIGH= OKAY...
WE'LL DO IT YOUR WAY.
WHAT--WHAT DID SHE--
BLOOD...FEELS LIKE IT'S ON FIRE.
HNNG...
CINDY...CINDY, SOMETHING'S WRONG...
CINDY?!
WHAT...? WHERE IS...
YOU KNOW, FOR THE DAUGHTER OF A LAWMAN, YOU ARE A TERRIBLE DETECTIVE, MS. STACY.
STORMING OVER HERE, WILD-EYED AND HALF-COCKED.
NOT ONE MOMENT TO EXAMINE THE CLUES. TO THINK ABOUT THE POSSIBILITIES.

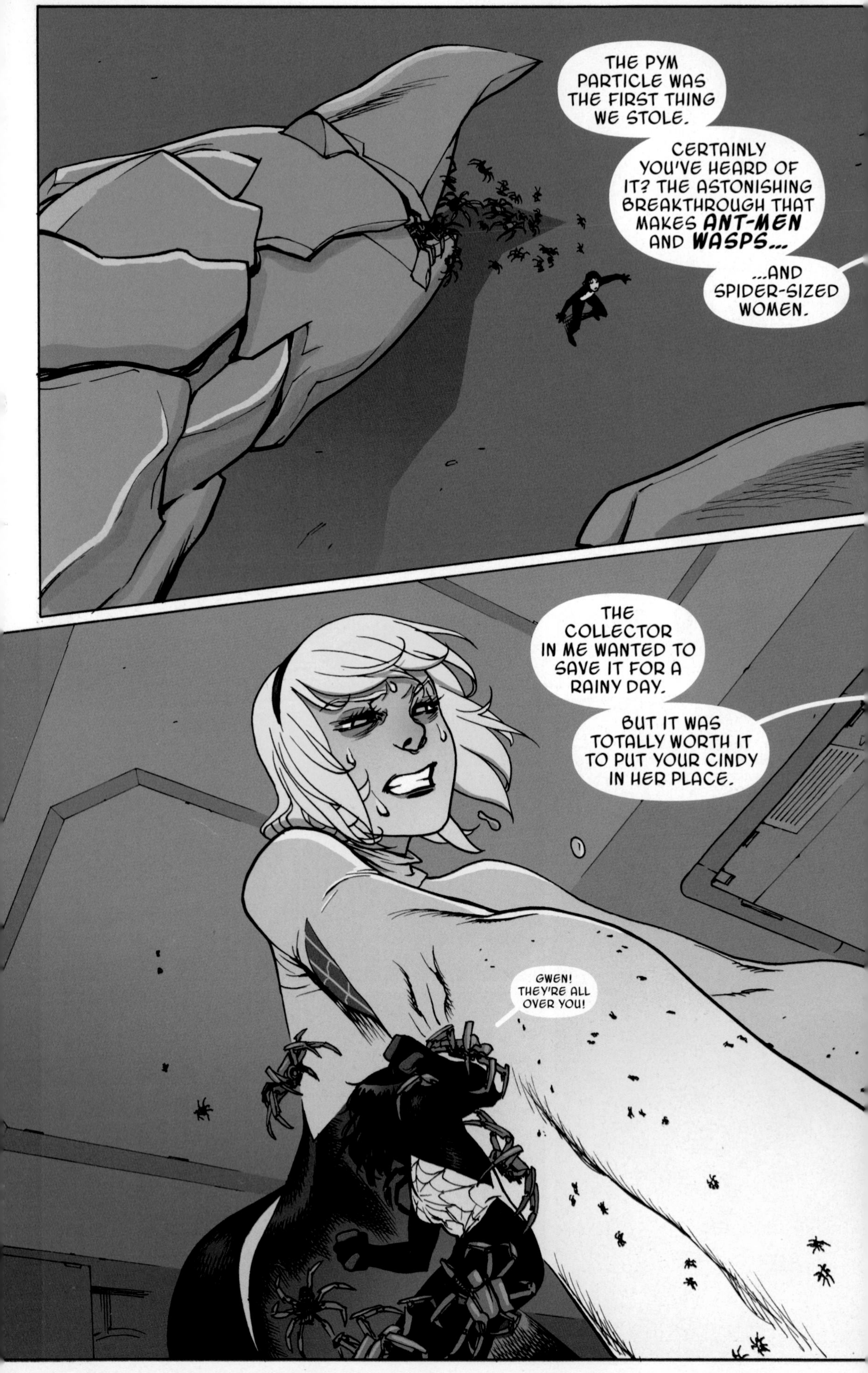
THE PYM PARTICLE WAS THE FIRST THING WE STOLE.
CERTAINLY YOU'VE HEARD OF IT? THE ASTONISHING BREAKTHROUGH THAT MAKES ANT-MEN AND WASPS...
...AND SPIDER-SIZED WOMEN.
THE COLLECTOR IN ME WANTED TO SAVE IT FOR A RAINY DAY.
BUT IT WAS TOTALLY WORTH IT TO PUT YOUR CINDY IN HER PLACE.
GWEN! THEY'RE ALL OVER YOU!

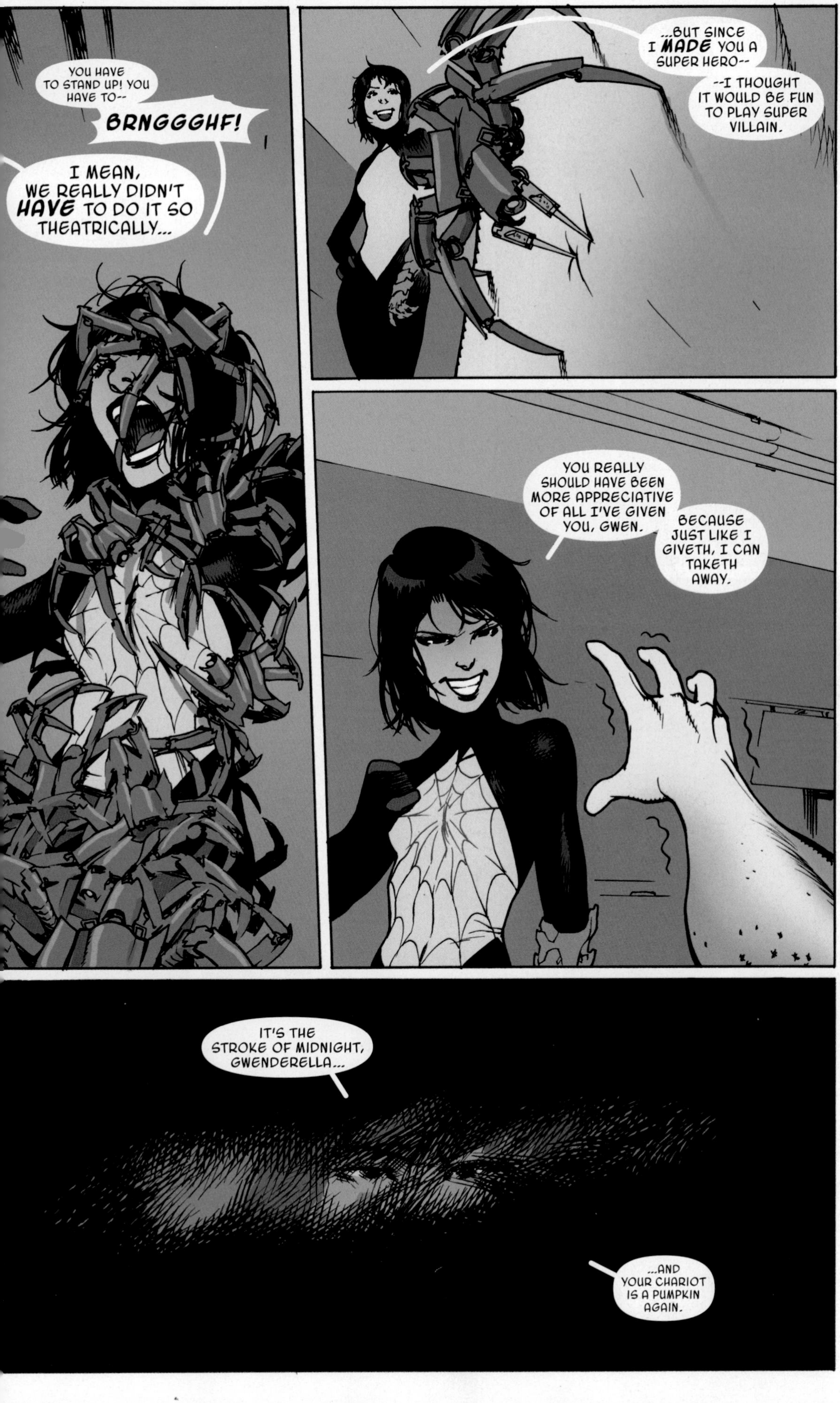
YOU HAVE TO STAND UP! YOU HAVE TO--
BRNGGGHF!
I MEAN, WE REALLY DIDN'T HAVE TO DO IT SO THEATRICALLY...
...BUT SINCE I MADE YOU A SUPER HERO--
--I THOUGHT IT WOULD BE FUN TO PLAY SUPER VILLAIN.
YOU REALLY SHOULD HAVE BEEN MORE APPRECIATIVE OF ALL I'VE GIVEN YOU, GWEN.
BECAUSE JUST LIKE I GIVETH, I CAN TAKETH AWAY.
IT'S THE STROKE OF MIDNIGHT, GWENDERELLA...
...AND YOUR CHARIOT IS A PUMPKIN AGAIN.

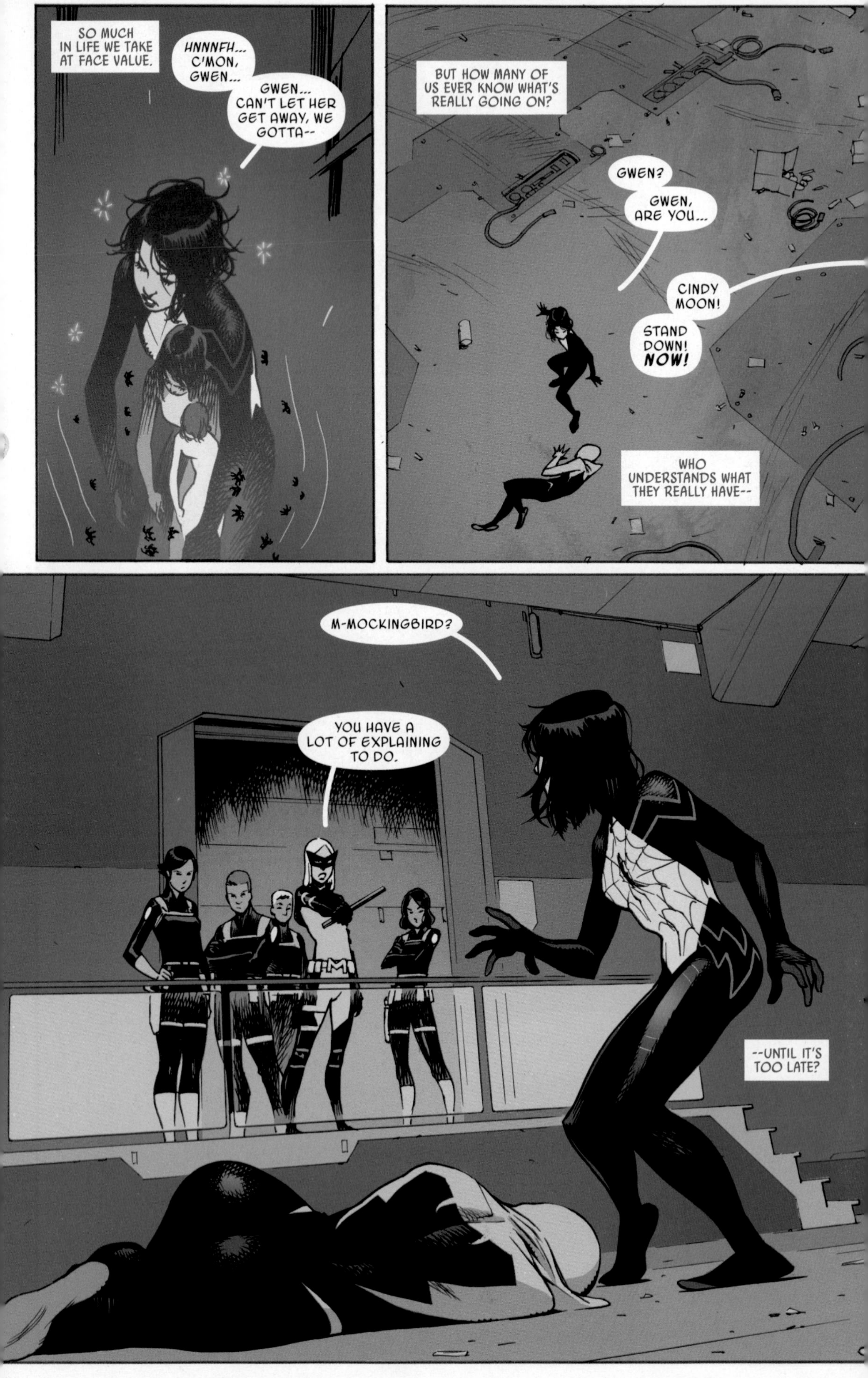
SO MUCH IN LIFE WE TAKE AT FACE VALUE.
HNNNFH... C'MON, GWEN...
GWEN... CAN'T LET HER GET AWAY, WE GOTTA--
BUT HOW MANY OF US EVER KNOW WHAT'S REALLY GOING ON?
GWEN?
GWEN, ARE YOU...
CINDY MOON!
STAND DOWN! NOW!
WHO UNDERSTANDS WHAT THEY REALLY HAVE--
M-MOCKINGBIRD?
YOU HAVE A LOT OF EXPLAINING TO DO.
--UNTIL IT'S TOO LATE?

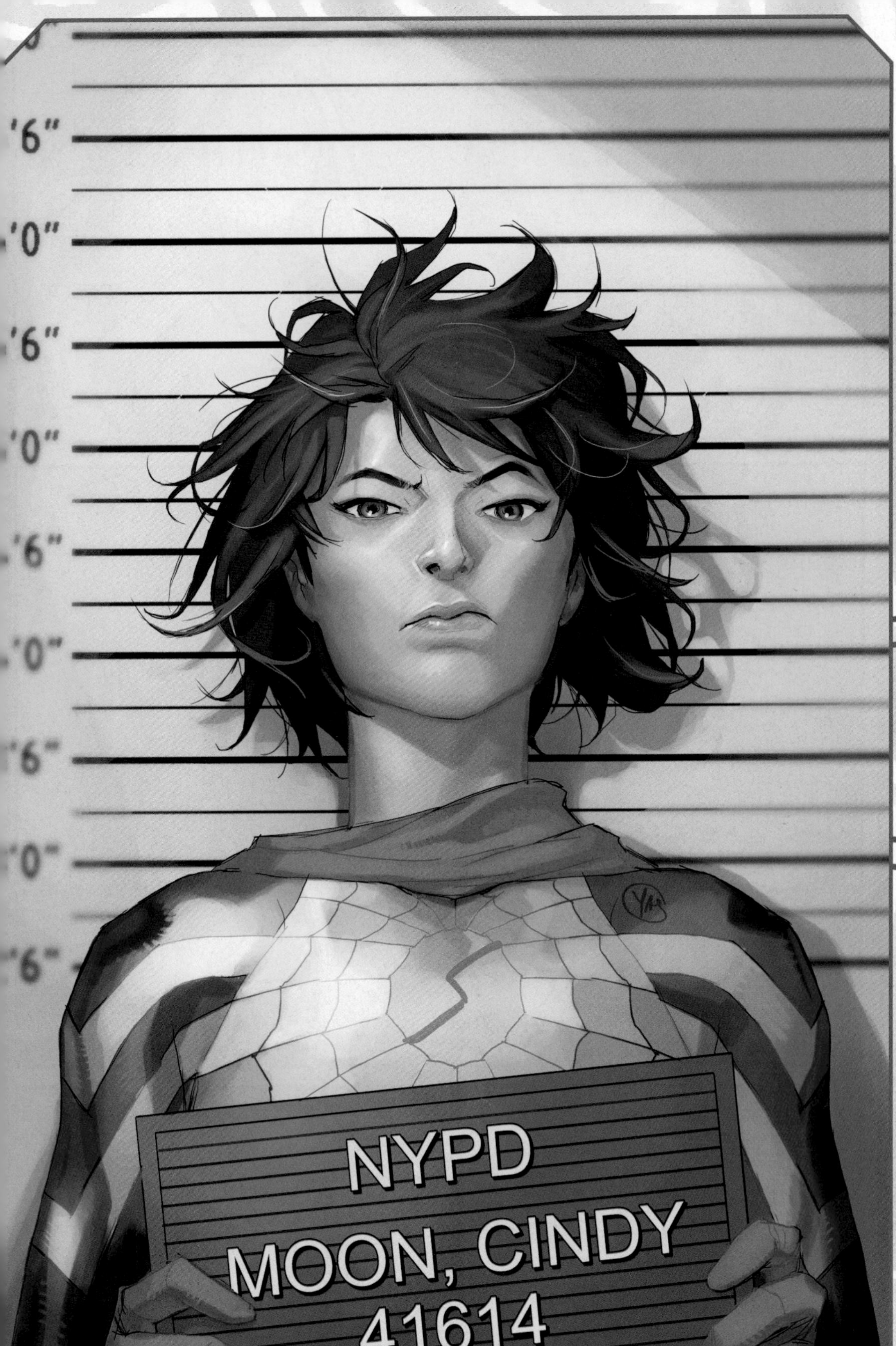
'6"
'0"
'6"
'0"
'6"
'0"
'6"
'0"
'6"
NYPD
MOON, CINDY
41614

SILK #8

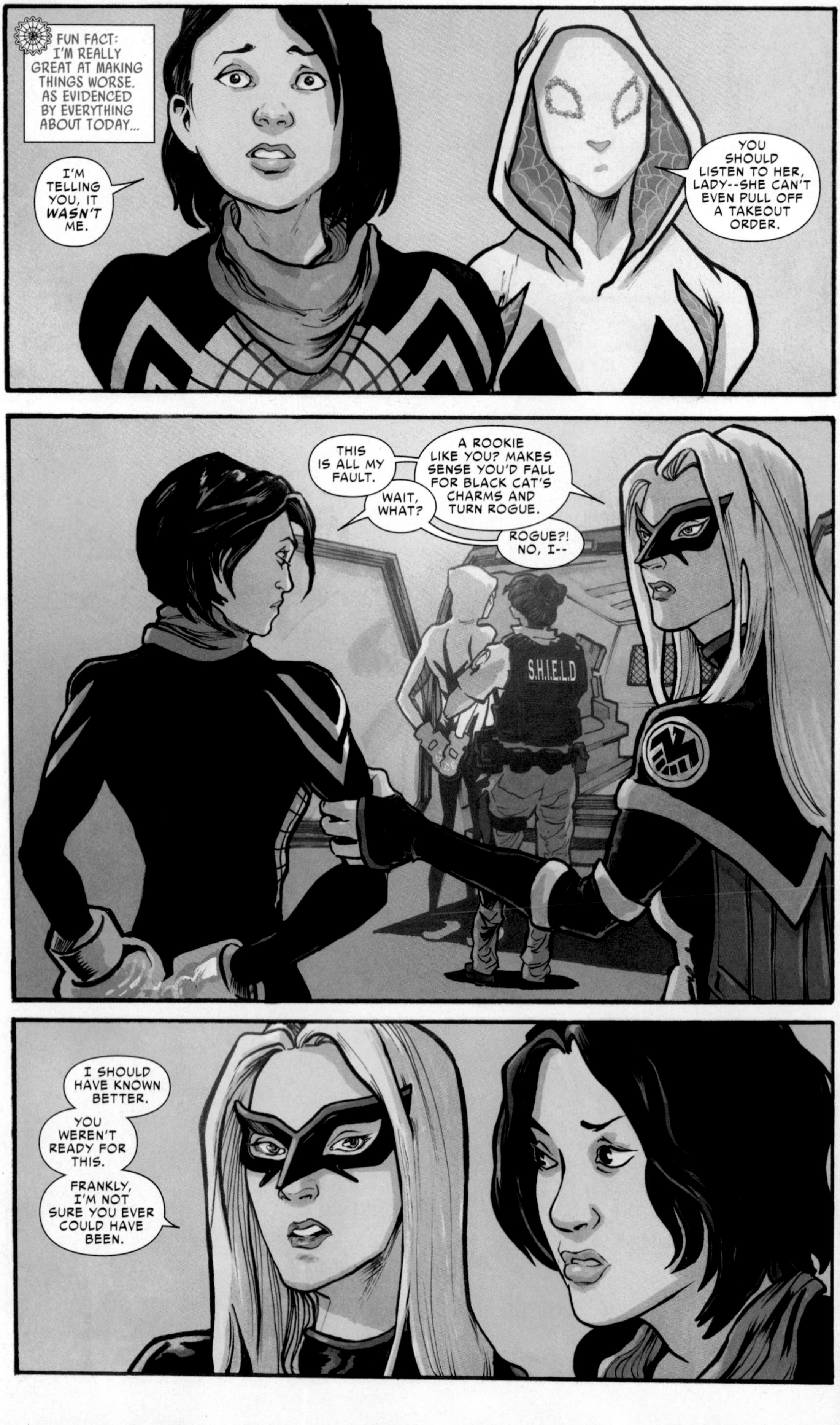
FUN FACT: I'M REALLY GREAT AT MAKING THINGS WORSE. AS EVIDENCED BY EVERYTHING ABOUT TODAY...
I'M TELLING YOU, IT WASN'T ME.
YOU SHOULD LISTEN TO HER, LADY--SHE CAN'T EVEN PULL OFF A TAKEOUT ORDER.
THIS IS ALL MY FAULT.
A ROOKIE LIKE YOU? MAKES SENSE YOU'D FALL FOR BLACK CAT'S CHARMS AND TURN ROGUE.
WAIT, WHAT?
ROGUE?! NO, I--
S.H.I.E.L.D
I SHOULD HAVE KNOWN BETTER.
YOU WEREN'T READY FOR THIS.
FRANKLY, I'M NOT SURE YOU EVER COULD HAVE BEEN.

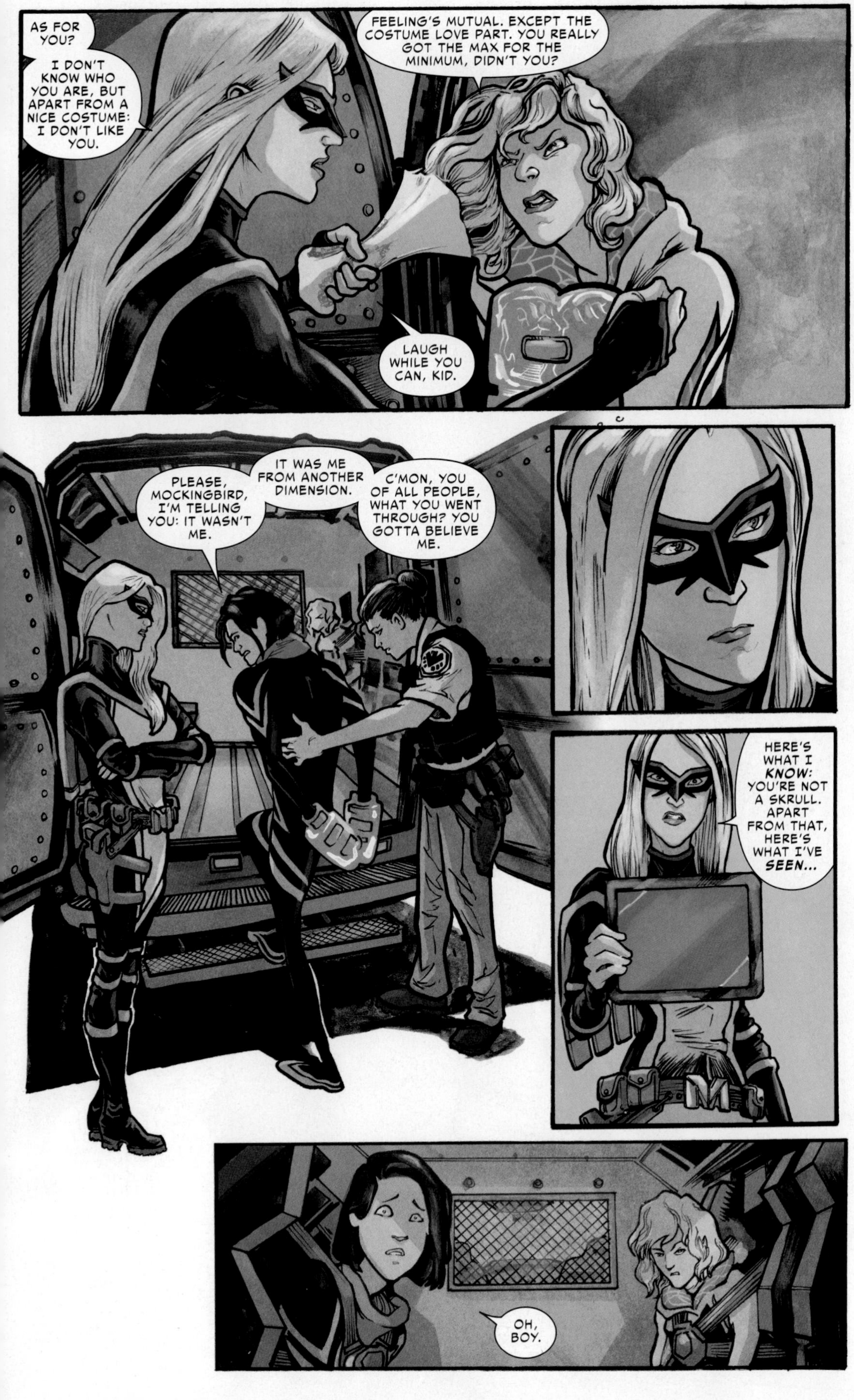
AS FOR YOU?
I DON'T KNOW WHO YOU ARE, BUT APART FROM A NICE COSTUME: I DON'T LIKE YOU.
FEELING'S MUTUAL. EXCEPT THE COSTUME LOVE PART. YOU REALLY GOT THE MAX FOR THE MINIMUM, DIDN'T YOU?
LAUGH WHILE YOU CAN, KID.
PLEASE, MOCKINGBIRD, I'M TELLING YOU: IT WASN'T ME.
IT WAS ME FROM ANOTHER DIMENSION.
C'MON, YOU OF ALL PEOPLE, WHAT YOU WENT THROUGH? YOU GOTTA BELIEVE ME.
HERE'S WHAT I KNOW: YOU'RE NOT A SKRULL. APART FROM THAT, HERE'S WHAT I'VE SEEN...
OH, BOY.

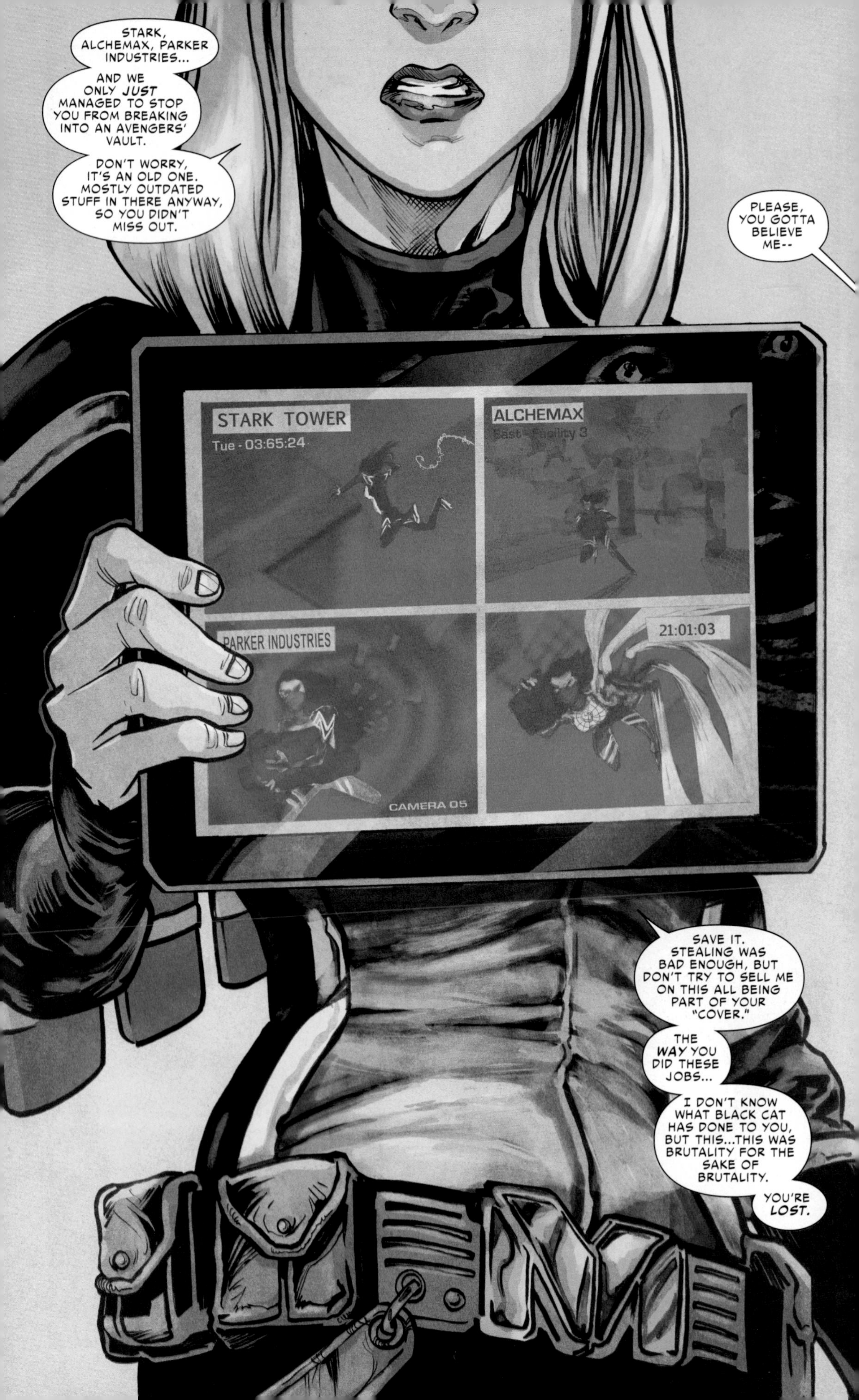
STARK, ALCHEMAX, PARKER INDUSTRIES...
AND WE ONLY JUST MANAGED TO STOP YOU FROM BREAKING INTO AN AVENGERS' VAULT.
DON'T WORRY, IT'S AN OLD ONE. MOSTLY OUTDATED STUFF IN THERE ANYWAY, SO YOU DIDN'T MISS OUT.
PLEASE, YOU GOTTA BELIEVE ME--
STARK TOWER
Tue - 03:65:24
ALCHEMAX
East - Facility 3
PARKER INDUSTRIES
CAMERA 05
21:01:03
SAVE IT. STEALING WAS BAD ENOUGH, BUT DON'T TRY TO SELL ME ON THIS ALL BEING PART OF YOUR "COVER."
THE WAY YOU DID THESE JOBS...
I DON'T KNOW WHAT BLACK CAT HAS DONE TO YOU, BUT THIS...THIS WAS BRUTALITY FOR THE SAKE OF BRUTALITY.
YOU'RE LOST.

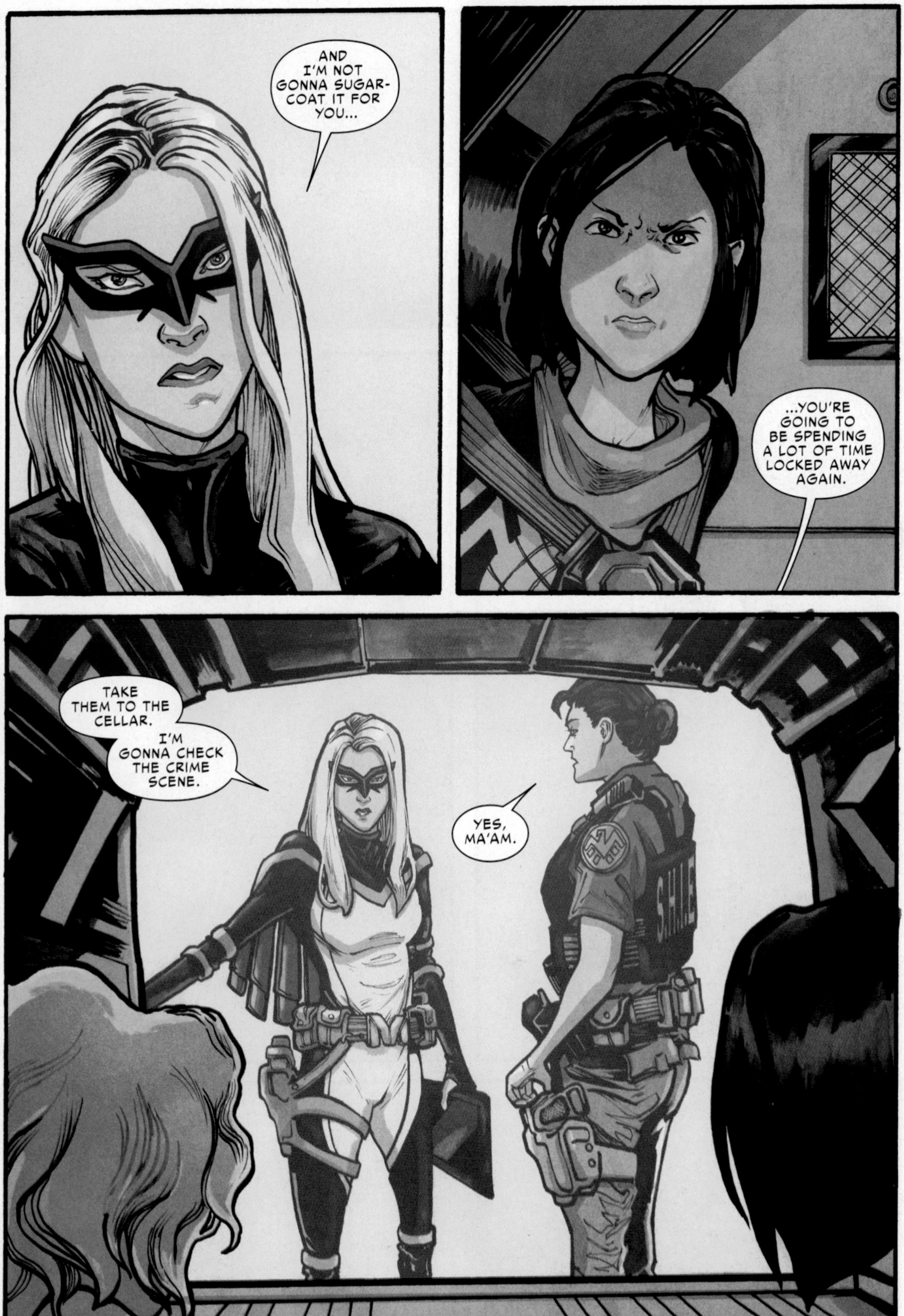
AND I'M NOT GONNA SUGAR-COAT IT FOR YOU...
...YOU'RE GOING TO BE SPENDING A LOT OF TIME LOCKED AWAY AGAIN.
TAKE THEM TO THE CELLAR.
I'M GONNA CHECK THE CRIME SCENE.
YES, MA'AM.

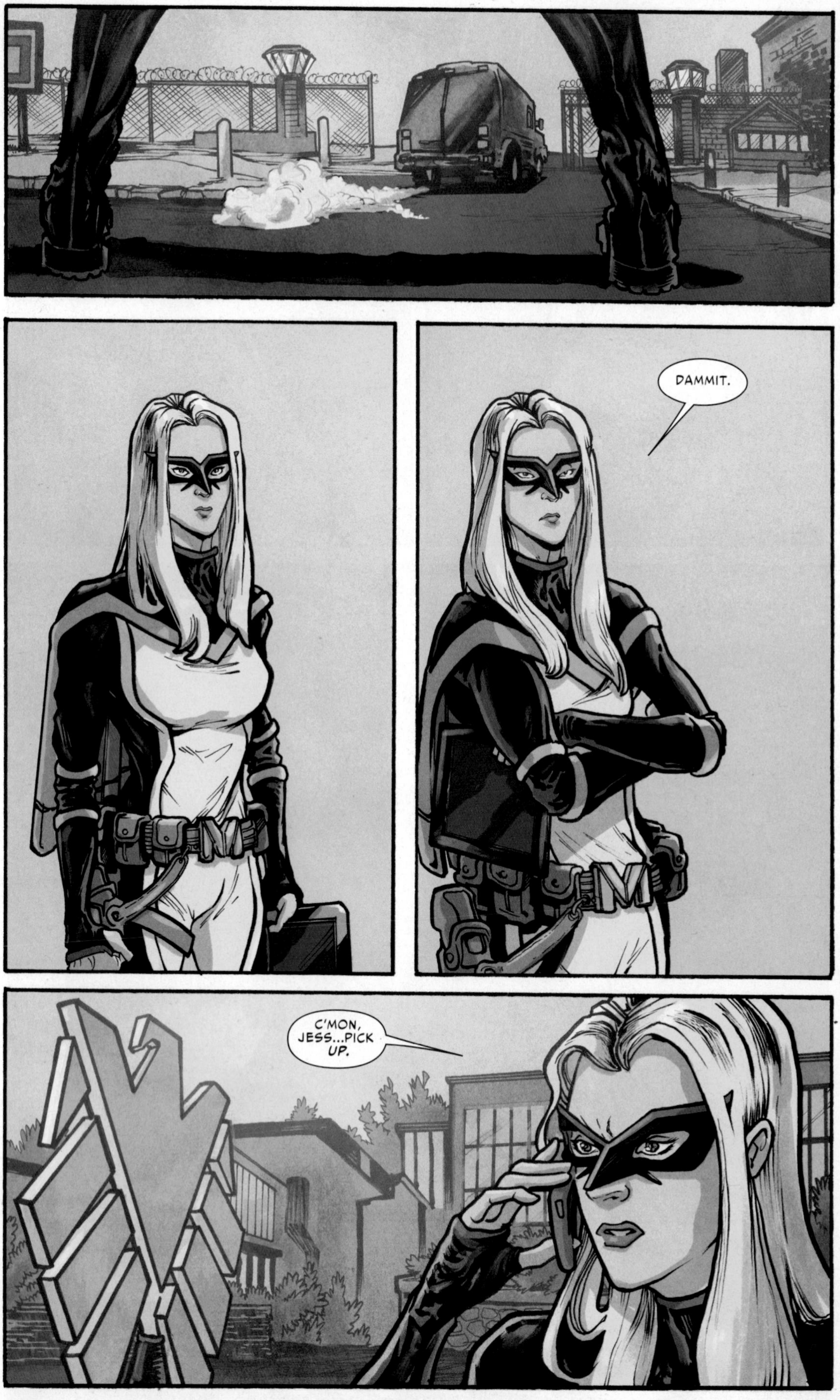
DAMMIT.
C'MON, JESS...PICK UP.

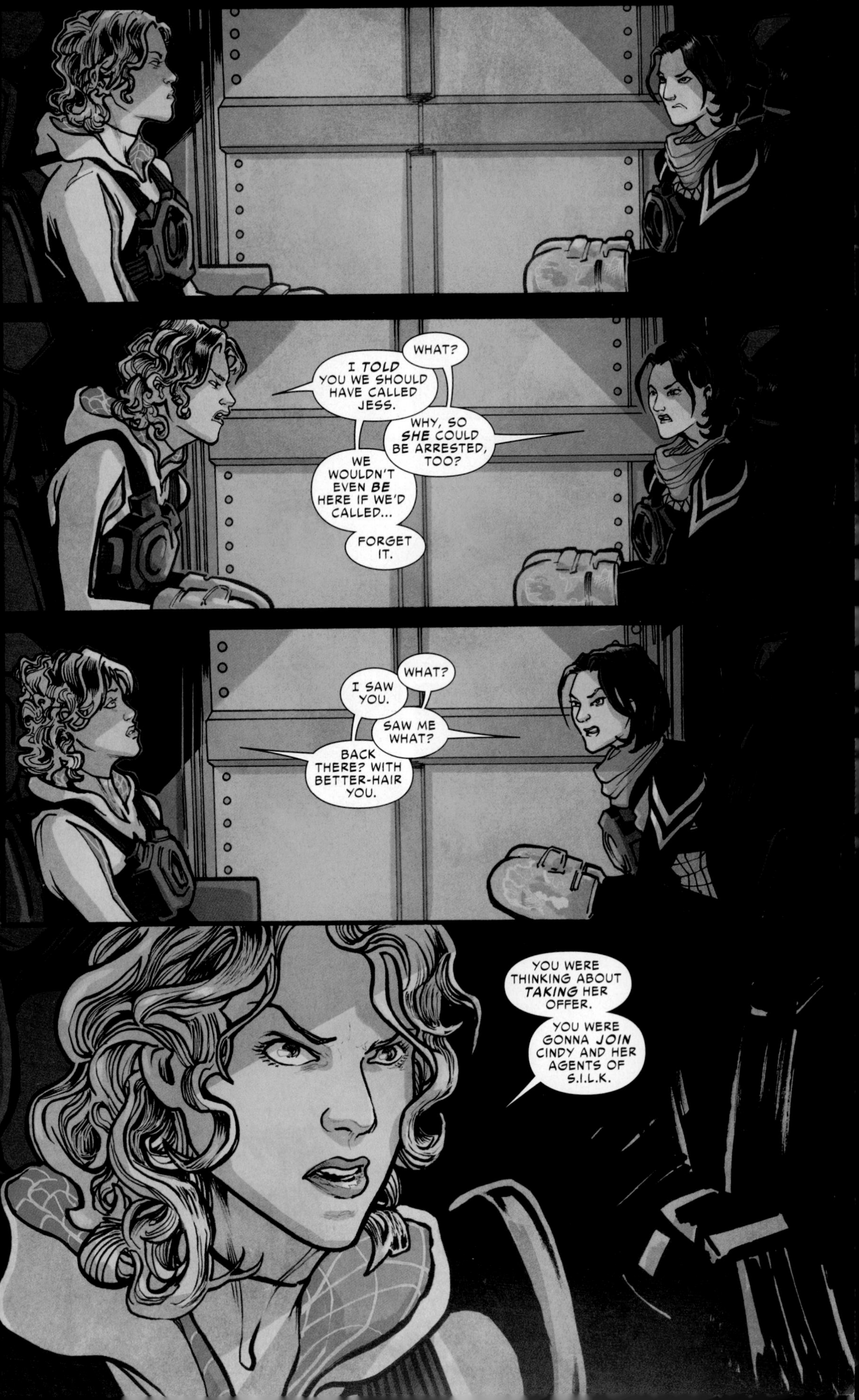
WHAT?
I TOLD YOU WE SHOULD HAVE CALLED JESS.
WHY, SO SHE COULD BE ARRESTED, TOO?
WE WOULDN'T EVEN BE HERE IF WE'D CALLED...
FORGET IT.
WHAT?
I SAW YOU.
SAW ME WHAT?
BACK THERE? WITH BETTER-HAIR YOU.
YOU WERE THINKING ABOUT TAKING HER OFFER.
YOU WERE GONNA JOIN CINDY AND HER AGENTS OF S.I.L.K.

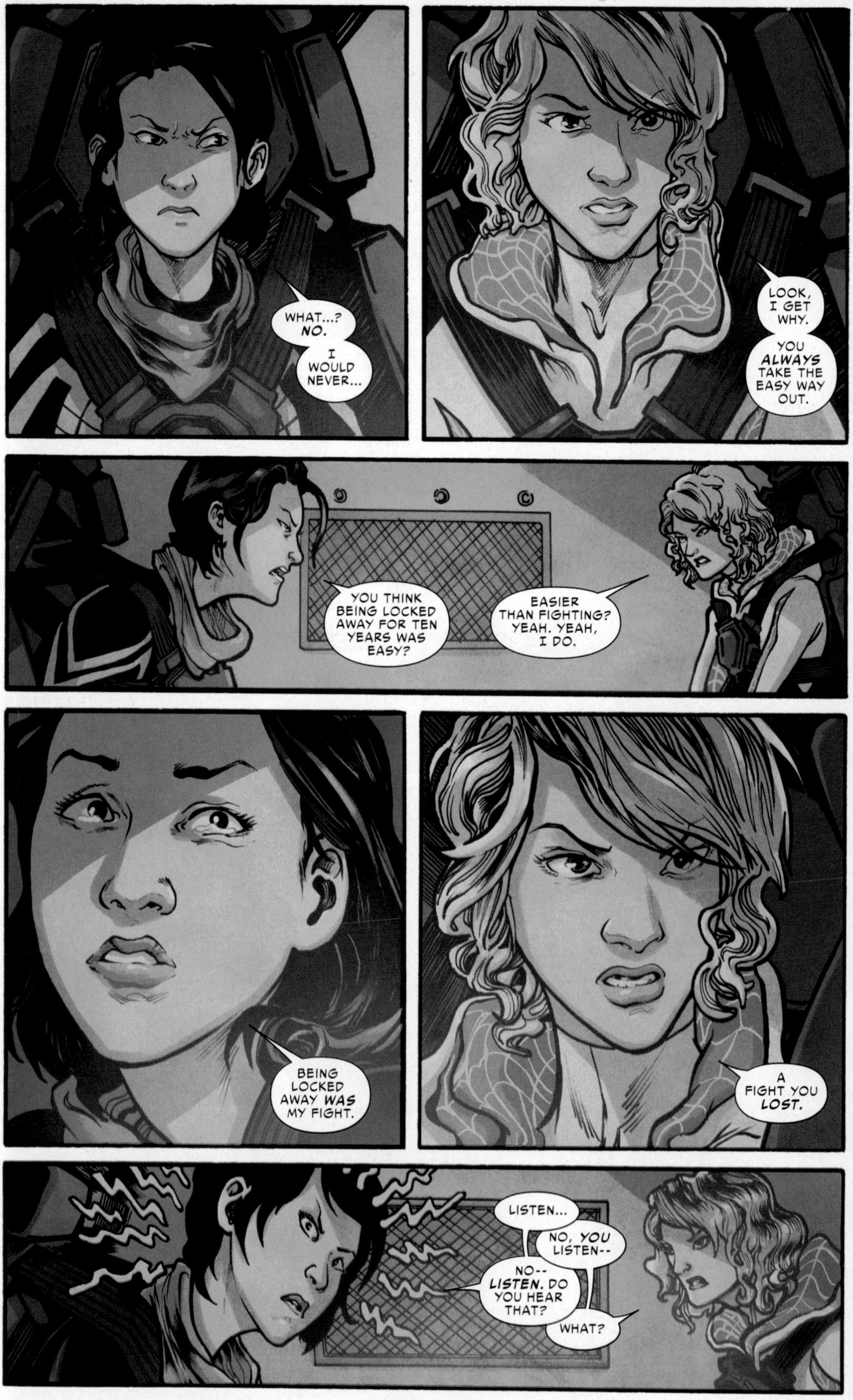
WHAT...? NO.
I WOULD NEVER...
LOOK, I GET WHY.
YOU ALWAYS TAKE THE EASY WAY OUT.
YOU THINK BEING LOCKED AWAY FOR TEN YEARS WAS EASY?
EASIER THAN FIGHTING? YEAH. YEAH, I DO.
BEING LOCKED AWAY WAS MY FIGHT.
A FIGHT YOU LOST.
LISTEN...
NO, YOU LISTEN--
NO-- LISTEN. DO YOU HEAR THAT?
WHAT?

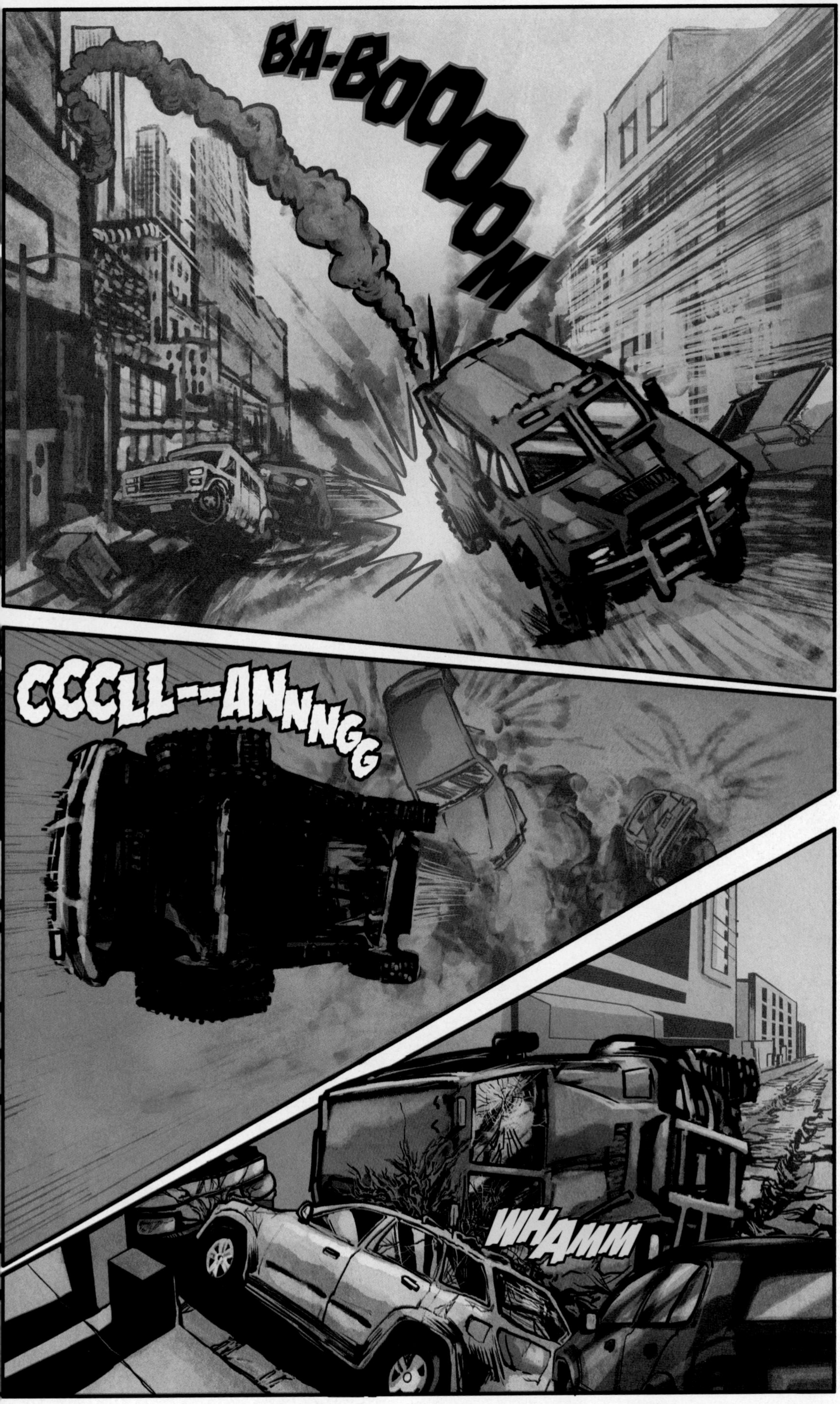
BA-BOOOOOM
CCCLL--ANNNGG
WHAMM

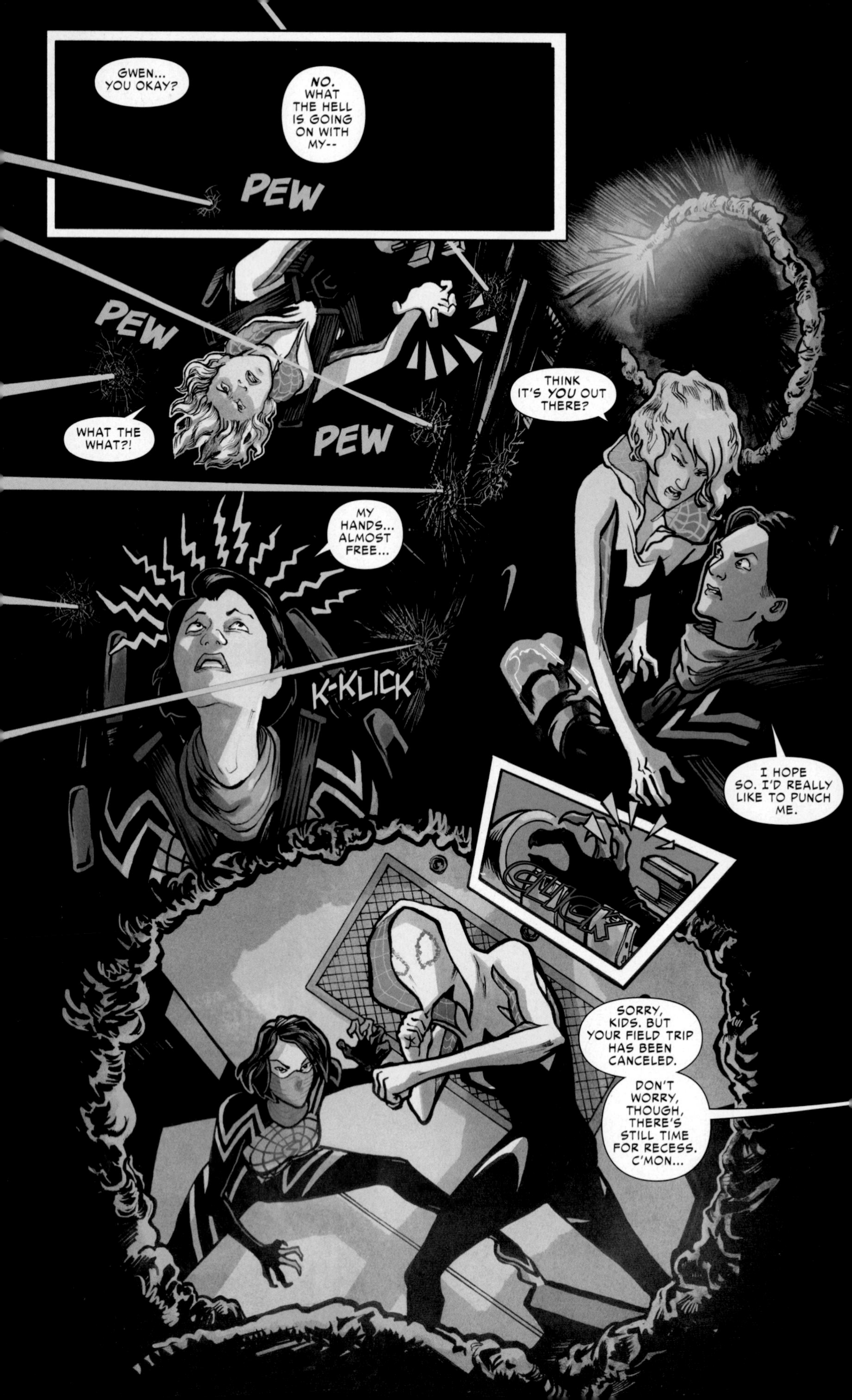
GWEN... YOU OKAY?
NO. WHAT THE HELL IS GOING ON WITH MY--
PEW
PEW
WHAT THE WHAT?!
PEW
THINK IT'S YOU OUT THERE?
MY HANDS... ALMOST FREE...
K-KLICK
I HOPE SO. I'D REALLY LIKE TO PUNCH ME.
CLICK
SORRY, KIDS. BUT YOUR FIELD TRIP HAS BEEN CANCELED.
DON'T WORRY, THOUGH, THERE'S STILL TIME FOR RECESS. C'MON...

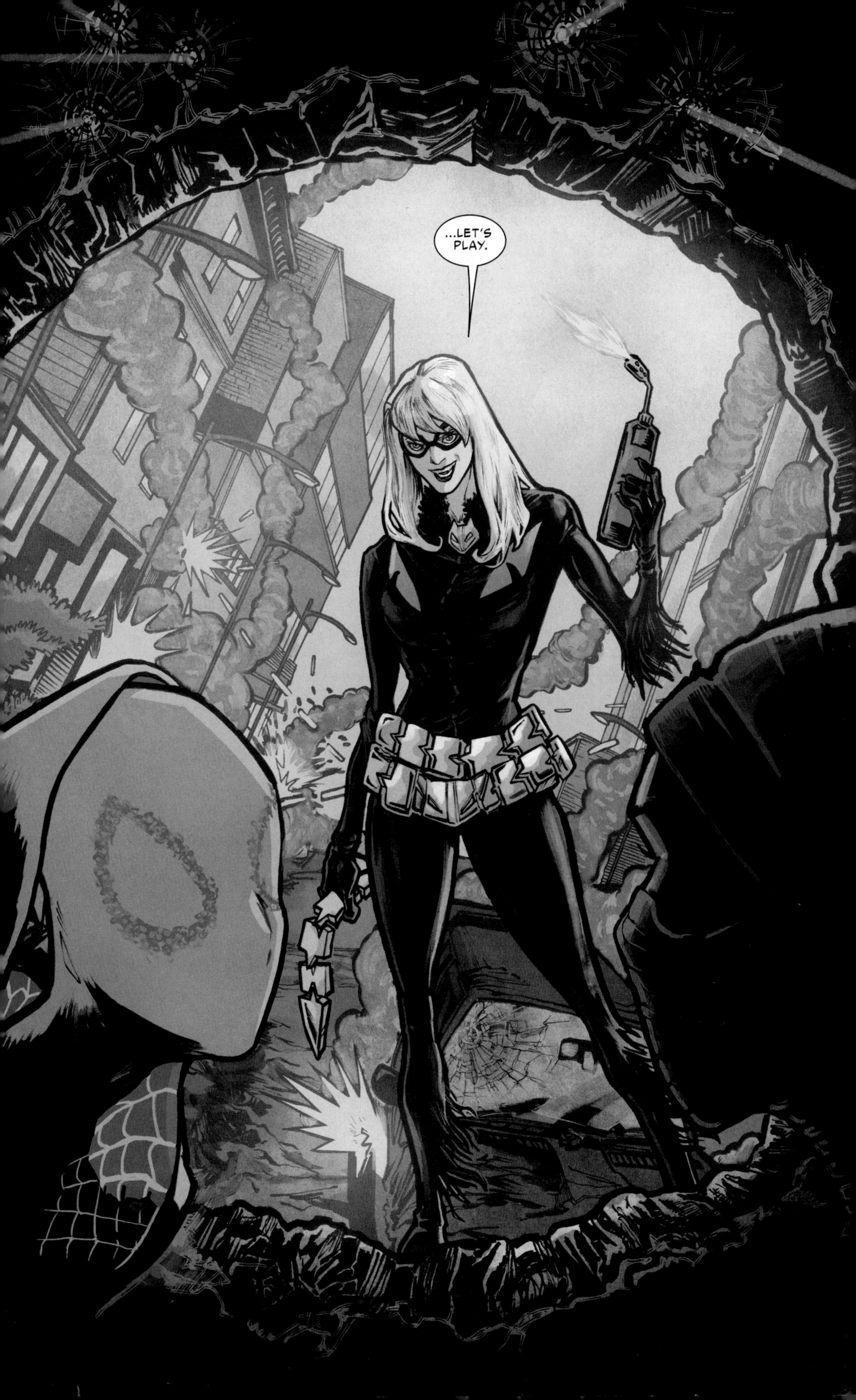
...LET'S PLAY.

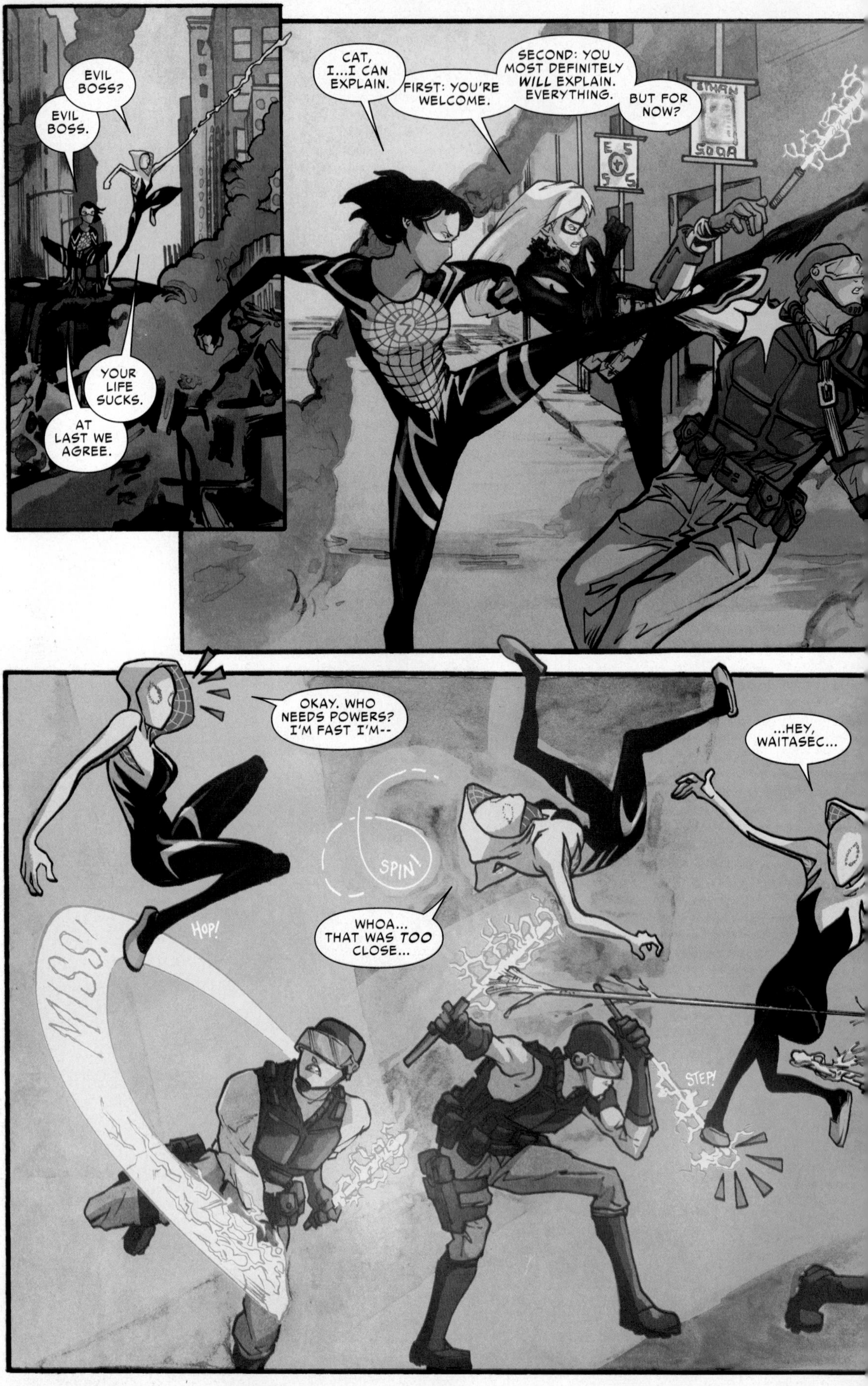
EVIL BOSS?
EVIL BOSS.
YOUR LIFE SUCKS.
AT LAST WE AGREE.
CAT, I...I CAN EXPLAIN.
FIRST: YOU'RE WELCOME.
SECOND: YOU MOST DEFINITELY *WILL* EXPLAIN. EVERYTHING.
BUT FOR NOW?
OKAY. WHO NEEDS POWERS? I'M FAST I'M--
SPIN!
...HEY, WAITASEC...
HOP!
WHOA... THAT WAS *TOO* CLOSE...
MISS!
STEP!

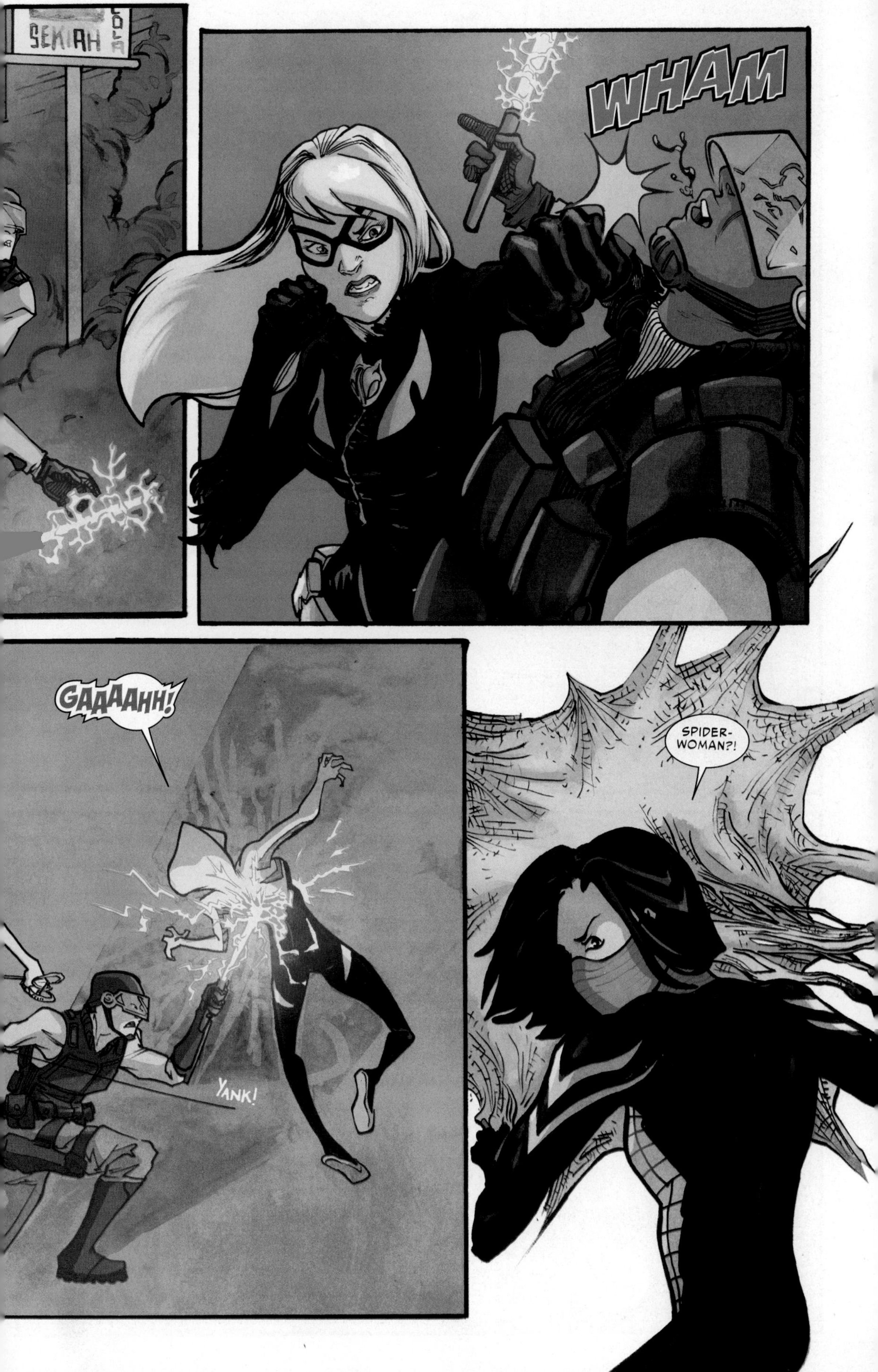
SEKIAH
COLA
WHAM
GAAAAHH!
YANK!
SPIDER-
WOMAN?!

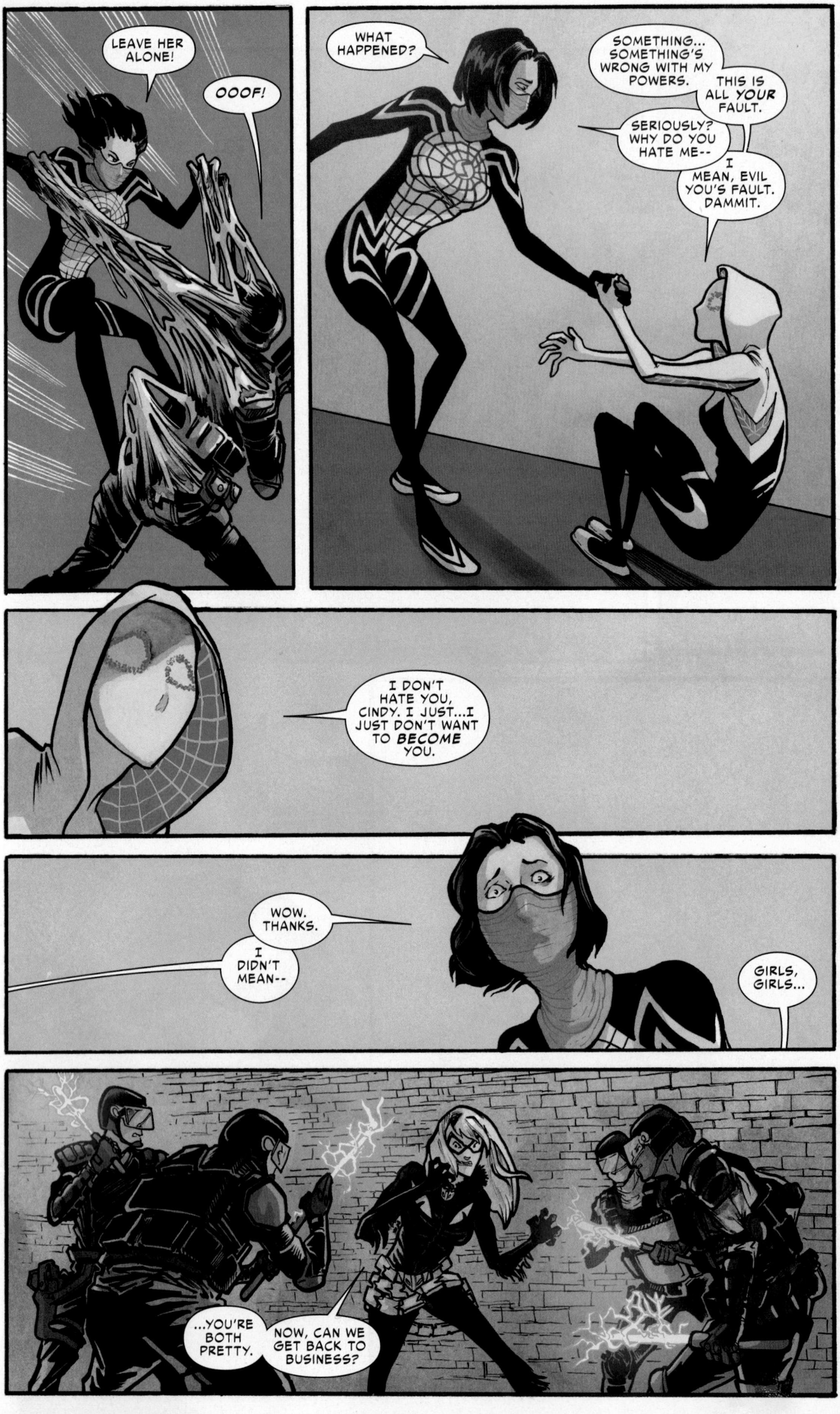
LEAVE HER ALONE!
OOOF!
WHAT HAPPENED?
SOMETHING... SOMETHING'S WRONG WITH MY POWERS.
THIS IS ALL YOUR FAULT.
SERIOUSLY? WHY DO YOU HATE ME--
I MEAN, EVIL YOU'S FAULT. DAMMIT.
I DON'T HATE YOU, CINDY. I JUST...I JUST DON'T WANT TO BECOME YOU.
WOW. THANKS.
I DIDN'T MEAN--
GIRLS, GIRLS...
...YOU'RE BOTH PRETTY.
NOW, CAN WE GET BACK TO BUSINESS?

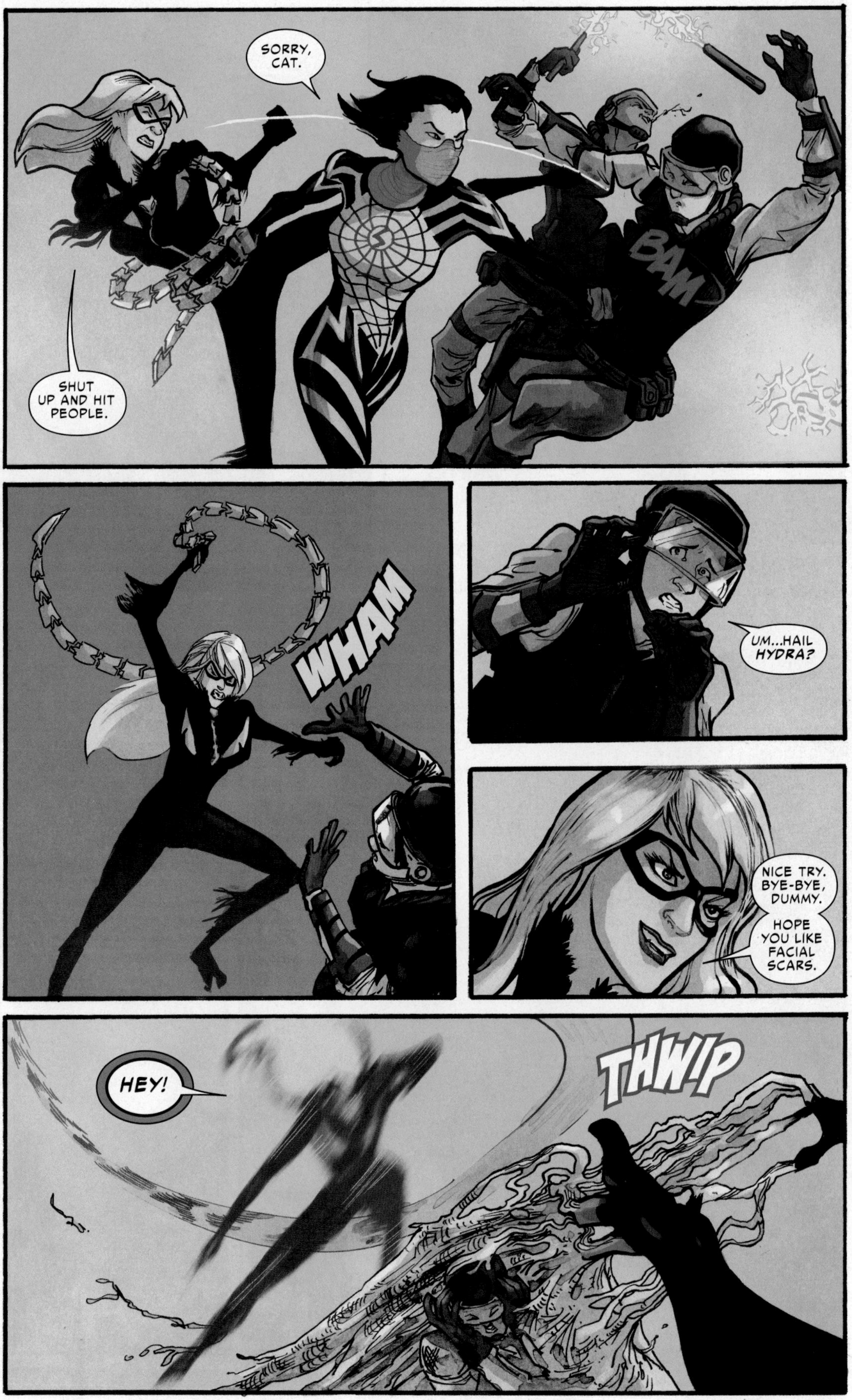
SORRY, CAT.
BAM
SHUT UP AND HIT PEOPLE.
WHAM
UM...HAIL HYDRA?
NICE TRY. BYE-BYE, DUMMY.
HOPE YOU LIKE FACIAL SCARS.
HEY!
THWIP

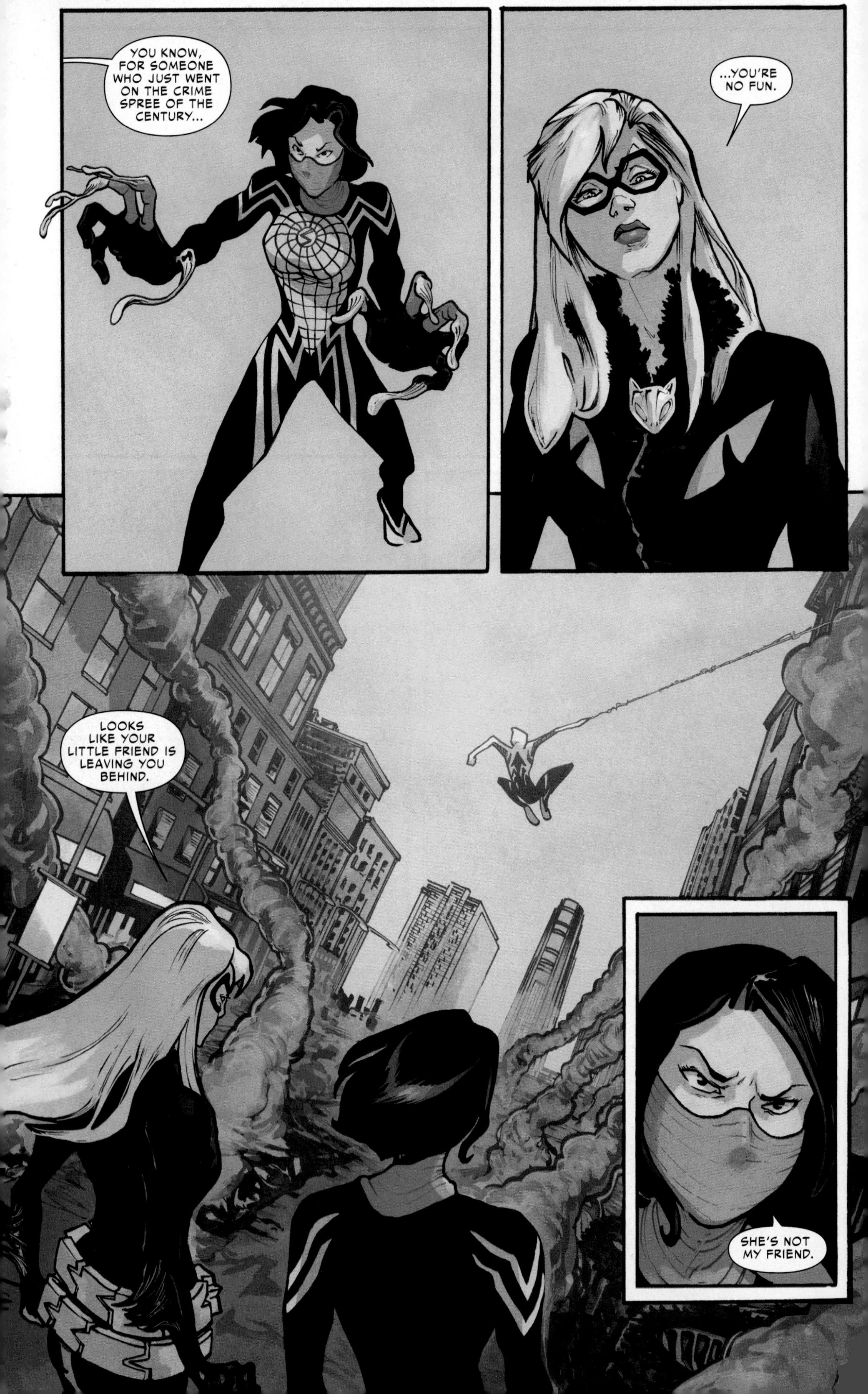
YOU KNOW, FOR SOMEONE WHO JUST WENT ON THE CRIME SPREE OF THE CENTURY...
...YOU'RE NO FUN.
LOOKS LIKE YOUR LITTLE FRIEND IS LEAVING YOU BEHIND.
SHE'S NOT MY FRIEND.

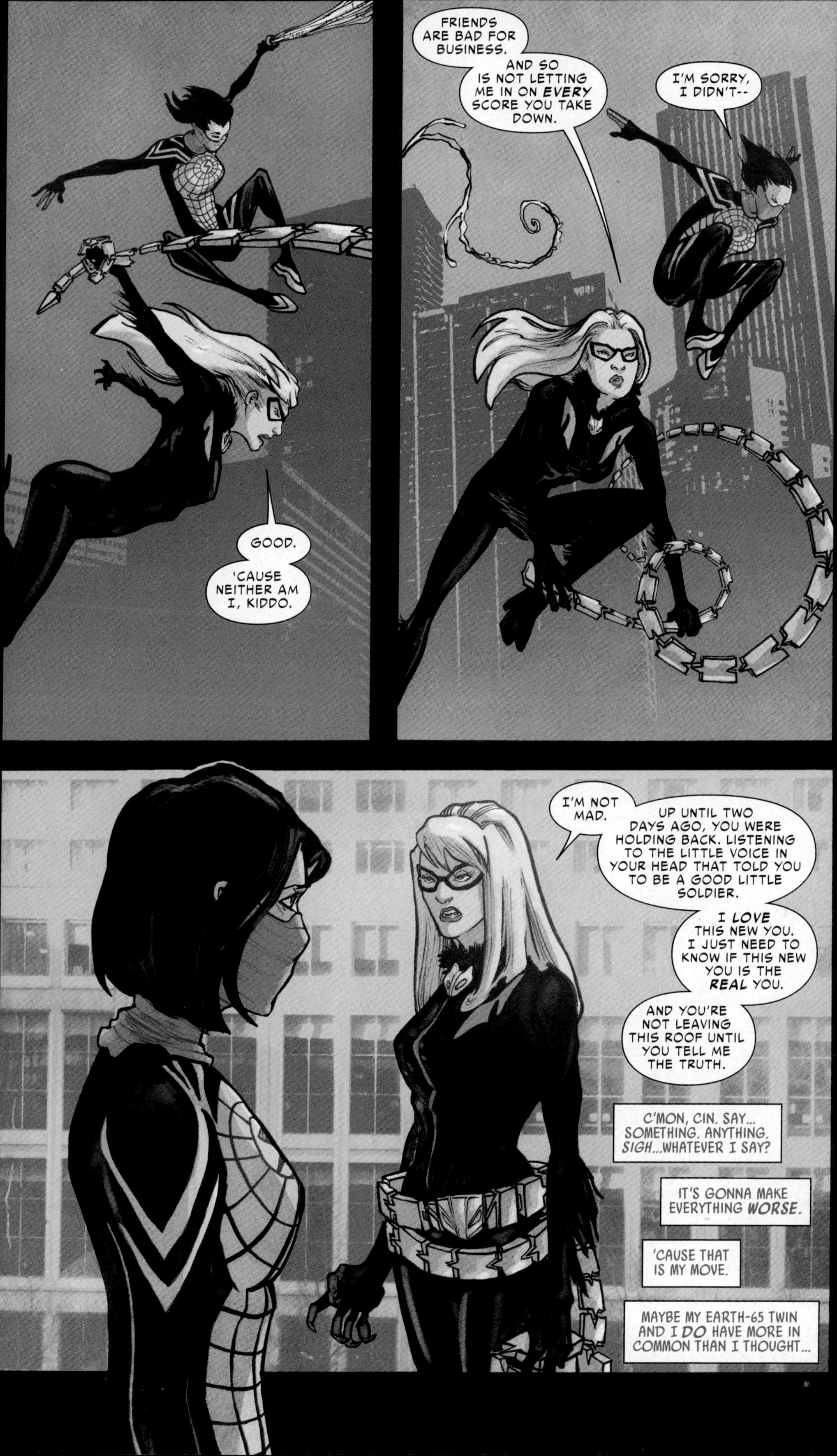

GOOD.
'CAUSE NEITHER AM I, KIDDO.
FRIENDS ARE BAD FOR BUSINESS.
AND SO IS NOT LETTING ME IN ON EVERY SCORE YOU TAKE DOWN.
I'M SORRY, I DIDN'T--
I'M NOT MAD.
UP UNTIL TWO DAYS AGO, YOU WERE HOLDING BACK. LISTENING TO THE LITTLE VOICE IN YOUR HEAD THAT TOLD YOU TO BE A GOOD LITTLE SOLDIER.
I LOVE THIS NEW YOU. I JUST NEED TO KNOW IF THIS NEW YOU IS THE REAL YOU.
AND YOU'RE NOT LEAVING THIS ROOF UNTIL YOU TELL ME THE TRUTH.
C'MON, CIN. SAY... SOMETHING. ANYTHING. SIGH...WHATEVER I SAY?
IT'S GONNA MAKE EVERYTHING WORSE.
'CAUSE THAT IS MY MOVE.
MAYBE MY EARTH-65 TWIN AND I DO HAVE MORE IN COMMON THAN I THOUGHT...

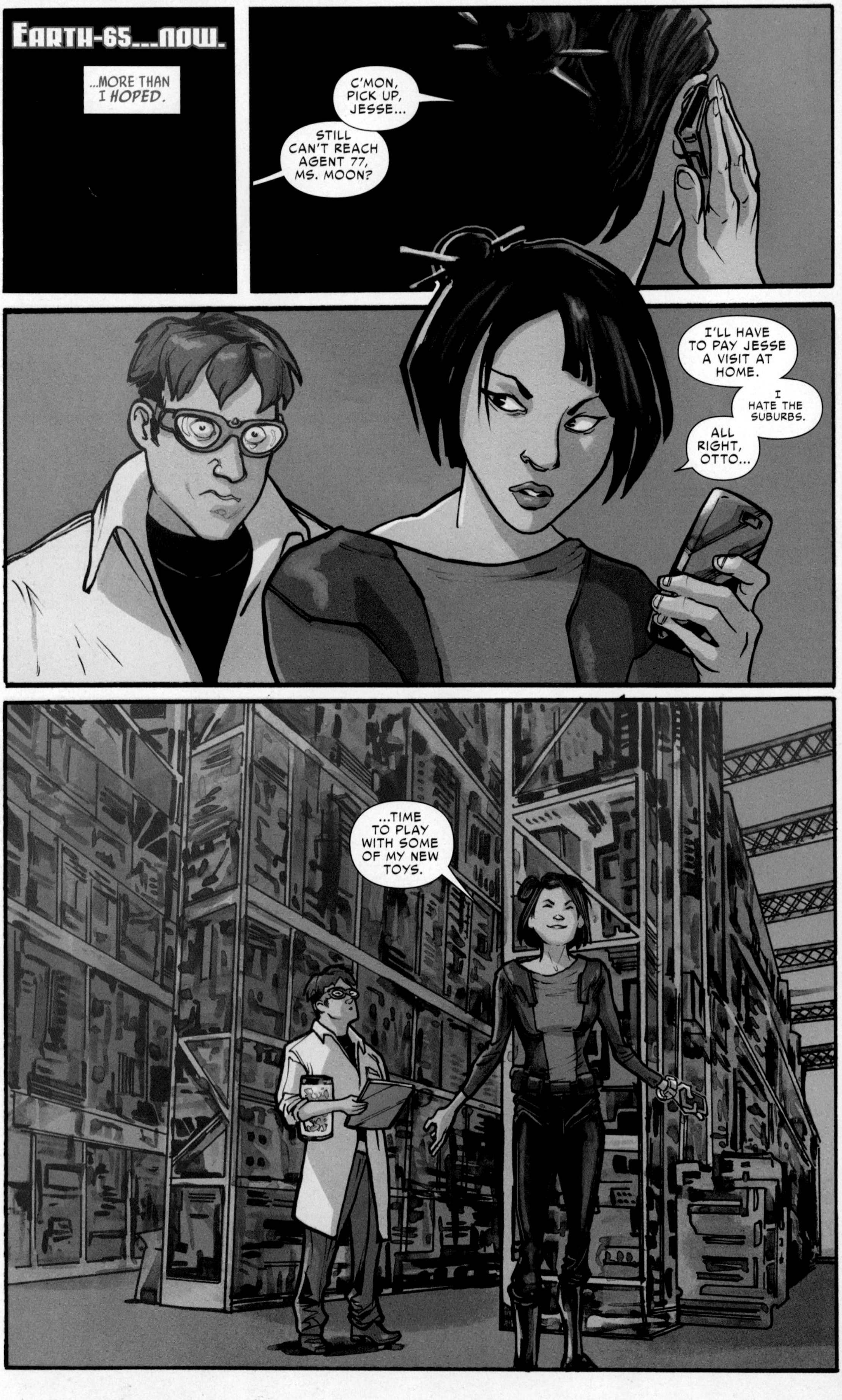
EARTH-65...NOW.
...MORE THAN I HOPED.
C'MON, PICK UP, JESSE...
STILL CAN'T REACH AGENT 77, MS. MOON?
I'LL HAVE TO PAY JESSE A VISIT AT HOME.
I HATE THE SUBURBS.
ALL RIGHT, OTTO...
...TIME TO PLAY WITH SOME OF MY NEW TOYS.

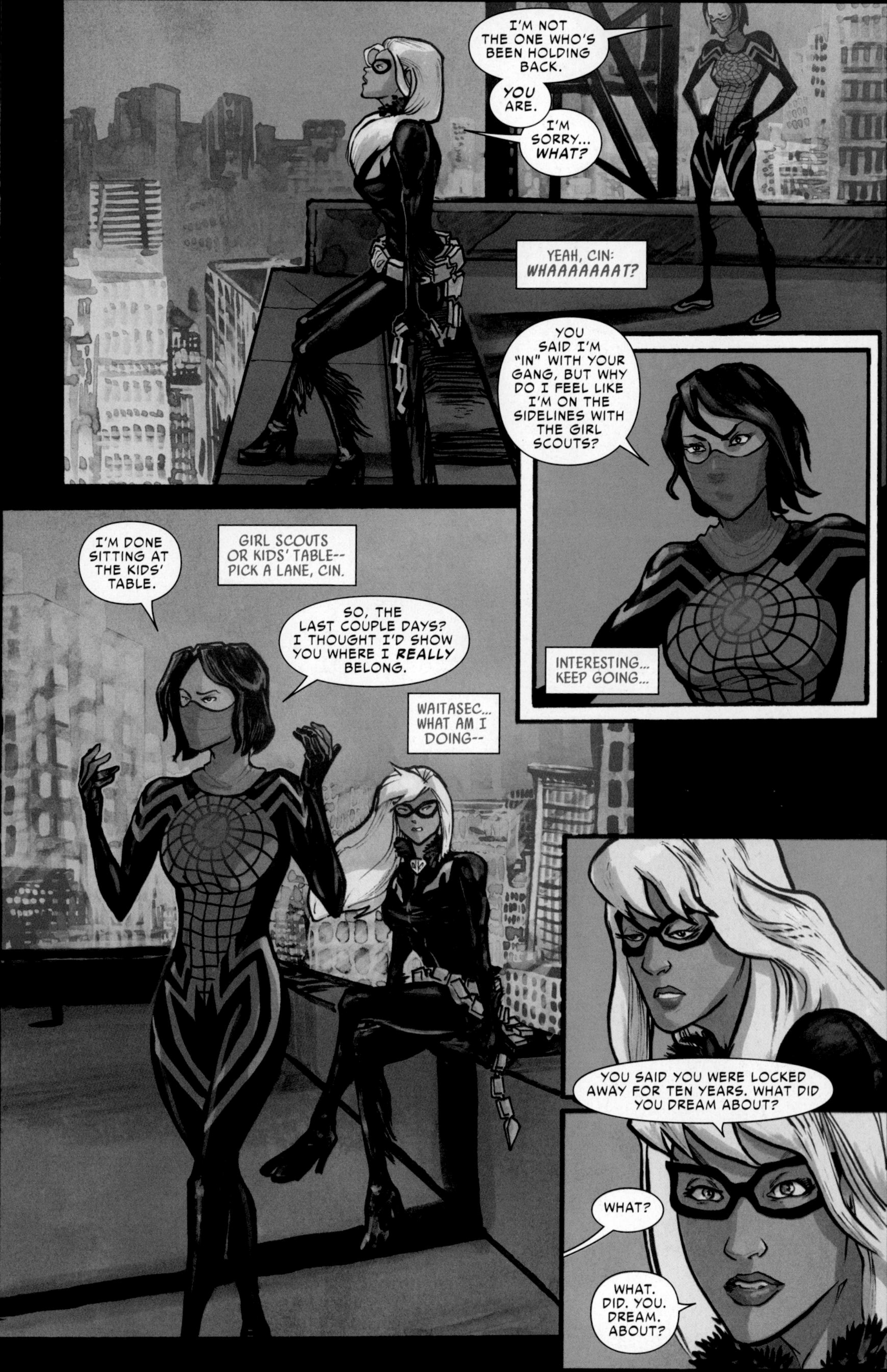

I'M NOT THE ONE WHO'S BEEN HOLDING BACK.
YOU ARE.
I'M SORRY... WHAT?
YEAH, CIN: WHAAAAAAAT?
YOU SAID I'M "IN" WITH YOUR GANG, BUT WHY DO I FEEL LIKE I'M ON THE SIDELINES WITH THE GIRL SCOUTS?
INTERESTING... KEEP GOING...
I'M DONE SITTING AT THE KIDS' TABLE.
GIRL SCOUTS OR KIDS' TABLE-- PICK A LANE, CIN.
SO, THE LAST COUPLE DAYS? I THOUGHT I'D SHOW YOU WHERE I REALLY BELONG.
WAITASEC... WHAT AM I DOING--
YOU SAID YOU WERE LOCKED AWAY FOR TEN YEARS. WHAT DID YOU DREAM ABOUT?
WHAT?
WHAT. DID. YOU. DREAM. ABOUT?

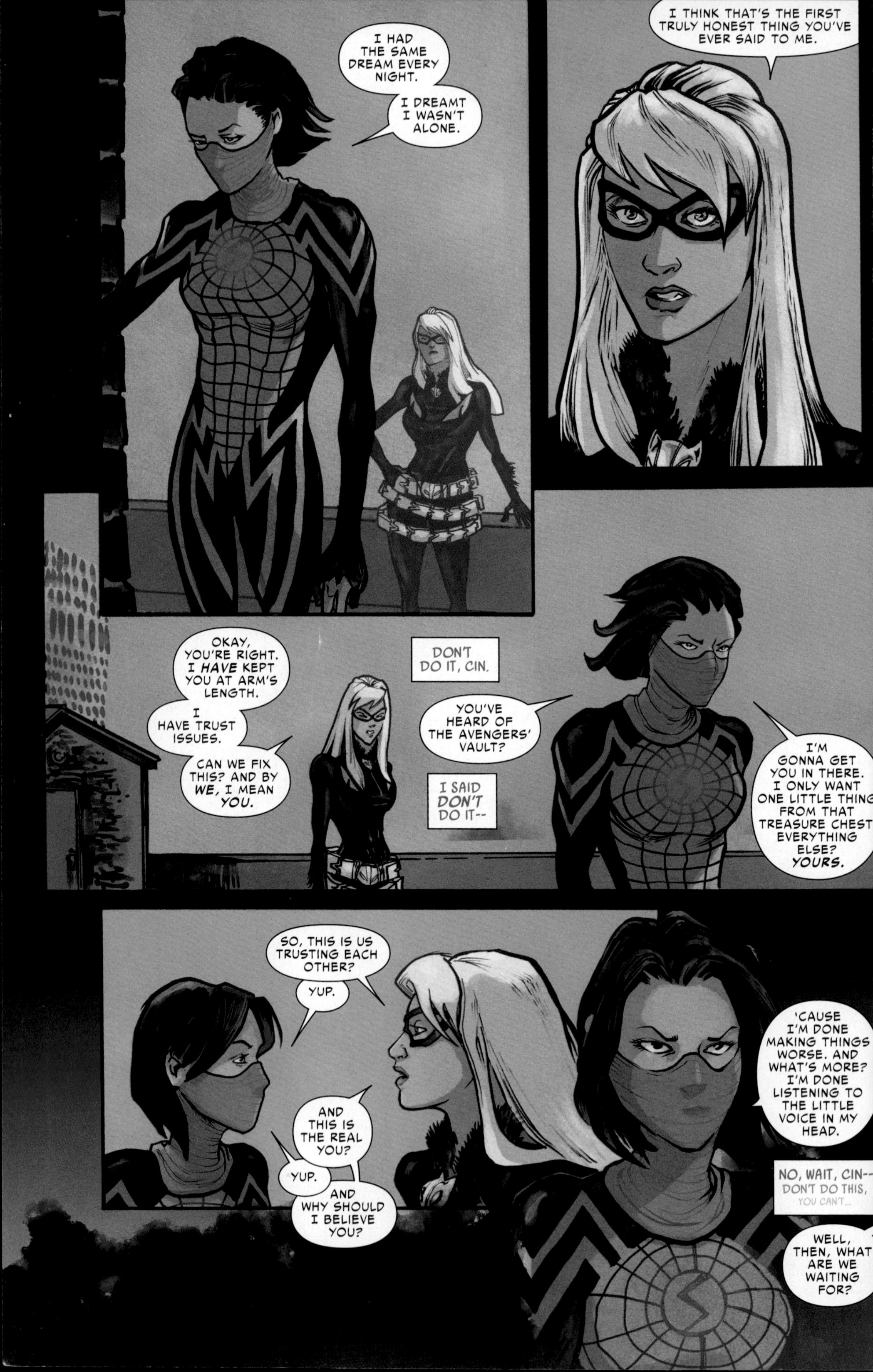
I HAD THE SAME DREAM EVERY NIGHT.
I DREAMT I WASN'T ALONE.
I THINK THAT'S THE FIRST TRULY HONEST THING YOU'VE EVER SAID TO ME.
OKAY, YOU'RE RIGHT. I *HAVE* KEPT YOU AT ARM'S LENGTH.
I HAVE TRUST ISSUES.
CAN WE FIX THIS? AND BY *WE*, I MEAN *YOU*.
DON'T DO IT, CIN.
YOU'VE HEARD OF THE AVENGERS' VAULT?
I SAID *DON'T* DO IT--
I'M GONNA GET YOU IN THERE. I ONLY WANT ONE LITTLE THING FROM THAT TREASURE CHEST. EVERYTHING ELSE? *YOURS.*
SO, THIS IS US TRUSTING EACH OTHER?
YUP.
AND THIS IS THE REAL YOU?
YUP.
AND WHY SHOULD I BELIEVE YOU?
'CAUSE I'M DONE MAKING THINGS WORSE. AND WHAT'S MORE? I'M DONE LISTENING TO THE LITTLE VOICE IN MY HEAD.
NO, WAIT, CIN-- DON'T DO THIS, YOU CAN'T...
WELL, THEN, WHAT ARE WE WAITING FOR?

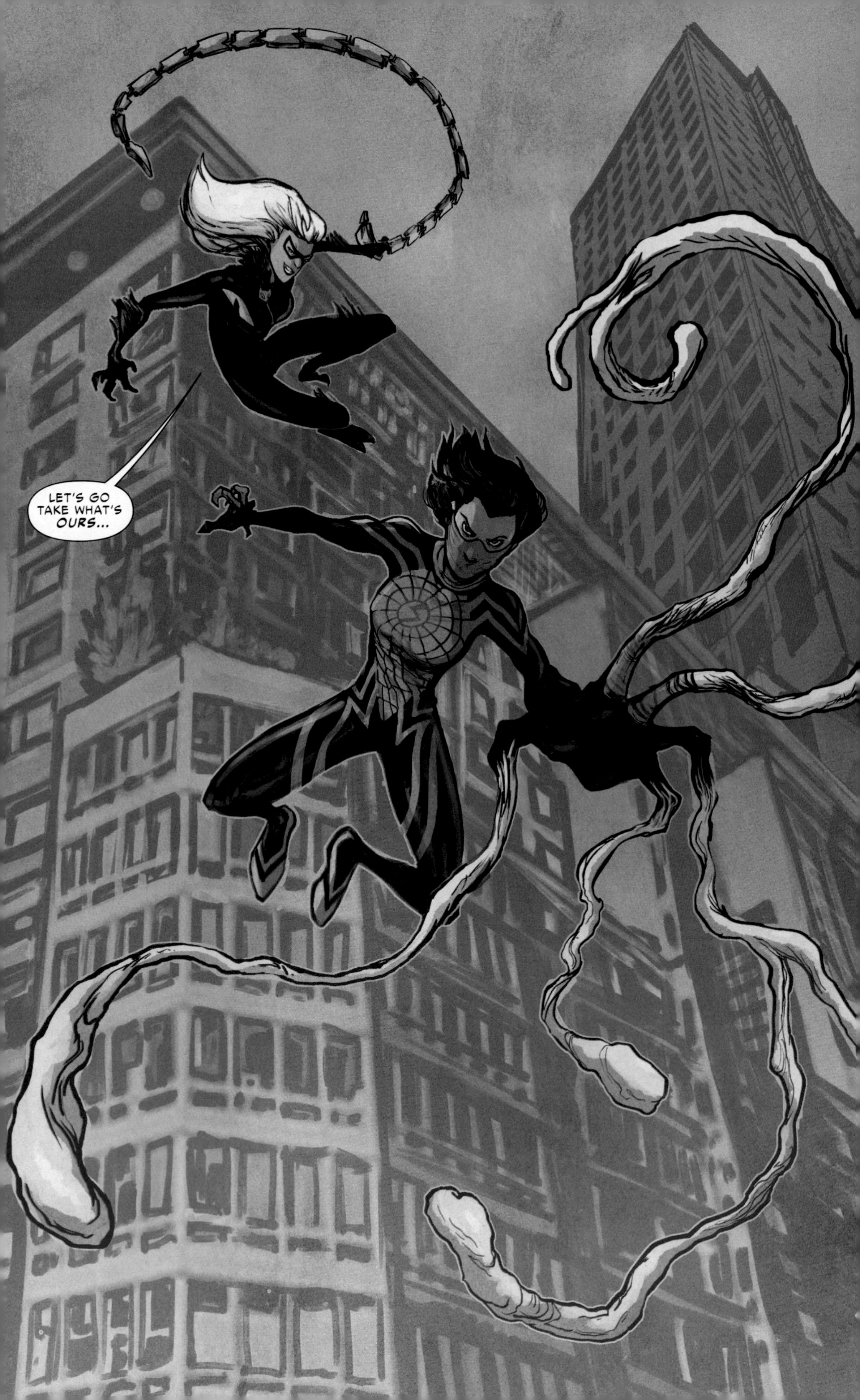
LET'S GO TAKE WHAT'S OURS...

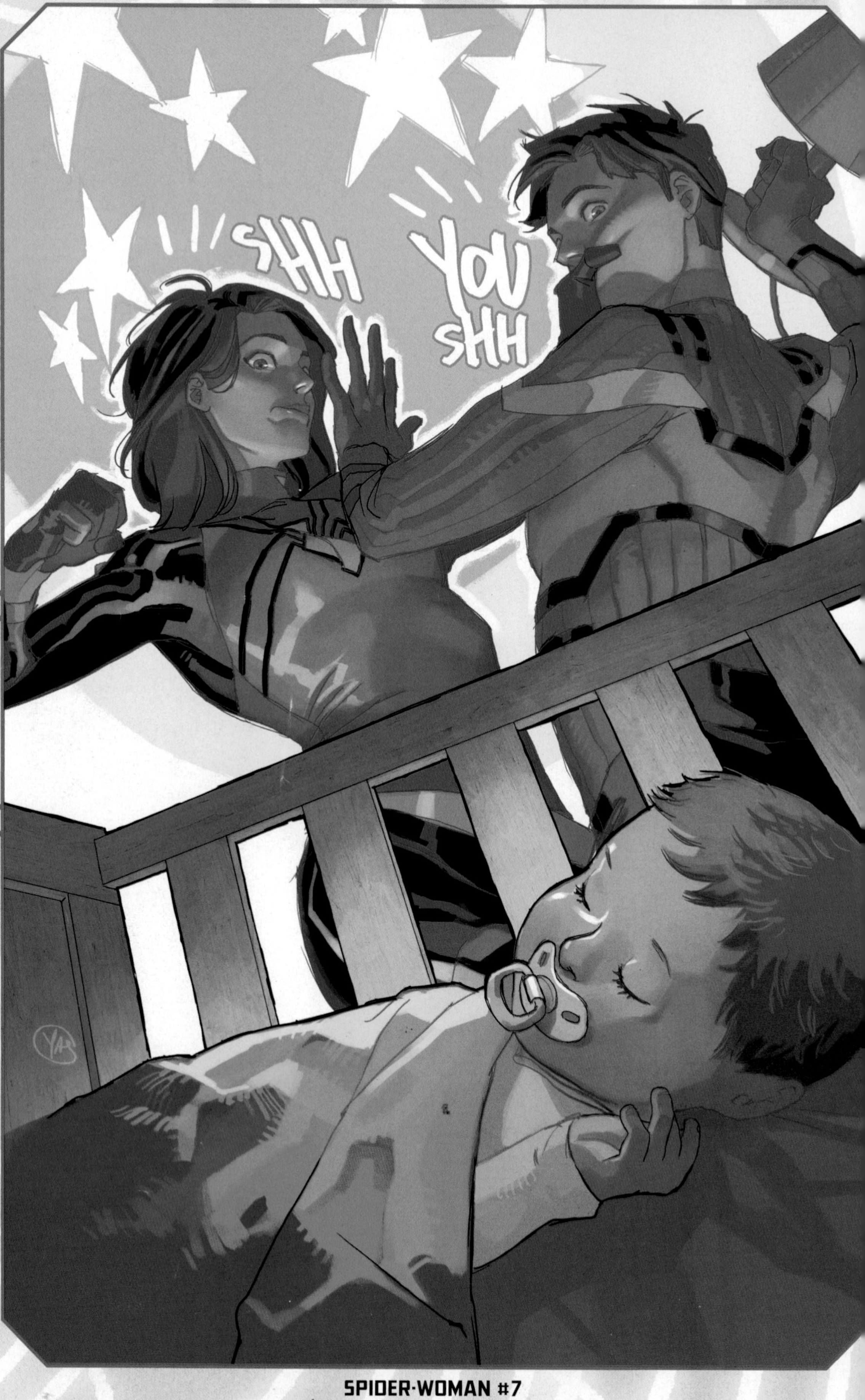
SHH
YOU SHH

SPIDER-WOMAN #7

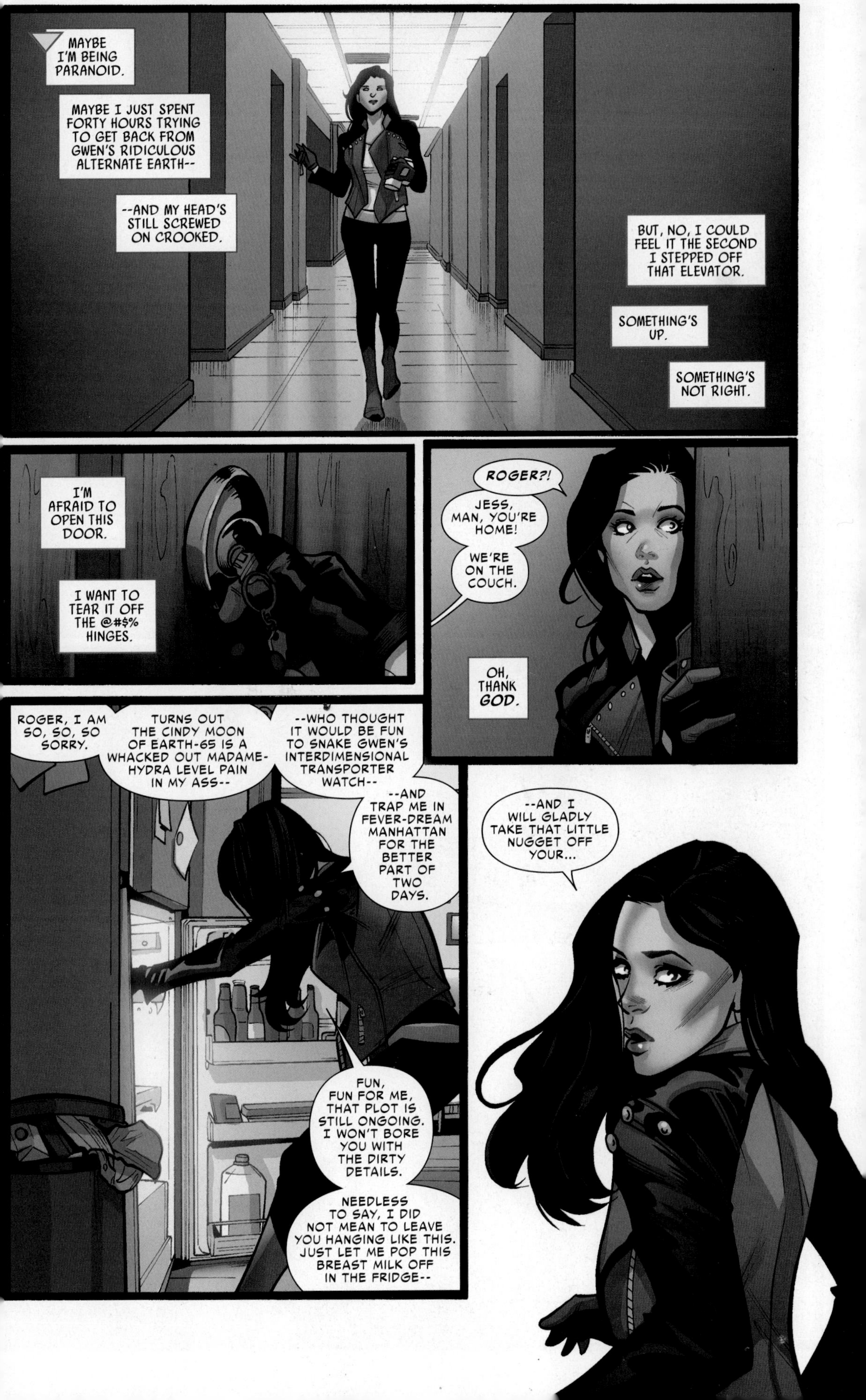

MAYBE I'M BEING PARANOID.
MAYBE I JUST SPENT FORTY HOURS TRYING TO GET BACK FROM GWEN'S RIDICULOUS ALTERNATE EARTH--
--AND MY HEAD'S STILL SCREWED ON CROOKED.
BUT, NO, I COULD FEEL IT THE SECOND I STEPPED OFF THAT ELEVATOR.
SOMETHING'S UP.
SOMETHING'S NOT RIGHT.
I'M AFRAID TO OPEN THIS DOOR.
I WANT TO TEAR IT OFF THE @#$% HINGES.
ROGER?!
JESS, MAN, YOU'RE HOME!
WE'RE ON THE COUCH.
OH, THANK GOD.
ROGER, I AM SO, SO, SO SORRY.
TURNS OUT THE CINDY MOON OF EARTH-65 IS A WHACKED OUT MADAME-HYDRA LEVEL PAIN IN MY ASS--
--WHO THOUGHT IT WOULD BE FUN TO SNAKE GWEN'S INTERDIMENSIONAL TRANSPORTER WATCH--
--AND TRAP ME IN FEVER-DREAM MANHATTAN FOR THE BETTER PART OF TWO DAYS.
FUN, FUN FOR ME, THAT PLOT IS STILL ONGOING. I WON'T BORE YOU WITH THE DIRTY DETAILS.
NEEDLESS TO SAY, I DID NOT MEAN TO LEAVE YOU HANGING LIKE THIS. JUST LET ME POP THIS BREAST MILK OFF IN THE FRIDGE--
--AND I WILL GLADLY TAKE THAT LITTLE NUGGET OFF YOUR...

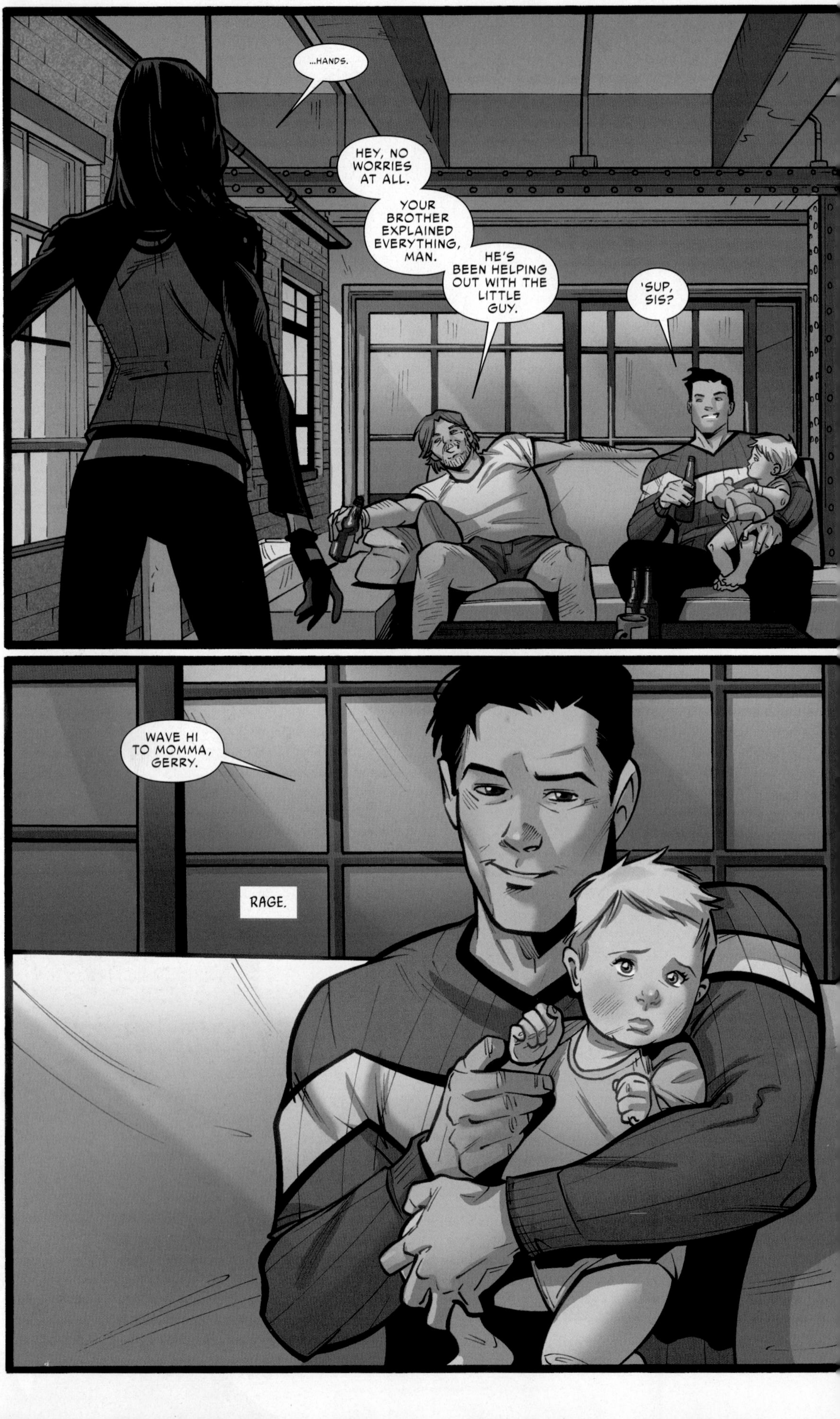
...HANDS.
HEY, NO WORRIES AT ALL.
YOUR BROTHER EXPLAINED EVERYTHING, MAN.
HE'S BEEN HELPING OUT WITH THE LITTLE GUY.
'SUP, SIS?
WAVE HI TO MOMMA, GERRY.
RAGE.

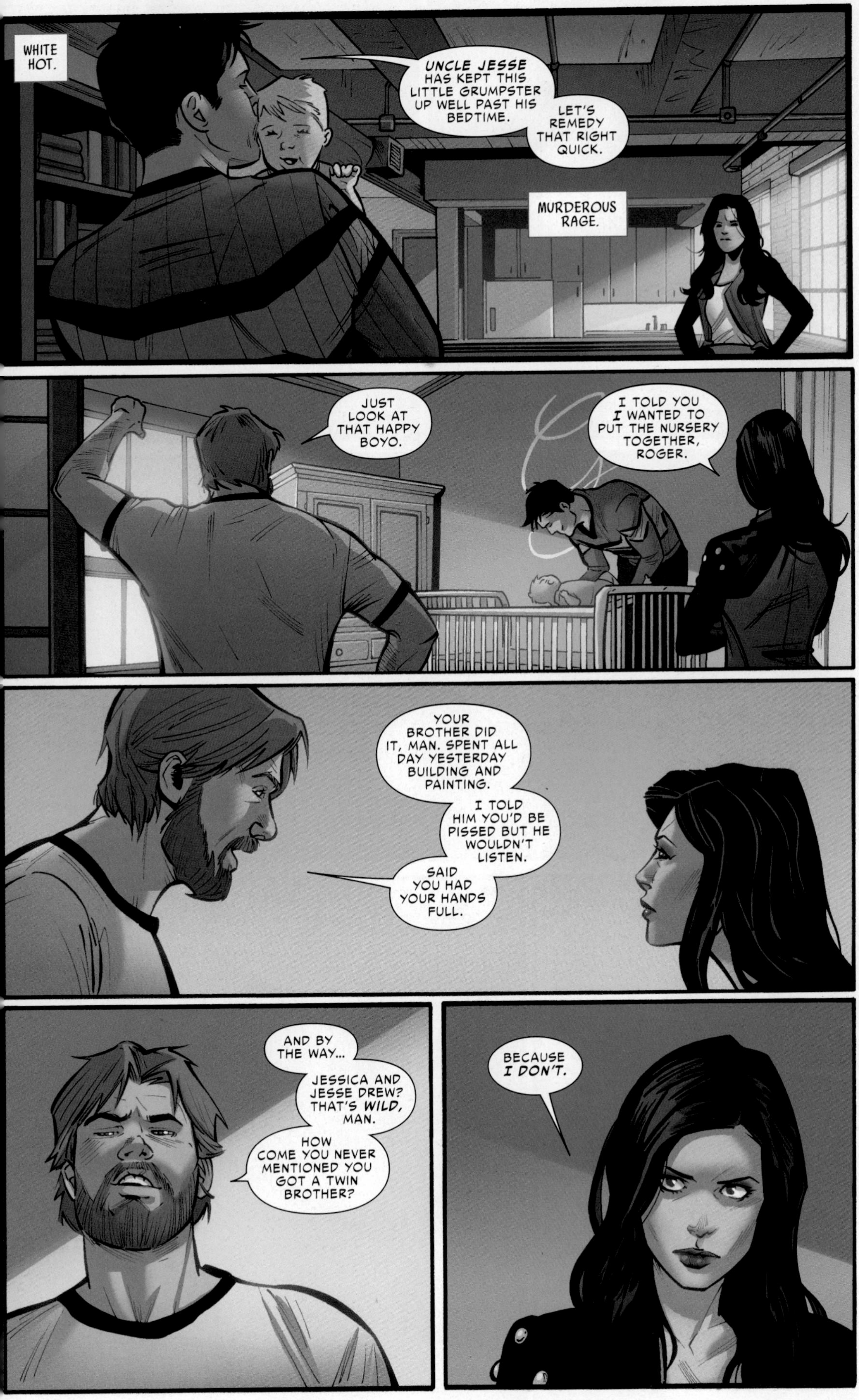
WHITE HOT.
UNCLE JESSE HAS KEPT THIS LITTLE GRUMPSTER UP WELL PAST HIS BEDTIME.
LET'S REMEDY THAT RIGHT QUICK.
MURDEROUS RAGE.
JUST LOOK AT THAT HAPPY BOYO.
I TOLD YOU I WANTED TO PUT THE NURSERY TOGETHER, ROGER.
YOUR BROTHER DID IT, MAN. SPENT ALL DAY YESTERDAY BUILDING AND PAINTING.
I TOLD HIM YOU'D BE PISSED BUT HE WOULDN'T LISTEN.
SAID YOU HAD YOUR HANDS FULL.
AND BY THE WAY...
JESSICA AND JESSE DREW? THAT'S WILD, MAN.
HOW COME YOU NEVER MENTIONED YOU GOT A TWIN BROTHER?
BECAUSE I DON'T.

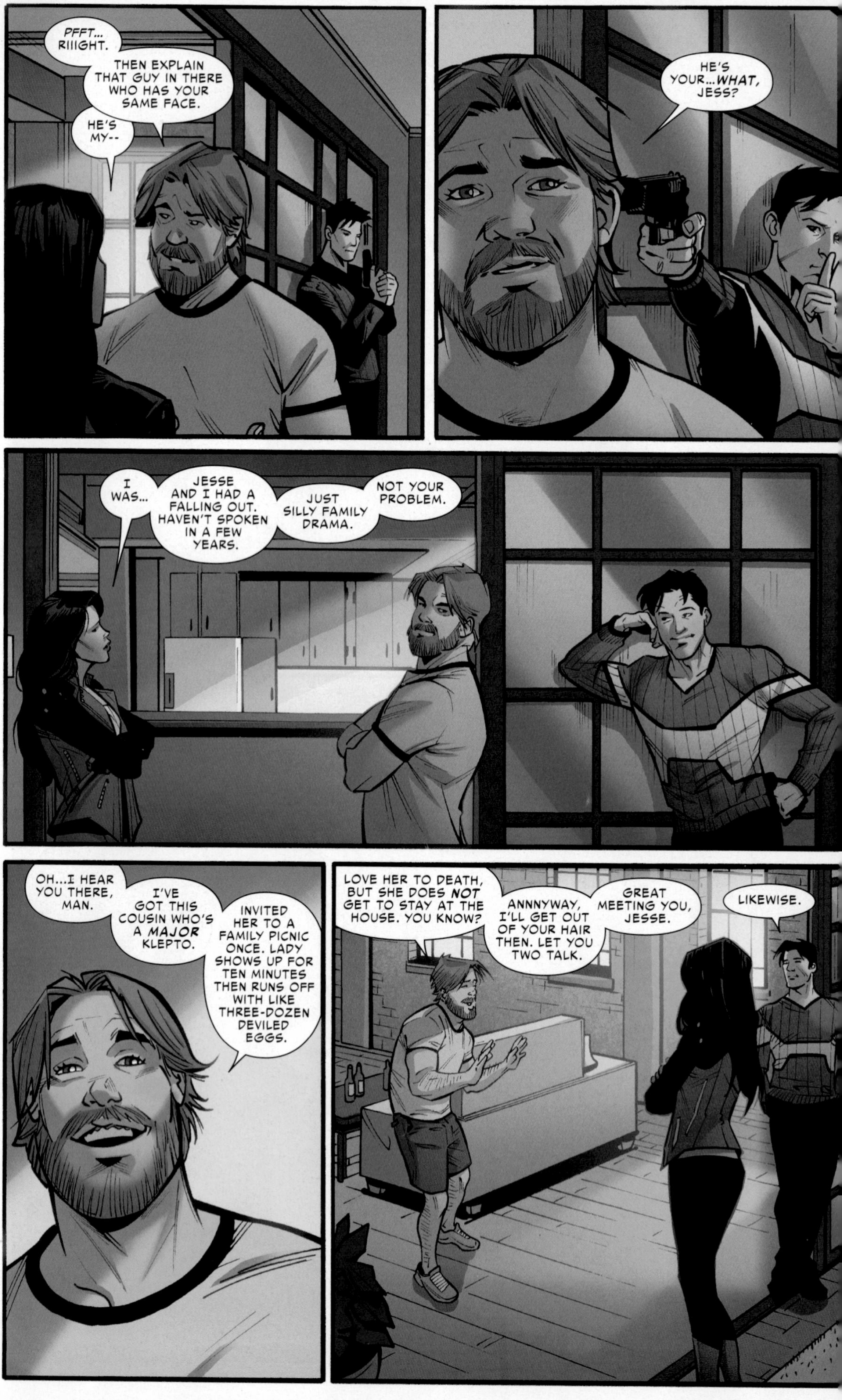
PFFT... RIIIGHT.
THEN EXPLAIN THAT GUY IN THERE WHO HAS YOUR SAME FACE.
HE'S MY--
HE'S YOUR...WHAT, JESS?
I WAS...
JESSE AND I HAD A FALLING OUT. HAVEN'T SPOKEN IN A FEW YEARS.
JUST SILLY FAMILY DRAMA.
NOT YOUR PROBLEM.
OH...I HEAR YOU THERE, MAN.
I'VE GOT THIS COUSIN WHO'S A MAJOR KLEPTO.
INVITED HER TO A FAMILY PICNIC ONCE. LADY SHOWS UP FOR TEN MINUTES THEN RUNS OFF WITH LIKE THREE-DOZEN DEVILED EGGS.
LOVE HER TO DEATH, BUT SHE DOES NOT GET TO STAY AT THE HOUSE. YOU KNOW?
ANNNYWAY, I'LL GET OUT OF YOUR HAIR THEN. LET YOU TWO TALK.
GREAT MEETING YOU, JESSE.
LIKEWISE.

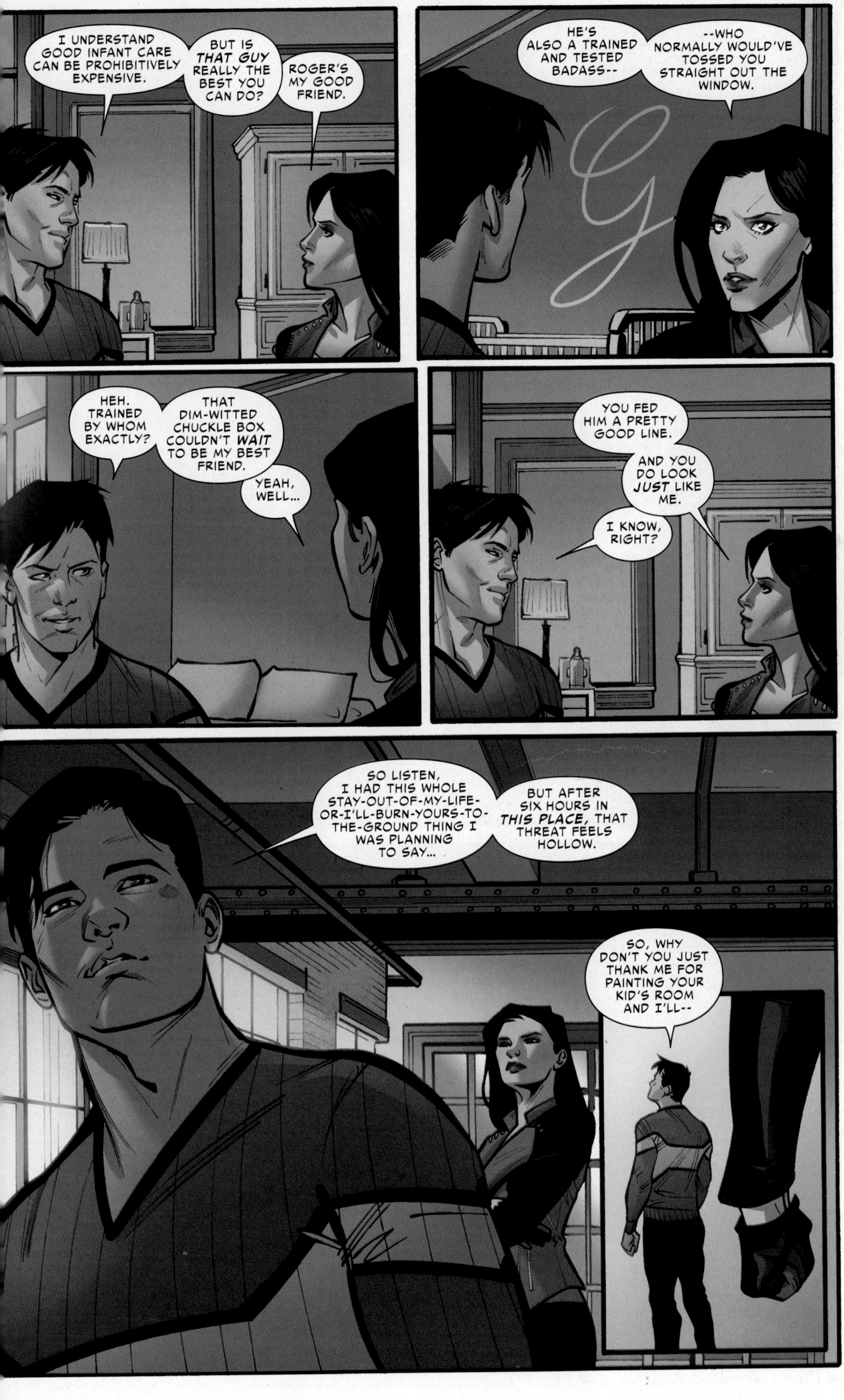
I UNDERSTAND GOOD INFANT CARE CAN BE PROHIBITIVELY EXPENSIVE.
BUT IS THAT GUY REALLY THE BEST YOU CAN DO?
ROGER'S MY GOOD FRIEND.
HE'S ALSO A TRAINED AND TESTED BADASS--
--WHO NORMALLY WOULD'VE TOSSED YOU STRAIGHT OUT THE WINDOW.
HEH. TRAINED BY WHOM EXACTLY?
THAT DIM-WITTED CHUCKLE BOX COULDN'T WAIT TO BE MY BEST FRIEND.
YEAH, WELL...
YOU FED HIM A PRETTY GOOD LINE.
AND YOU DO LOOK JUST LIKE ME.
I KNOW, RIGHT?
SO LISTEN, I HAD THIS WHOLE STAY-OUT-OF-MY-LIFE-OR-I'LL-BURN-YOURS-TO-THE-GROUND THING I WAS PLANNING TO SAY...
BUT AFTER SIX HOURS IN THIS PLACE, THAT THREAT FEELS HOLLOW.
SO, WHY DON'T YOU JUST THANK ME FOR PAINTING YOUR KID'S ROOM AND I'LL--

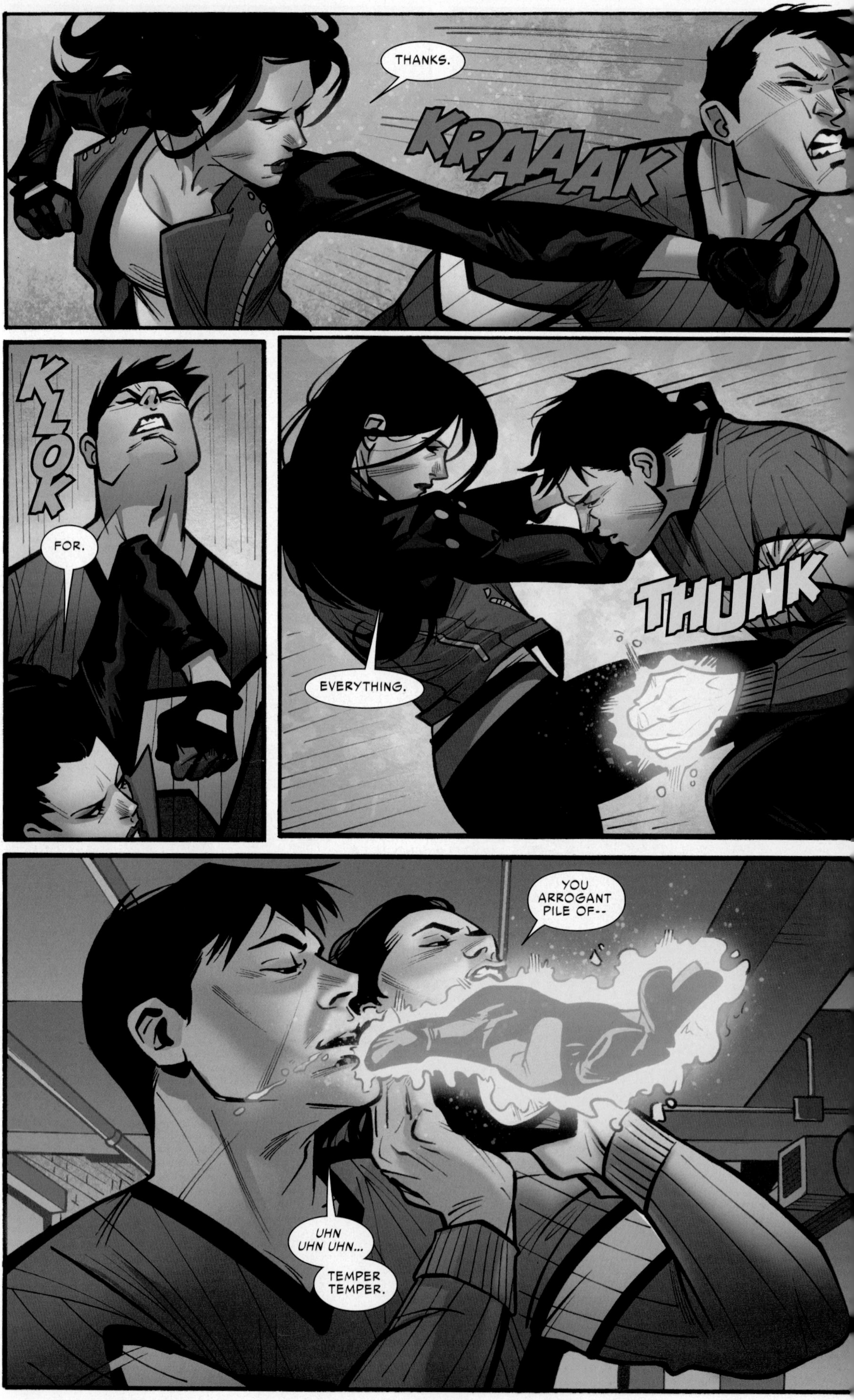
THANKS.
KRAAAK
KLOK
FOR.
EVERYTHING.
THUNK
YOU ARROGANT PILE OF--
UHN UHN UHN...
TEMPER TEMPER.

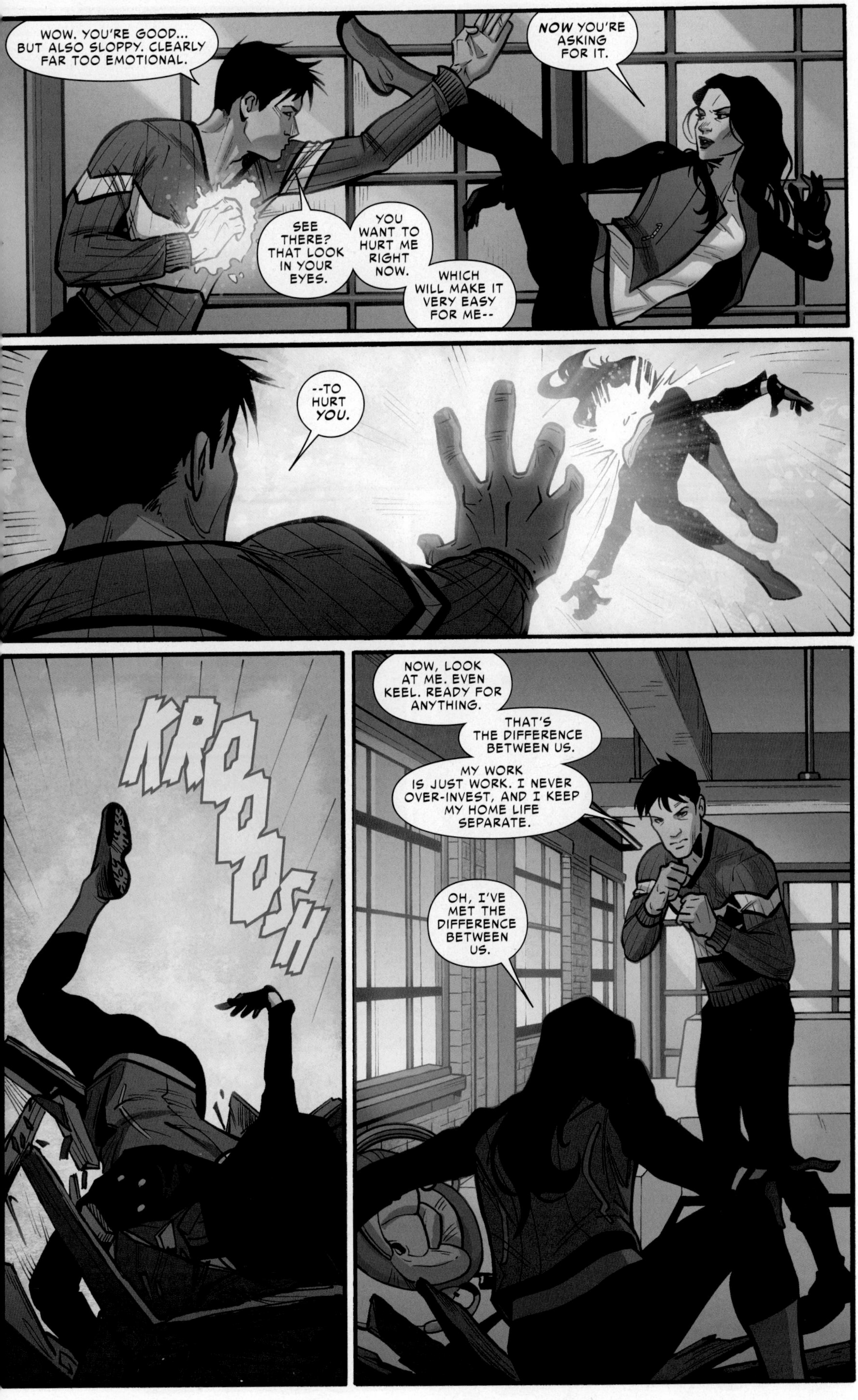
WOW. YOU'RE GOOD... BUT ALSO SLOPPY. CLEARLY FAR TOO EMOTIONAL.
NOW YOU'RE ASKING FOR IT.
SEE THERE? THAT LOOK IN YOUR EYES.
YOU WANT TO HURT ME RIGHT NOW.
WHICH WILL MAKE IT VERY EASY FOR ME--
--TO HURT YOU.
KROOSH
NOW, LOOK AT ME. EVEN KEEL. READY FOR ANYTHING.
THAT'S THE DIFFERENCE BETWEEN US.
MY WORK IS JUST WORK. I NEVER OVER-INVEST, AND I KEEP MY HOME LIFE SEPARATE.
OH, I'VE MET THE DIFFERENCE BETWEEN US.

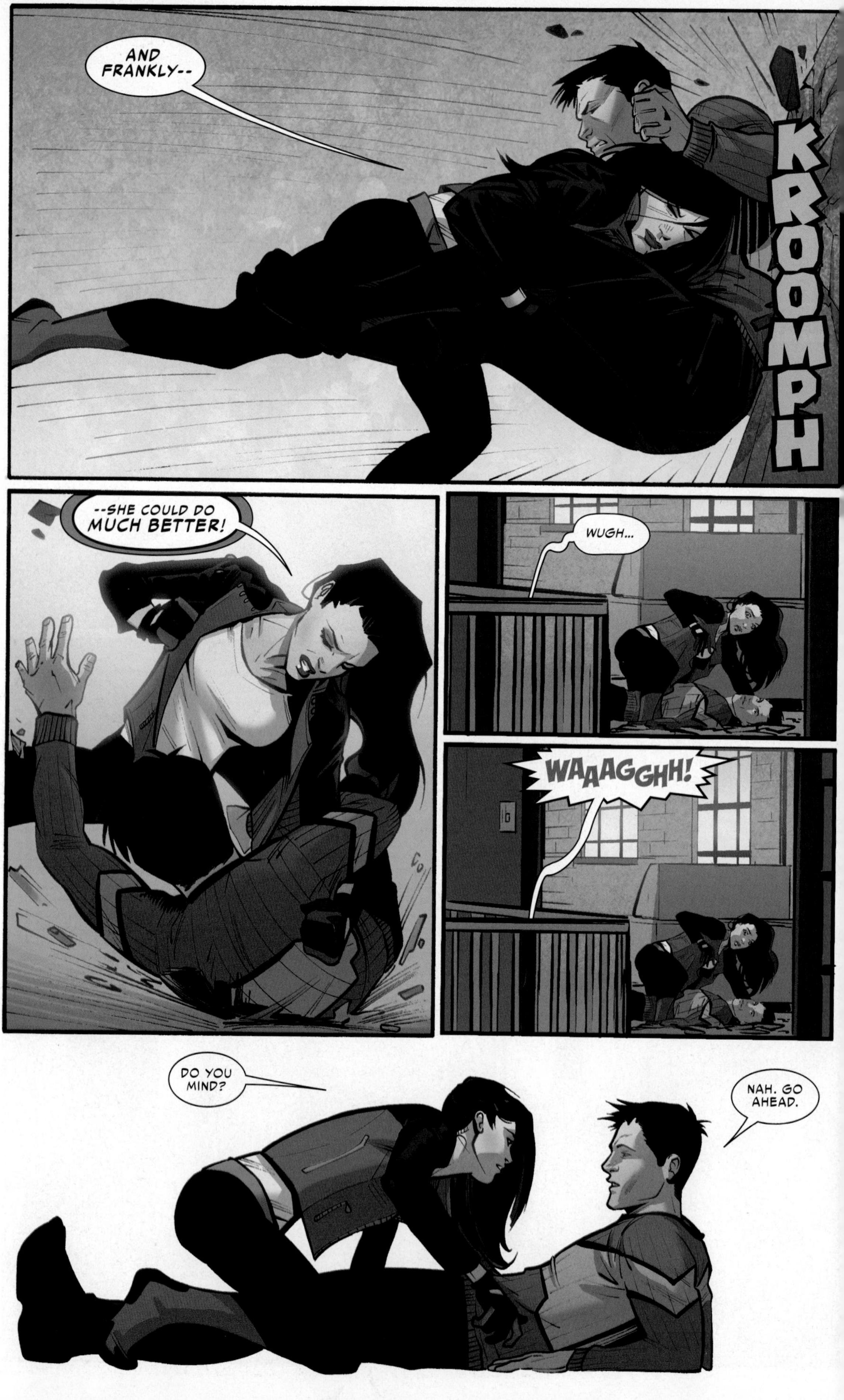
AND FRANKLY--
KROOMPH
--SHE COULD DO MUCH BETTER!
WUGH...
WAAAGGHH!
DO YOU MIND?
NAH. GO AHEAD.

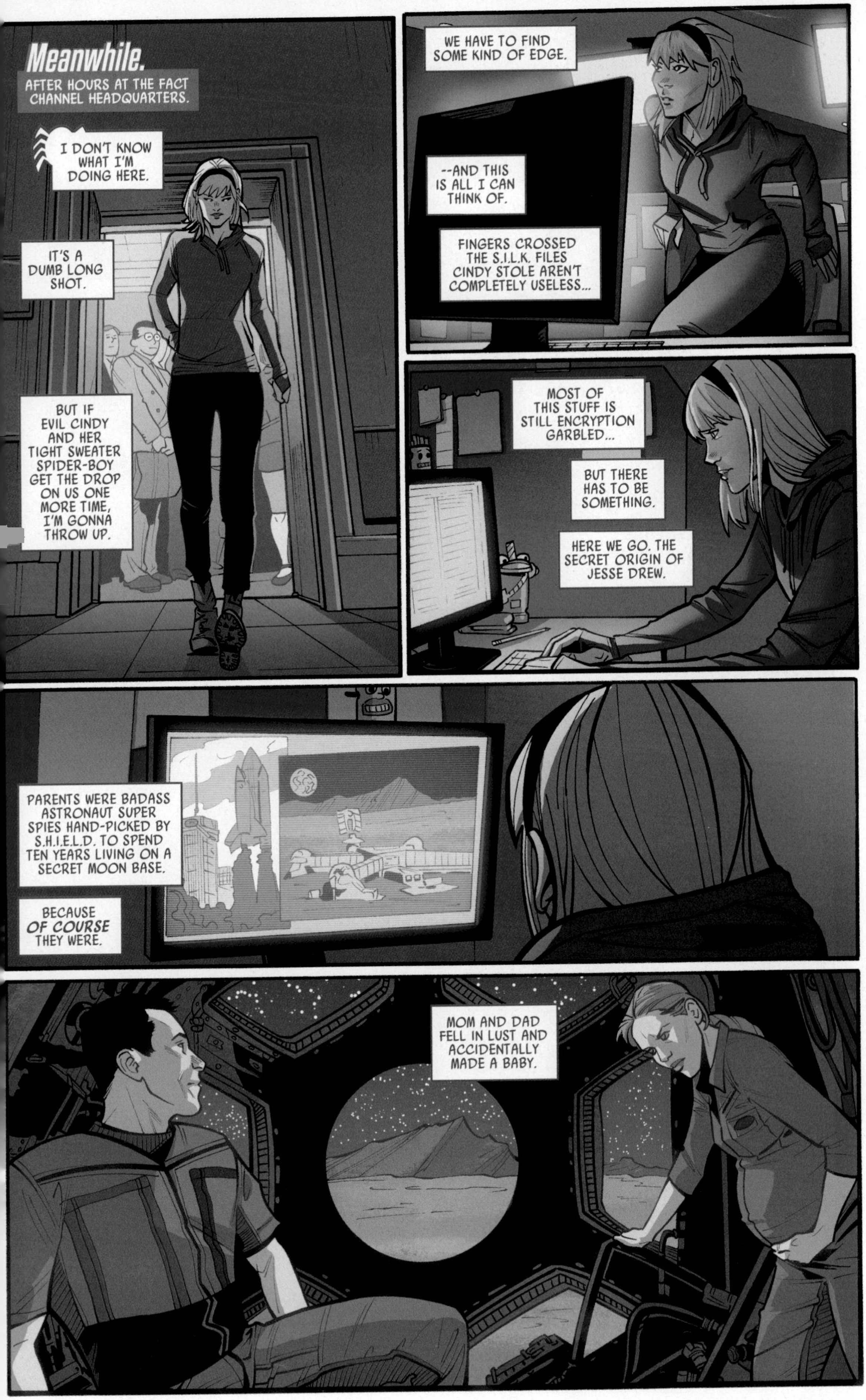
Meanwhile.
AFTER HOURS AT THE FACT CHANNEL HEADQUARTERS.
I DON'T KNOW WHAT I'M DOING HERE.
IT'S A DUMB LONG SHOT.
BUT IF EVIL CINDY AND HER TIGHT SWEATER SPIDER-BOY GET THE DROP ON US ONE MORE TIME, I'M GONNA THROW UP.
WE HAVE TO FIND SOME KIND OF EDGE.
--AND THIS IS ALL I CAN THINK OF.
FINGERS CROSSED THE S.I.L.K. FILES CINDY STOLE AREN'T COMPLETELY USELESS...
MOST OF THIS STUFF IS STILL ENCRYPTION GARBLED...
BUT THERE HAS TO BE SOMETHING.
HERE WE GO. THE SECRET ORIGIN OF JESSE DREW.
PARENTS WERE BADASS ASTRONAUT SUPER SPIES HAND-PICKED BY S.H.I.E.L.D. TO SPEND TEN YEARS LIVING ON A SECRET MOON BASE.
BECAUSE *OF COURSE* THEY WERE.
MOM AND DAD FELL IN LUST AND ACCIDENTALLY MADE A BABY.

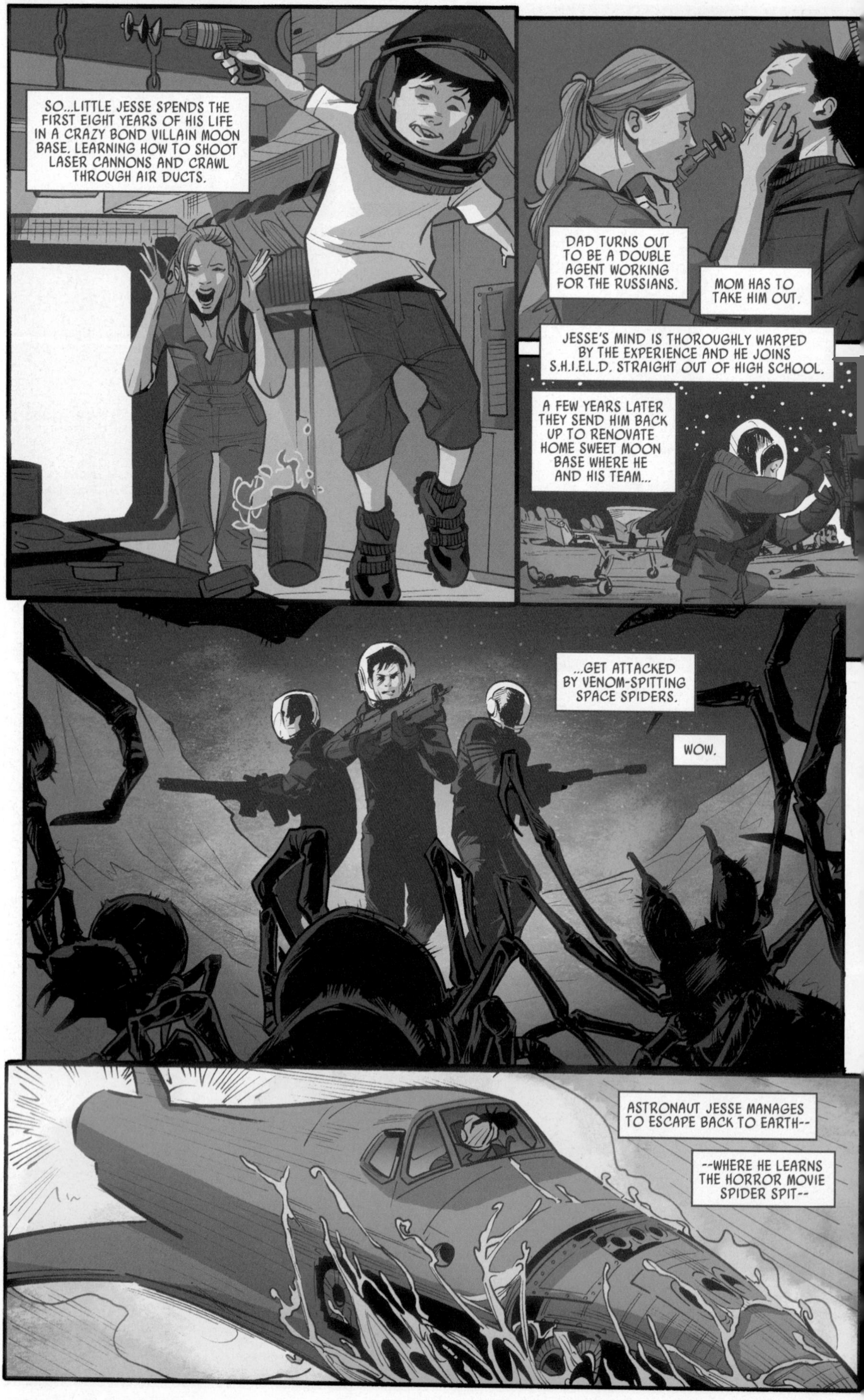
SO...LITTLE JESSE SPENDS THE FIRST EIGHT YEARS OF HIS LIFE IN A CRAZY BOND VILLAIN MOON BASE. LEARNING HOW TO SHOOT LASER CANNONS AND CRAWL THROUGH AIR DUCTS.
DAD TURNS OUT TO BE A DOUBLE AGENT WORKING FOR THE RUSSIANS.
MOM HAS TO TAKE HIM OUT.
JESSE'S MIND IS THOROUGHLY WARPED BY THE EXPERIENCE AND HE JOINS S.H.I.E.L.D. STRAIGHT OUT OF HIGH SCHOOL.
A FEW YEARS LATER THEY SEND HIM BACK UP TO RENOVATE HOME SWEET MOON BASE WHERE HE AND HIS TEAM...
...GET ATTACKED BY VENOM-SPITTING SPACE SPIDERS.
WOW.
ASTRONAUT JESSE MANAGES TO ESCAPE BACK TO EARTH--
--WHERE HE LEARNS THE HORROR MOVIE SPIDER SPIT--

--IS TURNING HIS BLOOD INTO POISONOUS BLACK GOO.

ENTER EVIL CINDY MOON.

SHE DEVELOPS SOME KIND OF ISOTOPE TO STABILIZE JESSE'S BLOOD.

WORKS LIKE A CHARM, SAVES HIS LIFE...

...AND GRANTS HIM STRANGE AND MYSTERIOUS SPIDER-POWERS.

WELCOME TO THE CLUB.

SHE STILL GIVES HIM TWO DOSES A DAY--

--ALL FOR THE LOW, LOW PRICE OF LIFELONG SERVITUDE.

GREAT. SO ALL I HAVE TO DO TO GET MY POWERS BACK IS LET SOME SPIDER ALIEN GET ALL UP ON MY FACE MEAT AND--

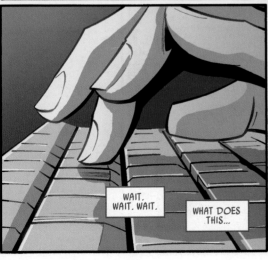

WAIT. WAIT. WAIT.

WHAT DOES THIS...

OH. SNAP.

THAT'S COLD-BLOODED.

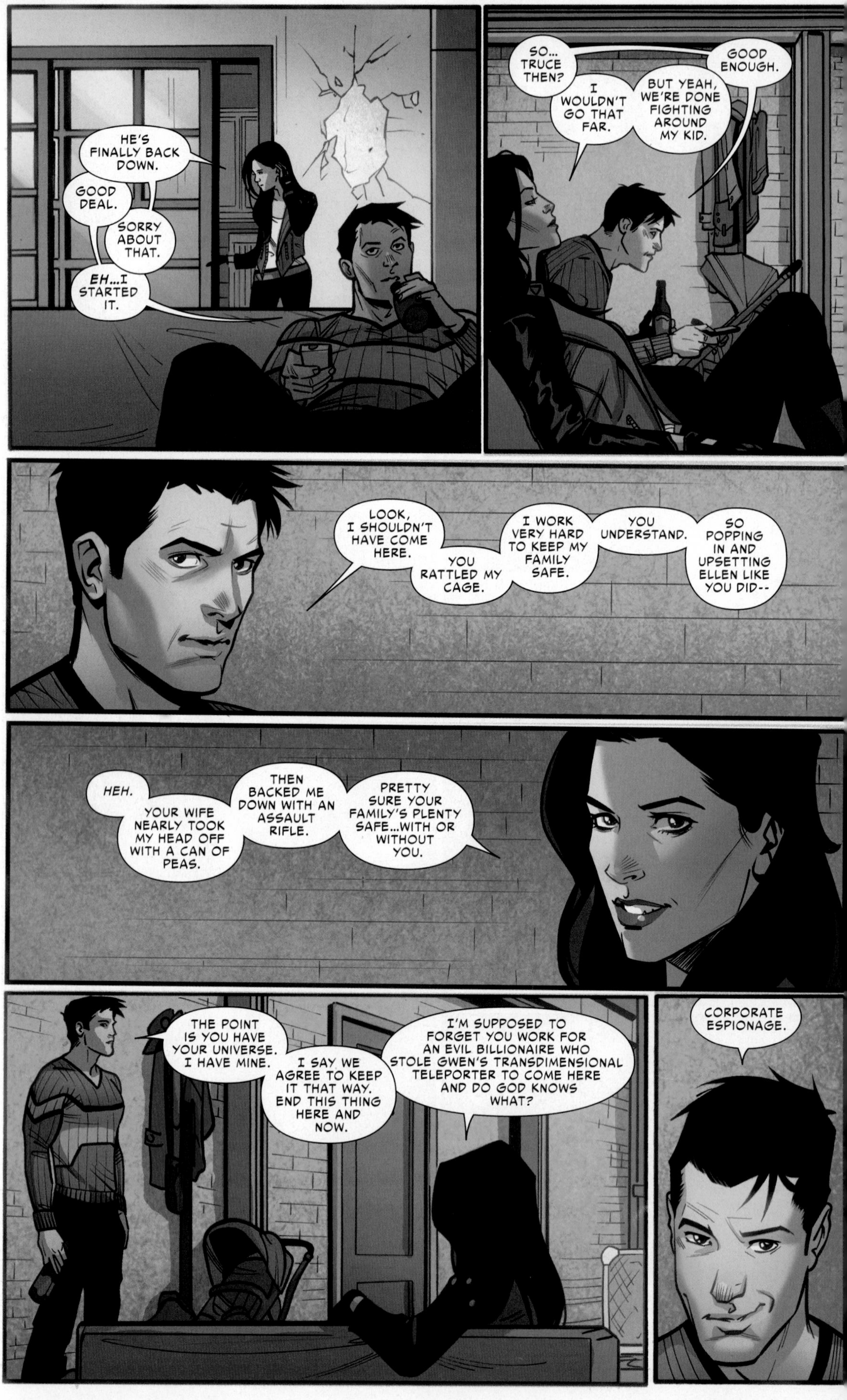
HE'S FINALLY BACK DOWN.
GOOD DEAL.
SORRY ABOUT THAT.
EH...I STARTED IT.
SO... TRUCE THEN?
I WOULDN'T GO THAT FAR.
BUT YEAH, WE'RE DONE FIGHTING AROUND MY KID.
GOOD ENOUGH.
LOOK, I SHOULDN'T HAVE COME HERE.
YOU RATTLED MY CAGE.
I WORK VERY HARD TO KEEP MY FAMILY SAFE.
YOU UNDERSTAND.
SO POPPING IN AND UPSETTING ELLEN LIKE YOU DID--
HEH.
YOUR WIFE NEARLY TOOK MY HEAD OFF WITH A CAN OF PEAS.
THEN BACKED ME DOWN WITH AN ASSAULT RIFLE.
PRETTY SURE YOUR FAMILY'S PLENTY SAFE...WITH OR WITHOUT YOU.
THE POINT IS YOU HAVE YOUR UNIVERSE. I HAVE MINE.
I SAY WE AGREE TO KEEP IT THAT WAY. END THIS THING HERE AND NOW.
I'M SUPPOSED TO FORGET YOU WORK FOR AN EVIL BILLIONAIRE WHO STOLE GWEN'S TRANSDIMENSIONAL TELEPORTER TO COME HERE AND DO GOD KNOWS WHAT?
CORPORATE ESPIONAGE.

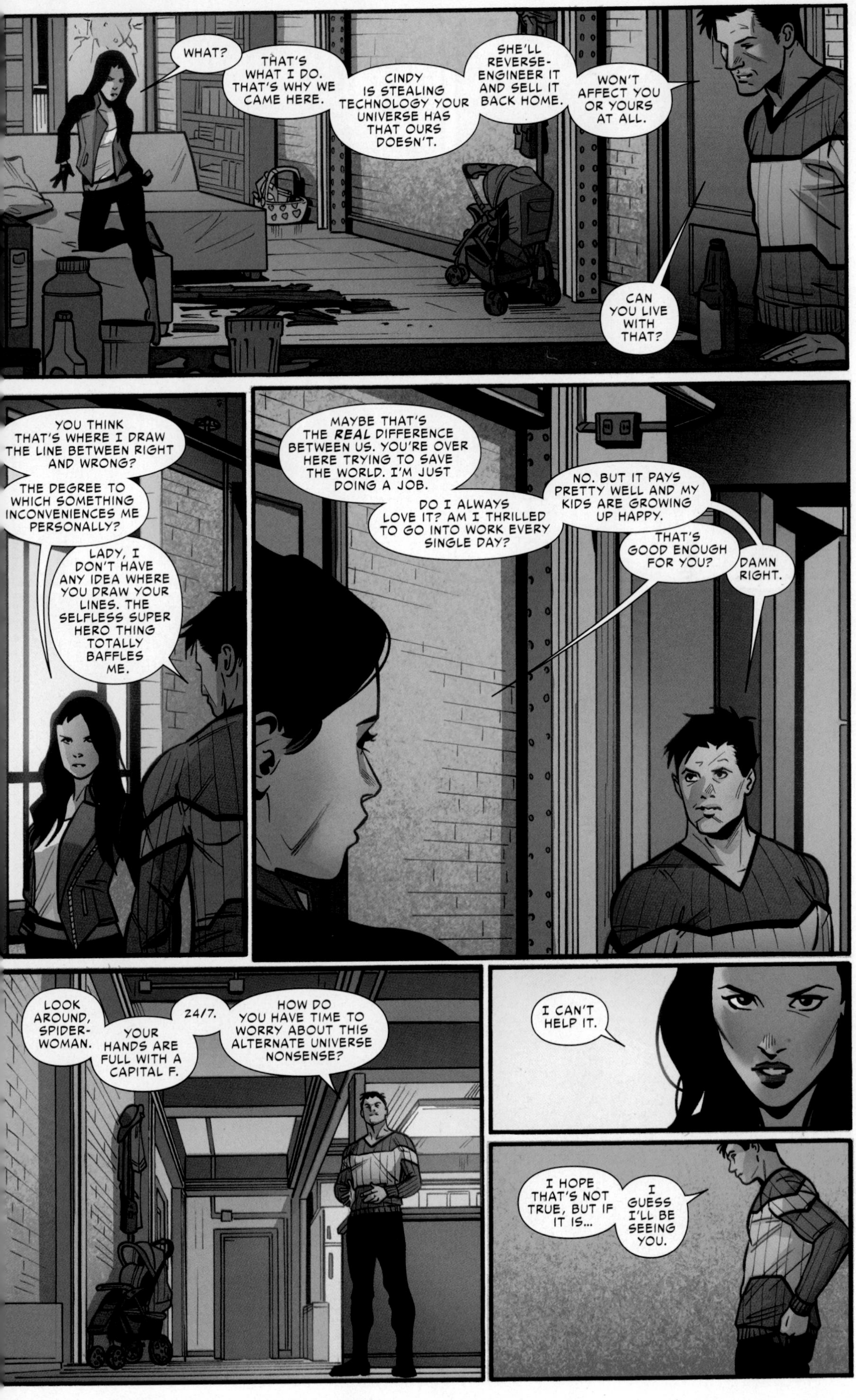
WHAT?
THAT'S WHAT I DO. THAT'S WHY WE CAME HERE.
CINDY IS STEALING TECHNOLOGY YOUR UNIVERSE HAS THAT OURS DOESN'T.
SHE'LL REVERSE-ENGINEER IT AND SELL IT BACK HOME.
WON'T AFFECT YOU OR YOURS AT ALL.
CAN YOU LIVE WITH THAT?
YOU THINK THAT'S WHERE I DRAW THE LINE BETWEEN RIGHT AND WRONG?
THE DEGREE TO WHICH SOMETHING INCONVENIENCES ME PERSONALLY?
LADY, I DON'T HAVE ANY IDEA WHERE YOU DRAW YOUR LINES. THE SELFLESS SUPER HERO THING TOTALLY BAFFLES ME.
MAYBE THAT'S THE REAL DIFFERENCE BETWEEN US. YOU'RE OVER HERE TRYING TO SAVE THE WORLD. I'M JUST DOING A JOB.
DO I ALWAYS LOVE IT? AM I THRILLED TO GO INTO WORK EVERY SINGLE DAY?
NO. BUT IT PAYS PRETTY WELL AND MY KIDS ARE GROWING UP HAPPY.
THAT'S GOOD ENOUGH FOR YOU?
DAMN RIGHT.
LOOK AROUND, SPIDER-WOMAN.
YOUR HANDS ARE FULL WITH A CAPITAL F.
24/7.
HOW DO YOU HAVE TIME TO WORRY ABOUT THIS ALTERNATE UNIVERSE NONSENSE?
I CAN'T HELP IT.
I HOPE THAT'S NOT TRUE, BUT IF IT IS...
I GUESS I'LL BE SEEING YOU.

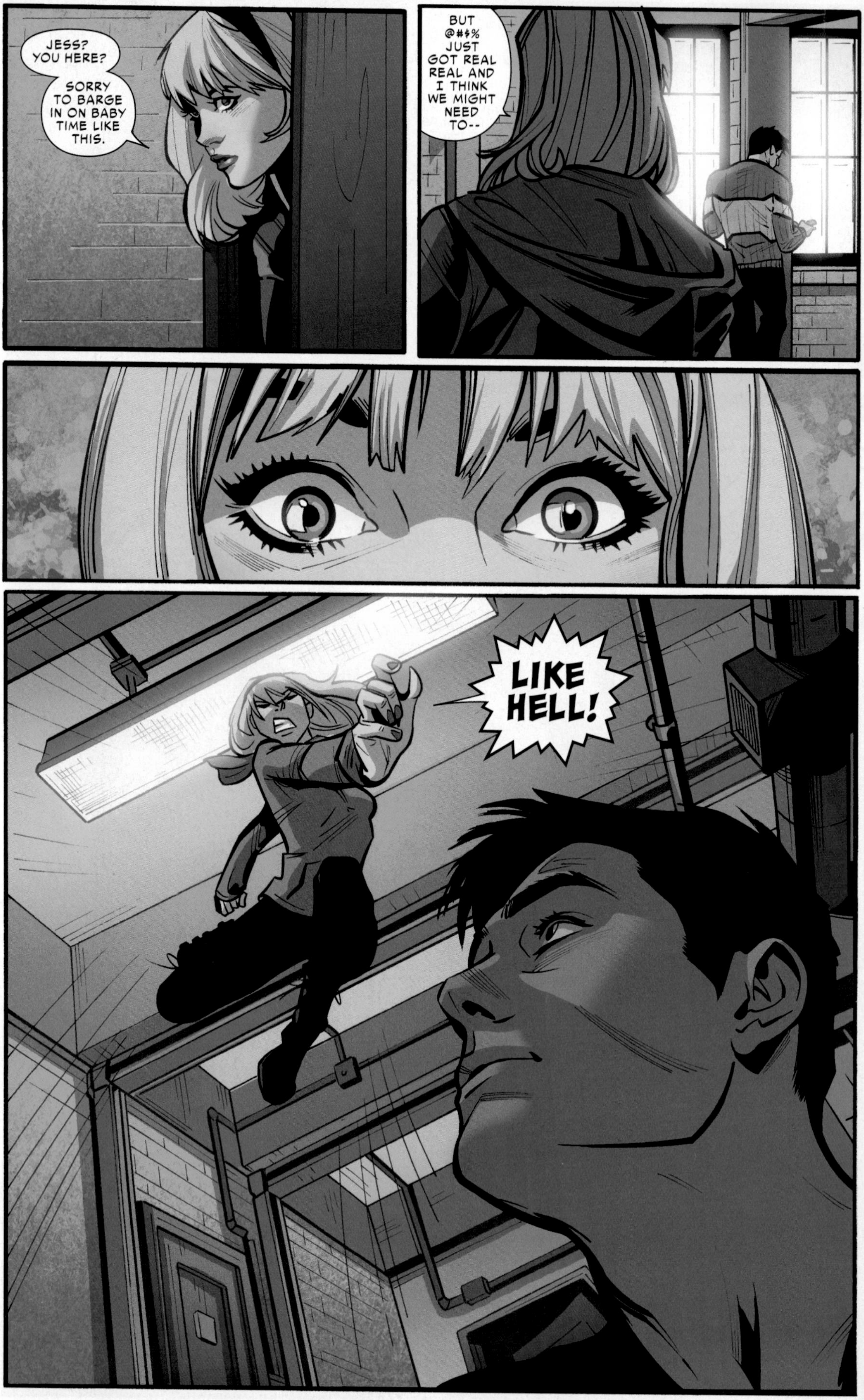
JESS? YOU HERE?
SORRY TO BARGE IN ON BABY TIME LIKE THIS.
BUT @#$% JUST GOT REAL REAL AND I THINK WE MIGHT NEED TO--
LIKE HELL!

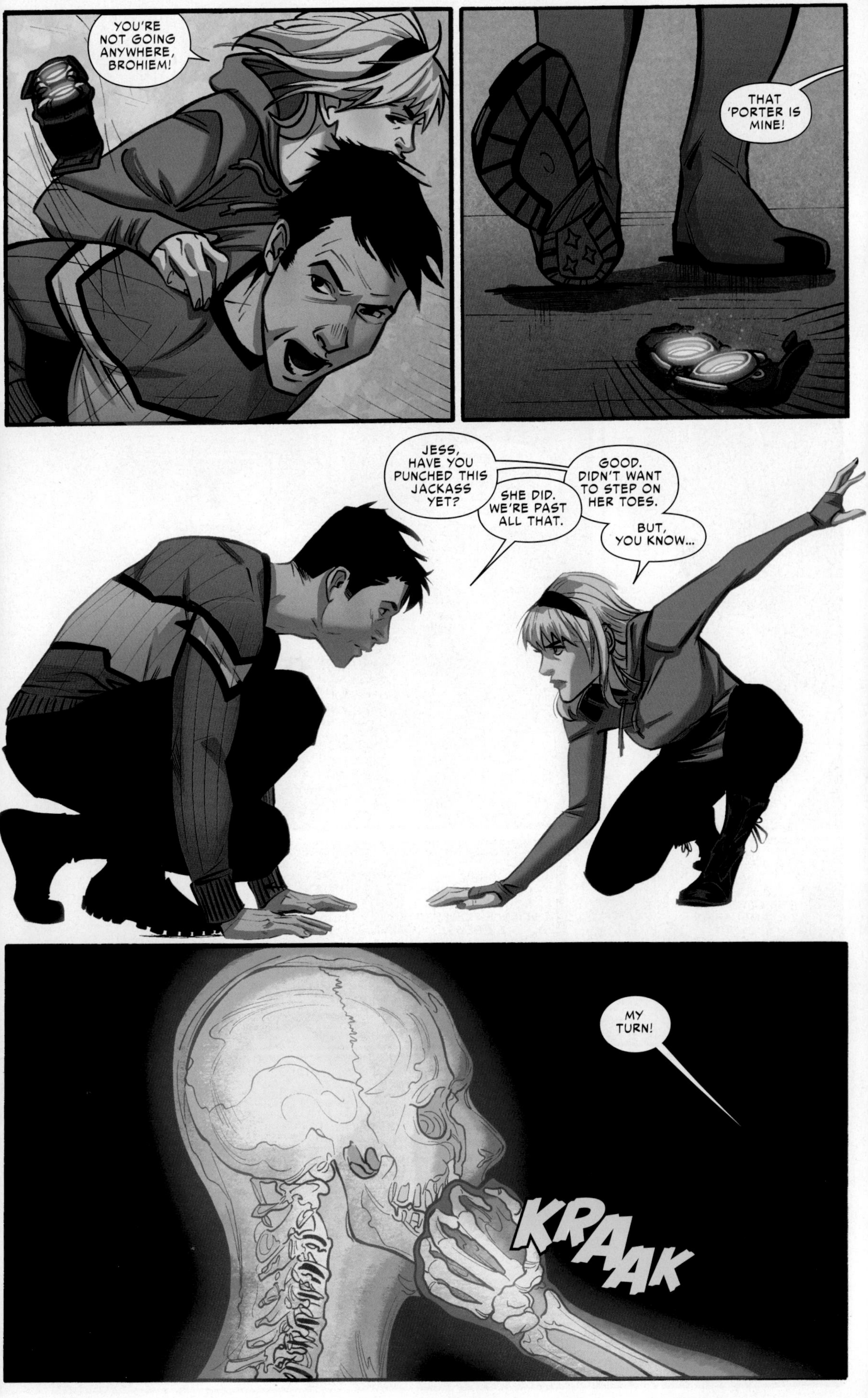
YOU'RE NOT GOING ANYWHERE, BROHIEM!
THAT 'PORTER IS MINE!
JESS, HAVE YOU PUNCHED THIS JACKASS YET?
SHE DID. WE'RE PAST ALL THAT.
GOOD. DIDN'T WANT TO STEP ON HER TOES.
BUT, YOU KNOW...
MY TURN!
KRAAAK

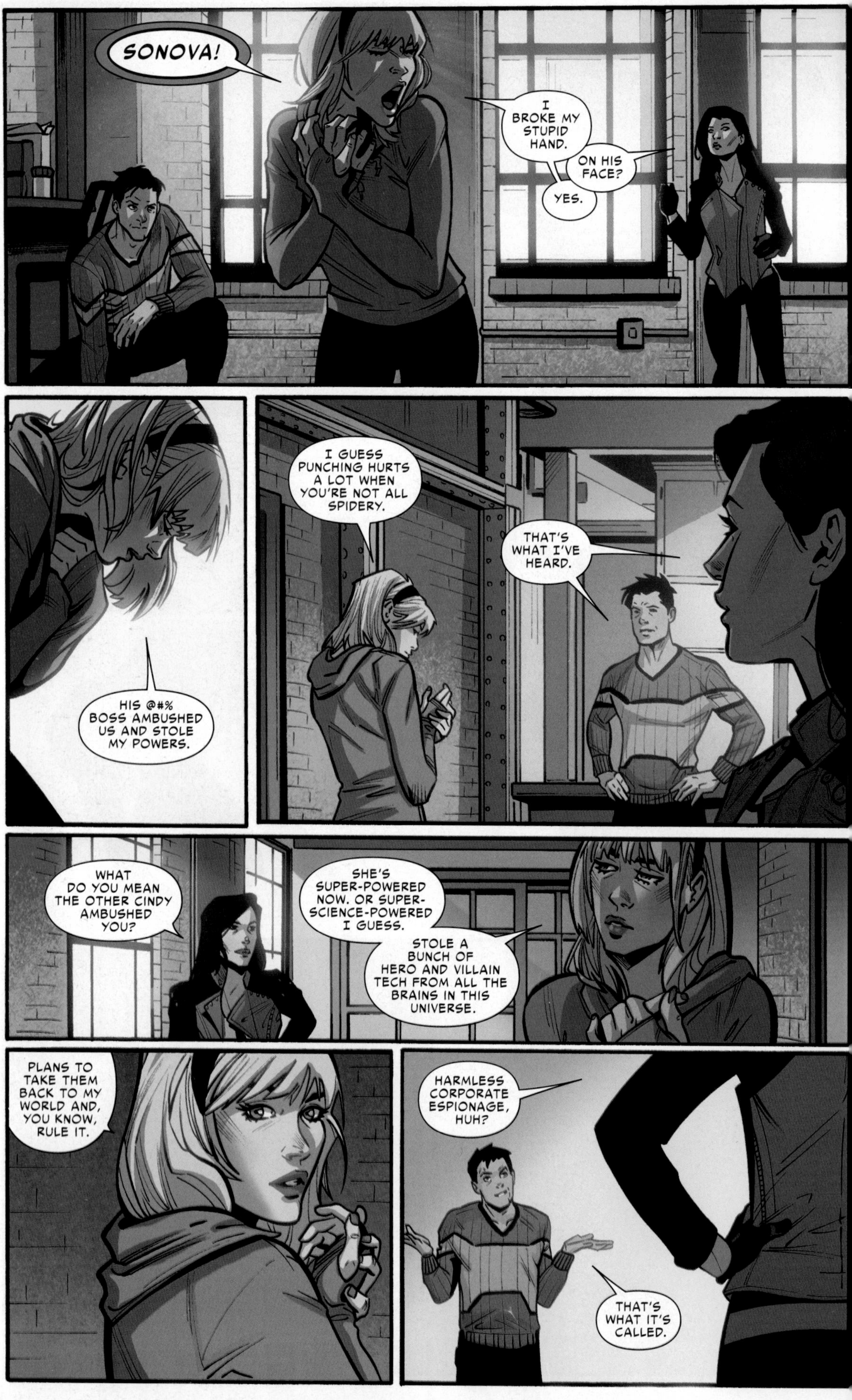
SONOVA!
I BROKE MY STUPID HAND.
ON HIS FACE?
YES.
HIS @#% BOSS AMBUSHED US AND STOLE MY POWERS.
I GUESS PUNCHING HURTS A LOT WHEN YOU'RE NOT ALL SPIDERY.
THAT'S WHAT I'VE HEARD.
WHAT DO YOU MEAN THE OTHER CINDY AMBUSHED YOU?
SHE'S SUPER-POWERED NOW. OR SUPER-SCIENCE-POWERED I GUESS.
STOLE A BUNCH OF HERO AND VILLAIN TECH FROM ALL THE BRAINS IN THIS UNIVERSE.
PLANS TO TAKE THEM BACK TO MY WORLD AND, YOU KNOW, RULE IT.
HARMLESS CORPORATE ESPIONAGE, HUH?
THAT'S WHAT IT'S CALLED.

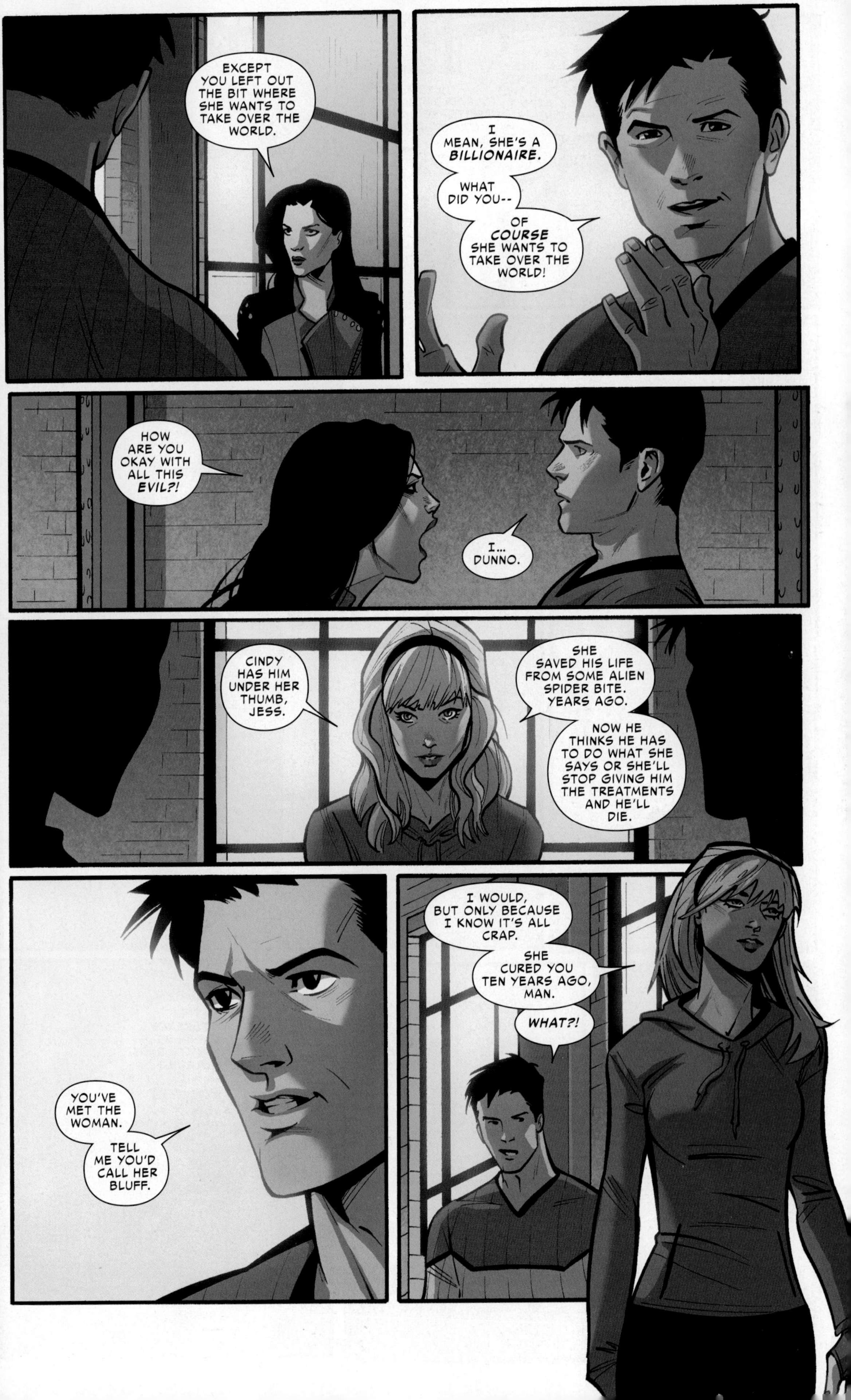
EXCEPT YOU LEFT OUT THE BIT WHERE SHE WANTS TO TAKE OVER THE WORLD.
I MEAN, SHE'S A *BILLIONAIRE.*
WHAT DID YOU--
OF *COURSE* SHE WANTS TO TAKE OVER THE WORLD!
HOW ARE YOU OKAY WITH ALL THIS *EVIL?!*
I... DUNNO.
CINDY HAS HIM UNDER HER THUMB, JESS.
SHE SAVED HIS LIFE FROM SOME ALIEN SPIDER BITE. YEARS AGO.
NOW HE THINKS HE HAS TO DO WHAT SHE SAYS OR SHE'LL STOP GIVING HIM THE TREATMENTS AND HE'LL DIE.
YOU'VE MET THE WOMAN.
TELL ME YOU'D CALL HER BLUFF.
I WOULD, BUT ONLY BECAUSE I KNOW IT'S ALL CRAP.
SHE CURED YOU TEN YEARS AGO, MAN.
WHAT?!

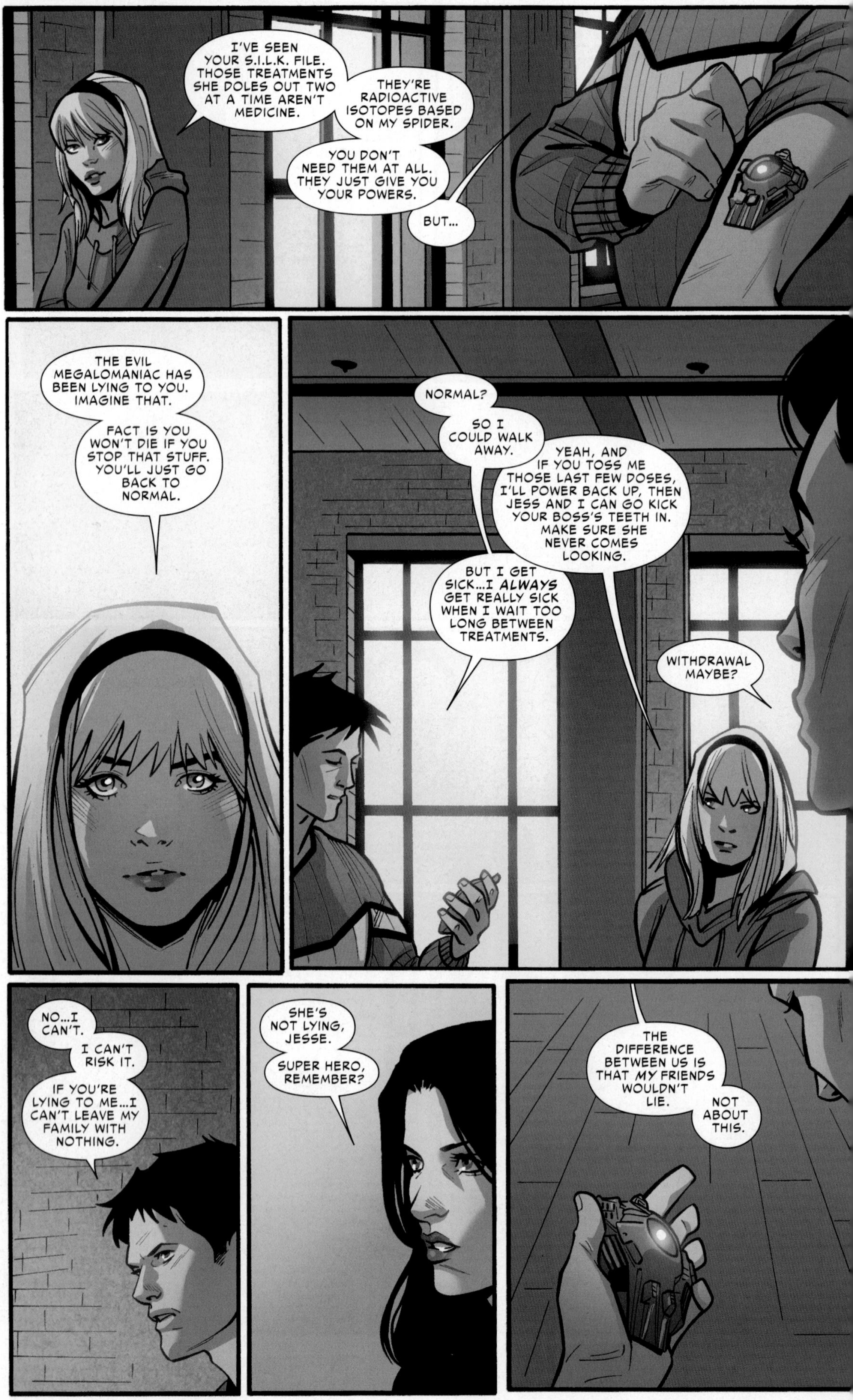
I'VE SEEN YOUR S.I.L.K. FILE. THOSE TREATMENTS SHE DOLES OUT TWO AT A TIME AREN'T MEDICINE.
THEY'RE RADIOACTIVE ISOTOPES BASED ON MY SPIDER.
YOU DON'T NEED THEM AT ALL. THEY JUST GIVE YOU YOUR POWERS.
BUT...
THE EVIL MEGALOMANIAC HAS BEEN LYING TO YOU. IMAGINE THAT.
FACT IS YOU WON'T DIE IF YOU STOP THAT STUFF. YOU'LL JUST GO BACK TO NORMAL.
NORMAL?
SO I COULD WALK AWAY.
YEAH, AND IF YOU TOSS ME THOSE LAST FEW DOSES, I'LL POWER BACK UP, THEN JESS AND I CAN GO KICK YOUR BOSS'S TEETH IN. MAKE SURE SHE NEVER COMES LOOKING.
BUT I GET SICK...I ALWAYS GET REALLY SICK WHEN I WAIT TOO LONG BETWEEN TREATMENTS.
WITHDRAWAL MAYBE?
NO...I CAN'T.
I CAN'T RISK IT.
IF YOU'RE LYING TO ME...I CAN'T LEAVE MY FAMILY WITH NOTHING.
SHE'S NOT LYING, JESSE.
SUPER HERO, REMEMBER?
THE DIFFERENCE BETWEEN US IS THAT MY FRIENDS WOULDN'T LIE.
NOT ABOUT THIS.

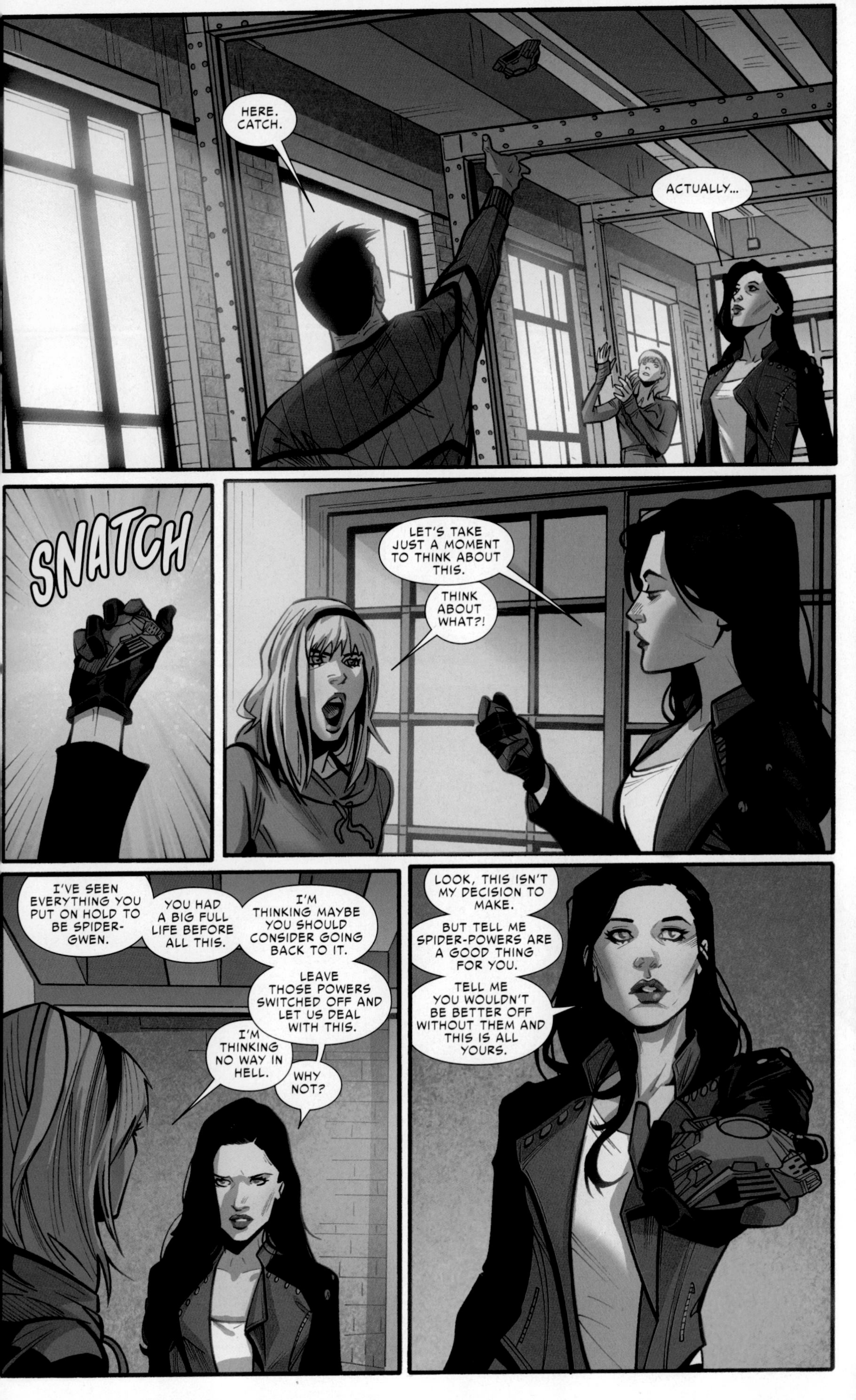
HERE. CATCH.
ACTUALLY...
SNATCH
LET'S TAKE JUST A MOMENT TO THINK ABOUT THIS.
THINK ABOUT WHAT?!
I'VE SEEN EVERYTHING YOU PUT ON HOLD TO BE SPIDER-GWEN.
YOU HAD A BIG FULL LIFE BEFORE ALL THIS.
I'M THINKING MAYBE YOU SHOULD CONSIDER GOING BACK TO IT.
LEAVE THOSE POWERS SWITCHED OFF AND LET US DEAL WITH THIS.
I'M THINKING NO WAY IN HELL.
WHY NOT?
LOOK, THIS ISN'T MY DECISION TO MAKE.
BUT TELL ME SPIDER-POWERS ARE A GOOD THING FOR YOU.
TELL ME YOU WOULDN'T BE BETTER OFF WITHOUT THEM AND THIS IS ALL YOURS.

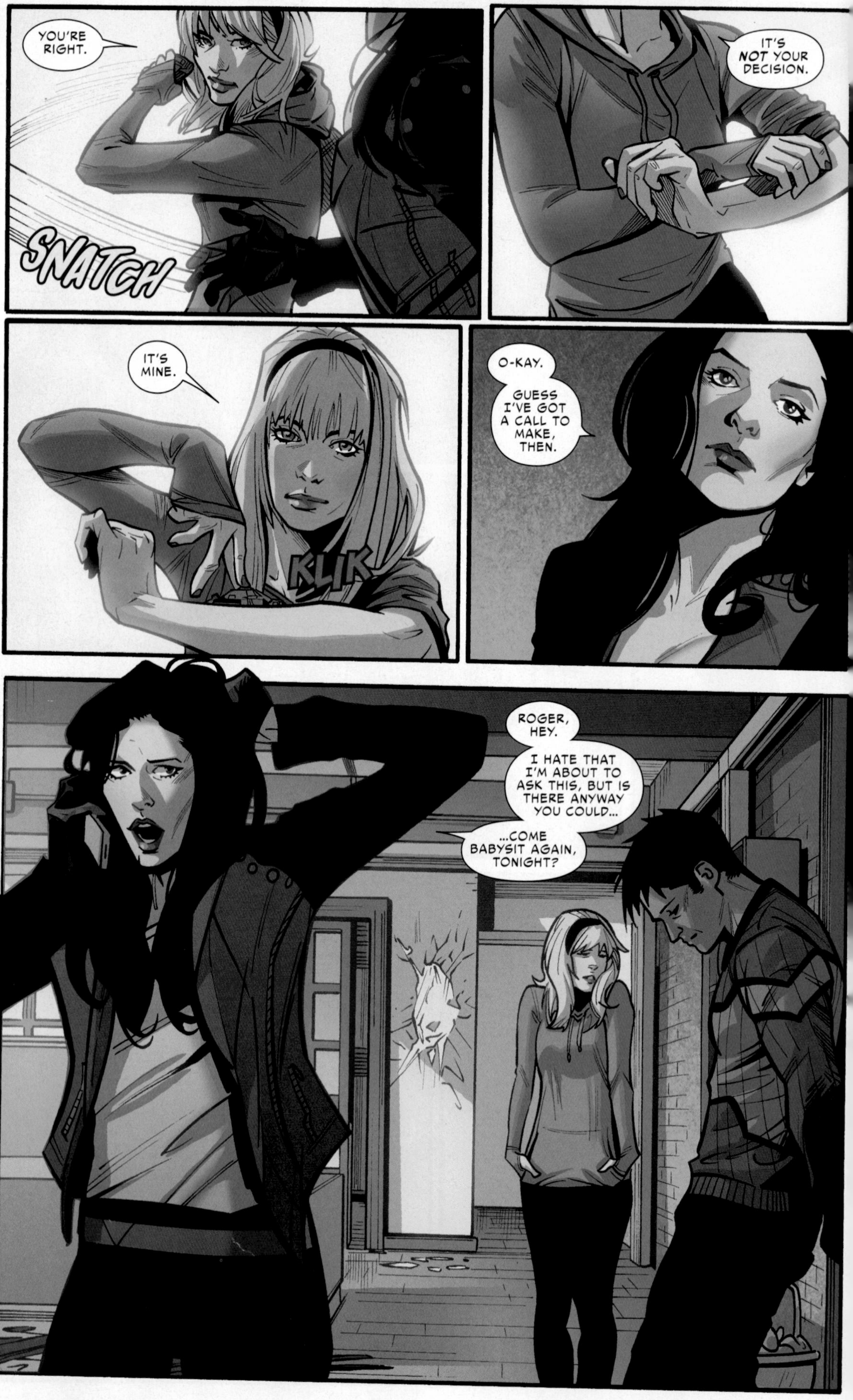
YOU'RE RIGHT.
SNATCH
IT'S NOT YOUR DECISION.
IT'S MINE.
KLIK
O-KAY.
GUESS I'VE GOT A CALL TO MAKE, THEN.
ROGER, HEY.
I HATE THAT I'M ABOUT TO ASK THIS, BUT IS THERE ANYWAY YOU COULD...
...COME BABYSIT AGAIN, TONIGHT?

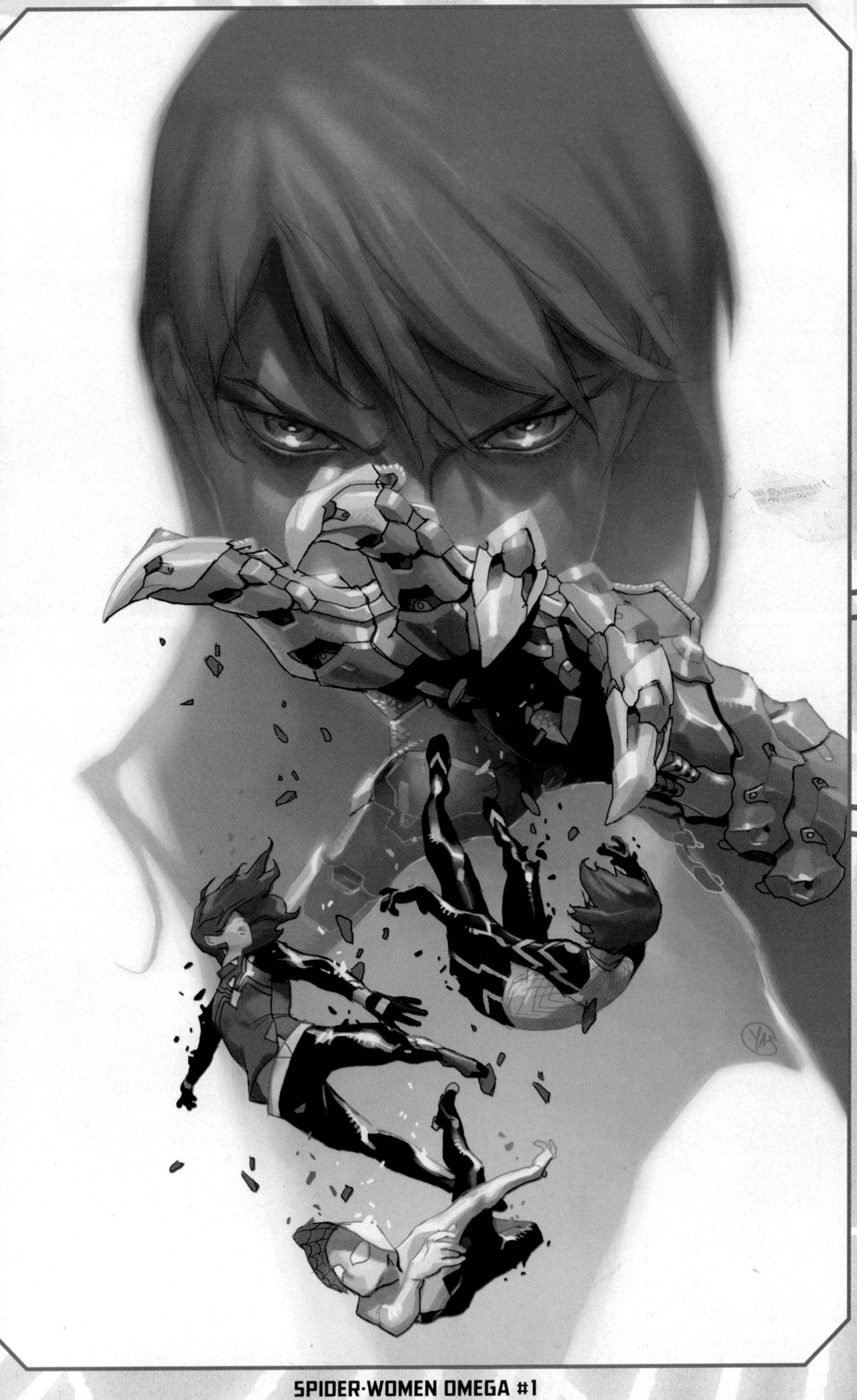

SPIDER-WOMEN OMEGA #1

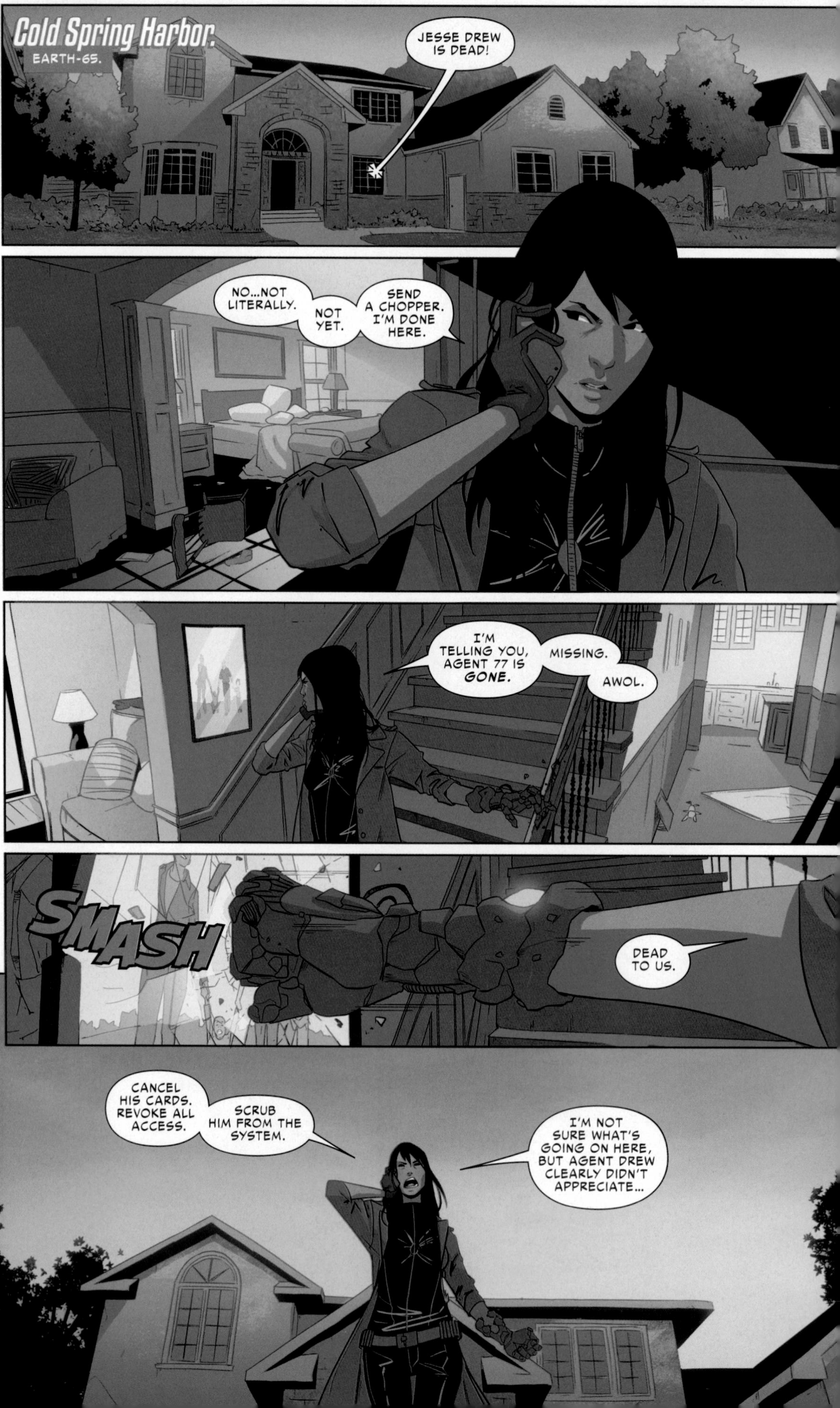
Cold Spring Harbor.
EARTH-65.
JESSE DREW IS DEAD!
NO...NOT LITERALLY.
NOT YET.
SEND A CHOPPER. I'M DONE HERE.
I'M TELLING YOU, AGENT 77 IS GONE.
MISSING.
AWOL.
SMASH
DEAD TO US.
CANCEL HIS CARDS. REVOKE ALL ACCESS.
SCRUB HIM FROM THE SYSTEM.
I'M NOT SURE WHAT'S GOING ON HERE, BUT AGENT DREW CLEARLY DIDN'T APPRECIATE...

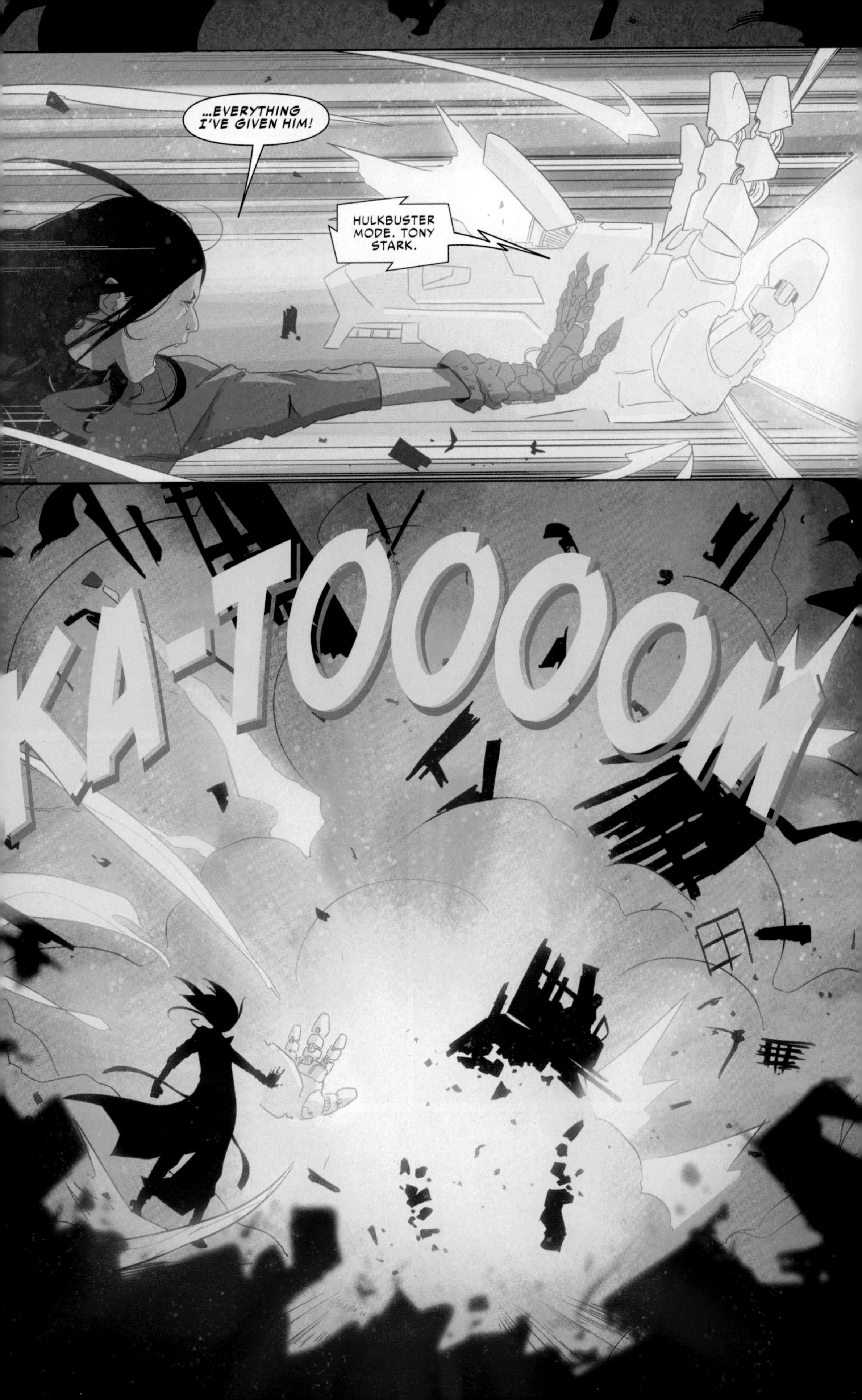
...EVERYTHING I'VE GIVEN HIM!
HULKBUSTER MODE. TONY STARK.
KA-TOOOOOM

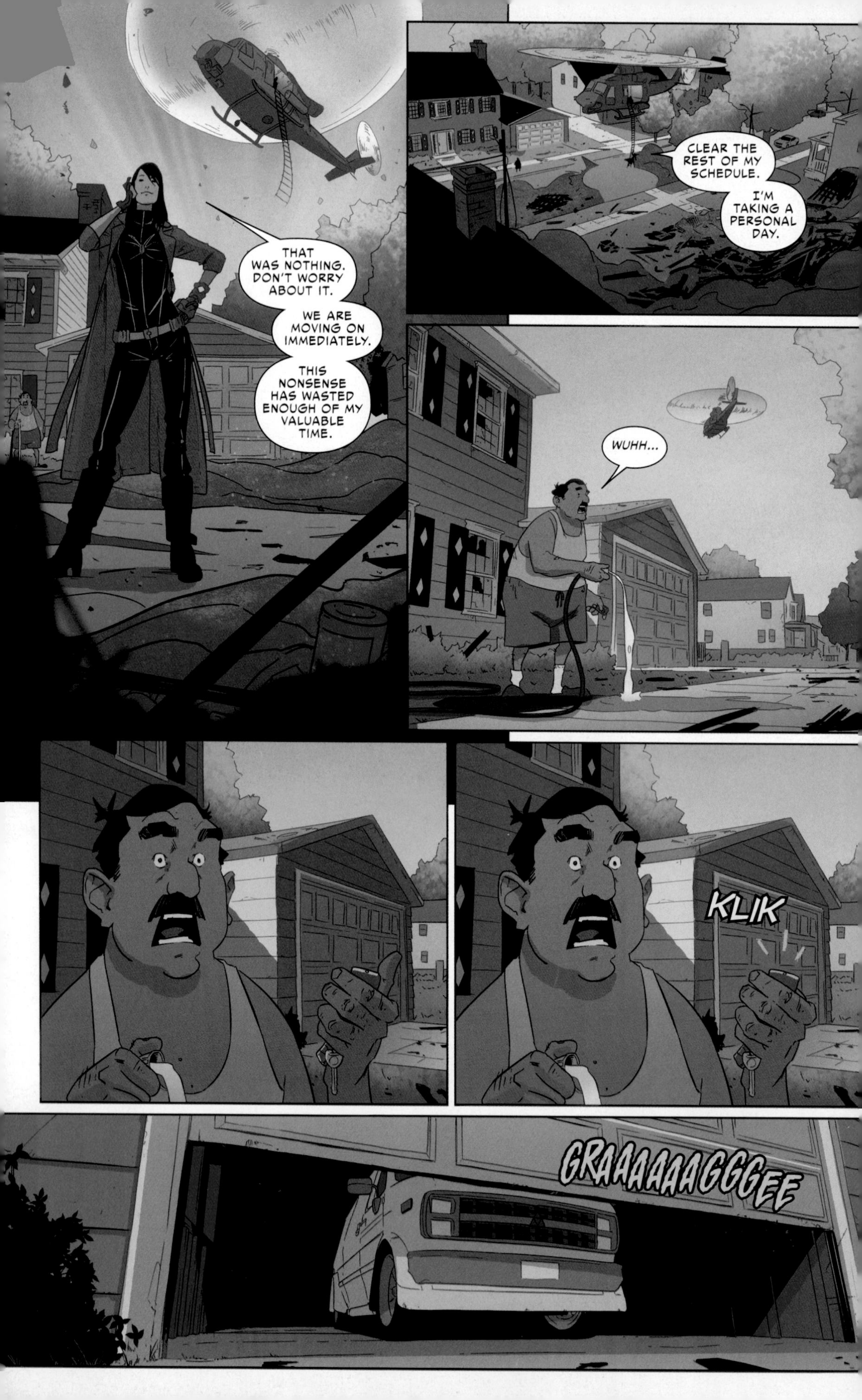
THAT WAS NOTHING. DON'T WORRY ABOUT IT.
WE ARE MOVING ON IMMEDIATELY.
THIS NONSENSE HAS WASTED ENOUGH OF MY VALUABLE TIME.
CLEAR THE REST OF MY SCHEDULE.
I'M TAKING A PERSONAL DAY.
WUHH...
KLIK
GRAAAAAAAGGGEE

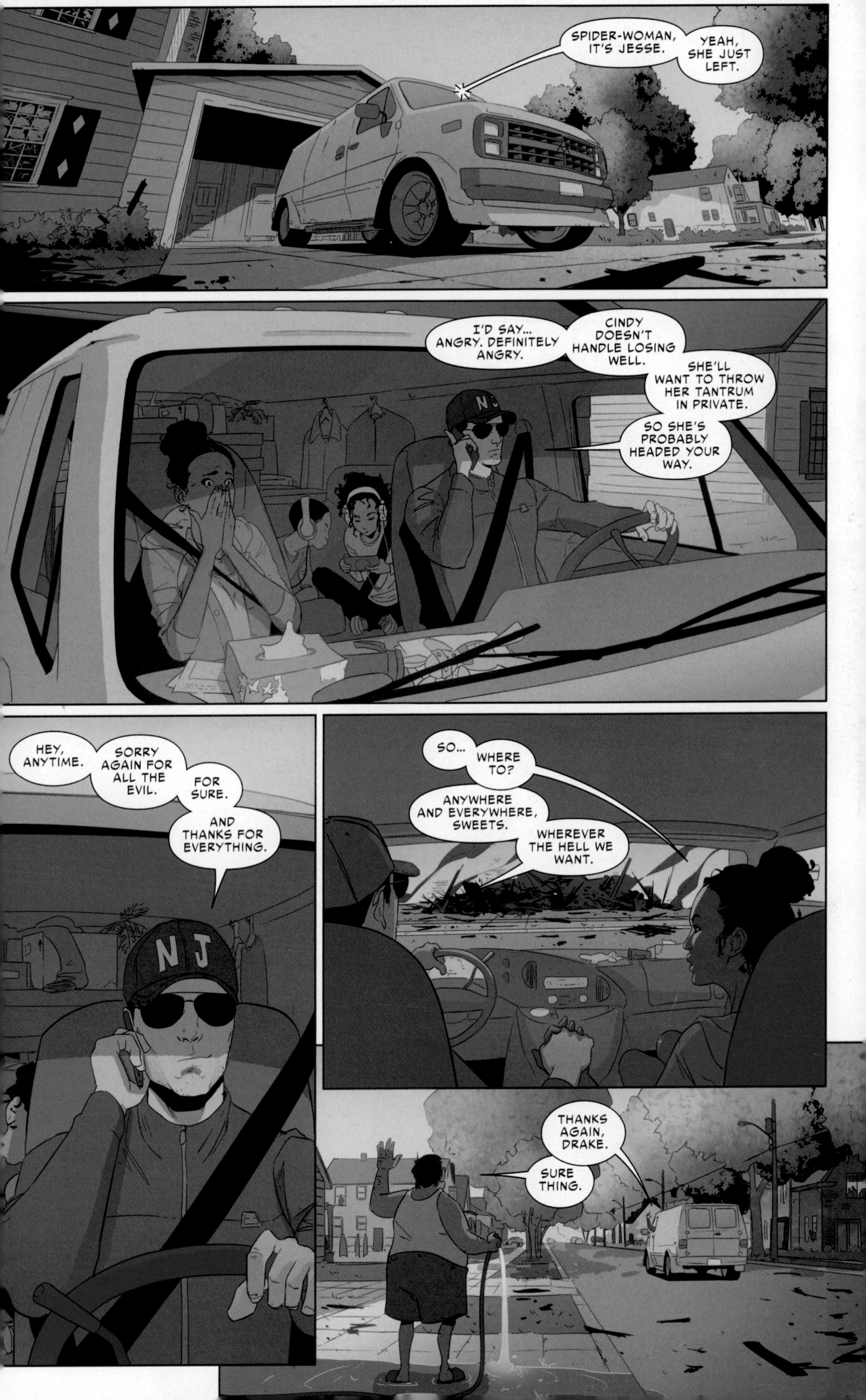
SPIDER-WOMAN, IT'S JESSE.
YEAH, SHE JUST LEFT.
I'D SAY... ANGRY. DEFINITELY ANGRY.
CINDY DOESN'T HANDLE LOSING WELL.
SHE'LL WANT TO THROW HER TANTRUM IN PRIVATE.
SO SHE'S PROBABLY HEADED YOUR WAY.
HEY, ANYTIME.
SORRY AGAIN FOR ALL THE EVIL.
FOR SURE.
AND THANKS FOR EVERYTHING.
SO...
WHERE TO?
ANYWHERE AND EVERYWHERE, SWEETS.
WHEREVER THE HELL WE WANT.
THANKS AGAIN, DRAKE.
SURE THING.

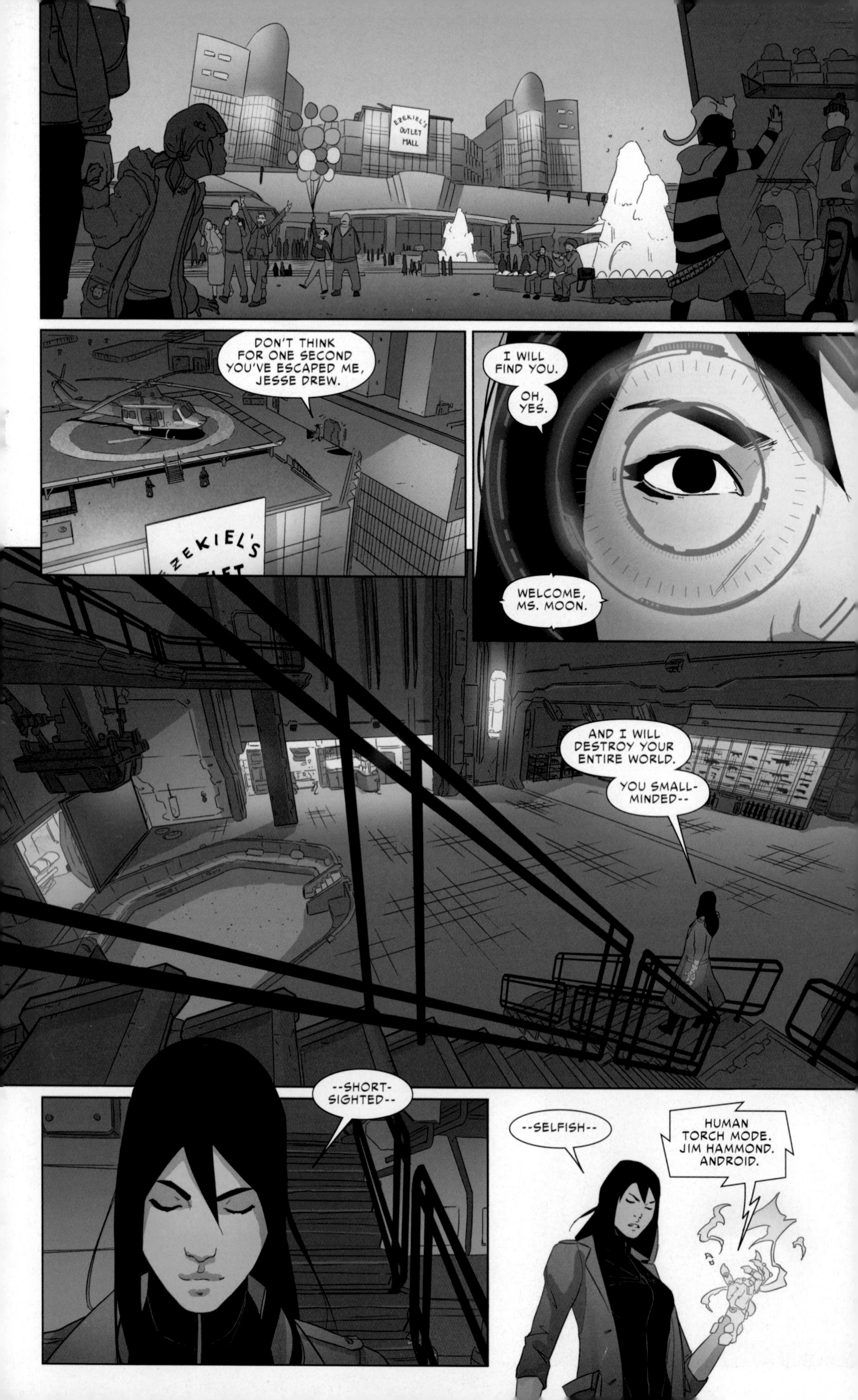
EZEKIEL'S OUTLET MALL
DON'T THINK FOR ONE SECOND YOU'VE ESCAPED ME, JESSE DREW.
EZEKIEL'S
I WILL FIND YOU.
OH, YES.
WELCOME, MS. MOON.
AND I WILL DESTROY YOUR ENTIRE WORLD.
YOU SMALL-MINDED--
--SHORT-SIGHTED--
--SELFISH--
HUMAN TORCH MODE. JIM HAMMOND. ANDROID.

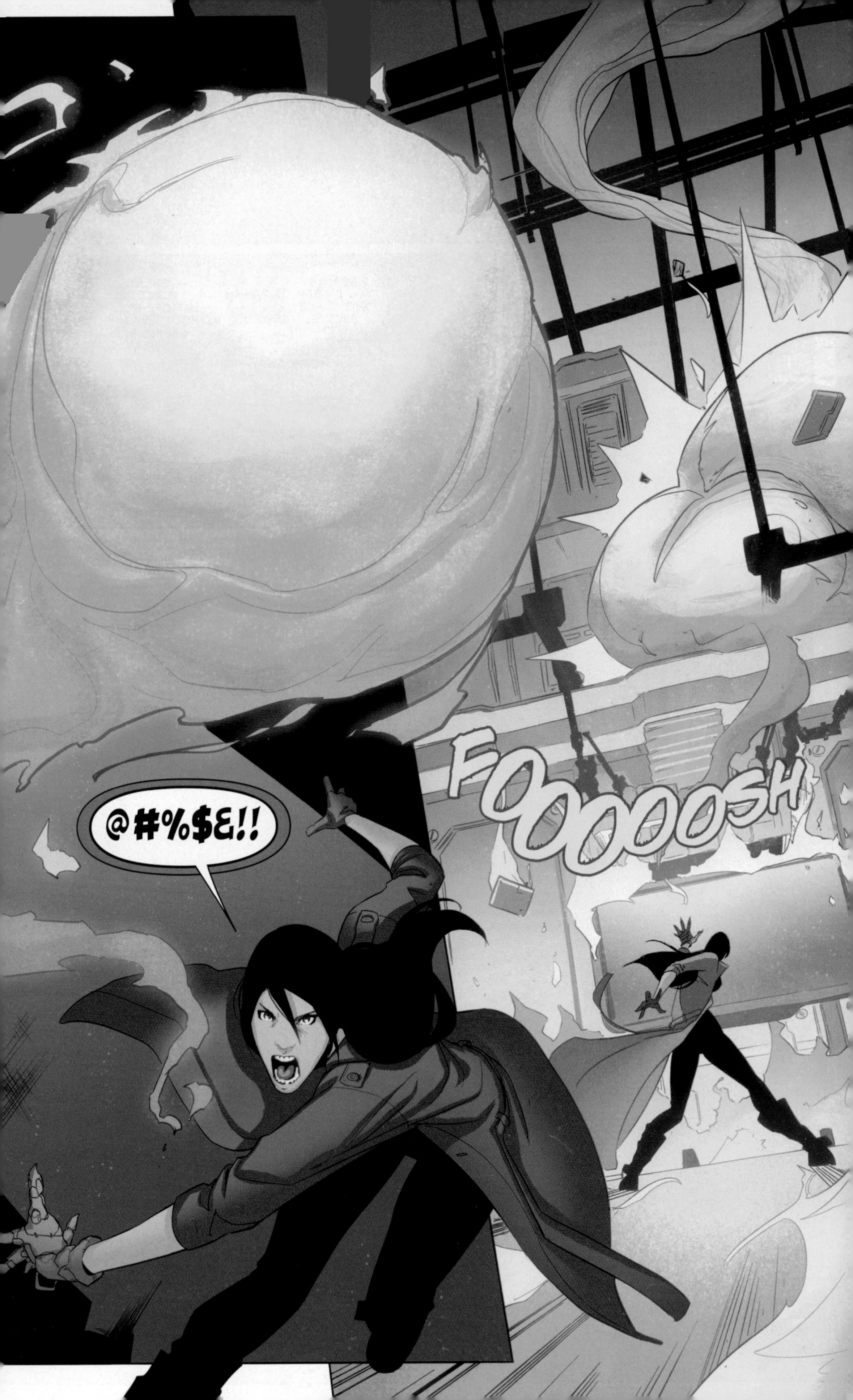

@#%$Ɛ!!
FOOOOOOSH

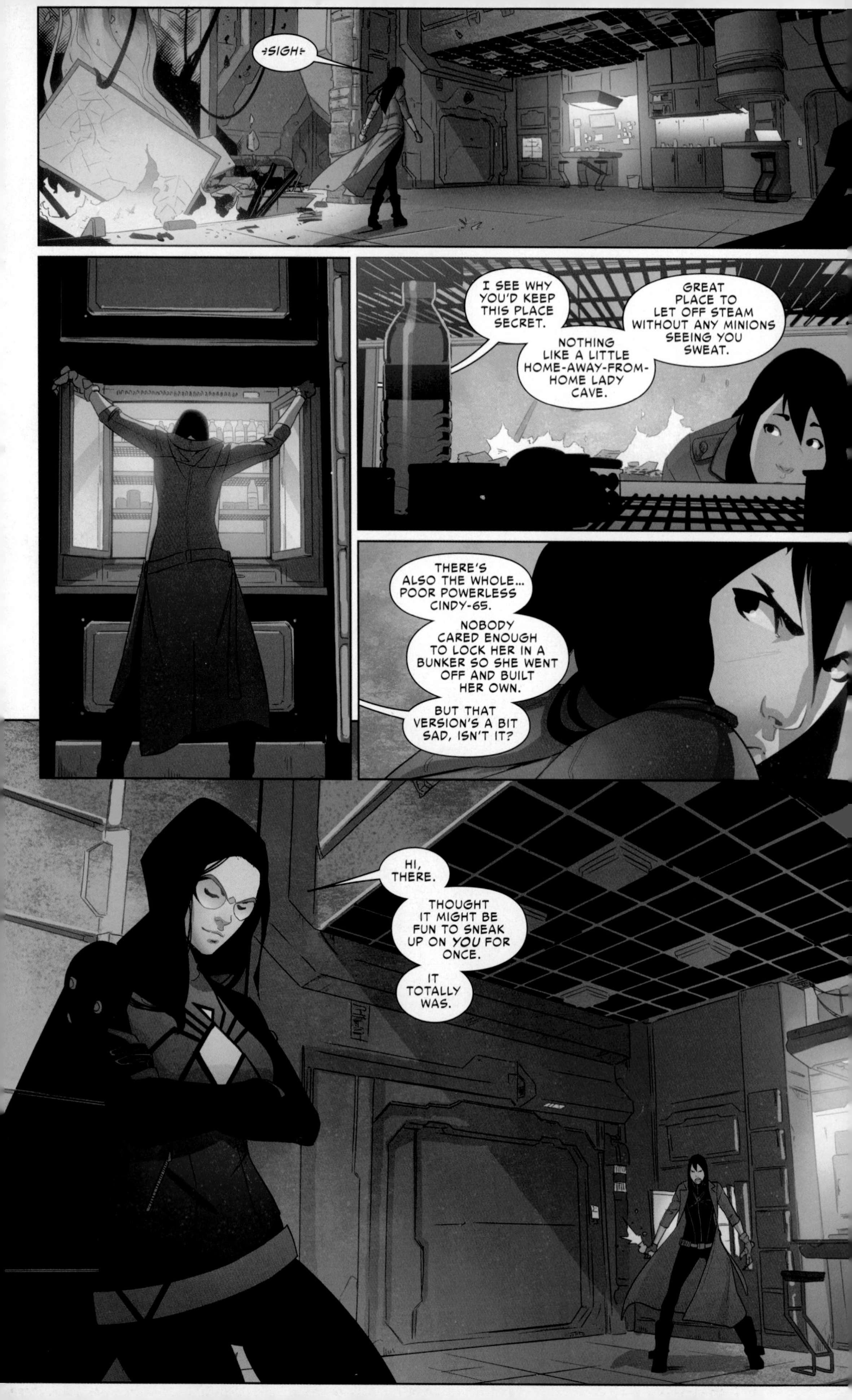

⇉SIGH⇇
I SEE WHY YOU'D KEEP THIS PLACE SECRET.
NOTHING LIKE A LITTLE HOME-AWAY-FROM-HOME LADY CAVE.
GREAT PLACE TO LET OFF STEAM WITHOUT ANY MINIONS SEEING YOU SWEAT.
THERE'S ALSO THE WHOLE... POOR POWERLESS CINDY-65.
NOBODY CARED ENOUGH TO LOCK HER IN A BUNKER SO SHE WENT OFF AND BUILT HER OWN.
BUT THAT VERSION'S A BIT SAD, ISN'T IT?
HI, THERE.
THOUGHT IT MIGHT BE FUN TO SNEAK UP ON *YOU* FOR ONCE.
IT TOTALLY WAS.

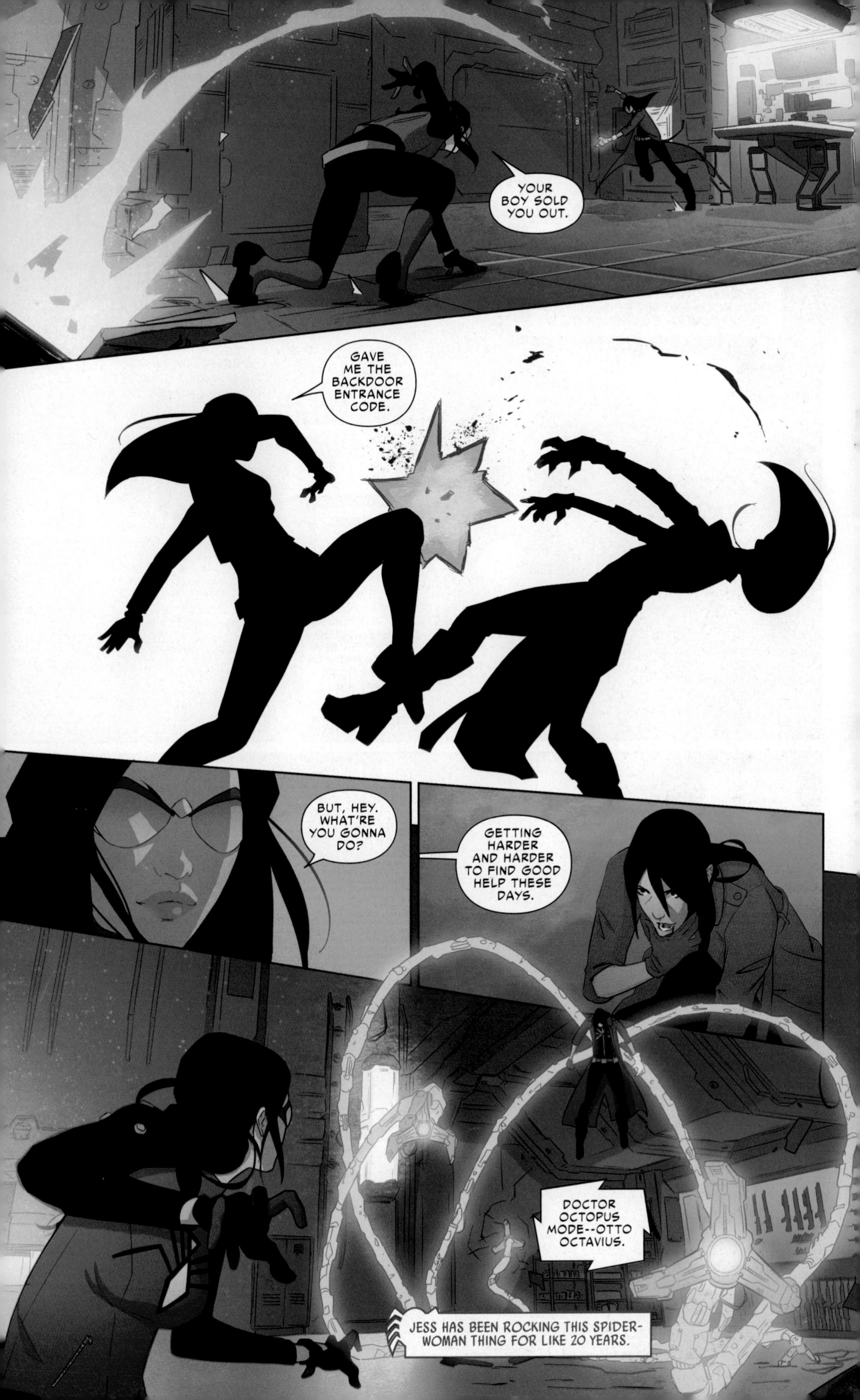
YOUR BOY SOLD YOU OUT.
GAVE ME THE BACKDOOR ENTRANCE CODE.
BUT, HEY. WHAT'RE YOU GONNA DO?
GETTING HARDER AND HARDER TO FIND GOOD HELP THESE DAYS.
DOCTOR OCTOPUS MODE--OTTO OCTAVIUS.
JESS HAS BEEN ROCKING THIS SPIDER-WOMAN THING FOR LIKE 20 YEARS.

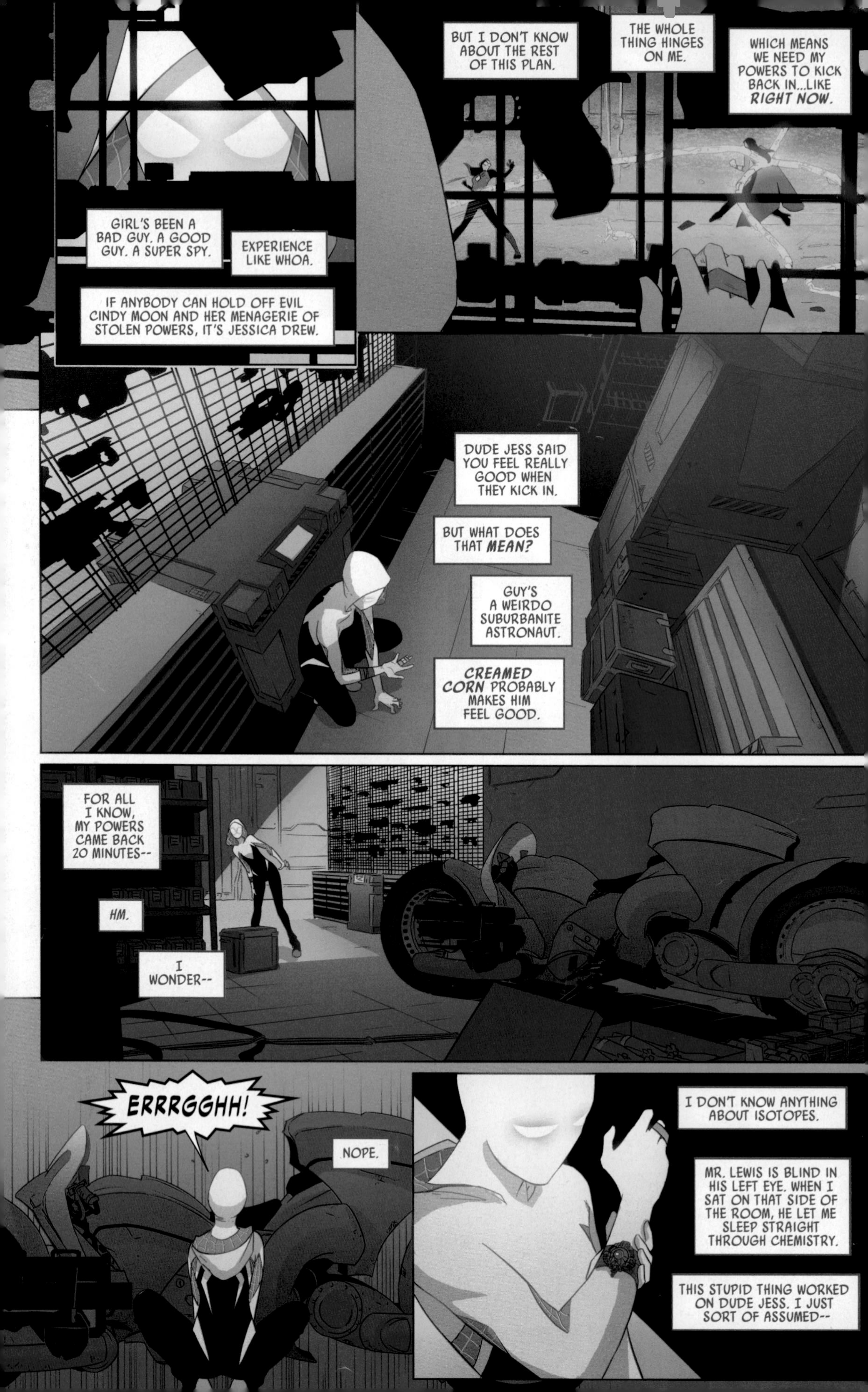
GIRL'S BEEN A BAD GUY. A GOOD GUY. A SUPER SPY.
EXPERIENCE LIKE WHOA.
IF ANYBODY CAN HOLD OFF EVIL CINDY MOON AND HER MENAGERIE OF STOLEN POWERS, IT'S JESSICA DREW.
BUT I DON'T KNOW ABOUT THE REST OF THIS PLAN.
THE WHOLE THING HINGES ON ME.
WHICH MEANS WE NEED MY POWERS TO KICK BACK IN...LIKE RIGHT NOW.
DUDE JESS SAID YOU FEEL REALLY GOOD WHEN THEY KICK IN.
BUT WHAT DOES THAT MEAN?
GUY'S A WEIRDO SUBURBANITE ASTRONAUT.
CREAMED CORN PROBABLY MAKES HIM FEEL GOOD.
FOR ALL I KNOW, MY POWERS CAME BACK 20 MINUTES--
HM.
I WONDER--
ERRRGGHH!
NOPE.
I DON'T KNOW ANYTHING ABOUT ISOTOPES.
MR. LEWIS IS BLIND IN HIS LEFT EYE. WHEN I SAT ON THAT SIDE OF THE ROOM, HE LET ME SLEEP STRAIGHT THROUGH CHEMISTRY.
THIS STUPID THING WORKED ON DUDE JESS. I JUST SORT OF ASSUMED--

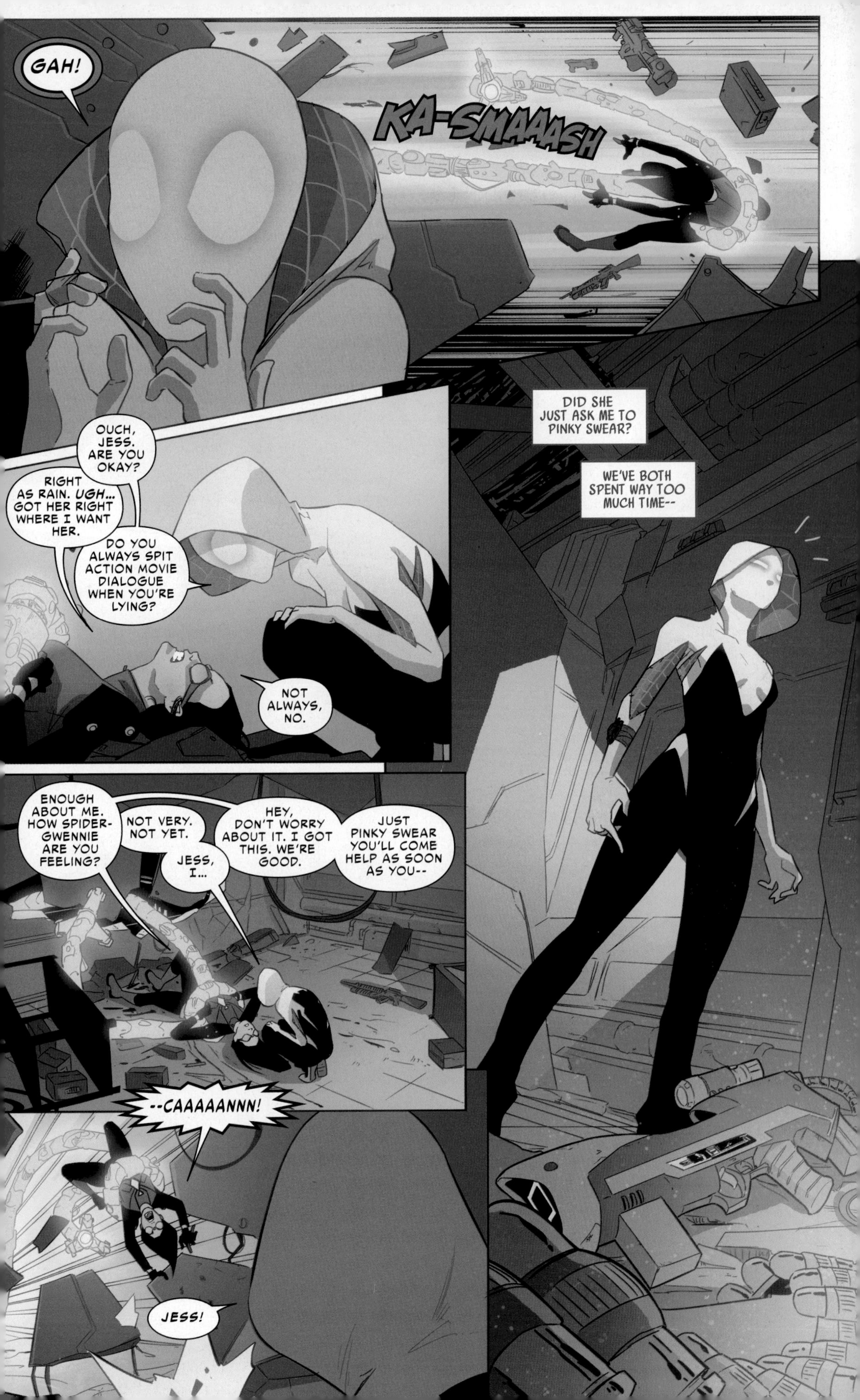
GAH!
KA-SMAAASH
OUCH, JESS. ARE YOU OKAY?
RIGHT AS RAIN. UGH... GOT HER RIGHT WHERE I WANT HER.
DO YOU ALWAYS SPIT ACTION MOVIE DIALOGUE WHEN YOU'RE LYING?
NOT ALWAYS, NO.
ENOUGH ABOUT ME. HOW SPIDER-GWENNIE ARE YOU FEELING?
NOT VERY. NOT YET.
JESS, I...
HEY, DON'T WORRY ABOUT IT. I GOT THIS. WE'RE GOOD.
JUST PINKY SWEAR YOU'LL COME HELP AS SOON AS YOU--
--CAAAAANNN!
JESS!
DID SHE JUST ASK ME TO PINKY SWEAR?
WE'VE BOTH SPENT WAY TOO MUCH TIME--

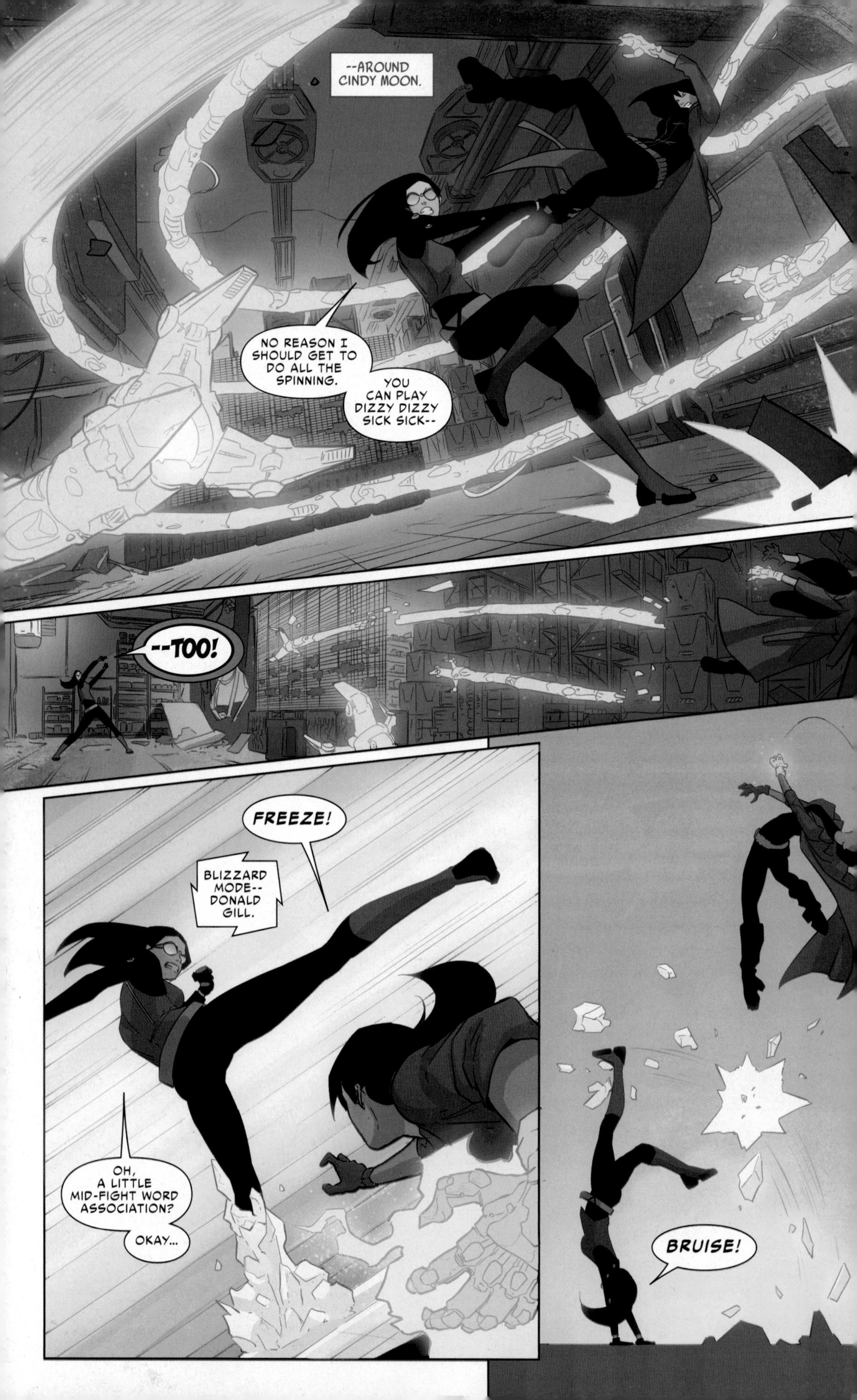
--AROUND CINDY MOON.
NO REASON I SHOULD GET TO DO ALL THE SPINNING.
YOU CAN PLAY DIZZY DIZZY SICK SICK--
--TOO!
FREEZE!
BLIZZARD MODE-- DONALD GILL.
OH, A LITTLE MID-FIGHT WORD ASSOCIATION?
OKAY...
BRUISE!

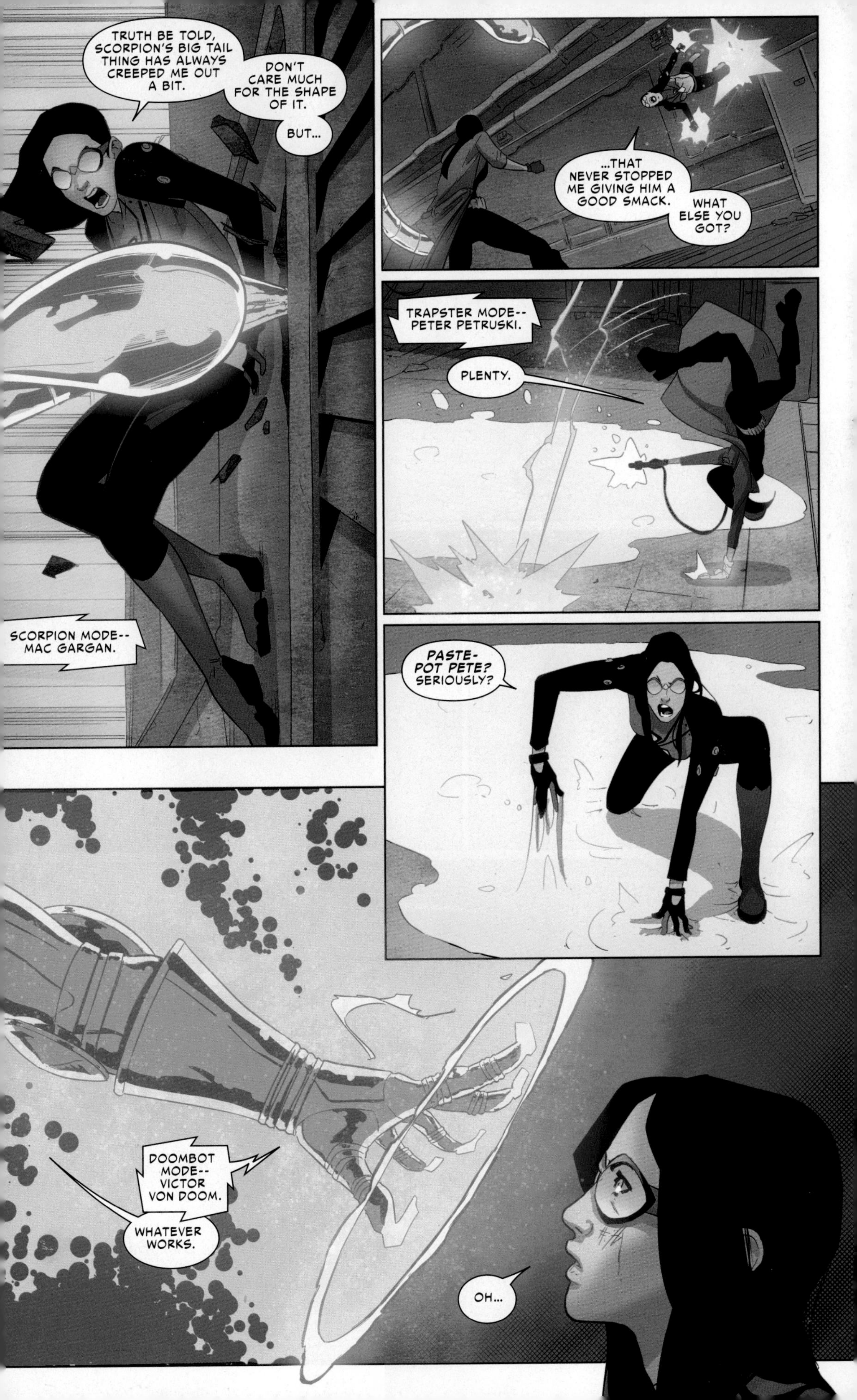
TRUTH BE TOLD, SCORPION'S BIG TAIL THING HAS ALWAYS CREEPED ME OUT A BIT.
DON'T CARE MUCH FOR THE SHAPE OF IT.
BUT...
SCORPION MODE-- MAC GARGAN.
...THAT NEVER STOPPED ME GIVING HIM A GOOD SMACK.
WHAT ELSE YOU GOT?
TRAPSTER MODE-- PETER PETRUSKI.
PLENTY.
PASTE-POT PETE? SERIOUSLY?
DOOMBOT MODE-- VICTOR VON DOOM.
WHATEVER WORKS.
OH...

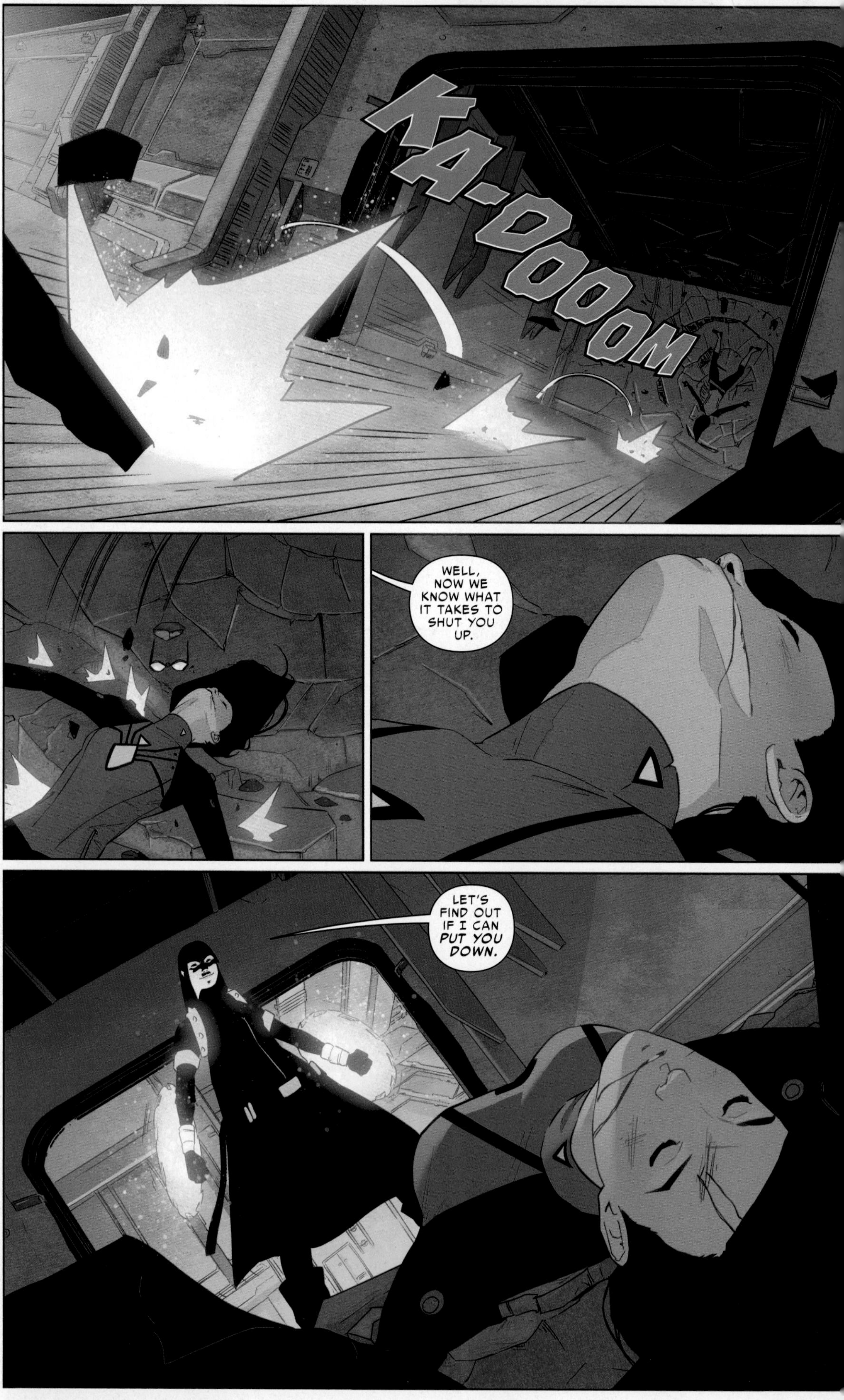
KA-DOOOM
WELL, NOW WE KNOW WHAT IT TAKES TO SHUT YOU UP.
LET'S FIND OUT IF I CAN PUT YOU DOWN.

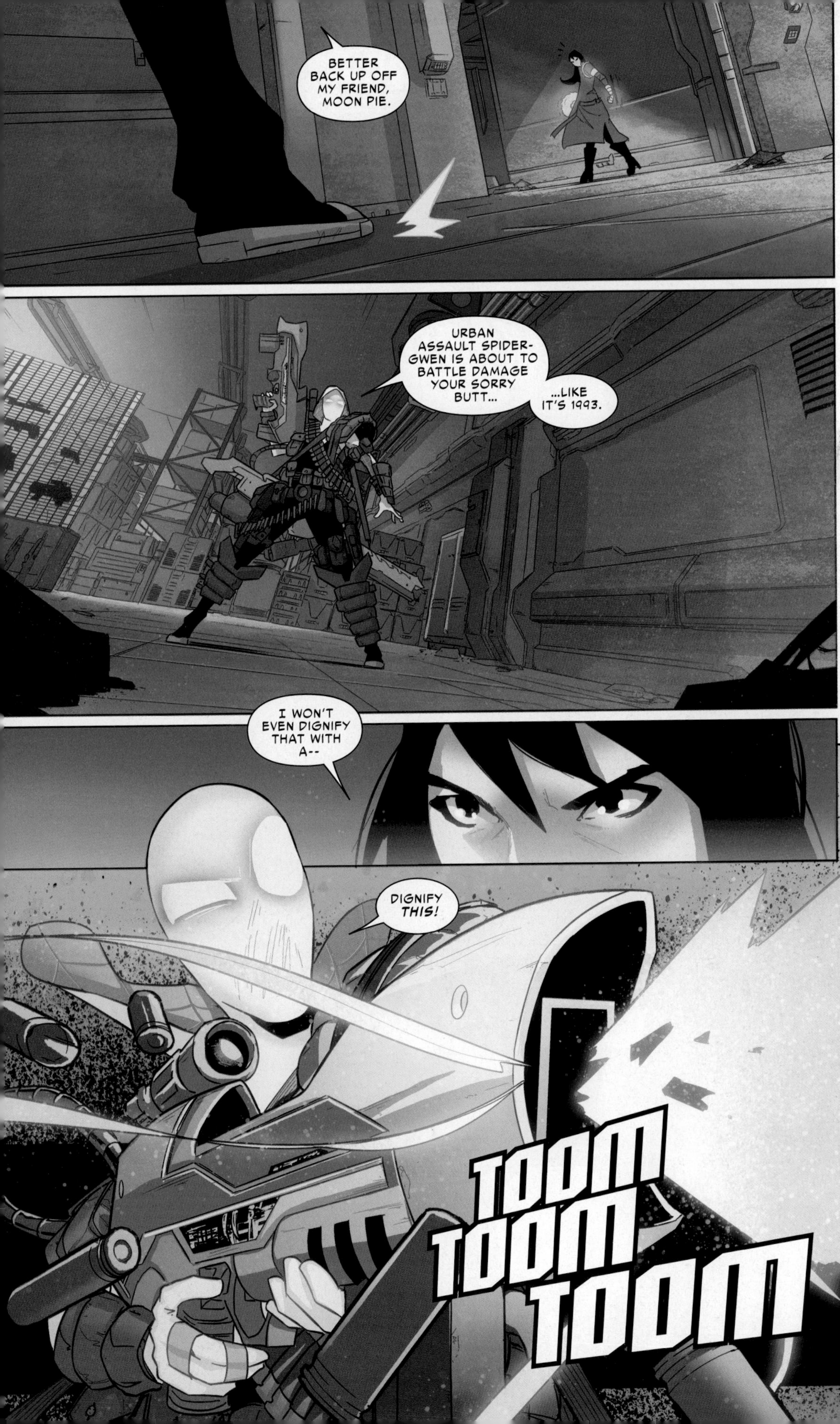
BETTER BACK UP OFF MY FRIEND, MOON PIE.
URBAN ASSAULT SPIDER-GWEN IS ABOUT TO BATTLE DAMAGE YOUR SORRY BUTT...
...LIKE IT'S 1993.
I WON'T EVEN DIGNIFY THAT WITH A--
DIGNIFY THIS!
TOOM TOOM TOOM

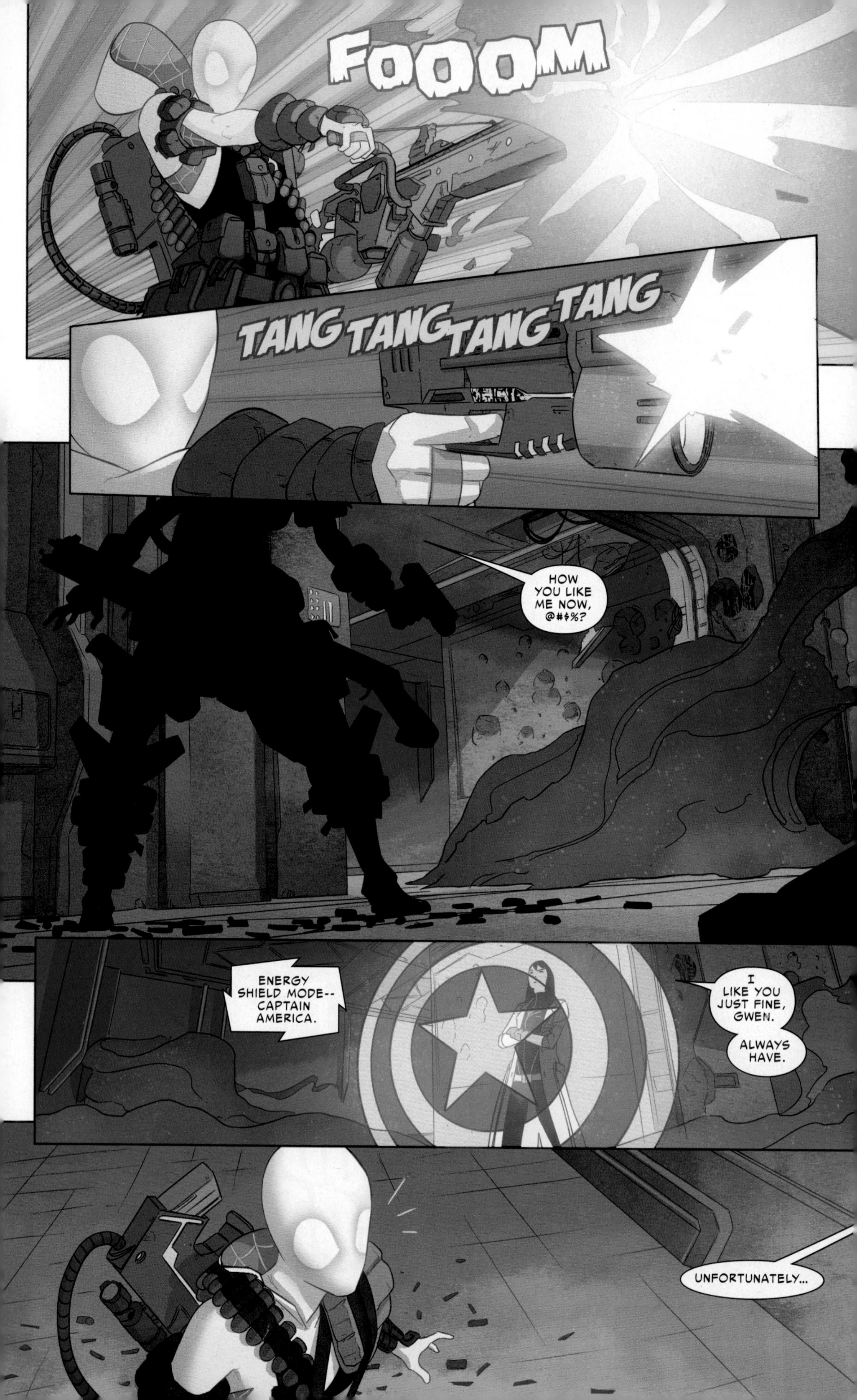
FOOOM
TANG TANG TANG TANG
HOW YOU LIKE ME NOW, @#$%?
ENERGY SHIELD MODE-- CAPTAIN AMERICA.
I LIKE YOU JUST FINE, GWEN.
ALWAYS HAVE.
UNFORTUNATELY...

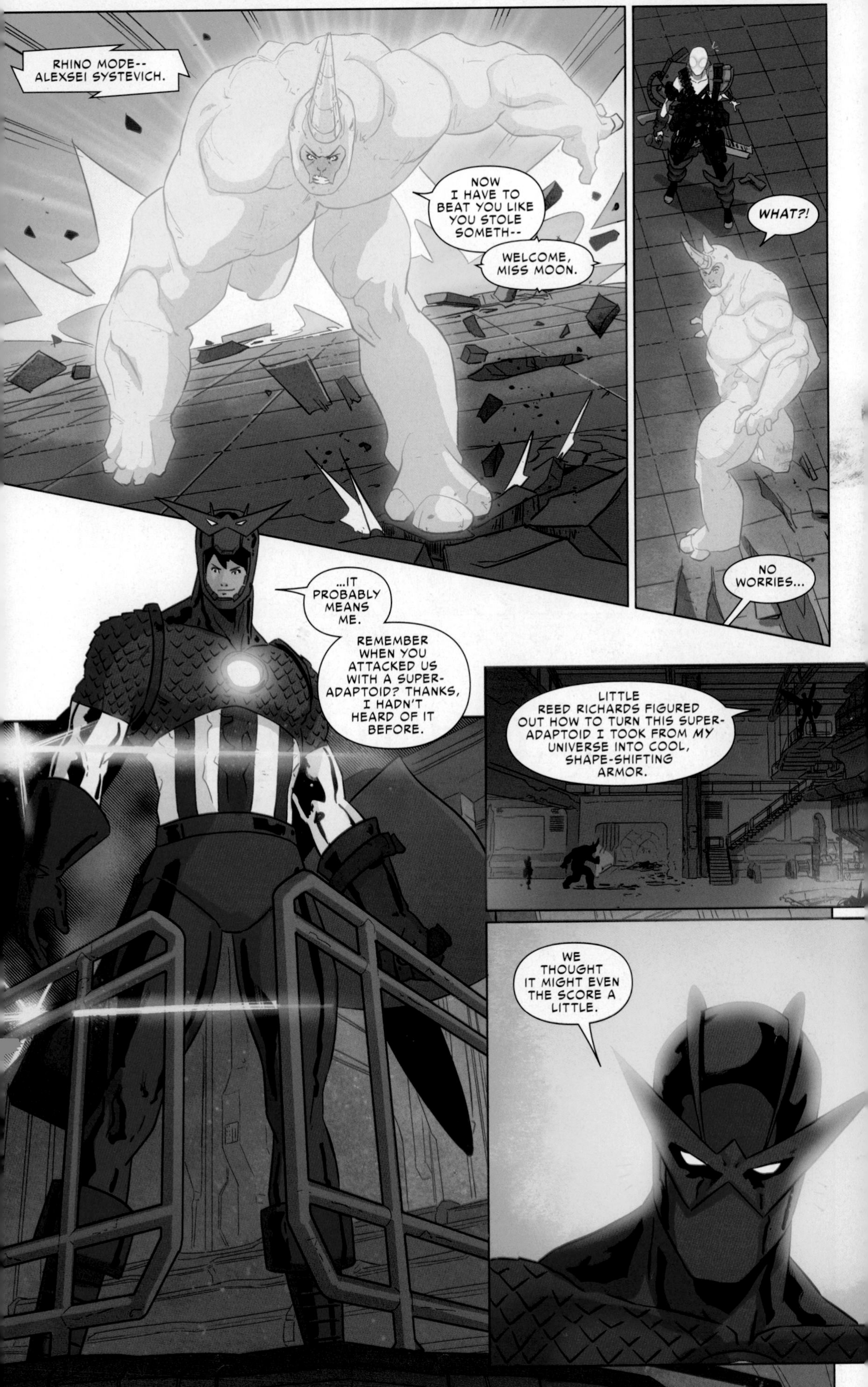
RHINO MODE--
ALEXSEI SYSTEVICH.
NOW I HAVE TO BEAT YOU LIKE YOU STOLE SOMETH--
WELCOME, MISS MOON.
WHAT?!
NO WORRIES...
...IT PROBABLY MEANS ME.
REMEMBER WHEN YOU ATTACKED US WITH A SUPER-ADAPTOID? THANKS, I HADN'T HEARD OF IT BEFORE.
LITTLE REED RICHARDS FIGURED OUT HOW TO TURN THIS SUPER-ADAPTOID I TOOK FROM MY UNIVERSE INTO COOL, SHAPE-SHIFTING ARMOR.
WE THOUGHT IT MIGHT EVEN THE SCORE A LITTLE.

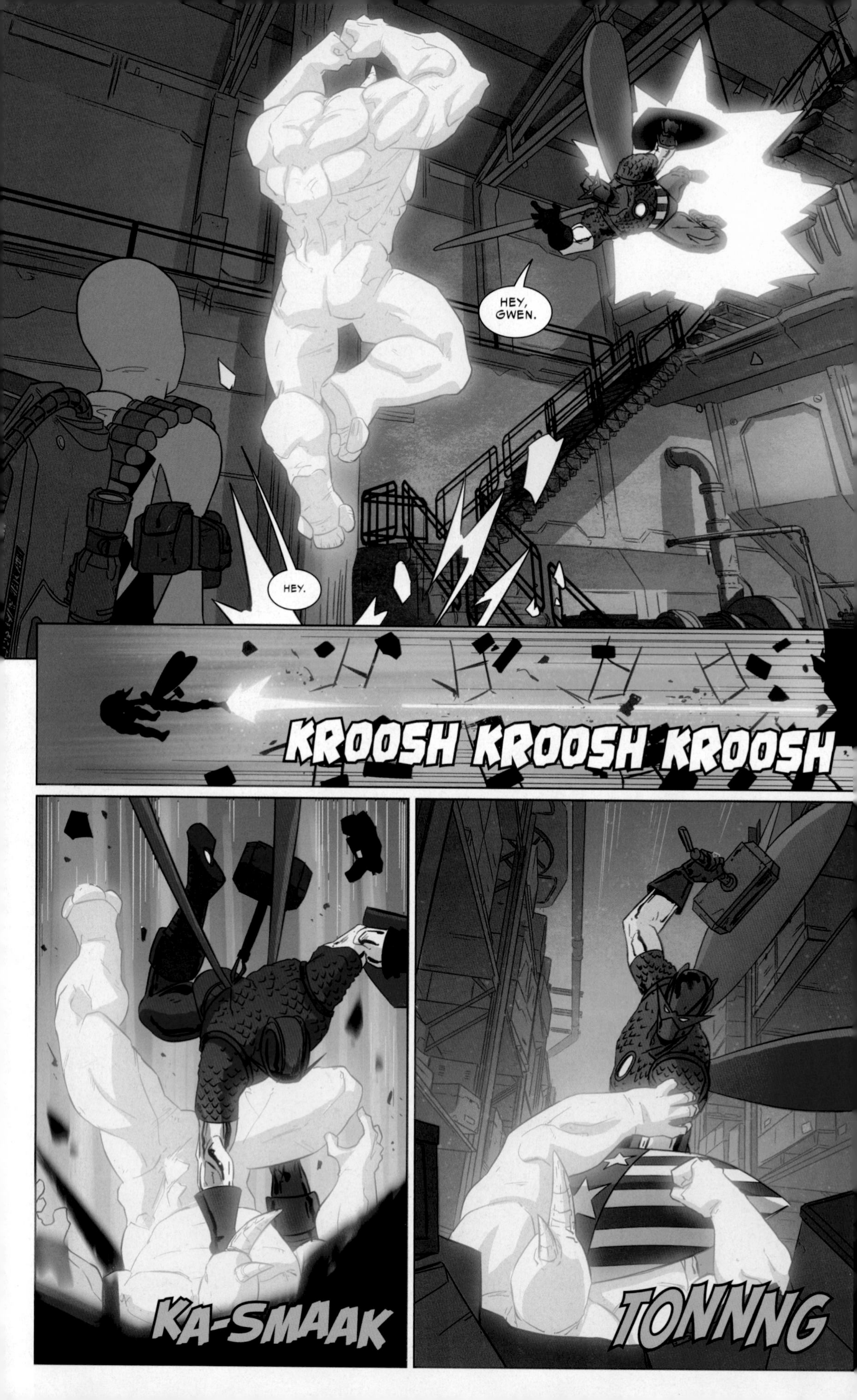
HEY, GWEN.
HEY.
KROOSH KROOSH KROOSH
KA-SMAAK
TONNNG

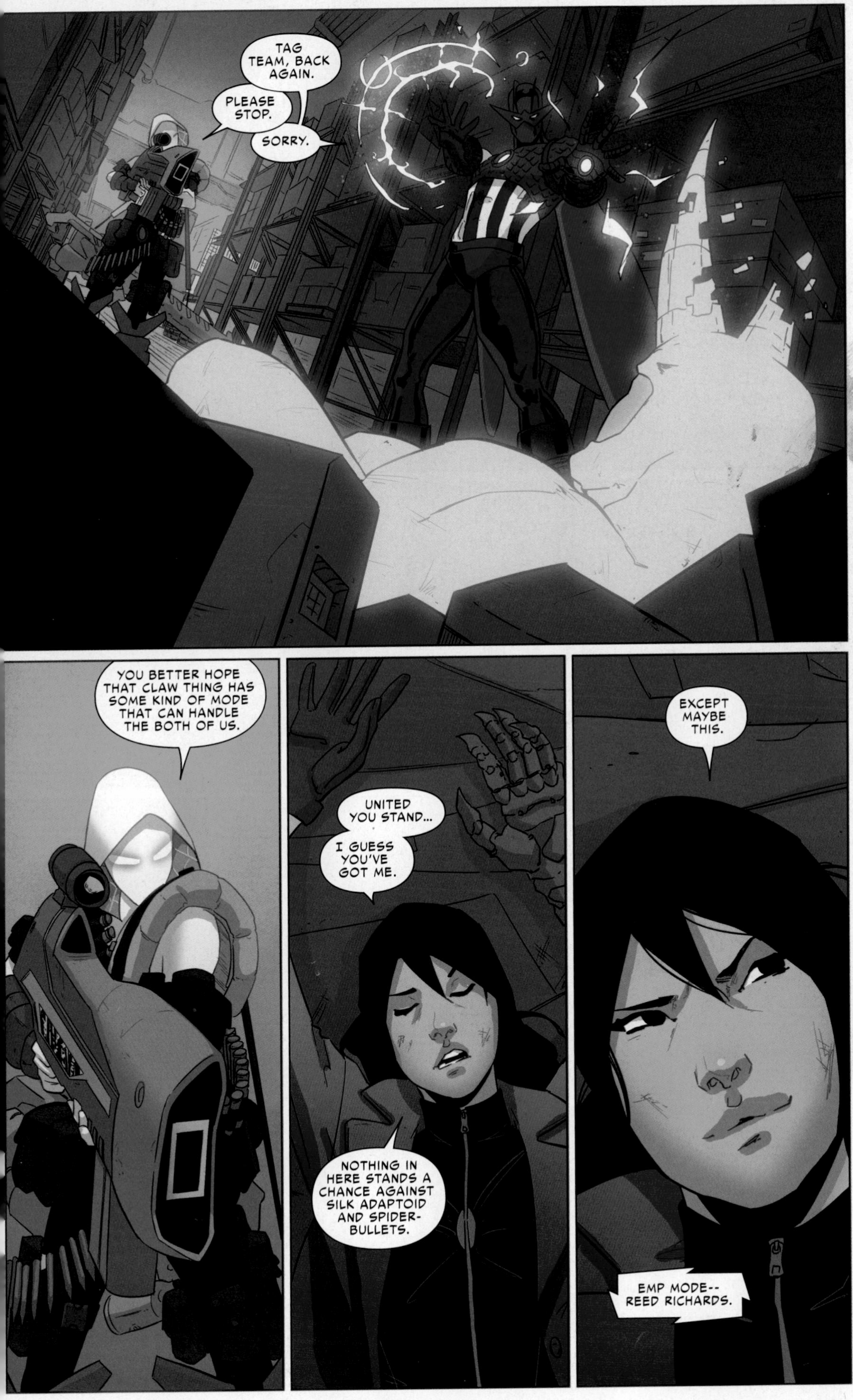
TAG TEAM, BACK AGAIN.
PLEASE STOP.
SORRY.
YOU BETTER HOPE THAT CLAW THING HAS SOME KIND OF MODE THAT CAN HANDLE THE BOTH OF US.
UNITED YOU STAND...
I GUESS YOU'VE GOT ME.
NOTHING IN HERE STANDS A CHANCE AGAINST SILK ADAPTOID AND SPIDER-BULLETS.
EXCEPT MAYBE THIS.
EMP MODE--REED RICHARDS.

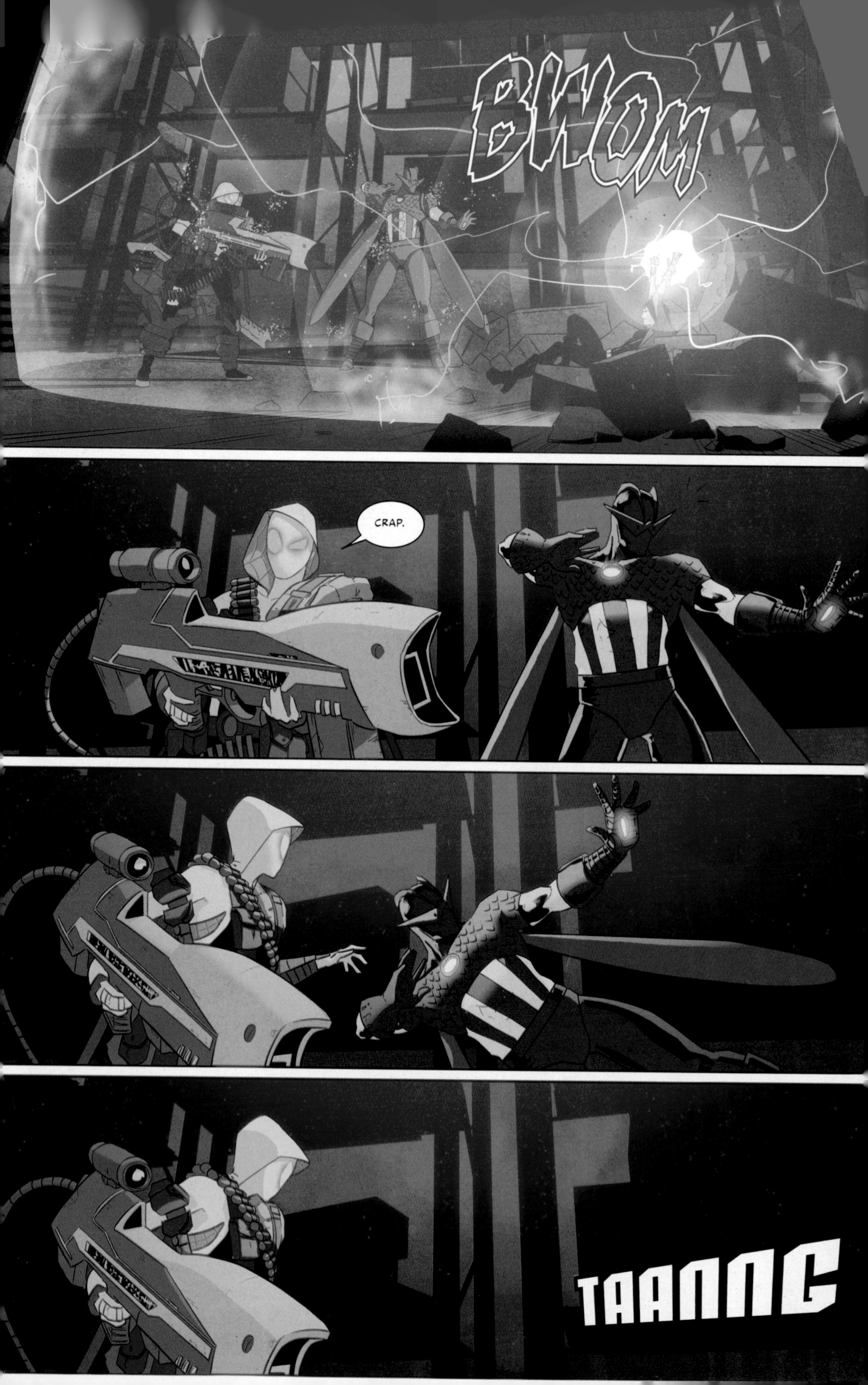
BWOM
CRAP.
TAANNG

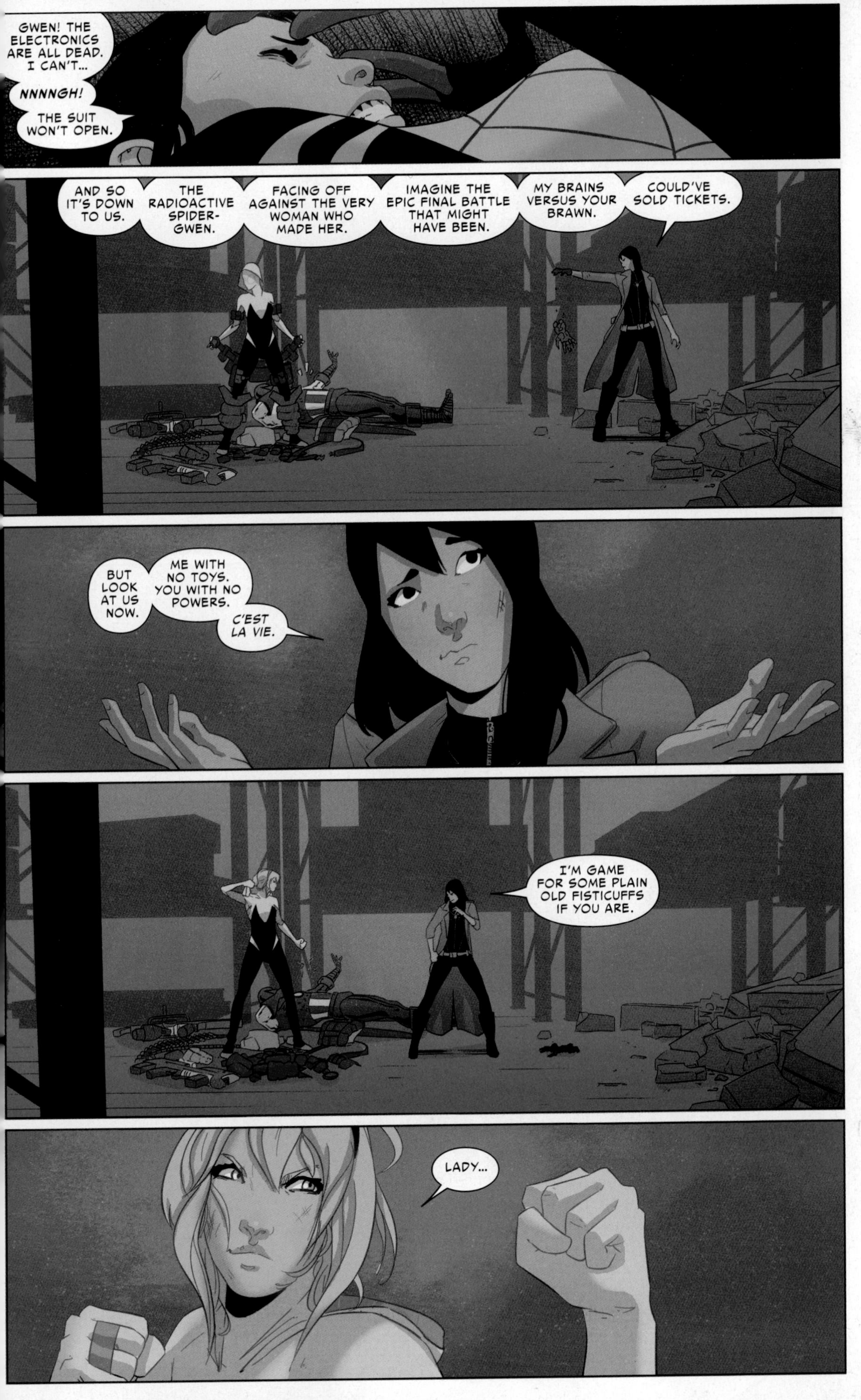
GWEN! THE ELECTRONICS ARE ALL DEAD. I CAN'T...
NNNNGH!
THE SUIT WON'T OPEN.
AND SO IT'S DOWN TO US.
THE RADIOACTIVE SPIDER-GWEN.
FACING OFF AGAINST THE VERY WOMAN WHO MADE HER.
IMAGINE THE EPIC FINAL BATTLE THAT MIGHT HAVE BEEN.
MY BRAINS VERSUS YOUR BRAWN.
COULD'VE SOLD TICKETS.
BUT LOOK AT US NOW.
ME WITH NO TOYS. YOU WITH NO POWERS.
C'EST LA VIE.
I'M GAME FOR SOME PLAIN OLD FISTICUFFS IF YOU ARE.
LADY...

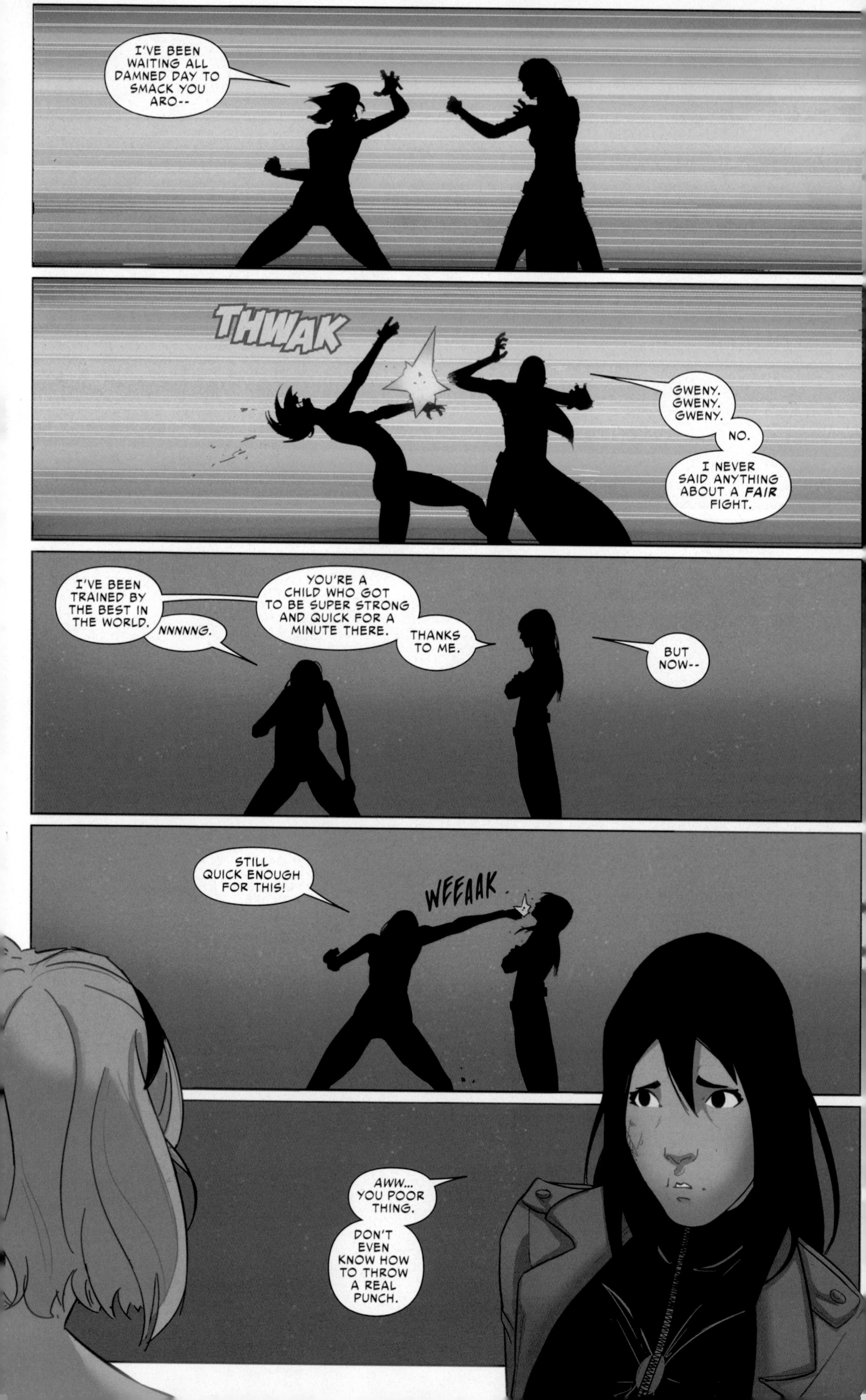
I'VE BEEN WAITING ALL DAMNED DAY TO SMACK YOU ARO--
THWAK
GWENY. GWENY. GWENY.
NO.
I NEVER SAID ANYTHING ABOUT A FAIR FIGHT.
I'VE BEEN TRAINED BY THE BEST IN THE WORLD.
NNNNNG.
YOU'RE A CHILD WHO GOT TO BE SUPER STRONG AND QUICK FOR A MINUTE THERE.
THANKS TO ME.
BUT NOW--
STILL QUICK ENOUGH FOR THIS!
WEEAAK
AWW... YOU POOR THING.
DON'T EVEN KNOW HOW TO THROW A REAL PUNCH.

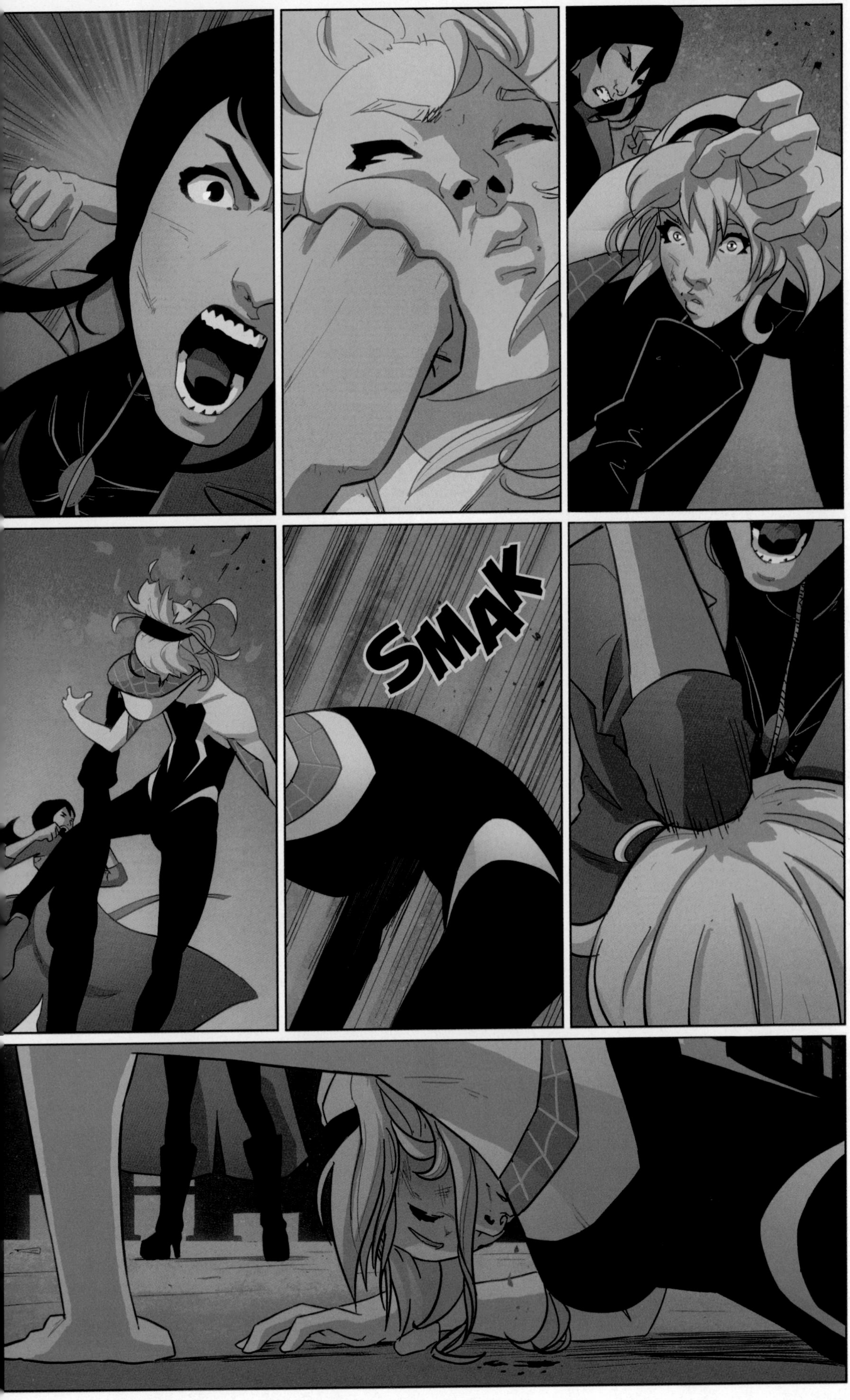
SMAK

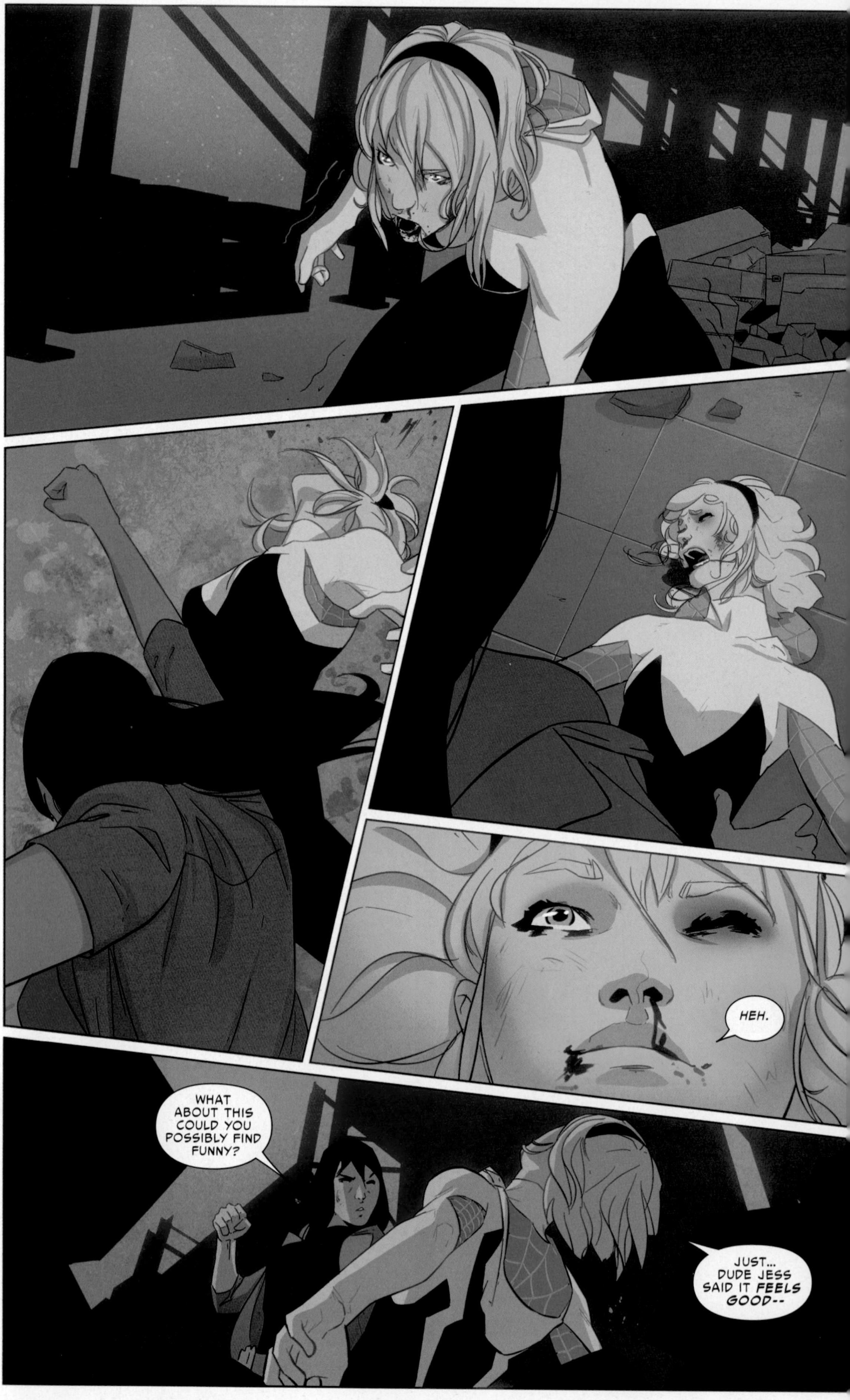
HEH.
WHAT ABOUT THIS COULD YOU POSSIBLY FIND FUNNY?
JUST... DUDE JESS SAID IT FEELS GOOD--

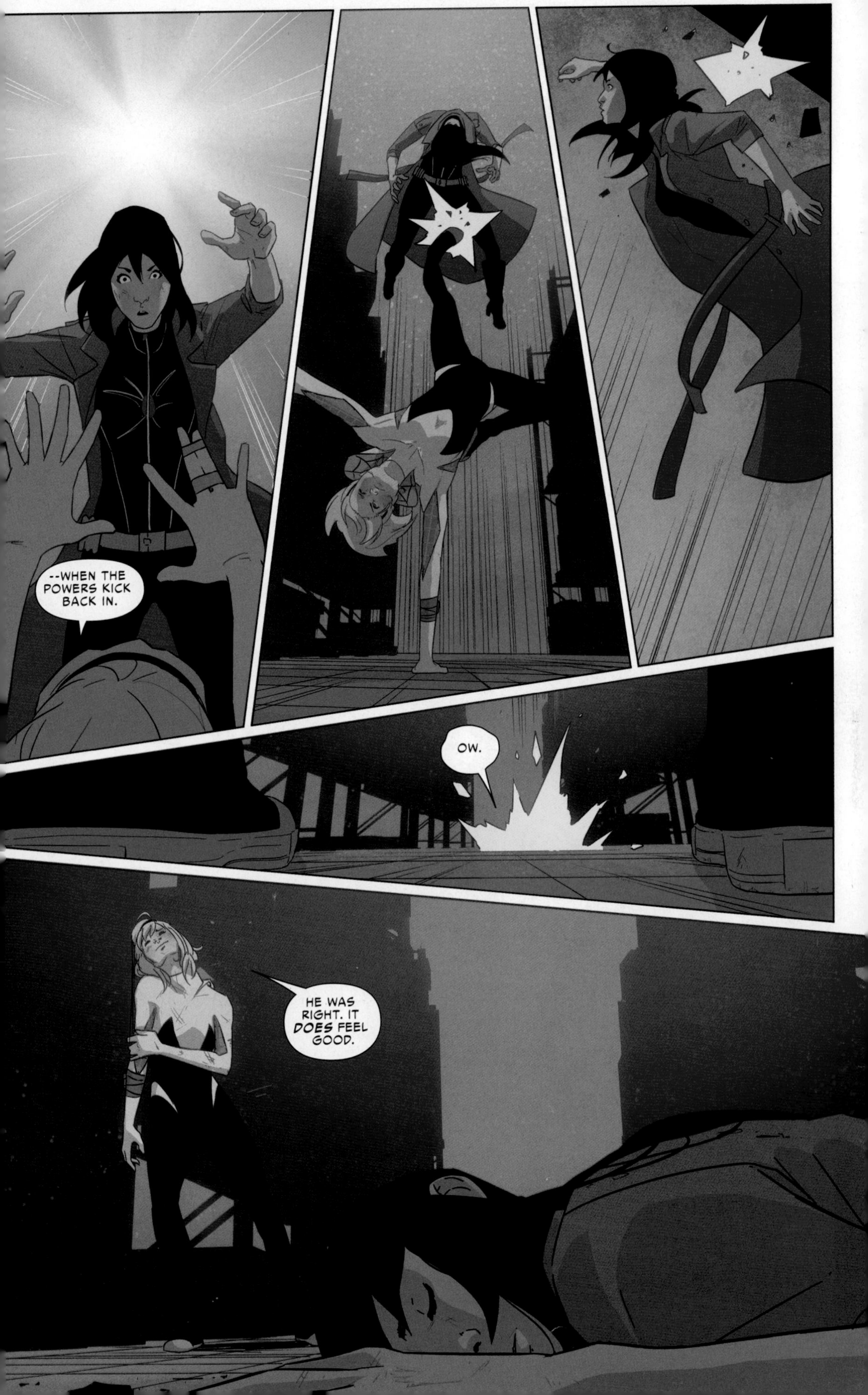
--WHEN THE POWERS KICK BACK IN.
OW.
HE WAS RIGHT. IT DOES FEEL GOOD.

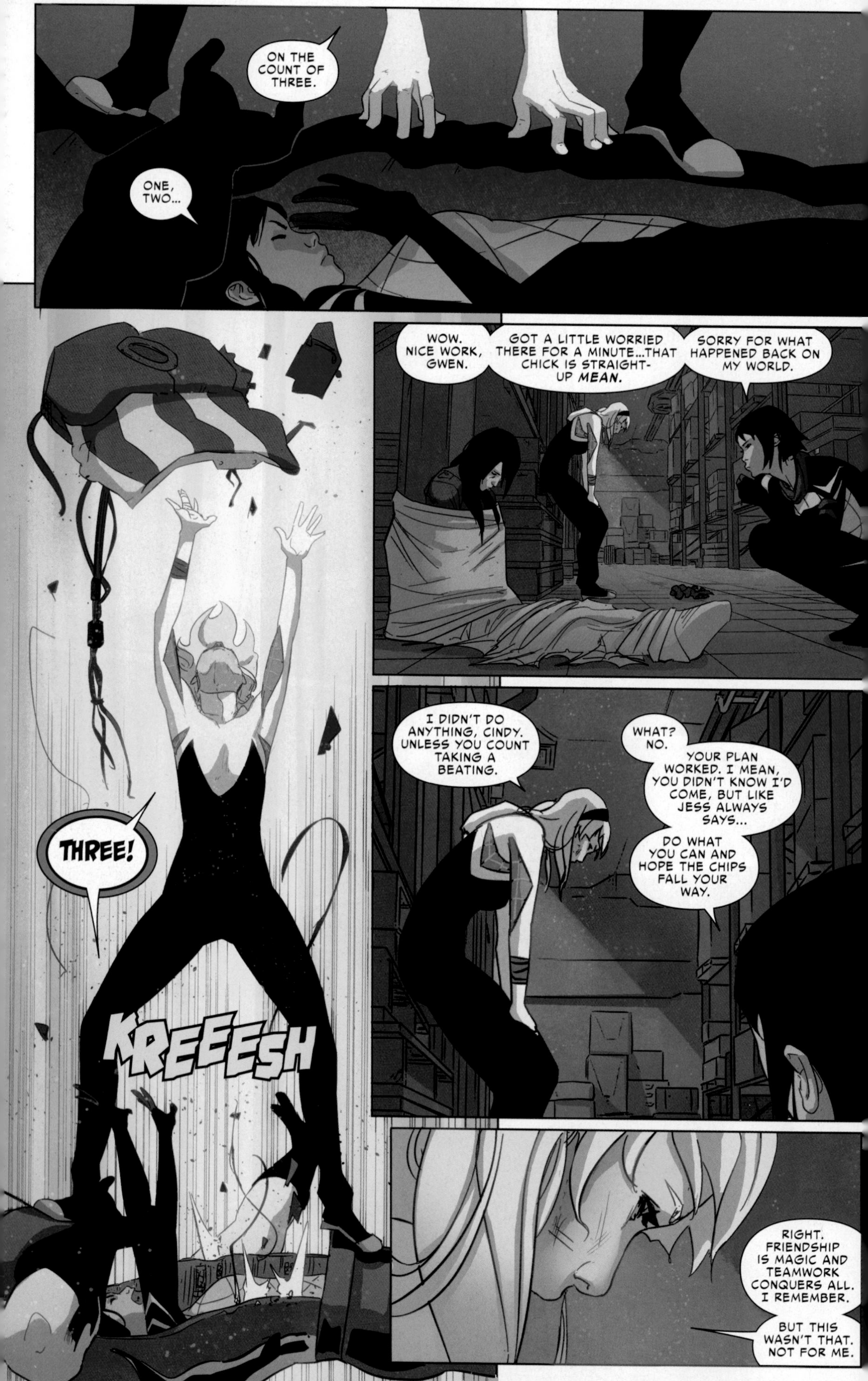

ON THE COUNT OF THREE.
ONE, TWO...
THREE!
KREEESH
WOW. NICE WORK, GWEN.
GOT A LITTLE WORRIED THERE FOR A MINUTE...THAT CHICK IS STRAIGHT-UP *MEAN.*
SORRY FOR WHAT HAPPENED BACK ON MY WORLD.
I DIDN'T DO ANYTHING, CINDY. UNLESS YOU COUNT TAKING A BEATING.
WHAT? NO.
YOUR PLAN WORKED. I MEAN, YOU DIDN'T KNOW I'D COME, BUT LIKE JESS ALWAYS SAYS...
DO WHAT YOU CAN AND HOPE THE CHIPS FALL YOUR WAY.
RIGHT. FRIENDSHIP IS MAGIC AND TEAMWORK CONQUERS ALL. I REMEMBER.
BUT THIS WASN'T THAT. NOT FOR ME.

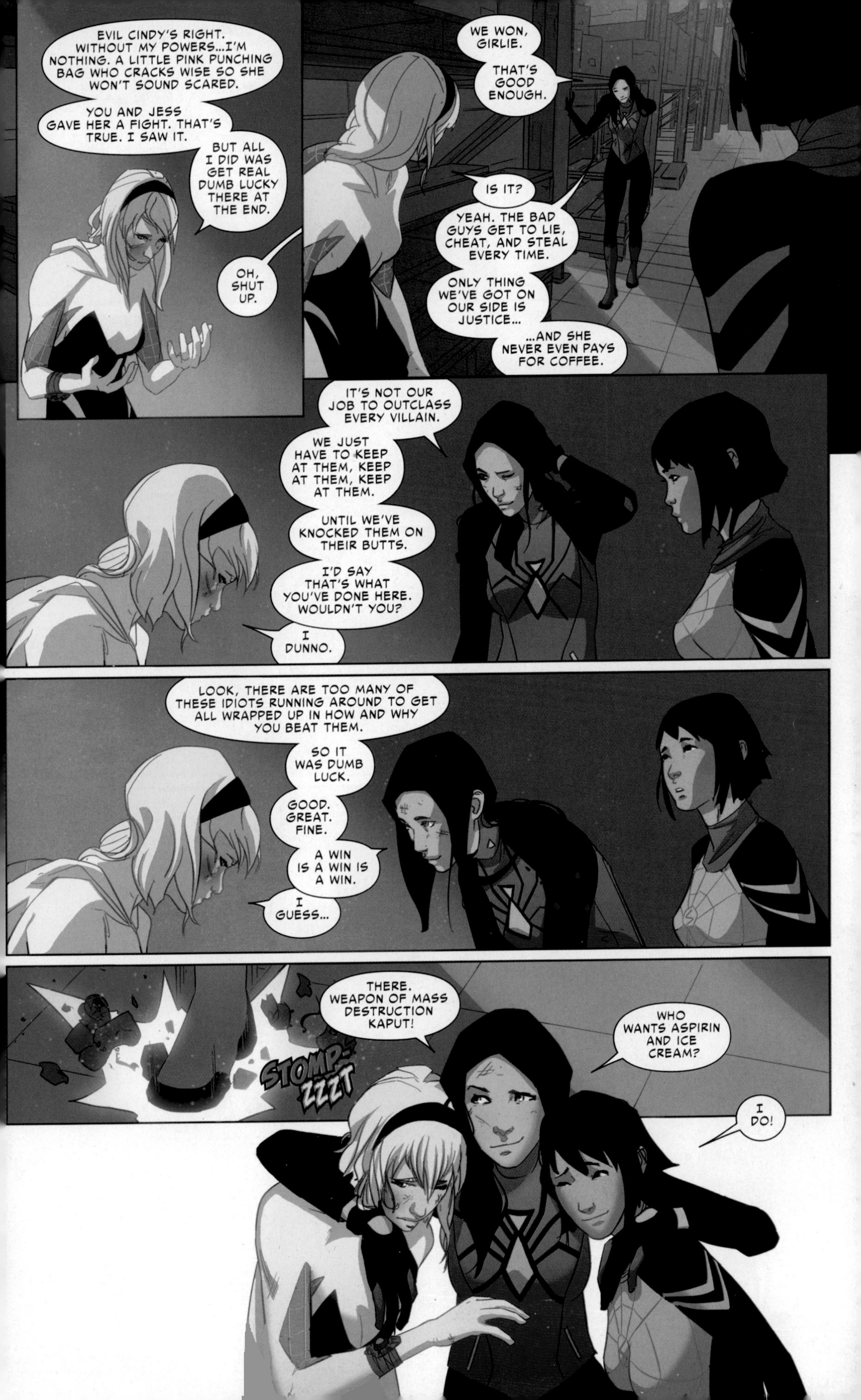
EVIL CINDY'S RIGHT. WITHOUT MY POWERS...I'M NOTHING. A LITTLE PINK PUNCHING BAG WHO CRACKS WISE SO SHE WON'T SOUND SCARED.
YOU AND JESS GAVE HER A FIGHT. THAT'S TRUE. I SAW IT.
BUT ALL I DID WAS GET REAL DUMB LUCKY THERE AT THE END.
OH, SHUT UP.
WE WON, GIRLIE.
THAT'S GOOD ENOUGH.
IS IT?
YEAH. THE BAD GUYS GET TO LIE, CHEAT, AND STEAL EVERY TIME.
ONLY THING WE'VE GOT ON OUR SIDE IS JUSTICE...
...AND SHE NEVER EVEN PAYS FOR COFFEE.
IT'S NOT OUR JOB TO OUTCLASS EVERY VILLAIN.
WE JUST HAVE TO KEEP AT THEM, KEEP AT THEM, KEEP AT THEM.
UNTIL WE'VE KNOCKED THEM ON THEIR BUTTS.
I'D SAY THAT'S WHAT YOU'VE DONE HERE. WOULDN'T YOU?
I DUNNO.
LOOK, THERE ARE TOO MANY OF THESE IDIOTS RUNNING AROUND TO GET ALL WRAPPED UP IN HOW AND WHY YOU BEAT THEM.
SO IT WAS DUMB LUCK.
GOOD. GREAT. FINE.
A WIN IS A WIN IS A WIN.
I GUESS...
STOMP-ZZZT
THERE. WEAPON OF MASS DESTRUCTION KAPUT!
WHO WANTS ASPIRIN AND ICE CREAM?
I DO!

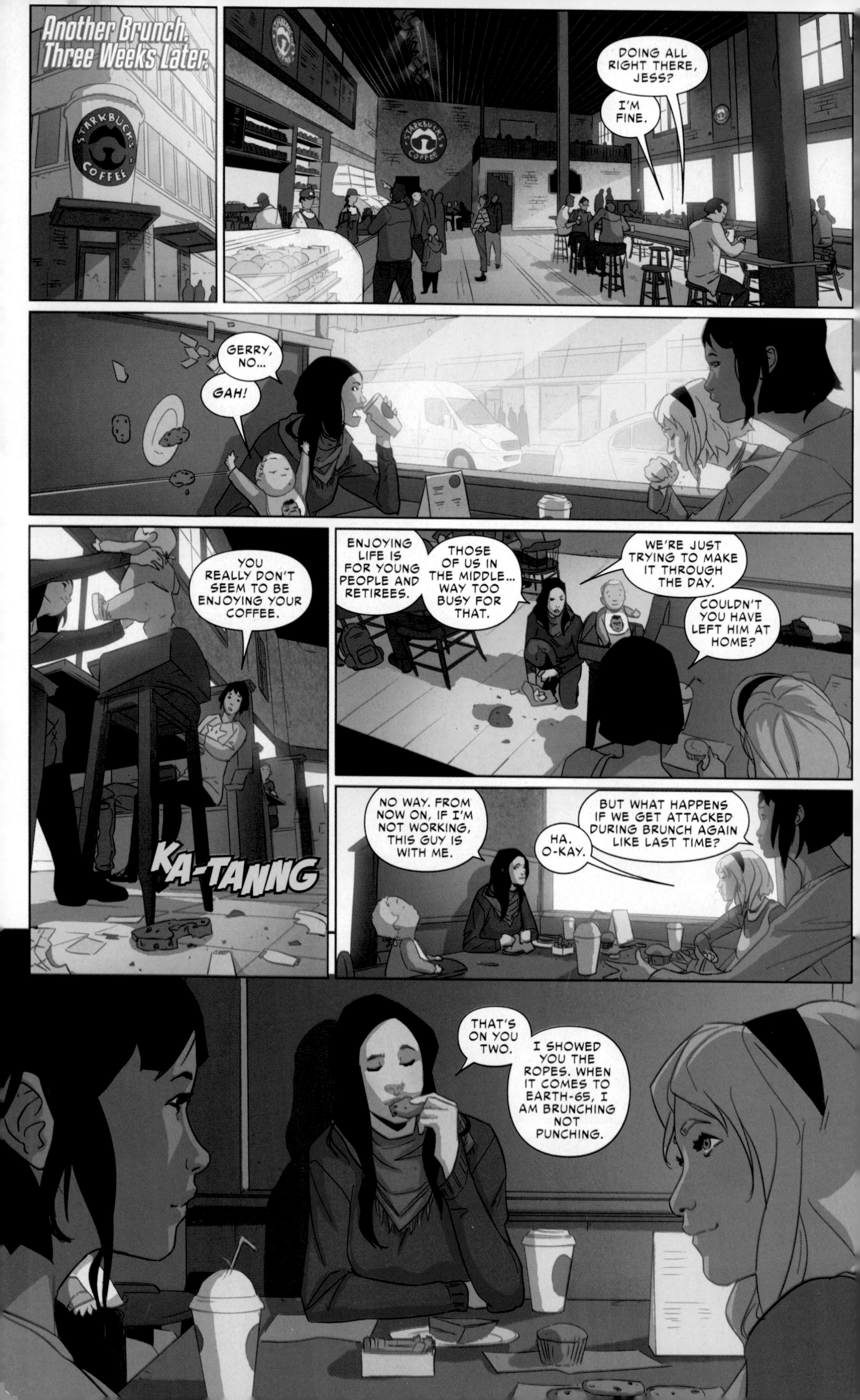
Another Brunch. Three Weeks Later.
STARKBUCKS COFFEE
DOING ALL RIGHT THERE, JESS?
I'M FINE.
GERRY, NO...
GAH!
YOU REALLY DON'T SEEM TO BE ENJOYING YOUR COFFEE.
KA-TANNG
ENJOYING LIFE IS FOR YOUNG PEOPLE AND RETIREES.
THOSE OF US IN THE MIDDLE... WAY TOO BUSY FOR THAT.
WE'RE JUST TRYING TO MAKE IT THROUGH THE DAY.
COULDN'T YOU HAVE LEFT HIM AT HOME?
NO WAY. FROM NOW ON, IF I'M NOT WORKING, THIS GUY IS WITH ME.
BUT WHAT HAPPENS IF WE GET ATTACKED DURING BRUNCH AGAIN LIKE LAST TIME?
HA. O-KAY.
THAT'S ON YOU TWO.
I SHOWED YOU THE ROPES. WHEN IT COMES TO EARTH-65, I AM BRUNCHING NOT PUNCHING.

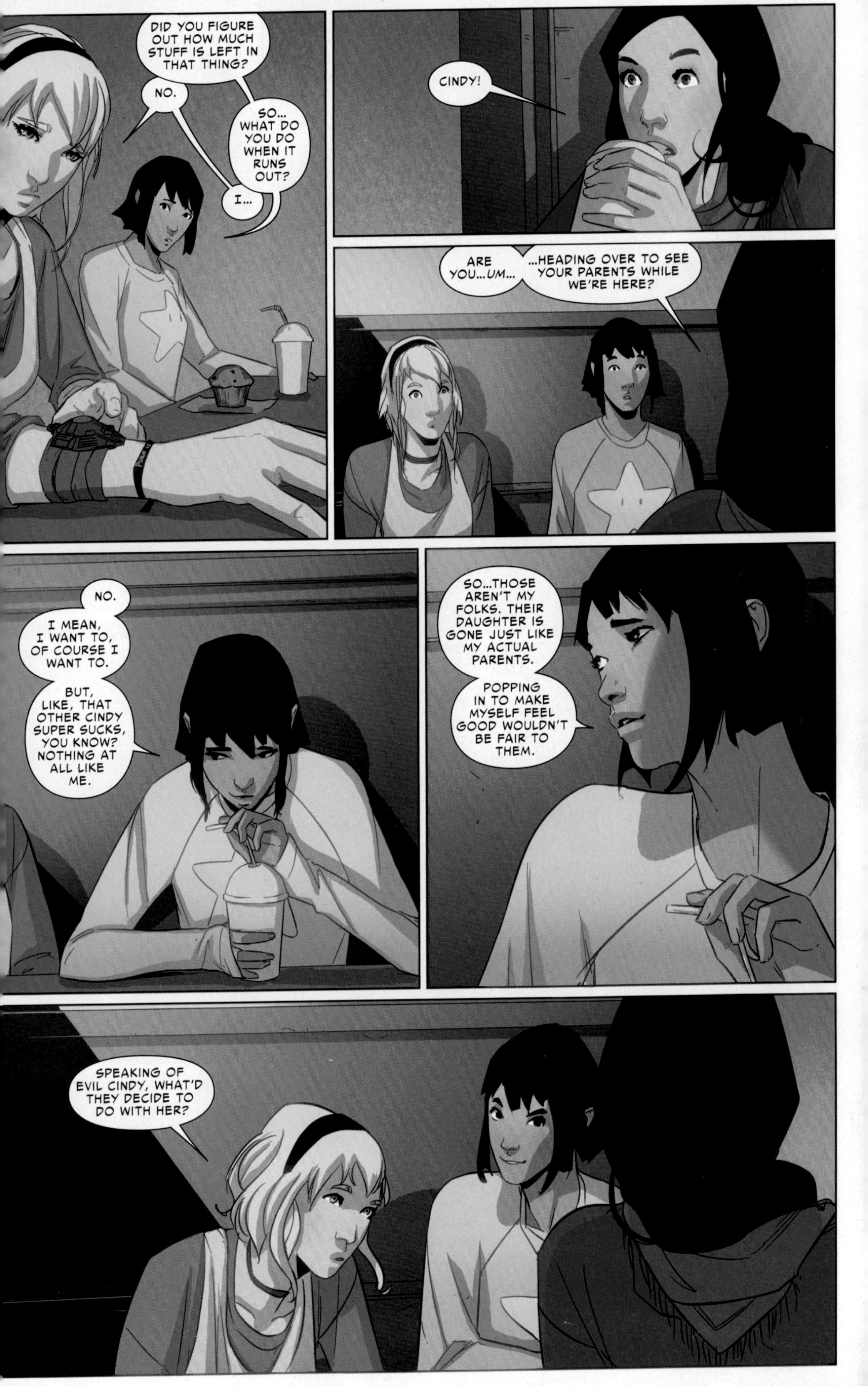

DID YOU FIGURE OUT HOW MUCH STUFF IS LEFT IN THAT THING?
NO.
SO... WHAT DO YOU DO WHEN IT RUNS OUT?
I...
CINDY!
ARE YOU...UM...
...HEADING OVER TO SEE YOUR PARENTS WHILE WE'RE HERE?
NO.
I MEAN, I WANT TO, OF COURSE I WANT TO.
BUT, LIKE, THAT OTHER CINDY SUPER SUCKS, YOU KNOW? NOTHING AT ALL LIKE ME.
SO...THOSE AREN'T MY FOLKS. THEIR DAUGHTER IS GONE JUST LIKE MY ACTUAL PARENTS.
POPPING IN TO MAKE MYSELF FEEL GOOD WOULDN'T BE FAIR TO THEM.
SPEAKING OF EVIL CINDY, WHAT'D THEY DECIDE TO DO WITH HER?

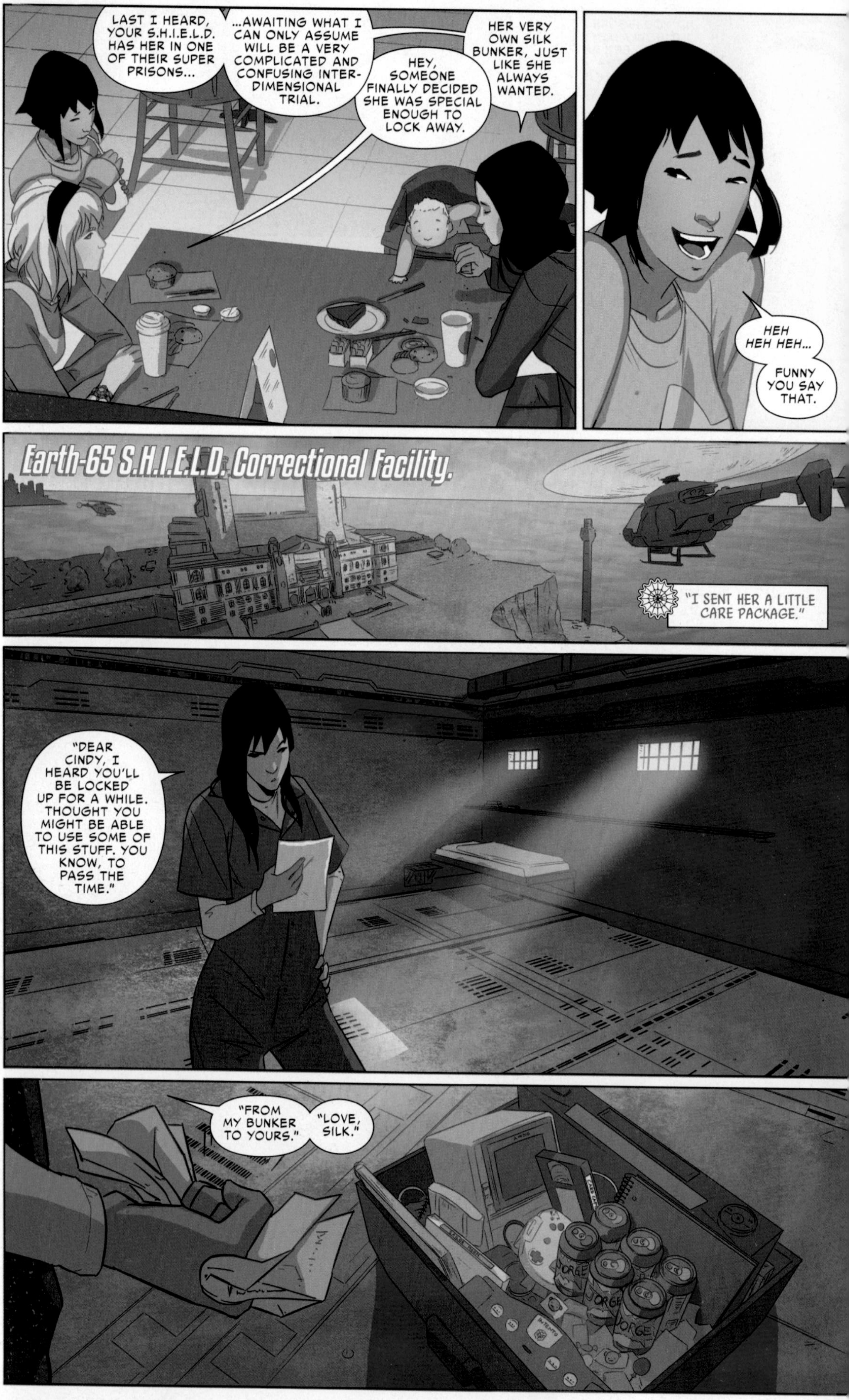
LAST I HEARD, YOUR S.H.I.E.L.D. HAS HER IN ONE OF THEIR SUPER PRISONS...
...AWAITING WHAT I CAN ONLY ASSUME WILL BE A VERY COMPLICATED AND CONFUSING INTER-DIMENSIONAL TRIAL.
HEY, SOMEONE FINALLY DECIDED SHE WAS SPECIAL ENOUGH TO LOCK AWAY.
HER VERY OWN SILK BUNKER, JUST LIKE SHE ALWAYS WANTED.
HEH HEH HEH...
FUNNY YOU SAY THAT.
Earth-65 S.H.I.E.L.D. Correctional Facility.
"I SENT HER A LITTLE CARE PACKAGE."
"DEAR CINDY, I HEARD YOU'LL BE LOCKED UP FOR A WHILE. THOUGHT YOU MIGHT BE ABLE TO USE SOME OF THIS STUFF. YOU KNOW, TO PASS THE TIME."
"FROM MY BUNKER TO YOURS."
"LOVE, SILK."
JORGE
JORGE
JORGE

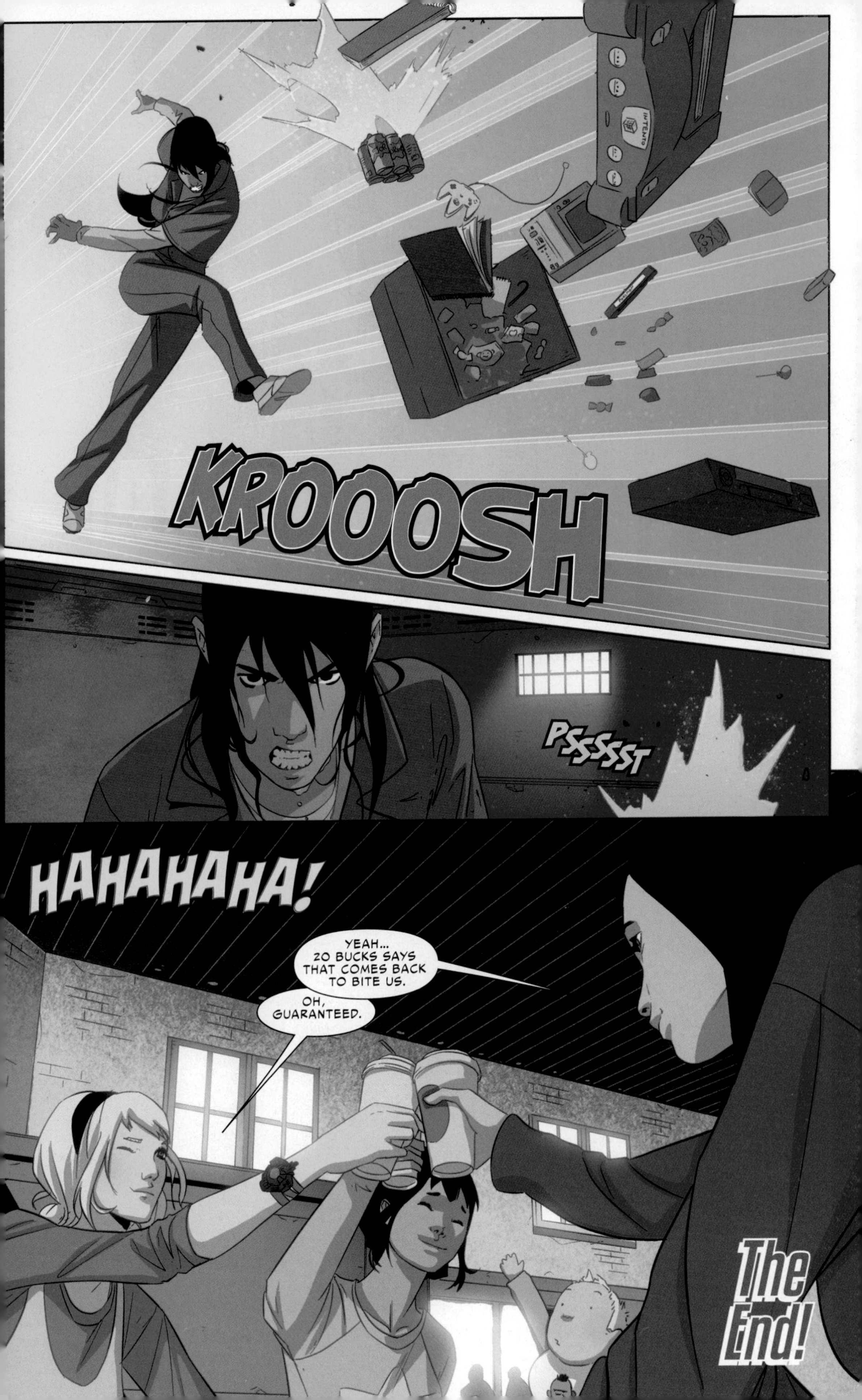
KROOOSH
PSSSSST
HAHAHAHA!
YEAH... 20 BUCKS SAYS THAT COMES BACK TO BITE US.
OH, GUARANTEED.
The End!

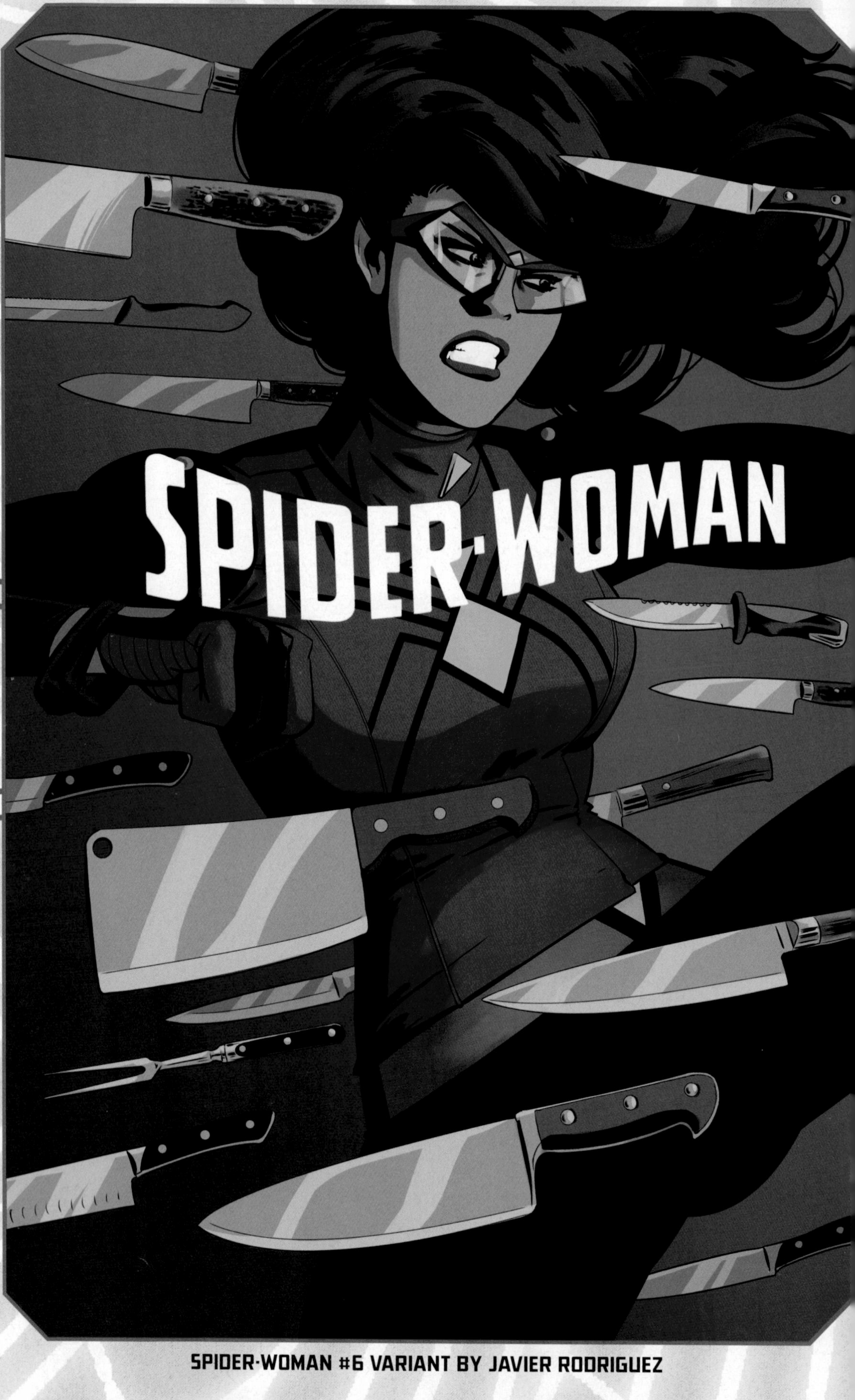
SPIDER-WOMAN

SPIDER-WOMAN #6 VARIANT BY JAVIER RODRIGUEZ

SPIDER-GWEN #8 BY ROBBI RODRIGUEZ

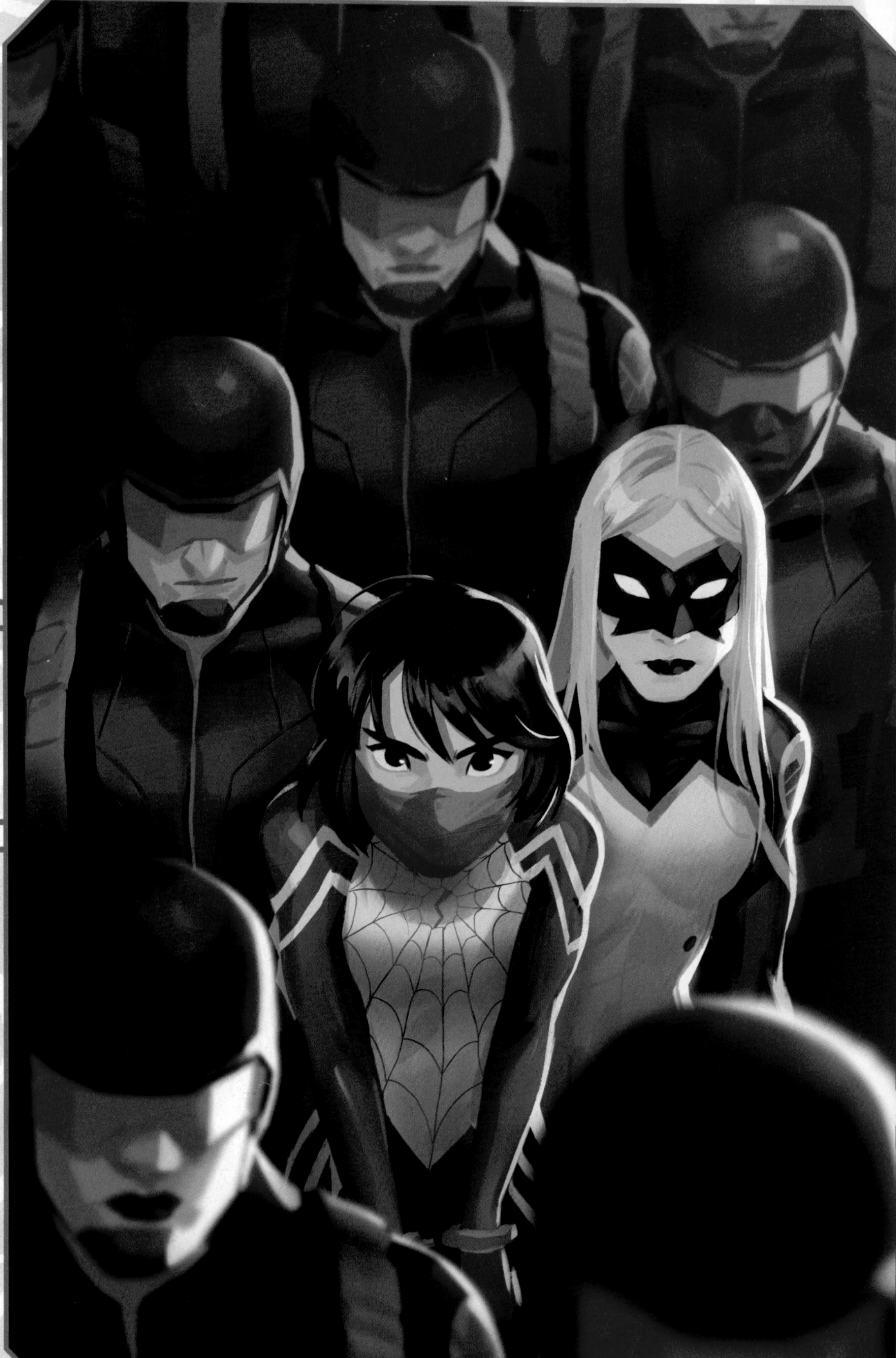

SILK #8 VARIANT BY HELEN CHEN

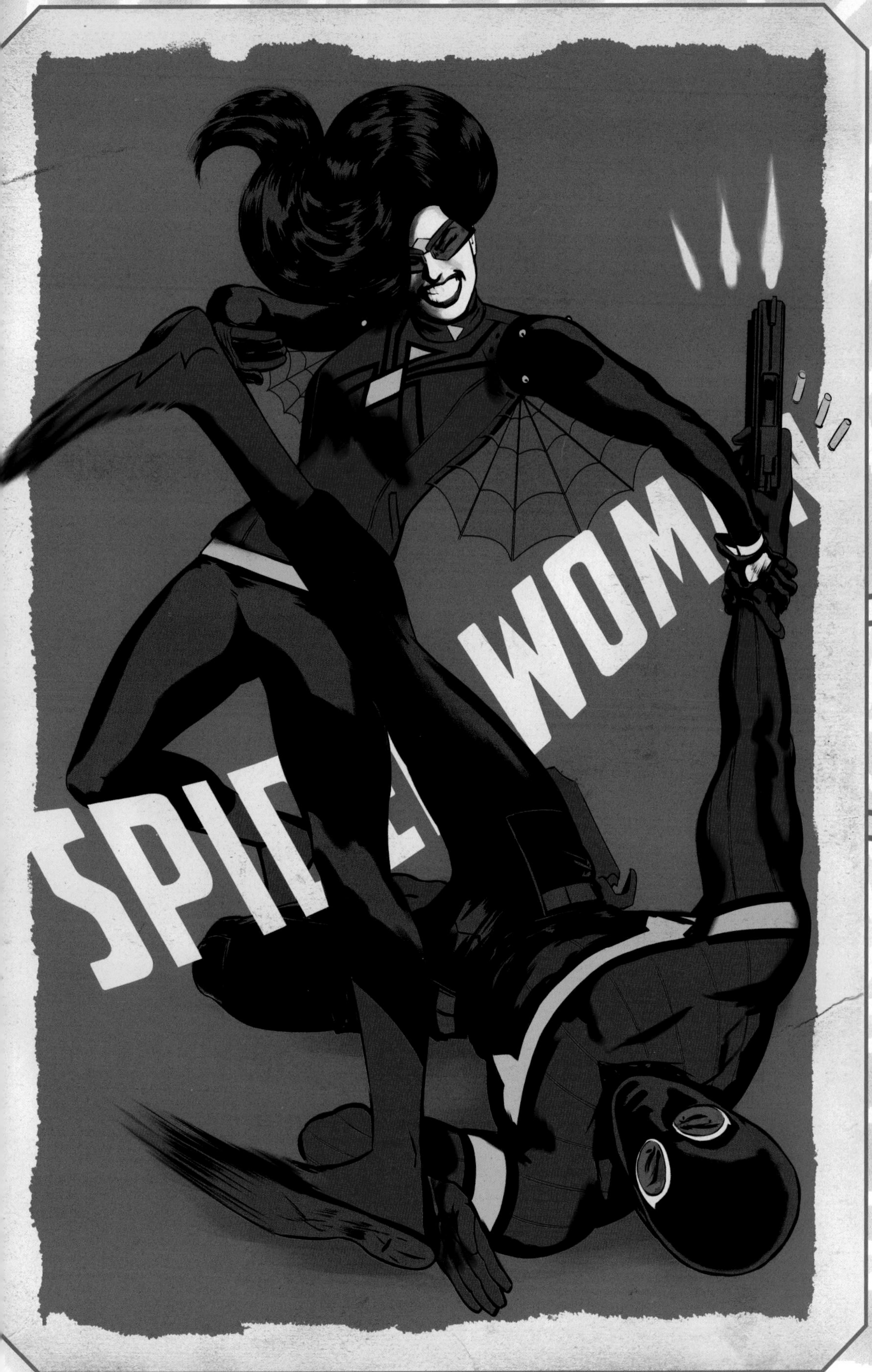

SPIDER-WOMEN #7 VARIANT BY JAVIER RODRIGUEZ

SPIDER-GWEN #8
HORSEMEN OF APOCALYPSE VARIANT
BY WILL SLINEY & FRANK D'ARAMTA

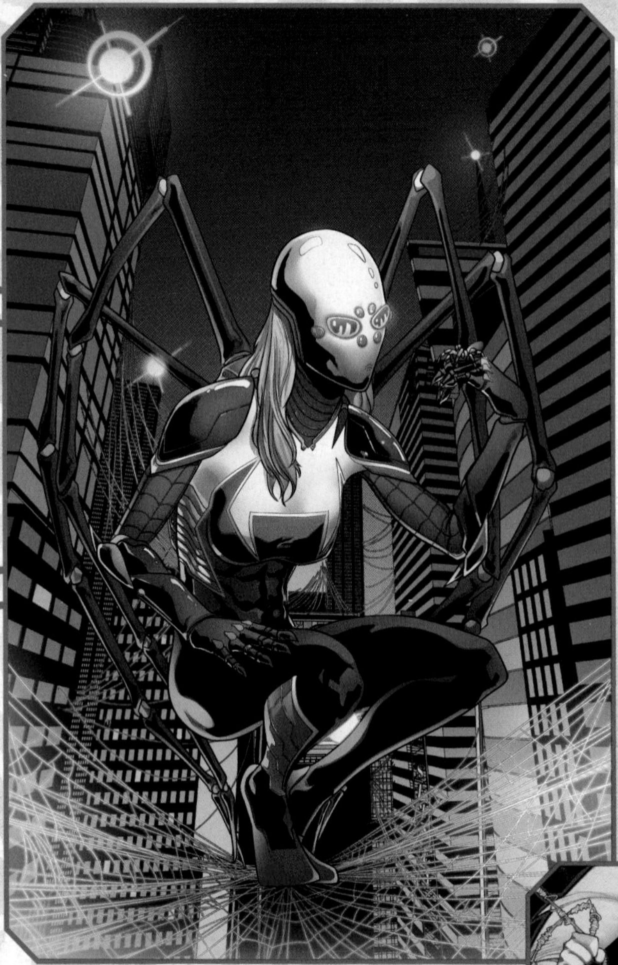

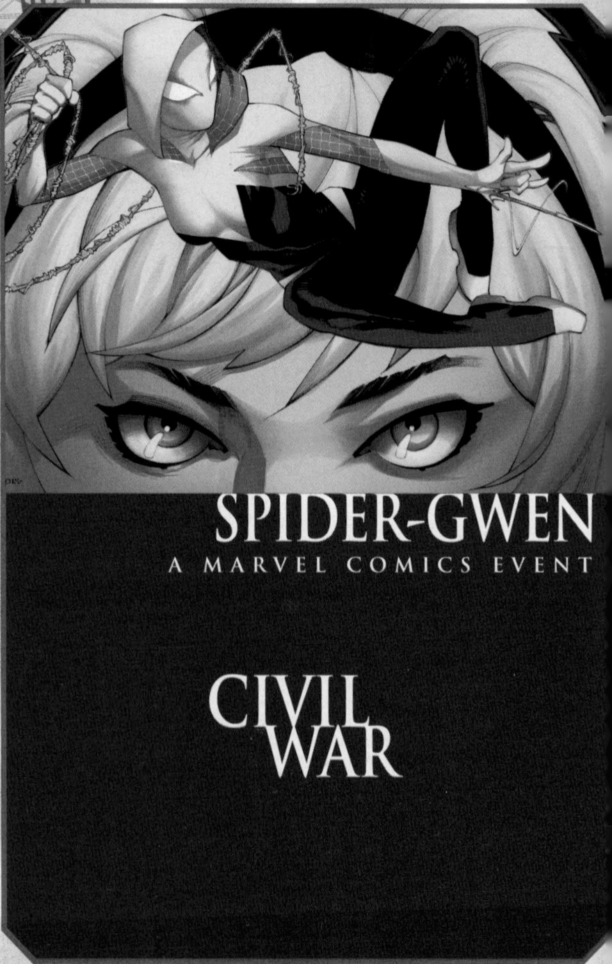
SPIDER-GWEN
A MARVEL COMICS EVENT
CIVIL WAR

SPIDER-GWEN #7 CIVIL WAR
VARIANT BY CHRISTOPHER STEVENS
& FRANK MARTIN

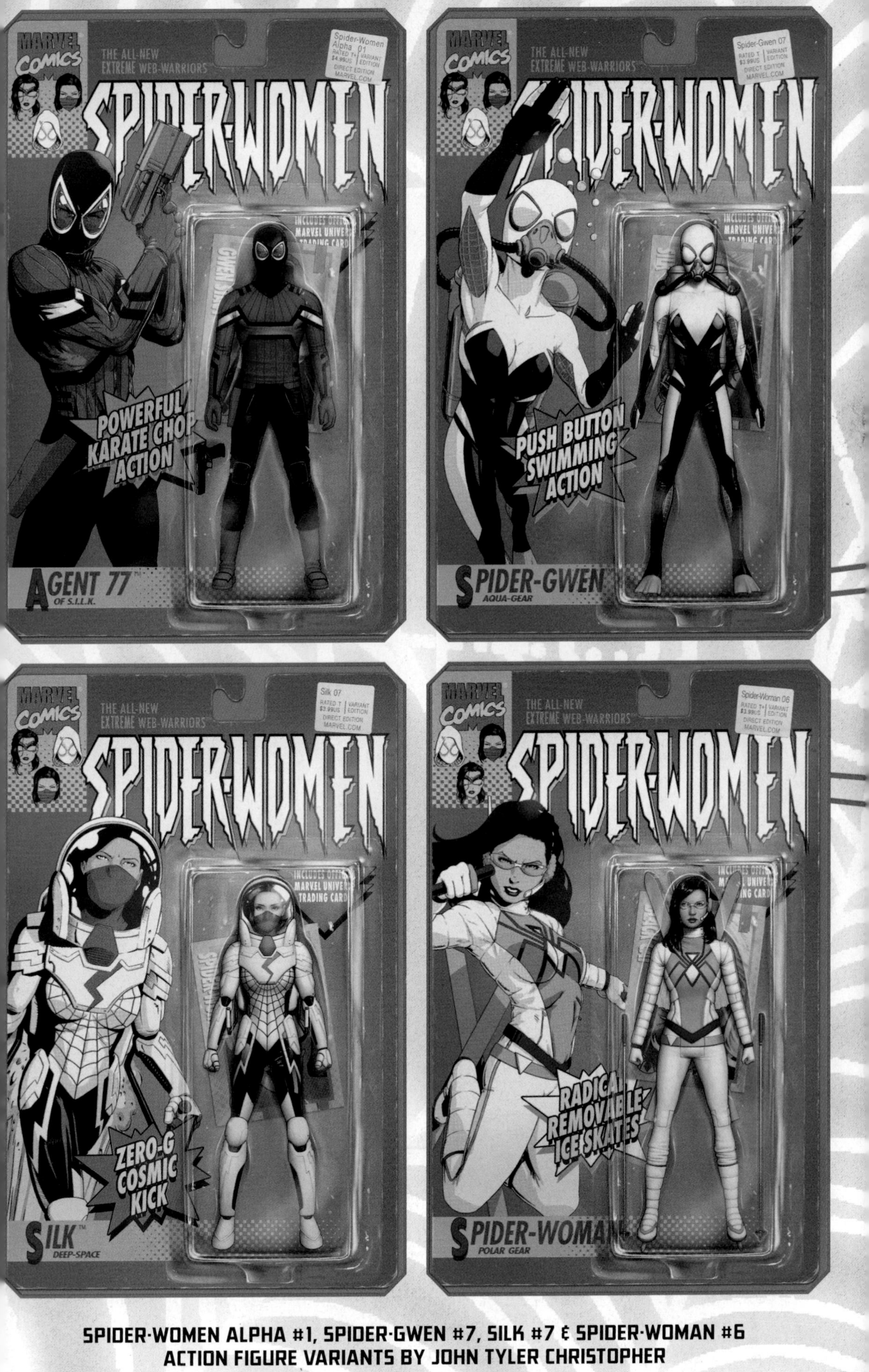
MARVEL COMICS
THE ALL-NEW EXTREME WEB-WARRIORS
SPIDER-WOMEN
Spider-Women Alpha 01 RATED T+ $4.99US VARIANT EDITION DIRECT EDITION MARVEL.COM
POWERFUL KARATE CHOP ACTION
AGENT 77
OF S.I.L.K.
MARVEL COMICS
THE ALL-NEW EXTREME WEB-WARRIORS
SPIDER-WOMEN
Spider-Gwen 07 RATED T+ $3.99US VARIANT EDITION DIRECT EDITION MARVEL.COM
PUSH BUTTON SWIMMING ACTION
SPIDER-GWEN
AQUA-GEAR
MARVEL COMICS
THE ALL-NEW EXTREME WEB-WARRIORS
SPIDER-WOMEN
Silk 07 RATED T $3.99US VARIANT EDITION DIRECT EDITION MARVEL.COM
ZERO-G COSMIC KICK
SILK
DEEP-SPACE
MARVEL COMICS
THE ALL-NEW EXTREME WEB-WARRIORS
SPIDER-WOMEN
Spider-Woman 06 RATED T+ $3.99US VARIANT EDITION DIRECT EDITION MARVEL.COM
RADICA REMOVABLE ICE SKATES
SPIDER-WOMA
POLAR GEAR

SPIDER-WOMEN ALPHA #1, SPIDER-GWEN #7, SILK #7 & SPIDER-WOMAN #6
ACTION FIGURE VARIANTS BY JOHN TYLER CHRISTOPHER

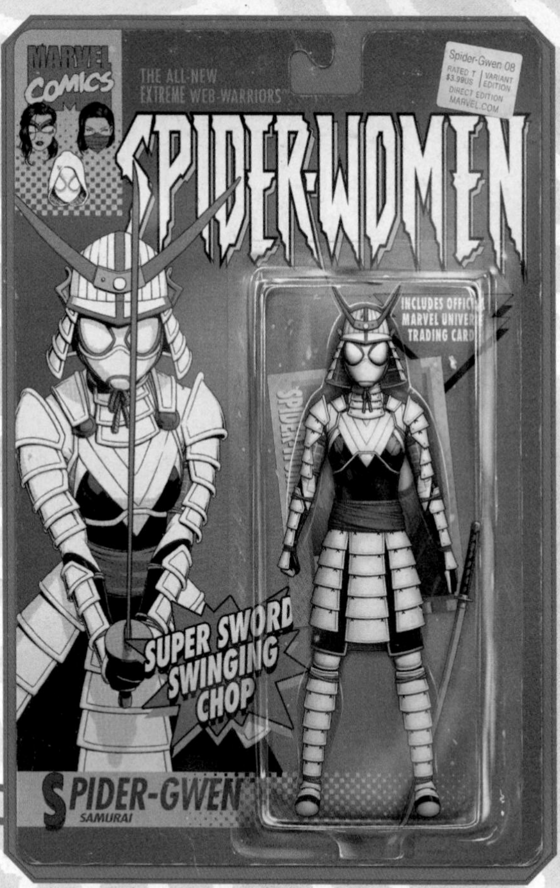
MARVEL COMICS
THE ALL-NEW EXTREME WEB-WARRIORS
Spider-Gwen 08
RATED T $3.99US VARIANT EDITION
DIRECT EDITION MARVEL.COM
SPIDER-WOMEN
SUPER SWORD SWINGING CHOP
SPIDER-GWEN
SAMURAI

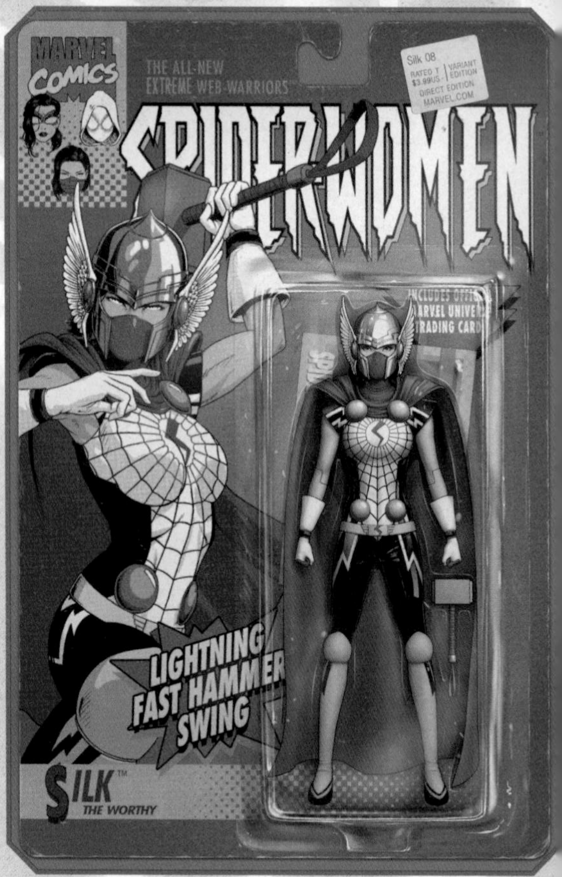
MARVEL COMICS
THE ALL-NEW EXTREME WEB-WARRIORS
Silk 08
RATED T $3.99US VARIANT EDITION
DIRECT EDITION MARVEL.COM
SPIDER-WOMEN
INCLUDES OFFICIAL MARVEL UNIVERSE TRADING CARD
LIGHTNING FAST HAMMER SWING
SILK
THE WORTHY

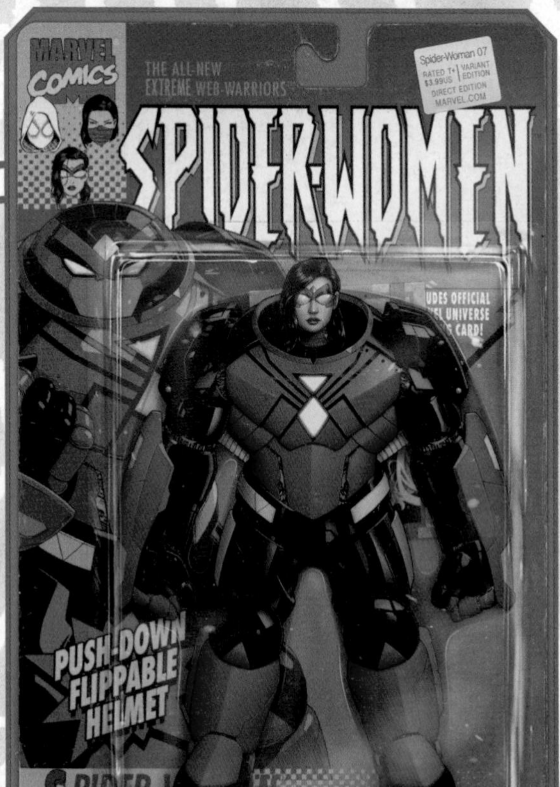
MARVEL COMICS
THE ALL-NEW EXTREME WEB-WARRIORS
Spider-Woman 07
RATED T+ $3.99US VARIANT EDITION
DIRECT EDITION MARVEL.COM
SPIDER-WOMEN
PUSH-DOWN FLIPPABLE HELMET

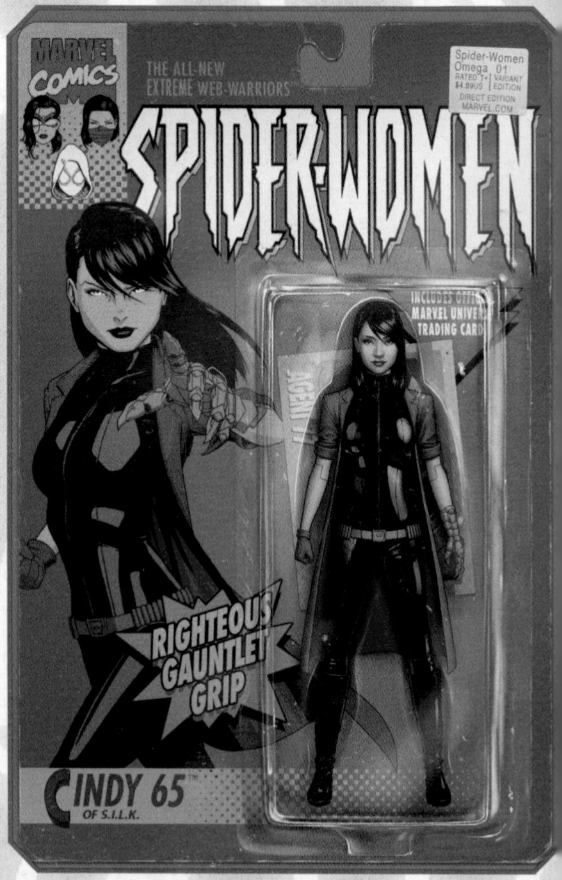
MARVEL COMICS
THE ALL-NEW EXTREME WEB-WARRIORS
Spider-Women Omega 01
RATED T+ $4.99US VARIANT EDITION
DIRECT EDITION MARVEL.COM
SPIDER-WOMEN
INCLUDES OFFICIAL MARVEL UNIVERSE TRADING CARD
RIGHTEOUS GAUNTLET GRIP
CINDY 65
OF S.I.L.K.

SPIDER-GWEN #8, SILK #8, SPIDER-WOMAN #7 & SPIDER-WOMEN OMEGA #1
ACTION FIGURE VARIANTS BY JOHN TYLER CHRISTOPHER